Environmental Psychology

BPS Textbooks in Psychology

BPS Wiley presents a comprehensive and authoritative series covering everything a student needs in order to complete an undergraduate degree in psychology. Refreshingly written to consider more than North American research, this series is the first to give a truly international perspective. Written by the very best names in the field, the series offers an extensive range of titles from introductory level through to final year optional modules, and every text fully complies with the BPS syllabus in the topic. No other series bears the BPS seal of approval!

Many of the books are supported by a companion website, featuring additional resource materials for both instructors and students, designed to encourage critical thinking, and providing for all your course lecturing and testing needs.

For other titles in this series, please go to **http://psychsource.bps.org.uk**

Environmental Psychology

An Introduction

Second Edition

Edited by

LINDA STEG

and

JUDITH I. M. DE GROOT

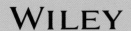

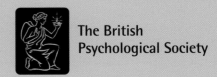

The British
Psychological Society

Registered Offices
John Wiley & Sons, Inc., 111 River Street, Hoboken, NJ 07030, USA
John Wiley & Sons Ltd, The Atrium, Southern Gate, Chichester, West Sussex, PO19 8SQ, UK

Editorial Office
John Wiley & Sons, Inc., 90 Eglinton Ave. E., Suite 300, Toronto, Ontario M4P 2Y3, Canada

For details of our global editorial offices, customer services, and more information about Wiley products visit us at www.wiley.com.

Wiley also publishes its books in a variety of electronic formats and by print-on-demand. Some content that appears in standard print versions of this book may not be available in other formats.

Library of Congress Cataloging-in-Publication Data
Names: Steg, Linda, editor. | de Groot, Judith I. M., editor.
Title: Environmental psychology : an introduction / edited by Linda Steg,
    Groningen University, Netherlands, Judith I. M. de Groot, Bournemouth
    University, Bournemouth.
Description: Second edition. | Hoboken, NJ : Wiley, 2019. |
    Series: BPS textbooks in psychology | Includes index. |
Identifiers: LCCN 2018026889 (print) | LCCN 2018028741 (ebook) |
    ISBN 9781119241041 (Adobe PDF) | ISBN 9781119241119 (ePub) |
    ISBN 9781119241089 (pbk.)
Subjects: LCSH: Environmental psychology.
Classification: LCC BF353.5.N37 (ebook) | LCC BF353.5.N37 E585 2018 (print) |
    DDC 155.9–dc23
LC record available at https://lccn.loc.gov/2018026889

Cover design by Wiley
Cover image: ©Tatiana Popova /Shutterstock

Set in 11/12.5pts Dante MT by SPi Global, Pondicherry, India
Printed and bound in Singapore by Markono Print Media Pte Ltd

10 9 8 7 6 5 4 3 2 1

Brief Contents

Contents

List of Figures

WOKJE ABRAHAMSE
Victoria University of Wellington, New Zealand

SEBASTIAN BAMBERG
FH Bielefeld University of Applied Science, Germany

CECILIA J. BERGSTAD
University of Gothenburg, Sweden

ELENA BILOTTA
Sapienza University of Rome, Italy

GISELA BÖHM
University of Bergen, Norway

JAN WILLEM BOLDERDIJK
Rijksuniversiteit Groningen, the Netherlands

MIRILIA BONNES
Sapienza University of Rome, Italy

GIUSEPPE CARRUS
University of Rome Tre, Italy

NADJA CONTZEN
University of Groningen, the Netherlands

JUDITH I. M. DE GROOT
University of Groningen, the Netherlands

PATRICK DEVINE-WRIGHT
University of Exeter, United Kingdom

SJERP DE VRIES
Wageningen University and Research, the Netherlands

GARY W. EVANS
Cornell University, USA

KELLY FIELDING
University of Queensland, Australia

FERDINANDO FORNARA
University of Cagliari, Italy

BIRGITTA GATERSLEBEN
University of Surrey, United Kingdom

E. SCOTT GELLER
Virginia Polytechnic Institute and State University, United States

ROBERT GIFFORD
University of Victoria, Canada

NICK GOTTS
Independent Researcher, United Kingdom

CAROLINE M. HAGERHALL
Swedish University of Agricultural Sciences, Sweden

JAAP HAM
Eindhoven University of Technology, the Netherlands

MAARTEN H. JACOBS
Wageningen University, the Netherlands

WANDER JAGER
University of Groningen, the Netherlands

LISE JANS
University of Groningen, the Netherlands

LARS-OLOF JOHANSSON
University of Gothenburg, Sweden

YANNICK JOYE
University of Groningen, the Netherlands

KEES KEIZER
University of Groningen, the Netherlands

CHRISTIAN A. KLÖCKNER
Norwegian University of Science and Technology, Norway

CECIL C. KONIJNENDIJK
University of British Columbia, Canada

SILVIE KRAEMER-PALACIOS
EAWAG, Switzerland

PHILIP K. LEHMAN
Salem VA Medical Center, USA

SIEGWART LINDENBERG
University of Groningen, the Netherlands

JOLANDA MAAS
Vrije Universiteit Amsterdam, the Netherlands

MICHAEL J. MANFREDO
Colorado State University, United States

LYNNE C. MANZO
University of Washington, Seattle, WA, United States

ELLEN MATTHIES
Otto von Guericke University, Germany

LINDSAY J. MCCUNN
University of Washington Tacoma, Unites States

CEES MIDDEN
Eindhoven University of Technology, the Netherlands

HANS-JOACHIM MOSLER
EAWAG, Switzerland

EMILIO MOYANO-DÍAZ
Talca University, Chile

ANDREAS NILSSON
University of Gothenburg, Sweden

ANNIKA NORDLUND
Umea University, Sweden

GODA PERLAVICIUTE
University of Groningen, the Netherlands

ÅSA ODE SANG
Swedish University of Agricultural Sciences, Sweden

GEERTJE SCHUITEMA
University College Dublin, Ireland

MAXIE SCHULTE
FH Bielefeld University of Applied Science, Germany

P. WESLEY SCHULTZ
California State University, United States

MASSIMILIANO SCOPELLITI
Libera Universita Mariaa Ss Assunta, Italy

LINDA STEG
University of Groningen, the Netherlands

JANET K. SWIM
Pennsylvania State University, USA

KARIN TANJA-DIJKSTRA
Vrije Universiteit Amsterdam, the Netherlands

CARMEN TANNER
University of Zurich, Switzerland

DANNY TAUFIK
Wageningen University and Research, the Netherlands

TARA L. TEEL
Colorado State University, United States

JOHN THØGERSEN
Aarhus University, Denmark

MARI S. TVEIT
Norwegian University of Life Sciences, Norway

JAVIER URBINA-SORIA
National Autonomous University of Mexico, Mexico

UCHITA VAID
Cornell University, USA

JERRY J. VASKE
Colorado State University, United States

AGNES E. VAN DEN BERG
University of Groningen, the Netherlands

ELLEN VAN DER WERFF
University of Groningen, the Netherlands

JANKE VAN DIJK-WESSELIUS
Vrije Universiteit Amsterdam, the Netherlands

LEONIE VENHOEVEN
University of Groningen, the Netherlands

BAS VERPLANKEN
University of Bath, United Kingdom

CHRIS VON BORGSTEDE
University of Gothenburg, Sweden

LORRAINE WHITMARSH
Cardiff University, UK

1 Environmental Psychology: History, Scope, and Methods

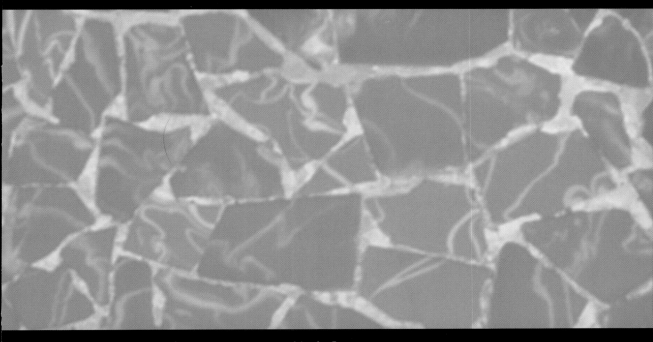

Linda Steg
University of Groningen, The Netherlands

Agnes E. van den Berg
University of Groningen, The Netherlands

Judith I. M. de Groot
University of Groningen, The Netherlands

CHAPTER OUTLINE

1.1 INTRODUCTION

This book aims to give an introduction in environmental psychology. We define **environmental psychology** as the discipline that studies the interplay between individuals and the built and natural environment. This means that environmental psychology examines the influence of the environment on human experiences, behaviour, and well-being, as well as the influence of individuals on the environment, that is, factors influencing environmental behaviour, and ways to encourage pro-environmental behaviour. This second edition of the book gives a state-of-the-art overview of theories and research on each of these topics.

In this introductory chapter we first give a brief overview of the history of the field of environmental psychology, followed by a discussion of characteristics of the field and a description of the main methods used in research. The chapter ends with an outline and rationale of the book.

1.2 HISTORY OF THE FIELD

Environmental psychology has been recognized as a field of psychology since the late 1960s and is therefore a relatively 'new' field in psychology (Altman 1975; Proshansky et al. 1976; Stokols 1977, 1978). Hellpach was one of the first scholars who introduced the term 'environmental psychology' in the first half of the twentieth century (Pol 2006). Hellpach (1911) studied the impact of different environmental stimuli, such as colour and form, the sun and the moon, and extreme environments, on human activities. In his later work, he also studied urban phenomena, such as crowding and overstimulation, and distinguished different types of environments in his work, including natural, social, and historical-cultural environments (Pol 2006). Although the topics of Hellpach are typical of the field of environmental psychology as it has been practised from the 1960s onwards, it was still too early to speak of an independent field of systematic research into human–environment interactions.

Brunswik (1903–1955) and Lewin (1890–1947) are generally regarded as the 'founding fathers' of environmental psychology (Gifford 2007). Neither of these scholars had significant empirical work that we would classify today as environmental psychology. However, their ideas, such as the interaction between physical environment and psychological processes and studying human behaviours in real-life settings instead of artificial environments, were influential for many later studies on human–environment interactions (see Box 1.1).

BOX 1.1 FOUNDING FATHERS OF ENVIRONMENTAL PSYCHOLOGY

Egon Brunswik (1903–1955) was one of the first psychologists who argued psychology should give as much attention to the properties of the organism's environment as it does to the organism itself. He believed that the physical environment affects psychological processes outside people's awareness. He strongly advocated research that includes all aspects of the environment of the person we are trying to understand rather than the fragmented and artificial environments that were more typical in psychological studies of the day.

Kurt Lewin (1890–1947) similarly argued that research should be driven by real-world social problems. He introduced the term 'social action research' including a non-reductionist, problem-focused approach that applies theories in practice and thereby emphasizes the importance of discovering ways to conduct research to solve social problems (Benjamin 2007). Moreover, like Brunswik, Lewin conceptualized the environment as a key determinant of behaviour. He argued that behaviour is a function of the person and the environment (Lewin 1951). Lewin mostly focused on the social or interpersonal influences instead of the physical environment (Wohlwill 1970), but he inspired different students to continue and expand on his ideas. These students included Barker and Bronfenbrenner, who are both seen as forerunners of environmental psychology.

1.2.1 Towards 'Architectural' Psychology

Around the late 1940s and 1950s, systematic research in everyday physical settings and psychological processes slowly increased with some pioneering studies on, for example, human factors in work performance (Mayo 1933), the lighting of homes (Chapman and Thomas 1944), and child behaviours in natural settings (Barker and Wright 1955). So, it was not until the late 1950s and early 1960s that human-environment interactions slowly received recognition as a full discipline. As most of the studies focused on how different environments influence people's perceptions and behaviours, they were labelled as studies in 'Architectural Psychology' to show the distinction from the more traditional forms of psychology (Canter 1970; Pol 2007; Winkel et al. 2009).

In this early period of the field of environmental psychology, much attention was given to the built physical environment (i.e. architecture, technology, and engineering) and how it affected human behaviour and well-being (Bonnes and Bonaiuto 2002). This focus on the built environment was largely guided by the political and social context of the time. Modern architecture tried to respond to post-war challenges (Pol 2006), such as decent housing. Questions like how homes, offices, or hospitals could best be built for their potential users and how environmental stressors (e.g. extreme temperatures, humidity, crowding) would affect human performance and well-being were the focus of many environmental psychological studies (Wohlwill 1970). Environmental psychology as a study to design buildings that would facilitate behavioural functions was officially born.

1.2.2   Towards a Green Psychology

The second period of rapid growth in environmental psychology started during the late 1960s when people increasingly became aware of environmental problems. This resulted in studies on **sustainability** issues, that is, studies on explaining and changing environmental behaviour to create a healthy and sustainable environment. The first studies in this area focused on air pollution (De Groot 1967; Lindvall 1970), urban noise (Griffiths and Langdon 1968), and the appraisal of environmental quality (Appleyard and Craik 1974; Craik and Mckechnie 1974). From the 1970s onwards the topics further widened to include issues of energy supply and demand (Zube et al. 1975) and risk perceptions and risk assessment associated with (energy) technologies (Fischhoff et al. 1978). In the 1980s the first studies were conducted that focused on efforts promoting conservation behaviour, such as relationships between consumer attitudes and behaviour (Cone and Hayes 1980; Stern and Gardner 1981).

1.3   CURRENT SCOPE AND CHARACTERISTICS OF THE FIELD

From the beginning of the twenty-first century, it has become evident that environmental problems such as climate change, pollution, and deforestation are major challenges threatening the health, economic prospects, and food and water supply of people across the world (IPCC 2013). It is also generally recognized that human behaviour is one of the main causes of these environmental problems. A continuing and growing concern of environmental psychology is to find ways to change people's behaviour to reverse environmental problems, while at the same time preserving human well-being and quality-of-life. To this end, a broad concept of sustainability, which encompasses environmental as well as social and economic aspects, has been widely adopted (World Commission on Environment and Development 1987). This broad concept of sustainability has increasingly become a central guiding and unifying principle for research in environmental psychology (Giuliani and Scopelliti 2009). Indeed, it has been suggested that, over the past decades, the field of environmental psychology has gradually evolved into a 'psychology of sustainability' (Gifford 2007).

Below, we discuss four key features of environmental psychology that characterize the field as it stands today: a focus on human–environment interactions, an interdisciplinary approach, an applied focus, and a diversity of methods.

1.3.1   Interactive Approach

As the definition of environmental psychology already indicates, environmental psychology is primarily interested in the interaction between humans and the built and natural environment; it also explicitly considers how the environment influences behaviour as well as which factors affect behaviour that can help improve environmental quality. For example, environmental conditions such as the presence of nature in the environment of childhood may influence people's connectedness to nature and willingness to support nature conservation measures. In turn, people's support for nature conservation measures may influence environmental conditions such as biodiversity. As another example, the available infrastructure for public and private transport may influence the level of car use, while in turn, the level of car use may influence the seriousness of environmental problems such as air pollution and global warming. So humans and the environment are related in a reciprocal, dynamic way.

The reciprocal relationship between humans and the environment serves as a starting point for the structure of this book. Part I discusses the negative as well as positive influences of environmental conditions on humans, with a focus on environmental impacts on human health and well-being. Part II discusses factors that influence human behaviour that affect environmental quality, with a focus on pro-environmental behaviour. Part III discusses which factors affect the outcomes and acceptability of strategies to encourage pro-environmental behaviour for creating sustainable environments.

1.3.2   *Interdisciplinary Collaboration*

Many environmental psychologists work in interdisciplinary settings, and closely collaborate with scholars from other disciplines. Each discipline provides a different view on the phenomenon under study, while in combination, they provide a comprehensive picture on the problem in question. As outlined in the historical overview, interdisciplinary collaboration has mostly occurred in three domains. First, environmental psychology has always worked closely with the disciplines of architecture and geography to ensure a correct representation of the physical-spatial components of human–environment relationships (see Part I of this book). Second, theoretical and methodological development in environmental psychology has been influenced strongly by social and cognitive psychology (see Part II of this book). Third, when studying and encouraging pro-environmental behaviour (see Part III of this book), environmental psychologists have collaborated with environmental scientists, among others, to correctly assess the environmental impact of different behaviours.

1.3.3   *Problem-Focused Approach*

Environmental psychologists do not conduct studies merely out of scientific curiosity about some phenomenon, but also to try to contribute towards solving real-life problems. This does not mean that environmental psychologists are not interested in theories. As evidenced in this book, a great deal of attention is paid to building and testing theories in order to understand, explain, and predict human–environment interactions. However, an important aim of theory development in environmental psychology lies in identifying the most effective solutions to real-life problems.

Environmental psychology studies human–environment interactions at different scale levels, from domestic surroundings and the neighbourhood to cities, nature reserves and countries, and even the planet as a whole. The problems and associated solutions that are studied vary across these levels. For example, at the local level, problems like littering and solutions like recycling may be a focus of research. At regional and national levels, problems like species loss and solutions like ecological restoration can be studied. At the global level, problems like climate change and solutions like the adoption of new technologies to combat climate change are of interest. Environmental psychology is concerned with problems at all scales, from local to global.

1.3.4 *Diversity of Methods*

Environmental psychology largely uses the same **quantitative** and **qualitative methods** as other psychological disciplines. However, whereas other psychological disciplines often have one dominant research paradigm, environmental psychology is characterized by the use of a wide diversity of methods (see Section 1.4 for an overview). Each research method has its strengths and weaknesses (see Table 1.1). Choosing a method typically involves a trade-off between **internal** and **external validity**. Internal validity reflects the extent to which cause–effect relationships can be established. External validity reflects the extent to which the results of a study can be generalized to other populations or settings. Low external validity of a finding may be problematic if the goal is designing an intervention to solve a specific applied problem. However, it may be less relevant if the purpose of the research is testing theory because in this case the main concern is to achieve a high internal validity. Ideally, environmental psychologists try to replicate the findings of the same phenomenon using different research designs. In this way, weaknesses of one research design may be compensated by the strengths of another, thereby optimizing internal and external validity.

1.4 MAIN RESEARCH METHODS IN ENVIRONMENTAL PSYCHOLOGY

The main research methods used in environmental research include questionnaire studies, laboratory experiments, simulation studies, field studies, and case studies. Below we briefly discuss each of these methods. We first discuss methods that can be used independent of specific environmental settings, followed by methods employed in artificial settings. Finally, we discuss methods that are employed in real settings. The main strengths and weaknesses of each method are summarized in Table 1.1.

Table 1.1 *Summary of main research methods in environmental psychology.*

Setting	Method	Strengths	Weaknesses	Use
Environment independent setting	Questionnaire studies	High external validity Cost-effective method for reaching large populations	No manipulation of variables Hard to make causal inferences	Describing perceptions, beliefs, and behaviour Studying relationships among variables
Artificial setting	Laboratory experiments	High internal validity Control of variables	Low external validity Artificiality	Testing theories or hypotheses Identifying causal relationships
	Simulation studies	Good balance between external/internal validity Realistic visualization	Requires advanced skills and equipment Often perceived as 'fictitious'	Study complex human–environment dynamics Visualize and evaluate future developments
	Field studies	Good balance between external/internal validity Replicable	Limited experimental control Time-consuming data collection	Studying current behaviour Evaluating interventions
Real setting	Case studies	High external validity Rich data	Low internal validity Time demanding Limited generalizability	Descriptions Explorations Developing hypotheses

1.4.1   Questionnaire Studies

Questionnaire studies aim to describe behaviours and to gather people's perceptions, opinions, attitudes, and beliefs about different issues. They are also widely used to establish relationships between two or more variables. For example, by asking people how often they engage in littering and how satisfied they are with the number of garbage bins in their neighbourhood a relationship can be established between both variables. However, typically, causality cannot be established which weakens internal validity. First, it cannot be excluded that a third variable (i.e. confound) has caused the relationship. For example, an area with many garbage bins may be inhabited by a particular group of residents (e.g. highly educated individuals) who may systematically differ from groups that inhabit areas with few garbage bins. Second, the direction of the relationship is not clear: does the municipality decide to place bins because people tend to litter a lot in certain areas or do people litter because there are no bins available?

Questionnaire studies are popular in environmental psychology for several reasons. First, manipulation of environmental conditions (as in experimental research), is often unethical or impossible. For example, when studying the effects of transport pricing on car use, it is mostly not feasible to double fuel prices in one area, but not in another area. Furthermore, external validity of questionnaire studies tends to be high, which is often regarded as crucial in studies on environmental issues. Finally, questionnaire studies are relatively easy to apply at low cost.

1.4.2 *Laboratory Experiments*

Laboratory experiments are conducted in a controlled, mostly artificial, environment created for the purpose of the research. Laboratory experiments enable the establishment of causal relationships between variables, because of two basic features of experiments: manipulation and random assignment. Imagine that a researcher would like to examine whether variable X (independent variable, e.g. presence versus absence of garbage bins) influences variable Y (dependent variable, e.g. littering). When only the independent variable is manipulated and all other variables are kept the same, it can be concluded with reasonable certainty that any differences in responses between conditions are due to the manipulation. That is, in the example, if there is a difference in the amount people litter with and without a garbage bin, one of the causes for littering has been identified: the presence of bins. Because of this feature, internal validity of laboratory experiments is high.

Randomization implies that all participants in the experiment have an equal chance of being assigned to each experimental condition. Randomization minimizes the chance that differences between experimental groups are caused by confounding individual factors such as differences in socio-demographics or personality types. For example, if only male participants are assigned to the garbage bin condition and only females to the condition without the garbage bin, then differences between the conditions may be caused by gender rather than the presence or absence of a bin.

The strong control in experimental settings generally creates artificial situations. Therefore, true experiments are often low in external validity, that is, the result may not easily be generalized to what typically happens in the real world.

1.4.3 *Computer Simulation Studies*

Sometimes it is impossible to conduct research with real individuals or realistic environmental stimuli. Examples are studies that aim to learn about complex systems that involve thousands of people or studies on how people evaluate future environmental scenarios. Environmental psychologists are increasingly using environmental simulations for this reason. In this type of research aspects of environments and/or humans are simulated as accurately and realistically as possible. Simulations may include immersive virtual environments, created with computers, that give the participant a realistic impression of what it would be like to experience particular environments or events (e.g. De Kort et al. 2003,; also see Chapter 28), 3D visualization of data in Geographical Information Systems (see Chapter 5), or agent-based models of land use or resource use (see Chapter 31). In general, simulations make it possible to keep some control over the environment, thereby increasing internal validity, while external validity is not compromised too much.

1.4.4   Field Studies

In order to achieve high external validity without compromising too much on internal validity, many environmental psychologists use field studies and experiments. As field experiments are conducted in real-life settings, they are relatively high in external validity. Yet, internal validity is relatively high as well, as the experimenter tries to control the situation by systematically manipulating independent variables (e.g. placing or removing a bin in the environment), and/or by trying to randomly assign participants to different study conditions (e.g. environments with and without bins). By doing so, researchers can be reasonably sure that any differences between conditions are due to the manipulations (and not to, e.g. individual differences), securing internal validity. Nevertheless, because field experiments take place in real settings, it is difficult to control for possible confounding variables, such as changing weather conditions or unexpected interruptions. Furthermore, in many situations, random assignment is not possible.

1.4.5   Case Studies

A case study is an in-depth study of a particular situation. It is a method used to narrow down a very broad topic of research into one single case, i.e. a person, setting, situation, or event. For example, the broad topic of urban environmental quality may be studied in one particular neighbourhood where the municipality has recently installed garbage bins to tackle littering. Rather than employing a strict protocol and close-ended questions to study a limited number of variables, case study methods involve an exploratory, qualitative examination of a single situation or event: a case. Qualitative research uses words or other non-numerical indicators (such as images or drawings) as data. The main purpose of case studies and other types of qualitative research is to explore and understand the meaning that individuals or groups ascribe to a phenomenon. In a case study, people or events are studied in their own context, within naturally occurring settings, such as the home, playing fields, the university, and the street. These settings are 'open systems' where conditions are continuously affected by interactions with the social, physical, historical, and cultural context to give rise to a process of ongoing change, including ethnography, grounded theory, and phenomenology (see Wolcott 2001). Although there will not be one objective truth of the interpretation of the phenomenon (Willig 2001).

Many different strategies can be used in case studies. Qualitative research methods like case studies are gaining in importance in academic journals, while quantitative research methods (that use numbers rather than words as data) still dominate in environmental psychology. This is evidenced in this book, which relies mostly on quantitative research.

1.5 OVERVIEW OF THE BOOK

This book aims to introduce students, professionals, and the general audience to key topics in contemporary environmental psychology. The book comprises three parts. After this general introduction, the first part, comprising Chapters 2–15, provides an overview of research on the positive and negative influences of environmental conditions on experiences, well-being, and behaviour, as well as ways to promote well-being via environmental changes. Key topics include risk perception, environmental stressors, nature experience, health effects of nature, architecture, urban environmental quality, and quality-of-life effects of environmental conditions. In addition, in this second edition, two new chapters have been added addressing the topics of climate change risks and the importance of nature for children.

The second part, comprising Chapters 16–25, focuses on understanding environmental behaviour. Various ways to measure environmental behaviour and factors influencing this behaviour, such as values and norms, are discussed. Specifically, in this second edition, the newly added Chapter 19 is dedicated to the significant role emotions can play in people's engagement in pro-environmental behaviour, while Chapter 20 discusses symbolic aspects of environmental behaviour. Furthermore, newly added Chapter 23 reviews how group memberships and the group processes associated with these memberships can affect environmental behaviour. The chapters in Part II present different theories to explain environmental behaviour, among which are norm theory, value theory, theories on affect, social dilemma theory, social identity theory, the theory of planned behaviour, the norm activation theory, the value-belief-norm theory of environmentalism, and habit theory. Also, a Latin American perspective on studying interactions between humans and the environment is provided.

The third part of the book, comprising Chapters 26–32, discusses ways to encourage pro-environmental behaviour and well-being via informational strategies, changing the incentives, and technological innovations. It also discusses factors influencing the acceptability of policies, processes of change, and social simulation of behaviour changes. Besides, special attention is paid to encouraging pro-environmental actions in developing countries.

In the final chapter of this book, we draw some general conclusions, identify trends, and suggest viable avenues for future research.

GLOSSARY

environmental psychology   A subfield of psychology that studies the interplay between individuals and the built and natural environment.

external validity   The extent to which the results of a study can be generalized (applied) to other populations (population validity) or settings (ecological validity). External validity is also known as generalizability.

internal validity   The extent to which it can be concluded that an observed effect is caused by an independent variable.

qualitative methods   Methods of analysis that use data in the form of words or other non-numerical indicators (e.g. images, drawings).

quantitative methods   Methods of analysis that use data in the form of numbers.

sustainability   Using, developing, and protecting resources at a rate and in a manner that enables people to meet their current needs and also ensures that future generations can meet their own needs; achieving an optimal balance between environmental, social, and economic qualities.

SUGGESTIONS FOR FURTHER READING

Bechtel, R.B. and Churchman, A. (2002). *Handbook of Environmental Psychology*. New York, NY: Wiley.

Bell, P.A., Green, T.C., Fisher, J.D., and Baum, A. (2001). *Environmental Psychology*, 5e. Belmont, CA: Wadsworth/Thomson Learning.

Fleury-Bahi, G., Pol, E., and Navarro, O. (2017). *Handbook of Environmental Psychology and Quality of Life Research*. Cham: Springer.

Gifford, R. (2007). *Environmental Psychology: Principles and Practice*. Colville, WA: Optimal books.

Nickerson, R.S. (2003). *Psychology and Environmental Change*. Mahwah, NJ: Erlbaum.

REVIEW QUESTIONS

1. What is environmental psychology? Give a short definition.
2. Describe four key features of environmental psychology.
3. Which concept has increasingly become a guiding and unifying principle for research in environmental psychology? Define this concept.
4. Give three examples of problems studied by environmental psychologists.
5. Why do environmental psychologists use a diversity of research methods?

Part I
Environmental Influences on Human Behaviour and Well-Being

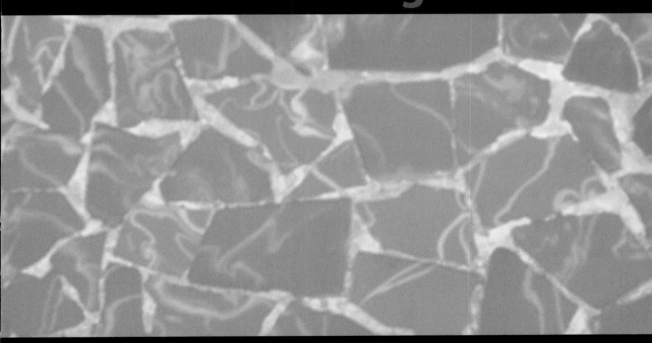

2 Environmental Risk Perception

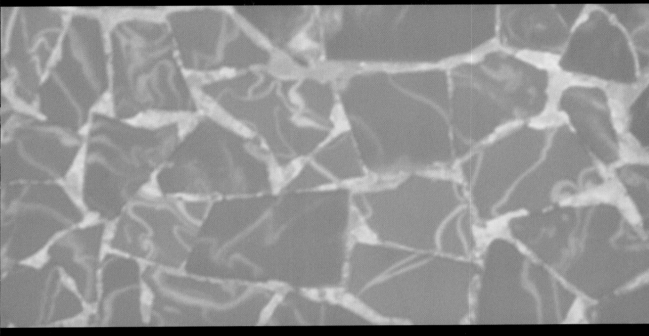

Gisela Böhm
University of Bergen, Norway

Carmen Tanner
University of Zürich, Switzerland

CHAPTER OUTLINE

2.1   INTRODUCTION

Environmental changes and pollution, as well as many human activities and technologies, bear the possibility of harmful and long-lasting consequences for both humans and nature. How people perceive such **risks** is a crucial question; **risk perceptions** can prompt or oppose actions to address particular risks. In this chapter, we will point out several factors that have been proposed to explain perceived risk in general, and perceived environmental risk in particular. First, we discuss **heuristics** and **biases**. This area has emphasized that subjective risk judgements are susceptible to cognitive biases. Second, we present the psychometric model, which seeks to identify key characteristics of risk that underlie risk perception. Third, we elaborate on characteristics of the individual that influence risk perception, in particular values and moral dimensions. Finally, we discuss emotions, which result from perceived risk but also shape risk perception.

2.2   WHAT ARE ENVIRONMENTAL RISKS?

In general, risk refers to a situation, event, or activity, which may lead to uncertain adverse outcomes affecting something that humans value. Thus, risk entails a causal chain between a risk source (a situation, event, activity, etc.) and an uncertain adverse outcome. The two essential components of risk are the severity and uncertainty of the adverse outcome (or loss). Characterizing an outcome as adverse involves a human evaluation. As Slovic puts it: 'danger is real, but risk is socially constructed' (1999, p. 689).

Environmental risks differ from other risks in a number of ways. We use climate change as a case in point. First, environmental risks are characterized by high complexity and uncertainty, entailing intricate causal relationships and multiple consequences. Consequently, they often encompass both risks *for* (e.g. acidification of oceans caused by anthropogenic carbon dioxide) and risks *from* (e.g. destruction of human habitat due to flooding) the environment. Second, environmental risks often emerge from the aggregated behaviours of many individuals (e.g. use of fossil fuels) rather than from a single activity. Therefore, mitigations cannot be easily attained, because they require actions of many people. Third, the consequences of environmental risks are often temporally delayed and geographically distant. The people who contribute to a risk (e.g. industrial countries) are not necessarily the ones who suffer the consequences (e.g. developing countries, future generations). Environmental risks, therefore, often raise ethical issues.

Environmental Psychology: An Introduction, Second Edition. Edited by Linda Steg and Judith I. M. de Groot.
© 2019 John Wiley & Sons Ltd. Published 2019 by John Wiley & Sons Ltd.

2.3   SUBJECTIVE RISK JUDGEMENTS

'Risk perception' refers to people's subjective judgement about the risk that is associated with some situation, event, activity, or technology. Research has developed several techniques to assess subjective risk judgements. First, respondents are asked to give an overall judgement by either rating or rank ordering various risks according to their overall riskiness or to the degree to which they experience concern, worry, or threat concerning these risks. A second approach is to ask people how much money they would be 'willing to pay' (WTP) to mitigate or how much they would be 'willing to accept' (WTA) to tolerate a particular risk. A third approach is to have respondents estimate the subjective probability of a given outcome (e.g. the probability of dying from lung cancer when exposed to asbestos).

2.3.1   *Heuristics and Biases in Risk Judgements*

Subjective risk judgements are rarely based on deliberate analyses. Instead, people often employ heuristics when making judgements, that is, simple, intuitive rules-of-thumb. Heuristics have traditionally been studied in the area of subjective probability estimates. Though heuristics often yield valid results, they can also lead to biased risk assessments.

One important example of biased risk assessment refers to people's tendency to overestimate small frequencies and to underestimate larger ones when judging the frequency of various dangers (Lichtenstein et al. 1978). Two prominent heuristics are the availability heuristic and the anchoring-and-adjustment heuristic (Tversky and Kahneman 1974). The **availability heuristic** posits that people are more likely to overestimate the occurrence of an event the easier it is for them to bring to mind examples of similar events. For example, our subjective probability of a car accident increases when we see a wrecked car at the side of the road. In the context of environmental risks, evidence for the availability heuristic is provided by a study which showed that people believed more in, and had greater concern about, global warming on days that they perceived to be warmer than usual (Li et al. 2011). Obviously, media coverage of accidents or other events can also affect how easily an event comes to mind and how risky an event is then perceived (Mazur 2006).

The **anchoring-and-adjustment heuristic** refers to the fact that, when making estimates, people often start out from a reference point that is salient in the situation (the anchor) and then adjust this first estimate to arrive at a final judgement. In most cases, the adjustment is insufficient and the final estimates are biased towards the anchor. For example, when asked to guess the percentage of African countries in the United Nations (UN), people's estimates were heavily influenced by an arbitrary number that showed up on a wheel of fortune in the participant's presence. The average estimate almost doubled from 25% to 45% when the wheel showed a 65 rather than a 10 (Tversky and Kahneman 1974). Similarly, people who were exposed to a high (10 °F) compared to a low (1 °F) initial anchor not only gave higher estimates for the increase in the Earth's temperature but were also more likely to believe in global warming and were WTP more to reduce global warming (Joireman et al. 2010).

Another pervasive finding is people's tendency to believe that they are more likely to experience positive events and less likely to experience negative events than others. This cognitive bias is known as **unrealistic optimism** (or optimism bias; Weinstein 1980), and has been found in various areas, including environmental or technological risks. For example, people tend to perceive risks of climate change, mobile phones, radioactive waste, and genetically modified food to be smaller for themselves than others (Costa-Font et al. 2009). Unrealistic optimism can have important implications, because individuals may fail to take preventive actions when they see no personal risk (Weinstein et al. 1990).

A factor that powerfully shapes risk evaluations is the framing of a problem. **Framing effects** refer to the finding that different descriptions of otherwise identical problems can alter people's decisions (Tversky and Kahneman 1981). Simple changes in wording – such as describing outcomes in terms of losses versus gains – can lead to different preferences. For example, people perceived environmental problems (e.g. river quality, air quality) as more important when the opportunity of restoring a previous better state (i.e. undoing a loss), rather than improving the current state (i.e. producing a gain), was given (Gregory et al. 1993; see Box 2.1).

Framing changes one's reference point of what would be a neutral outcome: no loss (when the outcome is expressed as a loss) versus no gain (when expressed as a gain). One common explanation for framing effects is that a loss is subjectively experienced as more devastating than the equivalent gain is gratifying (**loss aversion**; Tversky and Kahneman 1981).

While research on heuristics traditionally relied strongly on cognitive processes, later research has highlighted the importance of emotions for risk evaluations and decision-making (Pfister and Böhm 2008). The **affect heuristic**

BOX 2.1   FRAMING AND ENVIRONMENTAL DECISIONS

Hardisty et al. (2010, Study 2) demonstrated in an experiment how framing influences environmental decisions and how this process is shaped by individual differences such as political affiliation (i.e. Democrats, Independents, Republicans). Participants were asked to choose one of two airline tickets. The tickets were identical except that the 'green' option was more expensive, because it included a carbon fee. This fee was framed either negatively (as a tax) or positively (as an offset). As expected, the green option was chosen more frequently when it was framed as an offset rather than as a tax. Strikingly, this effect was moderated by political affiliation. In particular, when framed as a tax, the preference for the green option declined from Democrats to Independents and to Republicans, seemingly reflecting Republicans' dislike of taxes.

(Finucane et al. 2000) proposes that affective states serve as important informational inputs for risk judgements: If individuals feel positive about an activity, they tend to judge the risk as low and the benefit as high. Conversely, if they feel negative about an activity, they tend to judge the risk as high and the benefit as low. As a result, perceived risk and perceived benefit are inversely related – although, in reality, risks and benefits most probably correlate positively, because high risks are taken only if they promise great benefits.

2.3.2   *Temporal Discounting of Environmental Risks*

Temporal discounting refers to the psychological phenomenon that outcomes in the far future are subjectively less significant than immediate outcomes. Applied to environmental risk perception, this tendency would imply that environmental risks should be perceived as less severe when the consequences are delayed. Yet, studies looking at discounting in environmental risk evaluations found little evidence for it (Böhm and Pfister 2005; Gattig and Hendrickx 2007). For example, people find an oil spill equally risky whether it may happen in one month, in one year, or in ten years (Böhm and Pfister 2005). An explanation for these surprising findings could be that environmental risks tap into moral values, which apply irrespective of temporal aspects (Böhm and Pfister 2005; Gattig and Hendrickx 2007).

2.3.3   *The Psychometric Paradigm*

A well-established approach to studying risk perception is the **psychometric paradigm** (Slovic 1987). Its aim is to identify the 'cognitive map' of diverse risk events, activities, or technologies and its underlying psychological dimensions that lead individuals to perceive something as more or less risky.

Across a variety of studies, two dimensions have repeatedly emerged as a result of factor analyses, which constitute the basic dimensions of the cognitive map of perceived risk: dread risk and unknown risk. **Dread risk** describes the extent to which a risk is experienced as dreadful or as having severe, catastrophic consequences. **Unknown risk** refers to the extent to which the risk is experienced as new, unfamiliar, unobservable, or having delayed effects (see Box 2.2).

2.4   RISK, VALUES, AND MORALITY

Risk perception may also be driven by **values** and moral positions (see also Chapter 17). For example, people low on traditional values (i.e. family, patriotism, stability) and those high on altruism (concern with welfare of other humans and other species) tend to perceive greater global environmental risks (depletion of ozone layer and global warming; Whitfield et al. 2009). Similarly,

BOX 2.2   PSYCHOMETRIC STUDY OF ENVIRONMENTAL RISKS

McDaniels and his colleagues were the first who adapted the psychometric paradigm to the study of environmental risk perception. They conducted an extensive survey in which they asked respondents to evaluate 65 risks (associated with natural disasters, technologies, human activities, etc.) on 31 rating scales (McDaniels et al. 1995). These rating scales were later, through factor analysis, aggregated to five basic dimensions of environmental risk perception: impact on species (e.g. loss of animal species), human benefits (e.g. benefits to society), impact on humans (e.g. number of people affected), avoidability (e.g.

controllability of risk), and knowledge (e.g. understandability of impacts). Compared to previous risk perception studies, which usually yielded only two dimensions (i.e. dread risk and unknown risk), this study demonstrates the greater complexity of environmental risk perception. One interesting difference is that people clearly distinguish between impacts on humans and those on other species. A follow-up study compared expert and lay people's risk perceptions and showed that experts generally ascribed lower impacts (on both humans and species) to the presented risks than lay people (Lazo et al. 2000).

people who value nature in its own right (biospheric value orientation, see Chapter 17) show greater awareness while people with strong egoistic values show reduced awareness of environmental problems (Steg et al. 2005).

2.4.1   Values

A view dominant in environmental ethics maintains that some aspects of the environment (e.g. rare species, landscapes) have an inherent value, according to which the non-human world should be valued and respected 'for its own sake' (Taylor 1981; see also Chapter 17). In contrast to what environmental economics suggests, people are sometimes highly reluctant to make trade-offs among different values. For example, many think that it is morally wrong to sacrifice nature or endangered species for money. People think of such entities or values (e.g. human or animal life, unspoilt nature, human dignity) as absolute, not to be traded off for anything else, particularly not for economic values. Psychological theorizing speaks of **protected or sacred values** to refer to this phenomenon (Baron and Spranca 1997; Tetlock et al. 2000). Studies have shown that forcing people to trade off such values, or asking them to 'put a price' on things they consider protected (e.g. asking people for how much money they would be willing to accept the extinction of some species) can induce strong negative affective reactions (e.g. outrage) and trade-off reluctance (Hanselmann and Tanner 2008; Tetlock et al. 2000). Individuals holding protected values are more likely to reject market-based approaches to trading emission rights, despite their possible benefit in mitigating climate change (Sacchi et al. 2014).

Besides, sacred values seem to affect environmental risk perception: People holding sacred beliefs for the Indian river Ganges are less likely to perceive this river as polluted (Sachdeva 2016).

2.4.2 *Morality and Ethics*

Moral considerations also play an important role in risk evaluation (Böhm and Pfister 2005; Pfister and Böhm 2001). Moral philosophy usually contrasts **consequentialist principles** and **deontological principles**. The distinctive idea of deontological principles is that the focus is on the inherent rightness or wrongness of the act per se. Deontological principles refer to morally mandated actions or prohibitions (e.g. duty to keep promises, duty not to harm nature), despite their consequences. Consequentialist principles, in contrast, entail conclusions about what is morally right or wrong based on the magnitude and likelihood of outcomes. The aim of consequentialist principles is to maximize benefits and to minimize harms.

Consistent with the idea that deontological thinking focuses more on the inherent rightness or wrongness of actions than on the consequences, studies confirmed that people holding a deontological stance pay greater attention to whether harms or benefits derive from acts versus omissions (i.e. failures to act) than to the consequences (see Box 2.3). Such results have implications for environmental risk communication, suggesting that information about consequences is not equally relevant for all individuals.

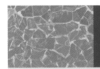

BOX 2.3   DEONTOLOGICAL REASONING, PROTECTED VALUES, AND ENVIRONMENTAL DECISION-MAKING

Tanner and colleagues found support for the role of deontological reasoning (see Section 2.4) and protected values in environmental decision tasks (Tanner and Medin 2004; Tanner et al. 2008). Participants were provided with several scenarios, each of them including a choice between an act and an omission (e.g. vaccinating versus not vaccinating children suffering from having drunk contaminated water). The consequences varied in terms of whether they were risky or certain, and whether they were framed in terms of losses or gains (see Section 2.1). It was assessed to what extent participants were treating nature, human, or animal lives as protected values, and to what extent they were more prone to a deontological or a consequentialist focus. The results revealed that protected values were strongly associated with deontological orientations, and with a stronger preference for acts than omissions. Most interestingly, participants more strongly endorsing protected values and deontological orientations were also immune to framing effects. Apparently, strong protected values make people focus on their duties for environmental acts rather than on the framing of outcomes. Participants with a highly consequentialist orientation, in contrast, were susceptible to the framing of the outcomes as gains or losses.

2.5 EMOTIONAL REACTIONS TO ENVIRONMENTAL RISKS

Emotions influence risk perceptions. We judge risks as higher when we feel negative about an activity, but we judge risks as lower when we feel positive about it (see affect heuristic, Section 2.3.1). There is more to emotions than their valence, though. Appraisal theories suggest that different specific emotions can have differential impacts on perceived risks even if they share the same valence (Keller et al. 2012). For example, fear increases and anger reduces risk perception, even though both are negative (Lerner and Keltner 2001). Fear and anger are associated with different tendencies to evaluate events (appraisals). Specifically, fear is associated with evaluating situations as uncertain and uncontrollable, leading individuals to perceive events as more risky. In contrast, anger predisposes individuals to evaluate events as highly certain and controllable, leading them to perceive events as less risky.

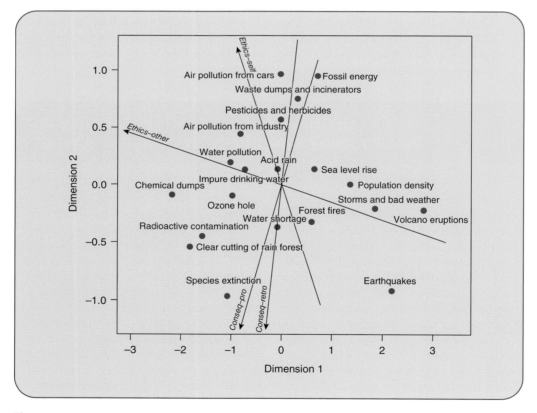

Figure 2.1 *Emotional reactions to environmental risks. Display of a multidimensional scaling of hazards based on emotional reactions to them. Vectors fitted into the configuration constitute emotion types.* Source: Reprinted from Böhm (2003), with permission of Elsevier.

Emotions can also occur as reactions to perceived risks (Böhm and Pfister 2015). When people focus on the consequences of a risk, they experience consequence-based emotions. These can be prospective (e.g. fear arising from the anticipation of harm) or retrospective (e.g. sadness triggered by an experienced loss). When people focus on moral rightness, they experience ethics-based emotions. These can be directed towards oneself (guilt when taking blame) or towards other people (outrage when blaming others). Böhm (2003) asked respondents to indicate for a list of environmental risks how intensely they experienced these four emotion types in response to the risks. The emotional profiles of the risks are shown in Figure 2.1. Ethics-based self-directed emotions (e.g. guilt) are particularly strong for individual behaviours such as car use. Ethics-based other-directed emotions (e.g. outrage) are experienced when responsibility can be ascribed more clearly to one agent (e.g. chemical dumps). Species extinction triggers mainly prospective (e.g. fear) and retrospective (e.g. sadness) consequence-based emotions (see also Chapter 9). Emotional reactions to natural risks (e.g. earthquakes) are generally weaker than those to risks that are caused by humans.

Positive emotions are also important in how people perceive and respond to environmental risks (Böhm and Pfister 2015). For example, support for climate change policies has been found to be strongly associated not only with worry but also with hope (Smith and Leiserowitz 2014).

2.6 SUMMARY

Examining how people perceive environmental risks is crucial for understanding their reactions to these risks. The aim of this chapter was to give an overview of prominent factors that are proposed in research and theory as determinants of environmental risk perception. Of course, by no means is this list of factors exhaustive. While past research was dominated by cognitive approaches and the question of how risks are perceived, current research emphasizes more the role of emotions in understanding risk perception. More emphasis is also given to the role of values and ethical dimensions in risk evaluation. Given that many environmental risks or new technologies are expected to have substantial impact on the Earth and our well-being, we expect that the discussion of ethical challenges will gain further importance in the future.

GLOSSARY

affect heuristic   The tendency to base judgements of risk and benefit on one's affective state.

anchoring-and-adjustment heuristic   Tendency to bias estimates towards anchors.

availability heuristic   Tendency to base judgements (e.g. concerning the probability of an event) on the 'ease' with which relevant instances of the event can be constructed or retrieved from memory.

bias   Judgements are biased if they are systematically distorted in one direction (e.g. away from a normative standard).

consequentialist principles   Perspective in moral philosophy, whereby the morality of an action depends on the consequences.

deontological principles   Perspective in moral philosophy, whereby the focus is on the inherent rightness or wrongness of an action (moral duties).

dread risk   The extent to which a risk is subjectively experienced as dreadful; one of the basic dimensions of risk perception that was identified in the psychometric paradigm (*see also* unknown risk).

framing effects   The finding that different descriptions of structurally identical problems can alter people's decisions.

heuristic   A simple rule-of-thumb to make a judgement that does not require deliberate and elaborate reasoning.

loss aversion   Tendency to prefer avoiding losses over acquiring gains.

protected or sacred values   Values that are seen as absolute and not tradeable.

psychometric paradigm   An approach of studying risk perception which aims at identifying the psychological dimensions underlying risk judgements.

risk   The possibility that a situation, event, or activity leads to an adverse outcome.

risk perception   People's subjective judgement about the risk associated with some activity, event, or technology.

temporal discounting   Tendency to value delayed outcomes less than immediate ones.

unknown risk   The extent to which a risk is subjectively experienced as new or unfamiliar; one of the basic dimensions of risk perception that was identified in the psychometric paradigm (*see also* dread risk).

unrealistic optimism (or optimism bias)   Tendency to believe that oneself will be more likely to experience positive, and less likely to experience negative, events than similar others.

values   Desirable trans-situational goals, varying in importance, which serve as guiding principles in the life of a person or other social entity.

SUGGESTIONS FOR FURTHER READING

Bernstein, P.L. (1996). *Against the Gods: The Remarkable Story of Risk*. New York, NY: Wiley.

Böhm, G., Nerb, J., McDaniels, T., & Spada, H. (Eds.). (2001). Environmental risks: perception, evaluation, and management [special issue]. *Research in Social Problems and Public Policy*, 9, xi–xx.

Breakwell, G.M. (2007). *The Psychology of Risk*. New York, NY: Cambridge University Press.

Slovic, P. (ed.) (2000). *The Perception of Risk*. London: Earthscan.

Slovic, P. (ed.) (2010). *The Feeling of Risk. New Perspectives on Risk Perception*. London: Earthscan.

REVIEW QUESTIONS

1. Do environmental risks differ from other types of risk, and if so, in which way?
2. Which heuristics do people use to derive risk judgements? Give an example for each heuristic that you know.
3. Describe the psychometric paradigm. Which dimensions have commonly been found to characterize perceived risk?
4. What is meant by protected values and deontological reasoning?
5. How can emotions affect risk perceptions?

3 Climate Change as a Unique Environmental Problem

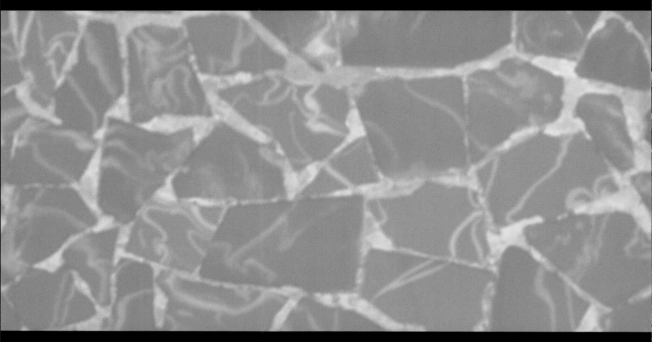

Janet K. Swim
Pennsylvania State University, USA

Lorraine Whitmarsh
Cardiff University, UK

CHAPTER OUTLINE

3.1 INTRODUCTION

The climate has always been changing, but, since the 1970s, physical scientists have raised alarms about **anthropogenic** (human-caused) **climate change** and its impacts on people, animals, and ecosystems. **Climate change** impacts include destabilization of ecological and human systems, and the rate of change outpacing humans' and other species' ability to adapt, creating displacement, disease, death, and extinction (IPCC 2013). These impacts have ethical implications since they disproportionately affect non-industrialized countries and poorer groups, while responsibility for causing climate change lies more with industrialized countries, which emit more heat-trapping gases.

Several unique qualities associated with human-caused climate change require psychologists to expand their ways of thinking about environmental problems. Climate change is global and has varied local impacts that contrast with the relatively more confined local nature of many problems that have been addressed by environmentalists, such as water and noise pollution. Climate change has uniquely multifaceted consequences with interlinking geophysical, biological, and human consequences that differ dependent upon location on the globe and vulnerability of the targets. Furthermore, the issue uniquely poses a challenge to economic and political systems reliant on growth and consumption and to many people's lifestyles and values because almost everything individuals in industrialized countries do directly or indirectly emits heat-trapping gases. Substantial economic, political, and lifestyle changes are needed to address the challenge. Finally, the causal links between individual decisions (e.g. to drive or eat meat) and the impacts on climate are not apparent. The complex, diffuse, distal, ethical, and political nature of climate change contributes to: (i) difficulties the public has in understanding climate change and (ii) their assessment of whether climate change is a risk and, subsequently, whether and how the public responds to the problem. We elaborate on each of these issues below.

3.2 PUBLIC UNDERSTANDING OF CLIMATE CHANGE

Awareness and understanding of climate change has increased since the 1980s when it first entered public consciousness (Capstick et al. 2015). Early assessments revealed conflation of climate change with **weather**, air pollution, and ozone depletion (e.g. Kempton 1991). Recently, erroneous association between ozone holes and climate change has diminished and recognition of the causal

Environmental Psychology: An Introduction, Second Edition. Edited by Linda Steg and Judith I. M. de Groot.
© 2019 John Wiley & Sons Ltd. Published 2019 by John Wiley & Sons Ltd.

link between fossil fuels and climate change has increased (Capstick et al. 2015). This improved knowledge about the role of individuals' energy use is potentially helpful because it removes a barrier to acting on climate change (Geiger et al. 2017).

Yet, gaps remain in the public's understanding of climate change. For example, there is little awareness of **ocean acidification** suggesting that the public does not understand the carbon cycle because human contribution to changes in the carbon cycle are causing both climate change and ocean acidification (Capstick et al. 2016). There also remains a tendency to identify others' energy use rather than one's own energy use as a cause of the problem, which may be due to lack of awareness or motivated reasoning (see below; Whitmarsh 2011).

For some, gaps in knowledge reflect lack of willingness to accept climate science rather than lack of knowledge. Despite growing scientific consensus about the reality and severity of climate change (IPCC 2013), there remains uncertainty and even denial amongst a minority of the public in some industrialized countries (Capstick et al. 2015). Acknowledgement of the seriousness of climate change has become increasingly polarized along party political lines. One of the strongest predictors of belief in climate change is whether people identify with a political party that accepts versus denies climate change (Hornsey et al. 2016). Providing more information about climate change is not necessarily effective for those who are most dismissive of it. For instance, conservatives who are generally scientifically literate are actually more likely to understand climate scientists' view of climate change than conservatives with less scientific knowledge but are also *more* likely to reject this science (Kahan et al. 2012). Consistent with this ideological filter through which information is assessed, providing information about the effectiveness of climate change policies leaves support for these policies unchanged (Rhodes et al. 2014) but instead reinforces existing opinions (Corner et al. 2012). Thus, 'much diversity in [public] understanding can be attributed not to what we learn about climate change but to how, and from whom, we learn: the sources of our information and how we evaluate those sources' (Clayton et al. 2015, p. 640).

3.3   ASSESSING THE RISK OF CLIMATE CHANGE

The extent to which people understand climate change is also reflected in perceptions of the risk it entails. Perceived risk from climate change in turn has implications for behavioural responses (McDonald 2016). To some, including those most vulnerable, climate change is an impending risk to people and the biosphere, requiring immediate action to mitigate and prepare for its impacts. To others, climate change is a distal risk of lesser importance than other, more well-defined, threats to humanity or to immediate personal life events. Thus, to this group, resources and personal attention should be directed to these other problems. To still others, anthropogenic climate change is a hoax generated by groups that latch on to it to promote a left-wing political agenda. As we discuss later, this view is rooted in ideology and actively promoted by certain right-wing organizations and vested interests. For these groups, this 'hoax' should be exposed and those that promote it educated or combated. These different beliefs are reflected in distinct climate change opinion groups or segments (see Box 3.1 and Figure 3.1).

Perceived risk from climate change involves both an assessment of the probability of harm and assessing how serious the problem is deemed to be (see Chapter 2). Both objective and **motivated reasoning**, whereby information processing and use is biased to support one's goals and beliefs, can influence these assessments. A useful way to understand risk assessment is to use the analogy of emergency response. That is, individuals must: (i) detect a problem, (ii) interpret the problem as an emergency or a threat, and (iii) accept and take responsibility for actions to address the problem action (Frantz and Mayer 2009).

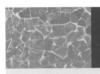

BOX 3.1 TYPOLOGIES OF CLIMATE CHANGE BELIEFS

Opinions about climate change statistically cluster or 'segment' the public into identifiable opinion groups (Roser-Renouf et al. 2015). Six such groups identified in the US ('Six Americas') are: the Alarmed (17% of the US population), Concerned (28%), Cautious (27%), Disengaged (7%), Doubtful (11%), and Dismissive (10%). As illustrated in Figure 3.1, membership in these groups is related to supporting climate change policies (Swim and Geiger 2017).

The size of these groups has remained basically stable over the last decade. Similar groups have been documented in Australia and Germany, though Germany has no Dismissive category possibly because climate change is less politicized there (Metag et al. 2015; Morrison et al. 2013). India, in contrast, has different segments: Informed, Experienced, Undecided, Unconcerned, Indifferent, and Disengaged (Leiserowitz et al. 2013).

Different climate change opinion groups suggest that tailored messages about climate change should be provided to these groups (see Chapter 26). One might provide the Alarmed with outlets for their concern, raise awareness about the risks of climate change to Cautious, Doubtful, and Disengaged groups, and reframe the issue along lines that are less ideologically threatening to the Dismissive group (see discussions on motivated reasoning).

More negative attributes are associated with the Alarmed and Dismissive than the other groups potentially because their relatively more extreme views make them seem non-normative (Swim and Geiger 2018). Yet, these negative impressions are lessened the more one's own opinions match the group's opinions (Swim and Geiger 2018). These impressions are potentially important because people may react against negatively viewed groups (Swim and Geiger 2018).

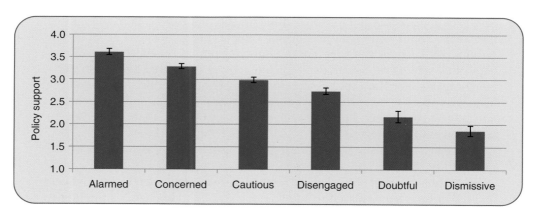

Figure 3.1 *Clusters of the public into identifiable opinion groups based on policy support towards climate change actions (see Box 3.1).*

3.3.1   *Detecting a Problem*

Many features of climate change and human psychological processes make climate change difficult to detect (Geiger et al. 2017). The anthropogenic nature of climate change is invisible, revealed, instead, through complex scientific methods and models. Further, climate change impacts go beyond weather impacts to less obvious effects such as food shortages, human migration, and post-traumatic stress (Clayton et al. 2014). Common construals of climate change also make climate change difficult to detect because it yields narrow definitions of impacts (Geiger et al. 2017; Smith and Leiserowitz 2012). For example, heavy snowfalls due to more moisture in the air counters the perception of climate change causing warming (e.g. melting icebergs); and increased spread of diseases due to migration of disease-carrying insects counters the idea that climate change is about mammals (e.g. polar bears) living in cold regions. Thus, even if a problem is detected, people will have a hard time knowing if the problem is a result of human-caused climate change.

Focal attention away from climate change impacts also makes it difficult to detect. Those living in industrialized areas of the world, with much time spent in climate-controlled spaces and being physically detached from nature, do not notice climate changes (Reser et al. 2014). People attend to weather patterns over short timescales, typically one or two seasons, rather than to longer-term climate changes, leading them to miss larger trends (Howe and Leiserowitz 2013). Due to the **availability heuristic**, climate change has less salience than other risks that are more amenable to direct and regular experience or to consistent media coverage. Motivated reasoning can accentuate this problem: people who believe climate change is not happening are less likely to accurately remember that they had experienced a warmer-than-usual summer during the previous year (Howe and Leiserowitz 2013).

3.3.2   Interpretations of Problems

Many do not interpret climate change and its impacts as a threat and do not feel worried about it (Capstick et al. 2015). Lack of perceived threat and worry can be attributed to ambiguity about whether climate change is responsible for particular problems, informational context, psychological distance from the problems, motivated reasoning that diminishes acceptance of the threat, and coping with intense emotions. We explain each of these below.

Attributional ambiguity about the causes and impacts of climate change increases uncertainty and potential doubt about the impacts of climate change (Swim and Bloodhart 2018). Attributional ambiguity occurs when there are multiple plausible alternative explanations making it difficult to know which explanation is most valid. Environmental or social (e.g. migration, health) problems are multiply determined. For instance, widespread forest fires are a result of both poor management of forest and climate change-induced vulnerability of the forests due to drought and greater survival of tree-eating insects that would otherwise have died when winters were colder. This can make it hard for much of the public to know how far it should be concerned about the relative contribution of climate change to particular problems.

Some argue that oil companies and political groups who do not want government policies that address climate change have purposely created uncertainty about human causes of climate change (Oreskes and Conway 2010). Without attributing the cause to humans, people will not feel responsible for causing it or solving it. One primary way they create uncertainty is by highlighting natural causes of climate change, thus creating attributional ambiguity about the causes of climate change. They also misrepresent 'facts' by various means such as noting that certain periods in history have been warm and ignoring the unique characteristics of current warming trends (Lewandowsky et al. 2013). Moreover, these groups create uncertainty by using scientists as information sources, creating the illusion of a dispute in the field and contributing to public impression of no scientific consensus on anthropogenic climate change. News media have contributed to this confusion via **false balance** – presenting two opposing positions in a way that implies that they represent two equally representative opinions (Boykoff and Boykoff 2004). A more accurate balance would be presenting differing views about whether particular policies would effectively address climate change rather than differing views on the validity of the science attributing recent climate change to humans.

Psychological distance, the perceived distance between oneself and the impacts of climate change (Trope and Liberman 2010), can influence perceived threat and worry (McDonald 2016). Perceiving climate change as having impacts years from now (temporal distance, see Chapter 2), in far-away places (geographic distance), and to people different from oneself (social distance) can decrease perceived threat from climate change. An **optimism bias** where negative consequences of climate change are believed to be more likely to be happening somewhere else and at some other time can diminish feeling at risk. Psychological distance is reduced when one personally experiences climate change; however, this experience is interpreted through the filter of prior beliefs. For example, experiencing a flood or heat-wave will particularly be seen as evidence of climate change if one already believes in climate change (Clayton et al. 2015).

Such motivated reasoning influences perceived threat of climate change, as well as detecting problems, as already noted. For example, when US Americans learn about excessive energy use in the US, they are more likely to attribute climate change to natural causes, than when they learn about an outgroup's (China) high energy consumption, and these attributions, in turn, impact on worry about climate change and policy support (Mo Jang 2013). This suggests that threat to positive evaluations of ingroups diminishes perceived climate change risk. Further, ideological beliefs can influence perceptions of the threats from climate change. For instance, conservatives are less likely to indicate climate change is a problem when solutions involve government regulation than when market-based solutions are proposed – solutions are consistent with their policy preferences (Campbell and Kay 2014). This tendency to discount problems because of a dislike of the solution rather than because of an assessment of the problem itself is known as **solution aversion**.

Even if one initially feels at risk, psychological coping responses may diminish these feelings (see Chapter 2). The consequences of climate change can be aversive, prompting avoidance of the topic (Norgaard 2011). Research on the impacts of fear appeals on taking actions indicates that, if people do not feel capable of reducing the risks, they cope with the seriousness by attenuating the perceived threat (O'Neill and Nicholson-Cole 2009). This suggests that, without effective solutions, worry about climate change will be attenuated. Thus, it is important to pair communication of seriousness of climate change with solutions to reduce the risks of climate change.

3.3.3   Accepting Responsibility and Taking Action

Perceived threat from climate change may not translate into actions for reasons outlined in part II of this book, including people not taking personal responsibility for the threat (e.g. value-belief-norm theory, see Chapter 22). Consistent with this model, accepting personal and collective responsibility are precursors to taking action to address climate change. Further, responsibility must also be paired with personal and community resources that provide opportunities for individual and group actions necessary to address climate change.

Climate change solutions involve, first, reducing heat-trapping gases in the atmosphere (e.g. by changing energy use and food choices; see part II of this book) to slow down and eventually stop climate change (**mitigation**), and, second, adjusting to and preparing for the inevitable impacts (**adaptation**), which involves both decreasing **vulnerability** (e.g. evacuating island nations) and increasing **resilience** (e.g. biodiversity can strengthen forests making them and their inhabitants more resilient to changes in climate impacts; IPCC 2013). We are at a point where mitigation cannot prevent upcoming changes, making adaptation critical. Resilience can be psychological, as well as physical, social, or economic. For instance, people can become more resilient when they know better how to act in an emergency, such as extreme weather events.

Current impacts and future planetary changes are more likely to affect animals than people and, when affecting people, most likely to affect populations such as the poor, elderly, and women, making the need for adaptation and mitigation a social justice (or '**environmental justice**') issue. Psychological research suggests that prejudice against outgroups may impair desire to take action to address climate change, for instance, leading people to be less concerned about harm to outgroup than ingroup members (Swim and Bloodhart 2018; see also Chapter 23). Plus, mitigation and adaption to climate change requires changing livelihoods and lifestyles in ways that are geographically distinct (e.g. changing diets to accommodate more drought-resistant crops in a region). Thus, it is important to consider place and cultural identity when developing responses (Clayton et al. 2015).

3.4 SUMMARY

This chapter highlighted unique psychologically-relevant aspects of climate change relative to other environmental problems that have been studied by environmental psychologists. Climate change is global, multifaceted, difficult to detect, and causally ambiguous. While the science is sound, public understanding and concern vary (e.g. by attitudinal segment and political ideology). Various psychological processes – including motivated reasoning, heuristics, attributional ambiguity, psychological distance, along with the informational context (e.g. media bias, politicized debate) and societal structures (e.g. limited opportunities for low-carbon choices) – influence (and often limit) the detection of the problem, feeling worried and perceptions of threat, as well as taking responsibility for and acting on the problem. Psychological research can reveal ways of mitigating and adapting to climate change, while highlighting and attending to environmental justice.

GLOSSARY

adaptation   Adjusting to and preparing for climate change.
anthropogenic climate change   Human-caused climate change due to increased heat-trapping gases in the atmosphere as a result of burning fossil fuels and changes in land use.
attributional ambiguity   Multiple plausible alternative explanations can be used to describe a behaviour or outcome making it difficult to know which explanation is most valid.

availability heuristic   A cognitive shortcut that relies on examples that immediately come to mind when evaluating a risk (or person, object, etc.), often based on recent or frequent experience with the example.

climate change   Any change in the average and variability of temperature and weather patterns over the long-term (decades or longer), due to natural or human causes. Climate is distinct from weather.

environmental justice   Policies affect people in order to prevent a negative impact on future generations, nature, and the environment.

false balance   Media representations of two opposing positions in a way that implies that the two opinions represent two equally representative opinions.

mitigation   Decreasing the amount of heat-trapping (aka, greenhouse) gases in the atmosphere to slow down climate change and ocean acidification.

motivated reasoning   The tendency to bias the assessment of information such that the assessments align with one's goals or beliefs.

ocean acidification   Decrease in the alkalinity (pH) of the oceans caused by increased absorption of atmospheric Carbon Dioxide (CO_2), which produces carbonic acid when combined with water.

optimism bias   The tendency to see one's own or one's groups' future in a positive light even if information suggests that the positive view is not justified.

psychological distance   The perceived distance between oneself and an event due to time, geographic difference, similarity with others experiencing an event, and/or likelihood. These four dimensions of spatial, temporal, social, and hypothetical distance form the basis of construal level theory (Trope and Liberman 2010).

resilience   Having resources, including psychological resources, that help one cope with negative experiences.

solution aversion   The tendency to discount problems when the solution is unappealing. This is a form of motivated reasoning.

vulnerability   The extent of being at risk from negative experiences.

weather   Short-term, often daily to weekly, changes in the average and variability of temperature, humidity, wind, etc.

SUGGESTIONS FOR FURTHER READING

Capstick, S., Whitmarsh, L., Poortinga, W. et al. (2015). International trends in public perceptions of climate change over the past quarter century. *WIREs: Climate Change* 6 (1): 35–61.

Clayton, S., Devine-Wright, P., Stern, P. et al. (2015). Psychological research and global climate change. *Nature Climate Change* 5: 640–646.

Geiger, N., Middlewood, B.L., and Swim, J.K. (2017). *Psychological, Social, and Cultural Barriers to Communicating About Climate Change*. Oxford Research Encyclopedia.

Swim, J.K., Clayton, S., and Howard, G.S. (2011). Human behavioral contributions to climate change: psychological and contextual drivers. *American Psychologist* 66 (4): 251–264. doi: 10.1037/a0023472.

REVIEW QUESTIONS

1. Why is providing more information about climate change not necessarily effective for changing beliefs about climate change?
2. A useful way to understand risk assessment is to use the analogy of emergency response. Name and describe the three parts of this analogy.
3. Many do not interpret climate change and its impacts as a threat and do not feel worried about it. Provide three psychological explanations why this may be the case.

4 Environmental Stress

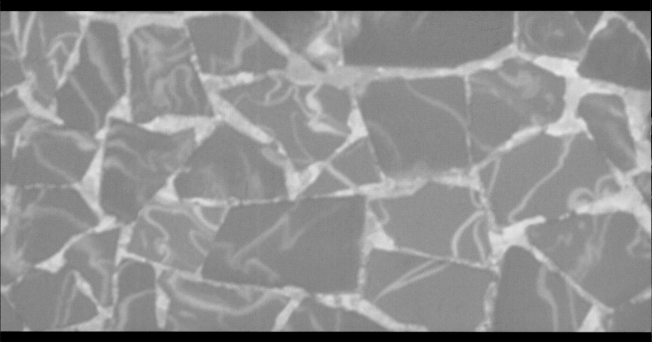

Elena Bilotta
Sapienza University of Rome, Italy

Uchita Vaid
Cornell University, USA

Gary W. Evans
Cornell University, USA

CHAPTER OUTLINE

4.1 INTRODUCTION

Human–environment transactions take different shapes, resulting in various outcomes. Given the human species' ability to survive, these transactions have largely positive outcomes. However, successful adaptation to environmental challenges and demands does not happen without costs. Suboptimal environmental conditions pose demands that may exceed individual capabilities. Such an imbalance between environmental demands and human response capabilities is referred to as **stress** (McGrath 1970; Evans and Cohen 2004). Stress has well-established links with ill-health that occur via alteration of the immune system (Sagerstrom and Miller 2004), increased cardiovascular responses (Steptoe and Kivimäki 2013), and alterations of inflammatory responses (Miller et al. 2002). Stress has also been consistently linked with psychological problems, like deteriorated mental health (Staufenbiel et al. 2013). Nonetheless, not every stressor is created equal, nor are the effects of every stressor harmful to both physical and psychological well-being.

Environmental stressors (e.g. noise, crowding, pollution) can be acute (e.g. pollution levels when stuck in a tunnel) or chronic (e.g. living near a trafficked highway). Chronic environmental stressors are more consequential for humans. For instance, a reliable link has been established between chronic stressors and impaired immunological responses, whilst acute stressors appear to have few consequences (Sagerstrom and Miller 2004). Environmental stressors are often chronic because individuals have limited possibility to escape or extinguish them. As an illustration, citizens living near an airport may not be able to afford the option of moving away. In this chapter we first provide a brief summary of general stress models, followed by a discussion of empirical evidence on the effects of a selection of five environmental stressors.

4.2 CONCEPTUALIZATIONS OF STRESS

Stress research owes much to the early works of Cannon (1932) and Selye (1956). Cannon studied animal and human reactions to dangerous situations. He noted that animals and humans displayed adaptive 'fight-or-flight' responses when they were confronted with emergency situations. He also showed that these fight-or-flight responses involve the activation of the **Sympathetic-Adrenal Medullary (SAM) system**. In case of emergencies, this physiological system regulates adrenaline release, prompting rapid increases in blood pressure, blood

Environmental Psychology: An Introduction, Second Edition. Edited by Linda Steg and Judith I. M. de Groot.
© 2019 John Wiley & Sons Ltd. Published 2019 by John Wiley & Sons Ltd.

coagulation, heart rate and sugar levels in the blood, decreasing the pace of digestion, and privileging allocation of energetic resources to the muscles. Importantly, once the emergency has passed, the system turns back to baseline levels, a process which Cannon dubbed **homeostasis**. Whereas Cannon was concerned with the response to acute threat, Selye was more interested in the adaptation of the body to chronic challenges. Selye proposed a three-stage pattern of response to stress which he called the **general adaptation syndrome (GAS)**. The three phases that the GAS goes through are: an alarm stage analogous to Cannon's fight-or-flight response, a resistance stage in which the body tries to cope with or adapt to the new demands, and an exhaustion stage during which bodily resources become depleted and system damage may occur.

Psychological models of stress have developed independently of biological models and have focused on the influence of psychological factors on stress responses. By far the best known of these models is the transactional model (Lazarus 1966; Lazarus and Folkman 1987). According to this model, stress is the product of the interaction between a person and the environment. Stress arises not only from the occurrence of an event, but also from people's **cognitive appraisal** of the event plus the **coping** strategies they use to deal with the event, both of which also influence stress levels.

More recently, **allostatic load** theory (McEwen 1998) has proposed a dynamic view of stress as the continuous effort of the body to achieve **allostasis** or stability through change. According to this theory there is not one ideal state of bodily functioning. Every time a person is confronted with a stressor, physiological stress systems are activated in order to find a new equilibrium that allows the individual to function in the changed situation. This process of allostasis has important benefits for the individual but is not without costs. Prolonged exposure to stressful conditions that require adjustments of base-line functioning may lead to cumulative wear and tear on the body. In general, the dominant conceptual framework in stress research has shifted from stability (homeostasis) to adaptive change (allostasis; Ganzel et al. 2010).

4.3   EFFECTS OF ENVIRONMENTAL STRESS

Humans face a wide-ranging array of environmental stressors in their daily life, especially in large cities. In this section we review five of the most common and widely studied environmental stressors: noise, crowding, poor housing quality, poor neighbourhood quality, and traffic congestion.

4.3.1   *Noise*

Noise is defined as unwanted sound and is typically characterized by intensity (e.g. decibel), frequency (e.g. pitch), periodicity (continuous or intermittent), and duration (acute or chronic). Sound is necessary but not sufficient to produce noise. The psychological component of sound (i.e. unwanted) and its physical components (i.e. intensity) play a central role in perceiving noise. Other important psychological characteristics of sound include its predictability and the degree of personal control over the source of the sound (Evans and Cohen 1987). Intense, unpredictable and uncontrollable noise can create negative feelings such as irritation and **annoyance** (Klatte et al. 2016).

Chronic noise produces physiological stress (Evans 2001; Van Kempen and Babisch 2012), and can result in significant increase in blood pressure in adults (Babisch and Kim 2011) and children (Van Kempen et al. 2010), an increase in prescriptions of cardiovascular medications, as well as an increase in heart disease and stroke (Münzel et al. 2014). Children attending schools near an airport had higher noradrenaline and other stress hormones and higher resting blood pressure over time compared to children living in quiet areas (Evans et al. 1998a). Additional evidence for physiological stress and noise comes from worksites. Persons working in noisier locations, particularly for many years, have higher blood pressure (Tomei et al. 2010).

Chronic noise negatively impacts people also at a psychological and behavioural level. It affects performance (see Box 4.1) and it may alter the ability to allocate attention, interfering in the detection of infrequent signals (Evans and Hygge 2007) and damaging memory (Van Kempen et al. 2006).

Noise also affects motivation. Children in noisier classrooms have been reported to have lesser achievement motivation (Gilavand and Jamshidnezhad 2016). It has long been found that individuals exposed to noise in a laboratory were less persistent on a motivational task performed after the noise was removed (Glass and Singer 1972). Because these effects were observed after the stressor was removed, these motivational effects have been interpreted as an **aftereffect** caused by the load of working under noise. When individuals were actually able to control the noise, the aftereffects were mitigated. Exposure to

BOX 4.1   EFFECTS OF NOISE ON READING ACQUISITION

Children's reading abilities were compared on two sides of a New York city school: one side of the school building was next to a noisy elevated train track, while the other side was protected from the noise (Bronzaft 1981). Primary school children in classrooms on the noisy side of the building had lower reading abilities compared to children on the quieter side of the building. This evidence is strong because children could not choose which classroom they were assigned to, approximating randomization. In a follow-up, Bronzaft took advantage of a naturally occurring experiment created by major sound reduction work at the school. After the work was completed, reading abilities no longer differed depending on classroom location.

other uncontrollable environmental stressors such as crowding and traffic congestion create similar motivational deficits (Evans and Stecker 2004).

4.3.2 Crowding

Crowding is a psychological state that occurs when a person perceives the number of people in the environment to be exceeding one's preference (Stokols 1972). The same density level may be experienced as more or less crowded because of individual differences (e.g. culture, personality, gender, age) or situational factors (e.g. temporal duration, activity, private versus public space; Stokols 1972). Crowding makes it difficult to regulate social interaction, limits behavioural options, and leads to invasions of **personal space**.

Laboratory studies show that crowding elevates physiological stress: the longer people experience crowding, the greater the elevations (Evans 2006). For example, crowding elevates skin conductance, blood pressure, and stress hormones (Evans 2001). Studies have shown household crowding as an important source of chronic stress (Riva et al. 2014). Living in a crowded home is also negatively associated with multiple aspects of child well-being, even after controlling for several dimensions of socioeconomic status (SES). There is a significant harmful effect of household crowding on academic achievement, on external behaviour problems and on physical health of children (Solari and Mare 2012).

When people feel crowded they also experience psychological stress: they show negative affect, tension, anxiety, and nonverbal signs of nervousness such as fidgeting or playing with objects repetitively (Evans and Cohen 1987). Crowding is consistently associated with **social withdrawal**, a coping mechanism characterized by reduced eye contact, greater interpersonal distancing and more pronounced inhibition in initiating a conversation (Box 4.2). Social withdrawal in turn may hamper such protective factors for mental health as development and maintenance of socially supportive relationships. Evidence on crowding, social withdrawal and social support emphasizes an interesting characteristic of human reactions to suboptimal environmental conditions. Human beings are adaptable but they pay a price for these adaptations (McEwen 2002). For instance, when they cope with crowding by withdrawal, they inadvertently damage social support, thus reducing resources to deal with other stressors, which may eventually translate into increased risks for mental health (Evans and Cohen 2004).

Gender can moderate crowding stressor effects. In general, men show stronger physiological reactions to crowding than women, such as elevated blood pressure (Evans et al. 1998b). Also women living in crowded homes are more likely to be depressed, while men report higher levels of withdrawal, and some males respond with both aggression and withdrawal (Regoeczi 2008). Hypothetically, gender differences in reactions to crowding could stem from men having larger personal space zones than women, or these differences could be due to men having fewer affiliative tendencies, and thus less tolerance for crowding, than women.

BOX 4.2   EFFECTS OF CROWDING ON SOCIAL WITHDRAWAL

In a series of studies, Baum and Valins (1977) examined students living in different types of dormitories. At one university, freshmen were randomly assigned by the housing office to one of two types of rooms: rooms located on both sides of long corridors with 36 students sharing a lounge and bathroom or suites where six students shared a lounge and bathroom. Despite the fact that both dormitories offered comparable floor area per person, over time students in the suites felt less crowded and got along better with people than students in the long corridors. They knew more dormitory residents, felt more strongly that they could regulate social interaction and experienced more social cohesion in their dormitories. This contrasted markedly with the experience of the students in the long-corridor dormitories. Furthermore, not only did the long-corridor residents evaluate the social climate more negatively, their behaviours changed accordingly. For example, when they were placed in an uncrowded waiting room in a laboratory, students from long corridors sat further away from another person in the room and were less likely to glance toward this person than students from the suites. Students living under crowded conditions had learned to cope by socially withdrawing. Such adaptations spilled over even to conditions that were not crowded. In general, these findings illustrate the importance of architecture and design to prevent crowding and negative effects of crowding (see also Chapter 11).

4.3.3   *Poor Housing Quality*

A study among low- and middle-income school children in rural areas in the eastern United States showed that children living in poor housing conditions (i.e. substandard quality of the house, high density, and noise in the house) displayed higher levels of stress hormones, independent of household SES, age or gender (Evans and Marcynyszyn 2004). In this study, housing conditions were assessed by trained raters who walked through the residence, noise was measured with a decibel meter and crowding as people per room. Similar effects of poor housing conditions on physiological indicators of stress have been found among adolescents (Evans et al. 1998a, b) and adults (Schaeffer et al. 1988). Poor housing quality is also related to symptoms of subjective stress (Gillis 1997) and mental health problems such as symptoms of anxiety (Hiscock et al. 2003) and depression (Shenassa et al. 2007). A longitudinal study showed that poor housing quality was associated with children's and adolescents' development, including worse emotional and behavioural functioning and lower cognitive skills (Coley et al. 2013). Improvements in housing conditions are also associated with increases in happiness and life satisfaction among residents who moved to better-quality housing or had their housing renovated (for a review see Thomson et al. 2013; see also Chapters 10 and 11).

4.3.4   Poor Neighbourhood Quality

Among the potentially salient physical characteristics of neighbourhoods that produce chronic stress are: quality of municipal and retail services, recreational opportunities, street traffic, accessibility of transportation, poor maintenance or poor visual surveillance, residential instability (i.e. changes in the local population), the physical quality of educational and healthcare facilities, noise, crowding, and toxic exposure (see also Chapter 11). For example, children displayed greater psychological distress in poorer physical quality urban neighbourhoods (Gifford and Lacombe 2006). Similar trends have been uncovered among adults in cross-sectional (Jones-Rounds et al. 2014) and longitudinal studies (Jokela 2015). Neighbourhood quality has also been shown to be associated with coronary heart disease risks and prevalence (Unger et al. 2014). Two studies in North American cities found that residence in a neighbourhood that is perceived as noisy, unclean, and crime-ridden is associated with poorer self-rated physical health (Hale et al. 2010; Hale et al. 2013). Also, there is some indirect evidence that residents of neighbourhoods of lower SES have poorer physical conditions on a wide array of variables. A randomized housing mobility experiment found that moving from a high-poverty to lower-poverty neighbourhood leads to long-term improvements in adult physical and mental health and subjective well-being (Ludwig et al. 2012). Since low-SES neighbourhood residents typically contend with a large number of environmental stressors compared with persons living in more affluent neighbourhoods (Evans 2004), it is reasonable to hypothesize that some of the observed elevated physiological stress in residents of poor neighbourhoods is likely due, at least in part, to greater environmental stressor exposure.

4.3.5   Traffic Congestion

High levels of traffic congestion may lead to elevated physiological stress and negative affect (e.g. Kozlowsky et al. 1995). Workers who experience traffic congestion more than three times a week report significantly higher levels of stress than those subject to infrequent congestion (Haider et al. 2013). A study among automobile commuters showed that levels of traffic congestion were linked to physiological stress, negative affect, and impaired task motivation (Novaco et al. 1991). This study also found that after a more demanding commute, drivers had more negative social interactions with their family members at home. This is an example of a **spillover effect**, a type of **cumulative fatigue** produced by environmental stressors which occurs when conditions in one setting influence a person's well-being in another setting (Evans and Cohen 2004). Another example of spillover effect is workplace aggression and absenteeism as outcomes of high commuter stress (Hennessy 2008). Research on traffic-related stress is becoming more relevant from both a psychological and a social standpoint because in most countries commuting times are increasing. In the US for example people spend on average almost 50 minutes a day commuting, and the fastest growing segment of commuting trips are those in excess of two hours, one way. Indeed, Americans on average now spend more annual time commuting than they do on holiday.

4.4 SUMMARY

Every day, people have to face a large number of environmental stressors. In this chapter we presented some evidence for the impact of noise, crowding, housing and neighbourhood quality, and traffic congestion on stress. Chronic exposure to these environmental stressors elevates physiological indicators of stress such as adrenaline, cortisol, and blood pressure, as well as psychological indicators of stress such as negative affect and annoyance. People living or working under conditions of noise, crowding, and traffic congestion also reveal deficits in motivation. The stressful impacts of suboptimal physical conditions on people are a joint consequence of physical parameters (e.g. sound intensity, density) plus psychological variables such as control over the environmental stressors. Moreover, stressors may have a series of negative aftereffects that persist even after the source of stress is removed. In order to better understand how chronic environmental stressors influence human health and well-being, physical characteristics of suboptimal settings need to be studied along with the sociocultural context in which they are embedded and how individuals appraise those situations and cope with them.

GLOSSARY

aftereffect The negative affect or motivational deficit, or fatigue that persists even when the environmental stressor is no longer present.

allostasis The process of achieving system stability through physiological and/or behavioural change.

allostatic load Long-term physiological costs of the organism's adaptations to repeated or chronic stressor exposure; an index of general wear and tear on the body.

annoyance Negative feelings and irritability associated with environmental stressors such as noise, pollution, and traffic congestion.

cognitive appraisal Cognitive interpretation of a situation or of an event.

coping Pattern of thoughts and actions individuals use to deal with stress.

crowding The subjective evaluation that the number of people in the environment exceeds the preferred or desired level. It differs from density, namely the objective ratio between number of people and size of environments.

cumulative fatigue The build-up of fatigue from expenditure of energy to cope with an environmental stressor.

environmental stressors Physical characteristics of the environment that produce stress.

general adaptation syndrome (GAS) A syndrome of responses to stress triggered by hormonal mediators.

homeostasis The tendency of a system to maintain internal stability.

noise Unwanted sound, typically measured as sound intensity by decibels.

personal space The area surrounding each person, which when entered by strangers causes discomfort.

social withdrawal Removing oneself from opportunities to engage in social interactions.

spillover effect   The negative affect, strained interpersonal relationships or fatigue, produced by exposure to an environmental stressor in one setting that carries over into another setting.

stress   Human responses to an imbalance between environmental demands and response capabilities of the person; responses to this imbalance may include physiology, negative affect, observational signs of nervousness, complex task performance, and motivation.

Sympathetic-Adrenal Medullary (SAM) system   The part of the sympathetic or involuntary nervous system that regulates the release of epinephrine and norepinephrine from the medullary cortex of the adrenal gland. The SAM system is best known for mediating the body's 'fight or flight' response to stress.

ACKNOWLEDGEMENTS

We thank Luigi Leone and Francesco Leone-Bilotta for their critical feedback and support.

SUGGESTIONS FOR FURTHER READING

Cohen, S., Evans, G.W., Stokols, D., and Krantz, D.S. (1986). *Behavior, Health, and Environmental Stress*. New York, NY: Plenum.

Evans, G.W. (2001). Environmental stress and health. In: *Handbook of Health Psychology* (ed. A. Baum, T. Revenson and J.E. Singer), 365–385. Hillsdale, NJ: Erlbaum.

Halpern, D. (1995). *Mental Health and the Built Environment*. London: Taylor & Francis.

Lopez, R. (2012). *The Built Environment and Public Health*. San Francisco: Jossey-Bass.

REVIEW QUESTIONS

1. List the common indicators of stress.
2. What is the adaptive function of stress responses? Relate your answer to short- and long-term impacts of stressors.
3. Which factors can make sound turn into noise? Name a physiological and a psychological factor.
4. Name two mental health correlates associated with poor housing quality.
5. Describe an example of a spillover effect. How might this phenomenon relate to coping with stressors?

5 Scenic Beauty: Visual Landscape Assessment and Human Landscape Perception

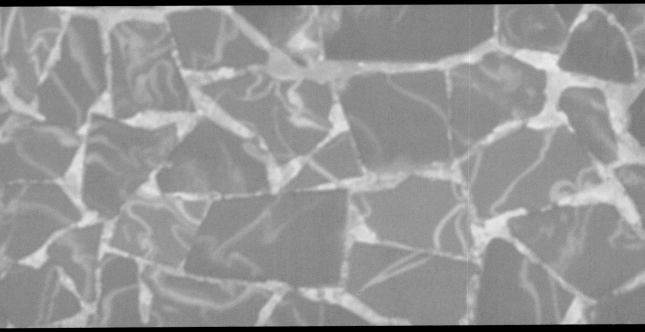

Mari S. Tveit
Norwegian University of Life Sciences, Norway

Åsa Ode Sang
Swedish University of Agricultural Sciences, Sweden

Caroline M. Hagerhall
Swedish University of Agricultural Sciences, Sweden

CHAPTER OUTLINE

5.1   INTRODUCTION

Landscapes are important to people. They form the backdrop of our everyday lives as dynamic expressions of the interaction between the natural environment and human activities (Antrop 1998; Council of Europe 2000). If you ask people to describe their favourite landscape or to tell you about a landscape they have lost, you will find that everyone has a story to tell and that landscapes can evoke strong feelings. Landscapes are important for people's identity and well-being, and exposure to landscapes can even help you recover from stressful or challenging situations (Velarde et al. 2007; see also Chapters 6 and 7).

The European Landscape Convention defines a **landscape** as 'an area, as perceived by people, whose character is the result of the action and interaction of natural and/or human factors' (Council of Europe 2000). Human **perception** is thus a central part of the definition of a landscape. The Convention is aimed at promoting landscape protection, management, and planning in both extraordinary and everyday landscapes. It includes people's landscape perception as well as their **landscape preferences** and **scenic beauty** assessments in policy and planning.

Increasing urbanization and changes in agricultural practices and policies have drastically changed European landscapes. Near-urban productive areas have become large-scale, while abandonment and reforestation occurs in marginal and less productive areas (Antrop 2004; Gómez-Limón and Lucío 1999; Jongman 2002). As a result of these developments, the concern for visual landscape quality in policy and planning has become stronger over the last decades, which has stimulated a rising interest in the scientific study of people's landscape perception.

In the following sections, we will first discuss different approaches to studying the visual quality of landscapes, followed by an overview of theories explaining landscape preferences as either innate or learnt. Then approaches to measuring and mapping scenic beauty are presented followed by methodological developments in this field.

5.2   VISUAL QUALITY ASSESSMENT

There are several approaches to studying visual landscape quality (Daniel 2001). Lothian (1999) proposed a distinction between the **objectivist approach** on the one hand, in which visual quality is viewed as inherent to the landscape and the **subjectivist approach** on the other hand, in which visual quality is considered a construct of the observer. This distinction parallels the long-standing debate in

Environmental Psychology: An Introduction, Second Edition. Edited by Linda Steg and Judith I. M. de Groot.
© 2019 John Wiley & Sons Ltd. Published 2019 by John Wiley & Sons Ltd.

the philosophy of aesthetics whether beauty is 'in the object' or 'in the eye of the beholder' (Meinig 1979). The practice of landscape aesthetics in environmental management has been largely dominated by an objectivist approach, in which visual landscape quality is assessed by experts based on formal knowledge. Research on visual landscape quality, however, has been dominated by the subjectivist approach, in which visual landscape quality is derived from lay people's perceptions and preferences.

Within the subjectivist approach, a distinction can be made between **positivistic models** that consider measurable physical features of landscapes as drivers of preference, and **phenomenological models** that focus on individual's personal experiences as a way to understand the underlying meanings of human–environment transactions (Ohta 2001; Thwaites and Simkins 2007). Both positivistic and phenomenological approaches generally accept that landscape quality derives both from what is in the landscape and from the observer. These approaches differ, however, in the relative importance they ascribe to these two components (landscape versus observer). Daniel and Vining (1983) have summarized the different approaches to studying visual landscape quality as being five 'models' that can be placed on a dimension ranging from objectivistic to subjectivistic (see Box 5.1).

5.3   THEORIES EXPLAINING LANDSCAPE PREFERENCES AS INNATE OR LEARNT

Evolutionary theories explain landscape preferences as a result of human evolution, with landscape preferences of today being innate reflections of landscape qualities enhancing survival in early humans. First, the **biophilia** hypothesis (Wilson 1984) states that humans possess an 'innate affinity for life and lifelike processes', which motivates them to seek contact with animals, plants, and landscapes. The biophilia hypothesis links diversity of species and landscape types to optimal human functioning, but does not specify which species or landscape types comply best with people's biophilic needs. A second evolutionary theory explains environmental preferences as the results of the search for a suitable **habitat** (Orians 1980). This habitat theory states that humans have an innate preference for savannah-like environments, as this was a suitable habitat for our ancestors. A third evolutionary theory is the prospect-refuge theory of Appleton (1975), focusing on the role of early humans as both predator and prey, thus needing to see (**prospect**) without being seen (**refuge**). According to Appleton, the presence of prospect and refuge in a landscape was favourable to survival in primitive human communities, which is still reflected in contemporary landscape preferences. Finally, the Preference Matrix developed by Stephen and Rachel Kaplan is probably the most quoted psychological theory explaining

BOX 5.1   FIVE MODELS OF VISUAL LANDSCAPE QUALITY

Daniel and Vining (1983) have distinguished five approaches or 'models' to studying visual landscape quality, which can be placed on a dimension ranging from objectivistic to subjectivistic:

1. The *ecological model*, an objectivist approach, defines landscape quality as independent of the observer and entirely determined by ecological or biological features in the landscape. Within this model the observer is seen as a user of the landscape and a potential disturbance.

2. The *formal aesthetic model*, also an objectivist approach, characterizes landscapes in terms of formal properties, such as form, line, unity, variety, etc. These properties are seen as inherent characteristics of the landscape that can be assessed by appropriately trained individuals (e.g. landscape architects).

3. The *psychophysical model* takes a position in between the objectivist and subjectivist approach. It aims to establish general relationships between measured physical characteristics of a scene (taken from photographs or geographical databases) and landscape preferences.

4. The *psychological model*, a subjectivist approach, characterizes the landscape in subjective terms by relying on human judgements of complexity, mystery, legibility, etc. These judgements are then related to an array of cognitive, affective, and evaluative dimensions of landscape experiences.

5. The *phenomenological model* is the most subjectivist model. It focuses on how each individual assigns personal relevance to landscape attributes in personal interpretations of landscape encounters.

After reviewing the strengths and weaknesses of each approach, Daniel and Vining (1983) concluded that a careful merger of the psychophysical and psychological approach 'might well provide the basis for a reliable, valid, and useful system of landscape-quality assessment' (p. 80).

landscape preferences (Kaplan and Kaplan 1989). Building on insights from prospect-refuge theory, this theory specifies two basic human needs that influence landscape preferences: the need for exploration and the need for understanding (see Box 5.2 and Table 5.1).

In contrast to the evolutionary approaches, **cultural theories** explain preferences as learnt and shaped by social, cultural, and personal characteristics. These theories often emphasize cognitive evaluation of functions offered by the landscape to individuals, instead of immediate affective responses (Bell 1999). Much quoted cultural theories include **topophilia** and the **ecological aesthetic**. First, topophilia implies that humans have a tendency to bond with what one knows well, meaning that familiarity and experience are important drivers of landscape preference (Tuan 1974). Second, the ecological aesthetic states that knowledge about the ecological functions of a landscape will lead to preference

BOX 5.2 THE PREFERENCE MATRIX

For prehumans who depended on hunting and gathering, the spatial understanding of areas they inhabited as well as the ability to explore new areas was probably highly important. Building on these insights, Kaplan and Kaplan (1989) proposed that visual information facilitating understanding and exploration has been very important in shaping human preferences, because appreciation of such landscapes would have been favoured by natural selection. The Preference Matrix combines these two informational needs with two different levels of immediacy or the degree of inference that is required in extracting the information (two-dimensional vs. three-dimensional space). The resulting matrix, as depicted in Table 5.1, identifies four landscape characteristics predicting landscape preference:

Coherence: Immediate understanding of how elements in the environment fit together.

Complexity: Visual richness that can be immediately explored.

Legibility: Understanding of what lies ahead and how you could find your way and not get lost.

Mystery: The promise of new things to explore if moving further into the landscape.

In a review of preference studies, Kaplan et al. (1989) found mystery to be the most consistent predictor of landscape preferences.

Table 5.1 *The preference matrix.*

Level of interpretation	Informational needs	
	Understanding	*Exploration*
Immediate (two-dimensional)	Coherence	Complexity
Inferred (three-dimensional)	Legibility	Mystery

Adapted from Kaplan and Kaplan (1989), see Box 5.2 for an explanation.

for it, making knowledge an important driver of preference (Carlson 2009; Gobster 1999; Nassauer 1992; see also Chapter 8). Other cultural theories include theories of sense or spirit of places, also known as **genius loci**, emphasizing the uniqueness and visually striking features of landscapes (Bell 1999; Norberg-Schulz 1980), **landscape heritage approaches** emphasizing visual signs of cultural heritage (e.g. Fairclough et al. 1999) and **aesthetics of care** emphasizing the importance of signs that a landscape is taken care of (Nassauer 1995, 1997).

Consistent with evolutionary theories, empirical research has shown a high degree of universality in landscape preferences (Bell 1999, p. 82; Kaplan and Kaplan 1989; Ulrich 1986; Van den Berg and Koole 2006). However, these evolutionary-based preferences are modified and shaped by cultural influences and experience, resulting in variations in preference ratings between groups and subcultures (Tveit 2009; Van den Berg et al. 1998; see also Chapter 8). Some landscape elements, such as water, seem to be rather universally appreciated whilst other aspects such as openness are evaluated differently according to observer characteristics (Sevenant and Antrop 2010; Tveit et al. 2006). These findings underline the importance of developing integrated theories that combine evolutionary, cultural, and personal bases for landscape preferences (Bell 1999; Bourassa 1991).

5.4   MEASURING AND MAPPING SCENIC BEAUTY

Several methods and frameworks for the assessment of scenic beauty and landscape quality have been developed to provide tools for decision support and landscape monitoring (see overviews in Tveit et al. 2006; Ode et al. 2008). Such methods and frameworks should be transparent, repeatable, and transferable between landscapes (Ode et al. 2008; Tveit et al. 2006). Some of these methods are largely expert based with rather weak links to the perception-based models explained above. However, other methods have explicitly taken people's preferences as a starting point. We will briefly discuss some of these latter models.

The **scenic beauty estimation (SBE) method** is a psychophysical method developed by the US Forestry Department (Daniel and Boster 1976). The SBE method estimates scenic beauty judgements for (images of) various natural scenes. These judgements are then statistically related to measurable landscape characteristics through regression analysis. The relationship between measurable landscape characteristics and perceived scenic beauty is used to predict or evaluate landscape management alternatives for their impact on scenic beauty. The SBE method has been applied mostly to forest stands. For example, Buhyoff et al. (1986) used the method to predict the scenic beauty of American southern pine stands. Results showed that physical variables related to age and size of the trees, such as the age of the dominant stand in years and average diameter at breast height of all trees in the plot stand, are positively related to scenic quality assessments by the general public. In total, 50% of the variance in the beauty ratings could be explained by these age- and size-related variables.

A more recent method is the **VisuLands framework** (see Tveit et al. 2006; Ode et al. 2008). This framework links visual indicators to theories of landscape perception and preference. It identifies nine key visual landscape aspects: naturalness, **stewardship, disturbance, historicity, visual scale, imageability, ephemera,** coherence, and complexity (see Box 5.2 for definitions of the latter two aspects). For each of these aspects, landscape attributes and elements contributing to its expression in the visual landscape are identified, as well as currently used visual indicators to assess it. The VisuLands framework presents a comprehensive approach to describing visual landscapes and assessing visual effects of land-scape change using data sources such as photographs, land cover data, aerial photographs, and field observations (Ode et al. 2010). Research has identified strong relationships between the nine key aspects and landscape preferences, although their relative importance and interpretation may vary across groups (Ode et al. 2008; Ode Sang and Tveit 2013). For example, disturbance is gener-ally perceived as negative. However, thresholds for when a change is perceived as disturbance may differ according to expectations, background, and motives (Shang and Bishop 2000; Sheppard and Picard 2006).

5.5   METHODOLOGICAL DEVELOPMENTS

The majority of landscape preference studies have used photographs as visual stimuli to assess preferences. On-site surveys are time-consuming, and photo-graphs have been found to be efficient and valid representations of real landscapes (Daniel and Meitner 2001; Palmer and Hoffman 2001). Recent developments include the use of computer **visualizations** and **virtual environments** in landscape preference surveys and scenario assessments (Bishop and Rohrmann 2003; Bishop et al. 2001; Ode et al. 2009). Studies have shown that realistic visualizations work as substitutes for photographs but that mixing different forms of stimuli should be avoided (Pihel et al. 2014). The use of computer-based visualizations and vir-tual environments allows for a high degree of control over the content of the environment, enabling the systematic testing of different aspects of the composi-tion of the environment (Ode Sang et al. 2014).

Significant advances in computer capability and improved access to high-resolution geodata have led to increased use of Geographical Information Systems in landscape assessment. A recent development is the ability to project map-based data onto a 3D terrain to create panoramic scenes of the visible area from certain points in the landscape, so-called **viewsheds**, making possible the development of indicators based on visual topology (e.g. Sang et al. 2015).

Eye tracking is a rather novel approach within landscape research (Dupont et al. 2013; Ode Sang et al. 2016), capturing the viewer's exploration of an image. The eye movements, including the order and length of fixations on specific parts of the image, are recorded as the respondent assesses the land-scape image on the screen. This method gives direct information about the features upon which the respondent bases the assessment. Pupil size gives an indication of relaxation and arousal responses, which can give information about the **restorative potential** of landscape elements (see also Chapter 7). The information from eye tracking strengthens the interpretation of results from preference surveys and complements them with more implicit, automatic meas-ures, of which landscape factors are important for perception and preference (Ode Sang et al. 2016).

5.6   SUMMARY

People's landscape perception is at the heart of the European Landscape Convention, which aims to promote landscape protection, management, and planning. This chapter presents some of the main approaches and theories of landscape perception and preferences. A distinction can be made between objectivist and subjectivist approaches which interpret landscape quality as either inherent in the landscape or in the eye of the beholder. Different models for studying visual landscape quality, ranging from an objectivist to a subjectivist approach, have been presented, along with evolutionary and cultural theories explaining landscape preferences as either innate or learnt. This chapter also provides an overview of methods for measuring and mapping scenic beauty, along with some recent methodological developments. The chapter shows that there is a substantial and growing knowledge base to meet the challenges of integrating knowledge about people's landscape perception in planning and policy according to the demands from the European Landscape Convention.

GLOSSARY

aesthetics of care   An approach to studying visual landscape quality that emphasizes the importance of signs that a landscape is taken care of, such as fences, mown edges, and tidy plantings.

biophilia   People's innate tendency to seek connections with nature and other forms of life.

cultural theories   Theories that view human nature as the result of social and cultural influences.

disturbance   Lack of contextual fit and coherence.

ecological aesthetic   An approach to landscape aesthetics which assumes that the more people learn about ecosystems, the more they will appreciate them.

ephemera   Changes with season and weather.

evolutionary theories   Theories that view human nature as a universal set of evolved psychological adaptations to recurring problems in the ancestral environment.

eye tracking   Measuring eye movements; either the point of gaze or the motion of an eye relative to the head.

genius loci   A location's distinctive atmosphere, or the 'spirit of place'.

habitat   The natural home or environment of an animal, plant, or other organism.

historicity   Historical continuity and historical richness, different time layers, amount and diversity of cultural elements.

imageability   Landscapes or landscape elements making landscapes distinguishable and memorable, creating a strong visual impression.

landscape   An area, as perceived by people, whose character is the result of the action and interaction of natural and/or human factors.

landscape heritage approach   A cultural approach to studying visual landscape quality that emphasizes the importance of visual signs of cultural heritage, such as archaeological ruins, ancient towns, grave sites, and sacred places.

landscape preference   The degree to which a landscape is liked.

objectivist approach   An approach to studying visual landscape quality that views scenic beauty as inherent to the landscape.

perception   The process by which an individual receives, selects, organizes, and interprets information to create a meaningful picture of the world.

phenomenological models   Models that focus on the individual's landscape experiences as a way to understand the underlying meanings of human–environment transactions.

positivistic models   Models that consider measurable physical features of landscapes as drivers of preference.

prospect   An outlook or view over a region or in a particular direction (direct prospect), or the promise that such an outlook or view can be attained if one could reach points farther off in the landscape (indirect prospect).

refuge   A place that serves as a shelter or as a hiding place.

restorative potential   The capability (of a landscape or other environment) to promote recovery from stress, mental fatigue, or other adverse conditions.

scenic beauty   The aesthetic experience of visual landscapes through perception.

scenic beauty estimation (SBE) method   A psychophysical method for the assessment of scenic beauty and landscape quality developed by the US Forestry Department as a decision support tool for government agencies.

subjectivist approach   An approach to studying visual landscape quality that views scenic beauty as a construct of the observer.

stewardship   Perceived human care for nature and landscape through active and careful management.

topophilia   A term used to describe emotional connections between human beings and places.

viewshed   Area visible to the human eye from a fixed viewpoint.

virtual environments   Computer-simulated environments that can simulate physical presence in places in the real world.

visual scale   Degree of openness, size of perceptual units.

Visualizations   A systematic process of describing landscape attributes, their spatial pattern, and their importance to people.

VisuLands framework   A decision-support model that predicts visual landscape quality from nine visual landscape characteristics: naturalness, stewardship, disturbance, historicity, visual scale, imageability, ephemera, coherence, and complexity.

SUGGESTIONS FOR FURTHER READING

Altman, I. and Wohlwill, J.F. (1983). Behavior and the natural environment. In: *Human Behavior and Environment: Advances in Theory and Research*. New York, NY: Plenum Press.

Kaplan, R. and Kaplan, S. (1989). *The Experience of Nature: A Psychological Perspective*. Cambridge: Cambridge University Press.

Wolfe, J.M., Kluender, K.R., Levi, D.M. et al. (2015). *Sensation & Perception*. Sunderland, MA: Sinauer Associates Inc.

REVIEW QUESTIONS

1. What is the main difference between objectivistic and subjectivistic approaches to visual landscape quality assessment?
2. List the five models of visual quality as distinguished by Daniel and Vining (1983).
3. The Preference Matrix by Kaplan and Kaplan (1989) distinguishes two basic informational needs that guide people's landscape preferences and four characteristics that fulfil these needs. Describe these needs and characteristics.
4. Which are the nine key aspects of visual landscapes according to the VisuLands framework?

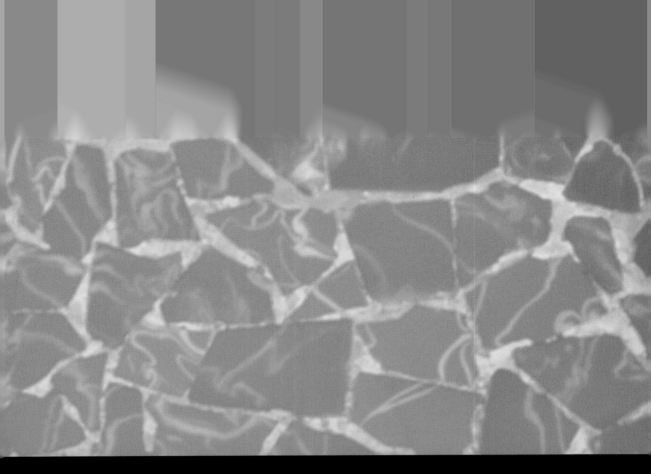

Agnes E. van den Berg
University of Groningen, The Netherlands

Yannick Joye
University of Groningen, The Netherlands

Sjerp de Vries
Wageningen University and Research, The Netherlands

CHAPTER OUTLINE

6.1 INTRODUCTION

The idea that contact with nature can promote health and well-being has a long history in Western as well as non-Western cultures (Box 6.1). This idea is still very much alive today. For example, in 2012, 96% of respondents in a representative Dutch sample indicated that they agreed with the statement 'a visit to nature gives me a healthy feeling' (Van den Berg 2012). People do not only believe that nature is healthy, they also act on these beliefs. Initiatives that make use of the healing powers of nature have emerged and prospered in many countries (Allen and Balfour 2014; Barton et al. 2016). Some well-known examples are the 'green gyms' in the UK, the 'udeskole' or outdoor education programs in Denmark) and 'shinrin-yoku', a popular Japanese practice which refers to the act of visiting nature areas for therapeutic reasons.

The idea that contact with nature is healthy appears so intuitively valid, that for a long time, people felt no need to demonstrate or quantify nature's contribution to their health and well-being. However, recent developments in **public health promotion** in Western countries have stimulated a growing interest in and demand for the scientific study of nature–health relations. Due to increased **stress** and a sedentary lifestyle, levels of cardiovascular disease, type II diabetes and respiratory conditions are rising at a rapid rate all across the Western world. Common sense knowledge suggests that natural environments can help to combat this health crisis by supporting an active, stress-free lifestyle. But does it really work? And if it works, how much nature of what size and type is needed, and where, to achieve certain health benefits? And for whom? To answer these questions, environmental psychologists have started to collect scientific

BOX 6.1 HISTORICAL BACKGROUND

One of the earliest references to the health-promoting qualities of nature is found on an ancient Sumerian clay tablet which described the paradisal garden of Dilmun as a place where 'human beings are untouched by illness'. The Greek text Air, Waters, and Places, attributed to Hippocrates (460–370 BCE), stresses the importance of climate, water quality, and a scenic environment for health. In later periods, references to physical and emotional benefits of nature can be found in historical texts about, among other things, mediaeval cloister gardens, romantic picturesque landscapes, and Victorian period urban parks. For example, in the early eighteenth century, British Prime Minister William Pitt aptly captured the health functions of the capital's parks with the phrase 'the lungs of London'.

Environmental Psychology: An Introduction, Second Edition. Edited by Linda Steg and Judith I. M. de Groot.
© 2019 John Wiley & Sons Ltd. Published 2019 by John Wiley & Sons Ltd.

evidence on nature–health relationships and possible mechanisms underlying these relationships. This chapter will give an overview of this research area, starting with a brief introduction to the concepts of health and nature.

6.2   WHAT IS HEALTH AND HOW CAN IT BE MEASURED?

The World Health Organization (WHO) definition of **health**, formulated in 1948, describes health as 'a state of complete physical, mental and social well-being and not merely the absence of disease or infirmity'. At that time this for-mulation was groundbreaking because of its focus on factors that support health and wellbeing (**salutogenesis**), instead of on factors that cause disease (**pathogenesis**). However, the WHO definition has been much criticized as being unmeasurable and unattainable. Indeed, the requirement for complete health would leave most people unhealthy most of the time. To overcome these limitations, a new dynamic concept of health was introduced, which describes health as 'the ability to adapt and to self-manage, in the face of social, physical and emotional challenges' (Huber et al. 2011). This concept provides a positive yet realistic and measurable view of health and, as such, it provides a suitable starting point for the study of health benefits of nature.

The health status of an individual or group can be measured by means of **health indicators**. A distinction can be made between clinical and public health indicators. **Clinical health indicators** cover objective and subjective measures of patient functioning, such as symptom severity, mortality, hospital days, medica-tion use, discomfort (pain, nausea), and patient satisfaction. **Public health indica-tors** give an indication of the health status of a population. These indicators include measures based on birth and death statistics, such as **mortality rates** and life expectancy; measures of the prevalence and incidence of disease and **illness** (also called **morbidity rates**); measures of self-reported general, mental and physical health; and measures of health-related quality of life. In addition to primary health indicators, **health risk factors**, such as smoking, inactivity, or stress, can be distinguished, which are associated with an increased probability of disease occurrence in the future.

6.3   WHAT IS NATURE AND HOW CAN IT BE MEASURED?

Within environmental psychology, the term **nature** is generally used to denote a broad category of natural environments and features of those environments, such as single trees or plants. Because visual experience plays an important role in human–nature interactions, representations of natural environments and features, such as photographs, films, video, and virtual nature, are also included in the concept of nature. The term **natural environment** is also broadly defined to include any kind of environment, place, or setting where vegetation and other natural elements (such as water) are dominantly present. However, different terms tend to be used depending on the degree of cultivation and the size of the setting. As discussed in Chapter 5, the term **landscape** is typically used for areas, often located in the countryside, that are the result of an interaction between human and natural factors. The term **nature area** is used to describe more large-scale natural settings that have developed through natural growth rather than design or planning. Finally, **green space** is a term that is mostly used by policy makers to refer to nature in and around urban areas, such as parks, trees along streets, and gardens.

Measures of the presence, amount or quality of green space in a certain area or place are commonly referred to as **green space indicators**. Just like health indicators, green space indicators can be assessed in an objective or subjective manner. Objective green space indicators, such as the percentage of an area covered by vegetation or water, can be calculated from maps, photos, or land-use databases, or by conducting systematic on-site observations. Subjective (or perceived) indicators can be derived from respondents' own descriptions of the amount and/or quality of green space in their own environment.

6.4   NATURE AND CLINICAL HEALTH

In 1984, Roger Ulrich published a study in the prestigious journal *Science* which, for the first time, provided empirical evidence that exposure to nature may improve human health (Ulrich 1984). Using the hospital files of patients recovering from gall bladder surgery, Ulrich demonstrated that patients in rooms overlooking a natural area with trees required somewhat shorter postoperative hospital stays, received fewer negative comments in nurses' notes, and needed fewer doses of strong painkillers than patients with a view of a brick wall, especially on days 2–5 after the surgery, when they had sufficiently recovered to be aware of their surroundings, but still suffered pain (Figure 6.1).

The findings of Ulrich's hospital-file study have been replicated in a series of clinical trials in a Korean hospital in which patients were, after surgery, assigned to rooms with and without potted plants (Park 2006). The results of these trials showed, among other things, that patients in rooms with plants had shorter hospital stays and needed fewer intakes of postoperative pain medication than patients in rooms without plants. Unlike the patients in Ulrich's hospital-file study, the patients in the Korean studies were randomly (that means by chance) allocated to rooms that were exactly similar except for the presence of plants. Therefore, the health differences between the groups who recovered in the two types of rooms can be unambiguously attributed to the presence of plants.

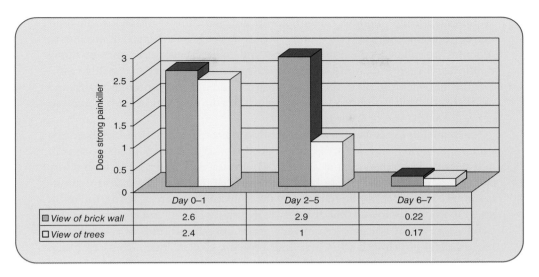

	Day 0–1	Day 2–5	Day 6–7
☐ View of brick wall	2.6	2.9	0.22
☐ View of trees	2.4	1	0.17

Figure 6.1 *Intake of doses of strong painkillers among patients recovering from gallbladder surgery in rooms with a view of nature or a view of a brick wall.*
Source: Adapted from Ulrich (1984).

Outside the hospital, a substantial amount of research has documented positive health impacts of **green care**, or nature-based therapies, such as care farming, horticultural therapy, or green exercise programs (Bragg and Atkins 2016). Unfortunately, this research has typically failed to include control groups that received the same kind of therapy in a non-natural environment. This makes it difficult to determine whether any health benefits were due to the natural environment, or to other factors, such as the structure, staffing, and activities of the programs. Consequently, research on green care provides mostly circumstantial evidence for a relationship between nature and health.

6.5 GREEN SPACE AND PUBLIC HEALTH

A more recent line of research has investigated the relationship between access to green space in the living environment and public health. This research has used large-scale population studies to compare the health and well-being of people living in green areas to the health and well-being of those living in less green areas (Van den Berg et al. 2015). Because attractive, natural neighbourhoods tend to attract wealthier and thus healthier people, advanced statistical techniques are used to control for confounding effects of socioeconomic background variables. A pioneering study among more than 10 000 residents of the Netherlands (De Vries et al. 2003) found that residents with a high percentage of green space in a 1 or 3 km radius around their home reported better general and mental health and fewer health complaints than those with a low percentage of green space around their home. These findings have been replicated with different populations, health measures, and green space indicators in many countries. A review of these studies revealed strong evidence for positive associations between the quantity of green space and perceived mental health and all-cause mortality, and moderate evidence for an association with perceived general health (Van den Berg et al. 2015).

Epidemiological studies have consistently indicated that relationships between green space and health are stronger for groups who tend to spend more time in and near their homes, such as the elderly, housewives, and people with a low socioeconomic status. As a result, health inequalities between different socio-economic groups might be reduced by the availability of green space. Indeed, a study in England showed that disparity in mortality rates between poor and rich people was about twice as low in very green neighbourhoods as compared to barren neighbourhoods (Mitchell and Popham 2008). Thus, access to green space may protect people from the negative health consequences of having a low income.

Research on relationships between green space and health has focused mostly on the presence or amount of green space in the living environment. However, there is growing recognition that the quality of the green space is also important for health (Van Dillen et al. 2011). The importance of quality above quantity was demonstrated in a study in two neighbourhoods in a Dutch city (Zhang et al. 2015). The two neighbourhoods differ in quality of green space, specifically accessibility and usability, but were matched for amount of green space and socio-demographic composition. Despite the similarity in amount of green space, residents of the neighbourhood with more accessible and usable green spaces reported better mental health and more attachment to the neighbourhood green space.

6.6 MECHANISMS LINKING NATURE TO HEALTH

How can a positive relationship between nature and health be explained?

We discuss four main mechanisms (Hartig et al. 2014): (i) improvement in **air quality,** (ii) stimulation of **physical activity**, (iii) facilitation of **social cohesion**, and (iv) stress reduction (Figure 6.2). This selection is not complete. There are many other plausible pathways via which nature can directly and indirectly influence health, including the buffering of noise, exposure to ultraviolet light which generates vitamin D, strengthening connectedness to nature, or the stimulation of spiritual experiences (Cleary et al. 2017; Kuo 2015). However, we focus on air quality, physical activity, social cohesion, and stress reduction as the most widely studied mechanisms.

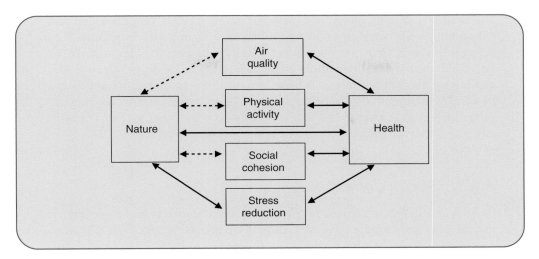

Figure 6.2 *Schematic representation of relationships among nature, health, and underlying mechanisms. Solid lines represent established relationships; dashed lines represent weaker or inconsistent relationships.*

6.6.1 Air Quality

Plants and trees are well-known for their capacity to remove pollutants from the air and to reduce heat by providing shade and increasing humidity levels (Zupancic et al. 2015). Plants and trees also give off essential oils, known as **phytoncides**, as a protection against harmful attacks by insects, fungi, and bacteria. Preliminary findings indicate that inhaling phytoncides and other substances found in nature like **negative air ions** can have beneficial effects on human physiology and mental health (Craig et al. 2016). However, plants and trees may also have a negative influence on air quality, by releasing pollens, or by impeding airflows in urban areas so that dust gets 'trapped' (Vos et al. 2013). Plants and trees thus can have positive as well as negative impacts on air quality. Whether the overall net health effect is favourable may depend on specific local circumstances.

6.6.2 Physical Activity

In popular discourse, the concept of 'healthy nature' is closely associated with the concept of 'being physically active'. It may therefore come as a surprise that epidemiological studies have often failed to demonstrate positive relationships between nature and physical activity levels (e.g. Maas et al. 2008). For some populations, especially children and the elderly, positive relations between physical activity levels and presence of and/or distance to green space have been reported. However, these relations may depend to a large extent on perceptions of (traffic) safety, rather than on the naturalness of the setting. A natural environment may, however, support physical activity by providing added benefits.

For example, people generally experience more positive emotions and less exhaustion while walking or cycling in natural environments compared to doing the same activities in built or indoor environments (Bowler et al. 2010). For children, playing in natural settings can encourage more creative and explorative play behaviour that is beneficial for their emotional, cognitive, and physical development (Wilson 2012). Hence, the relationship between the naturalness of a setting and physical activity is more complex than is often thought, and may vary with the type of activity and population subgroup.

6.6.3   Social Cohesion

Parks and other green spaces may promote social contacts and cohesion (or bonds) between neighbourhood members by providing attractive places to meet and socialize (Coley et al. 1997; De Vries et al. 2013). Especially, community and allotment gardens have been found effective in promoting social contacts and reducing feelings of loneliness (Van den Berg et al. 2010). However, in dense urban areas, enclosed green spaces, especially when they are ill-maintained, can also reduce social cohesion by making people feel unsafe (Kaźmierczak 2013).

6.6.4   Stress Reduction

Nature and green space are highly valued for their stress-reducing properties. As many people know from personal experience, taking in the sounds and sights of nature can almost instantly make one feel more relaxed and release mental and physical tension. It has been suggested that this stress-relieving capacity of nature is a remnant of human evolution in natural environments, during which the human brain may have become hardwired to respond positively to unthreatening natural settings (Ulrich 1999, see also Chapter 5). Nature's stress-relieving properties are supported by a large number of experimental studies, which have shown that natural environments promote faster and more complete restoration from physical and mental stress symptoms than most built environments (Collado et al. 2017) Moreover, epidemiological studies have shown that relationships between green space in the living environment and health can, to a large extent, be explained by the lower stress levels of residents of greener areas (De Vries et al. 2013). Even viewing nature from the window, or watching slides or videos of nature, can lead to measurable reductions in mental and physical stress levels. This latter finding suggests that the visual perceptual system plays an important role in nature's stress-relieving properties.

In sum, although health benefits of nature are likely to be regulated by multiple pathways, the psychological mechanism of stress reduction has thus far received the strongest and most unequivocal support. Empirical evidence regarding air quality, physical activity, and social cohesion as mechanisms underlying nature–health relationships remains more mixed and inconclusive. The details of the stress reduction mechanism are discussed in chapter 7.

6.7   SUMMARY

In this chapter we have provided an overview of empirical research aimed at verifying the long-standing and widely held notion that contact with nature can promote people's health and well-being. We have shown that there is increasing evidence from well-controlled studies for positive relationships between nature and clinical and public health indicators. However, the causal nature of these relationships needs to be further established. We have discussed four mechanisms that may explain a relationship between nature and health: (i) air quality, (ii) physical activity, (iii) social cohesion, and (iv) stress-reduction. Of these mechanisms, stress reduction appears the most unequivocally established pathway to health benefits of nature. In general, the scientific research and insights discussed in this chapter provide a scientific base for the formal acceptance and better practical use of health benefits of nature in policy and practice.

GLOSSARY

air quality   A measure of the condition of air relative to the requirements of humans or other species.

clinical health indicators   Objective and subjective measures of patient functioning.

epidemiological studies   Studies on the distribution and determinants of health-related states or events.

green care   An umbrella term for preventive and therapeutic interventions that use elements of nature to promote health.

green space   A term mostly used by policymakers to refer to nature in and around urban areas.

green space indicator   A measure of the presence, quantity or quality of green space.

health   A condition of well-being free of disease or infirmity.

health indicator   A measure of the health status of an individual or group.

health risk factor   Behaviour or other characteristics associated with an increased probability of future disease occurrence.

illness   The subjective state of 'unwellness' which can occur independently of, or in conjunction with, disease or sickness.

landscape   An area, as perceived by people, whose character is the result of the action and interaction of natural and human factors.

morbidity rate   The number of individuals suffering from a disease during a given time period (the prevalence rate) or the number of newly appearing cases of a disease per unit of time (incidence rate).

mortality rate   The number of deaths (in general, or due to a specific cause) in a population, typically expressed in units of deaths per 1000 individuals per year.

nature area   A natural setting, often large-scale and remotely located, that has developed through natural growth rather than design or planning.

natural environment   Any kind of environment, place, or setting where vegetation and other natural elements are dominantly present.

nature   A broad concept that encompasses natural areas such as forests as well as agricultural landscapes, urban greenery, and natural elements and features such as trees and lakes.

negative air ions   negatively charged particles in the air that are naturally formed by cosmic rays, lightning, waterfalls, rains or wind.

pathogenesis   An approach to health that focuses on the identification and elimination of factors that cause disease.

physical activity   Any bodily movement produced by skeletal muscles that causes your body to work harder than normal.

phytoncides   essential oils given off by trees to protect against harmful attacks by insects, fungi, and bacteria.

public health indicators   Objective and subjective measures of the health status of a population, such as measures based on the prevalence and incidence of disease, or self-reported health measures.

public health promotion   The science of protecting and improving the health of communities through education, promotion of healthy lifestyles, and research for disease and injury prevention.

salutogenesis   An approach to health that focuses on factors that support human health and well-being.

social cohesion   The degree to which members of a community feel committed to the community and other members of the community.

stress   A real or perceived threat or challenge to the integrity of the organism, which is often accompanied by fear or anxiety.

SUGGESTIONS FOR FURTHER READING

Barton, J., Bragg, R., Wood, C., and Pretty, J. (2016). *Green Exercise: Linking Nature, Health and Well-Being*. London / New York: Routledge.

Nilsson, K., Sangster, M., Gallis, C. et al. (2010). *Forests, Trees and Human Health and Well-Being*. Dordrecht: Springer Science Business and Media.

Van den Bosch, M. and Bird, W. (2017). *The Oxford Textbook of Nature and Public Health*. Oxford: Oxford University Press.

REVIEW QUESTIONS

1. Why is it important to empirically verify relationships between nature and health?
2. What is the main difference between the biomedical/pathogenic and biopsychosocial/salutogenic approach to health?
3. What are health inequalities and how can green space in the living environment reduce such inequalities?
4. How can a positive relationship between nature and health be explained? Describe the mechanisms that are commonly used to explain health benefits of nature.
5. What is known about the relationship between nature and physical activity?

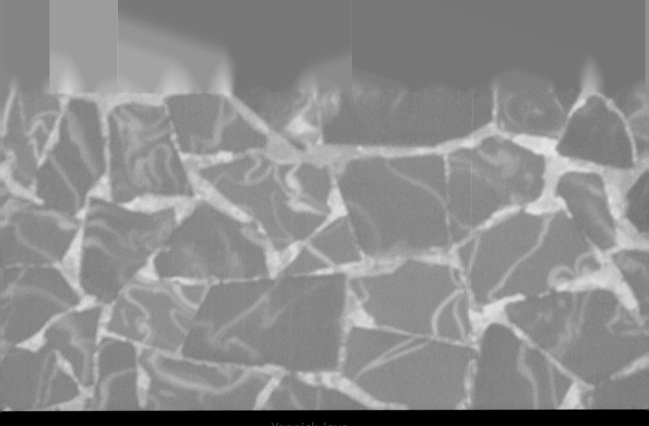

Yannick Joye
University of Groningen, The Netherlands

Agnes E. van den Berg
University of Groningen, The Netherlands

CHAPTER OUTLINE

7.1   INTRODUCTION

What would you recommend to a friend who is feeling stressed and worried? Go to sleep? See a funny movie? Or take a walk in the forest? Chances are high that you will pick the latter option. Indeed, going into nature is probably among the most widely practised ways of obtaining relief from stress and fatigue in modern Western societies. How can this be explained? More than 150 years ago, the American landscape architect Frederik Law Olmsted already noted that 'scenery worked by an unconscious process to produce relaxing and "unbending" of faculties made tense by the strain, noise, and artificial surroundings of urban life' (Beveridge 1977, p. 40). This analysis seems strikingly modern and prefigures recent theoretical formulations concerning the so-called 'restorative' or stress-relieving effects of nature. In this chapter, we will give an overview of theories on restorative effects of natural environments, along with a discussion of empirical findings and practical implications.

7.2   RESTORATIVE ENVIRONMENTS RESEARCH

The word **restoration** is an umbrella term that, within environmental psychology, refers to the experience of a psychological and/or physiological recovery process that is triggered by particular environments and environmental configurations, i.e. **restorative environments**. A substantial number of experiments have shown that natural environments tend to be more restorative than urban or built environments (see Box 7.1). Exposure to restorative natural environments may contribute to well-being and the prevention of disease and illness. As such, restorative environments are a prominent topic in the study of health benefits of nature (see Chapter 6).

Research into restorative environments has primarily been guided by two theoretical explanations, each with their own interpretation of the construct of restoration. First, **stress recovery theory** (SRT: Ulrich 1983; Ulrich et al. 1991) is concerned with restoration from the **stress** which occurs when an individual is confronted with a situation that is perceived as demanding or threatening to well-being. Second, **attention restoration theory** (ART: Kaplan and Kaplan 1989; Kaplan 1995) focuses on the restoration from attentional

Environmental Psychology: An Introduction, Second Edition. Edited by Linda Steg and Judith I. M. de Groot.

BOX 7.1   THE EXPERIMENTAL PARADIGM IN RESTORATIVE ENVIRONMENTS RESEARCH

Restorative effects of natural and urban environments are typically studied in an experimental paradigm. In this paradigm, healthy volunteers first receive a stress or fatigue induction treatment (e.g. watching a scary movie; performing mentally fatiguing tasks). Next, they are randomly exposed to real or simulated natural versus built environments. Stress and/or mental fatigue are measured at (at least) three points in time: at the start of the experiment (Time 1), after the stress-induction (Time 2), and after exposure to the natural or built environment (Time 3). Changes from Time 1 to Time 2 indicate the effectiveness of the stress induction, while changes from Time 2 to Time 3 indicate the restorative effect of the environment. The three main categories of dependent measures used in restorative environments research are:

1. *Affective measures* (e.g. how happy/sad/stressed do you feel at this moment?).

2. *Cognitive measures* (e.g. **attention** and memory tasks).

3. *Physiological measures* (e.g. heart rate, blood pressure, skin conductance, cortisol levels).

These experiments consistently demonstrate that stressed and/or fatigued individuals who are exposed to scenes dominated by natural content have more positive mood changes, perform better on attention tasks, and display more pronounced changes characteristic of physiological stress recovery than stressed individuals who are exposed to scenes dominated by built content. These restorative effects have been found for all kinds of natural environments including forests, rural scenery, waves on the beach, and golf courses (Velarde et al. 2007).

fatigue that occurs after prolonged engagement in demanding tasks. Although there has been discussion on the compatibility of SRT and ART (Ulrich et al. 1991; Kaplan 1995), the two theories are generally regarded as complementary perspectives that focus on different aspects of the restorative process (Hartig et al. 2003a). In the sections that follow the two theories are explained in more detail.

7.2.1   *Stress Recovery Theory*

Roger Ulrich laid the foundations for SRT in the 1983 article *Aesthetic and Affective Response to Natural Environment*. Based on the work of Zajonc (1980), he argued that people's initial response towards an environment is one of generalized affect (i.e. like, dislike), which occurs without conscious recognition or processing of the environment. Initial positive **affective** responses come about when specific environmental features or **preferenda** are present in the environment. These features include the presence of natural content (e.g. vegetation) as well as more structural features such as complexity, gross structural features (e.g. symmetries), depth/spatiality cues, an even ground surface texture, deflected vista (e.g. a path bending away), and absence of threats. Quick positive affective responses to these features initiate the restorative process because they provide a breather from stress, accompanied by liking and reduced levels of **arousal** and negative feelings such as fear. If the scene draws enough interest, more extensive **cognitive** processing of the environment may take place, which may be accompanied by memories and other conscious thoughts. According to SRT, however, such more deliberate restorative experiences are rare, and the vast majority of encounters with natural environments are dominated by the initial affective reaction and involve only elementary cognition.

7.2.2   *Attention Restoration Theory*

While SRT considers restoration primarily as a quick, affect-driven process, ART emphasizes the importance of slower, cognitive mechanisms in restoration. ART was fully described for the first time in 1989 by Rachel and Stephen Kaplan in the book *The Experience of Nature*. In this book, the Kaplans provide a broad overview of their long-time research on people's relationship with nature, which encompasses not only restorative experiences but also perception and visual preferences. In the latter domain, Kaplan and Kaplan (1989) are well-known for their 'Preference Matrix', a framework for predicting people's landscape preferences (see Chapter 5 for a detailed discussion of this model). The Preference Matrix is sometimes confused with ART, because both models consist of four components and were developed by the same authors. However, the Preference Matrix and ART should be considered as distinct models, each focusing on different aspects of the people–nature relationship.

A core assumption of ART is that people only have a limited capacity to direct their attention to something that is not in itself interesting. The cognitive mechanism necessary to inhibit or block out competing stimuli, called the **central executive**, becomes depleted with prolonged or intensive use (Kaplan and Berman 2010). Depletion of this central executive mechanism can result in **directed attentional fatigue (DAF)**. ART predicts that environments can counter DAF when the human–environment relationship is characterized by four qualities: **fascination** or the capacity of an environment to automatically draw attention without cognitive effort, a sense of **extent** or connectedness, **being away** from daily hassles and obligations, and a **compatibility** between the individual's inclinations and the characteristics of the environment (see also Box 7.2). Because the combination of these four qualities is most typical for human interactions with natural environments, these environments tend to be far more effective in countering DAF than most built settings. However, churches (Herzog et al. 2010) or museums (Kaplan et al. 1993) also tend to possess multiple restorative qualities and thereby may serve as a restorative environment, especially for experienced visitors who feel comfortable in these settings.

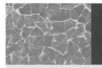

BOX 7.2   PERCEIVED RESTORATIVENESS

In addition to measuring actual changes in people's restorative state after exposure to environments (see Box 7.1), a second line of research has focused on measuring the perceived restorative potential of environments. Most of these studies have used the perceived restorativeness scale (PRS: Hartig et al. 1996, 1997) or some variation of it. The PRS consists of statements that tap the four restorative characteristics described by ART. For each statement, respondents are asked to indicate on a Likert-type scale the extent to which the statement fits their experience of a given environment (ranging from 'not at all' to 'completely'). Sample items are:

- *My attention is drawn to many interesting things (fascination);*

- *There is much going on (extent/ coherence);*
- *Spending time here gives me a break from my day-to-day routine (being away);*
- *I can do things I like here (compatibility).*

A recurrent finding is that perceived restorativeness increases with the level of naturalness (Carrus et al. 2013; Herzog et al. 2003; Hipp et al. 2016; Laumann et al. 2001). The scale has been successfully used to evaluate the restorativeness of landscape designs (Tenngart Ivarsson and Hagerhall 2008) and zoo attractions (Pals et al. 2009).

7.3   THE EVOLUTIONARY ORIGINS OF RESTORATIVE NATURE EXPERIENCES

Restorative responses are often interpreted as relics of human evolution in a natural world. Specifically, it has been proposed that certain natural features (e.g. verdant vegetation) and particular natural landscapes (e.g. savannahs) could offer ancestral humans resource opportunities and safety (e.g. trees as shelters), and in so doing, promoted human survival (Ulrich 1983; Ulrich et al. 1991). Consequently, humans may have developed a biologically prepared readiness to display positive affective responses to such elements (Ulrich 1999; see also Chapter 5).

Although widely held in the field of restorative environments research, this evolutionary account has been put into question (Joye and De Block 2011; Joye and Van den Berg 2011). One empirical criticism is that the few studies that do exist on restoration are often performed with undergraduate students in Western countries. The results obtained with such a limited group can hardly provide justification for the evolutionary, universalist assumptions underlying restoration theories. A more conceptual problem is that the human species has always inhabited more or less vegetated environments during its evolutionary history. Because this implies that greenery has always been available to everybody, it is unclear why there would have been any selection pressure for evolving preferences for these elements, as restoration theories seem to imply.

7.4 RECENT THEORETICAL AND EMPIRICAL DEVELOPMENTS

In this section, we will discuss three recent theoretical and empirical approaches that have focused on further unravelling the conditions and mechanisms underlying restorative environment experience.

7.4.1 Perceptual Fluency Account

The perceptual fluency account (PFA) is based on the phenomenon of **perceptual fluency** and aims to provide an integration of both SRT and ART (Joye et al. 2016). The central assumption of PFA is that natural environments are processed more fluently than urban settings, and that this fluency difference leads to a difference in restorative potential. Perceptually fluent processing of natural stimuli and scenes is thought to occur because the visual brain is more tuned in to the way in which visual information is structured in natural scenes than in built environments. Specifically, it is thought that due to their so-called **fractal** or self-similar patterns, natural scenes contain much more redundant information than urban scenes, making the former more fluent to process than the latter (see Figure 7.1). The notion that fractals are involved in restorative effects of nature is increasingly supported by experimental studies in which participants are exposed to real or computer-generated stimuli that vary in fractal characteristics (Taylor and Spehar 2016; Van den Berg et al. 2016a). Among other things, this research has shown that electroencephalogram (EEG) recorded alpha waves, an indicator of a wakefully relaxed state, tend to be larger during viewing of natural (statistical) fractals than during viewing of artificial (exact) fractals (Hägerhäll et al. 2015).

7.4.2 Connectedness to Nature

Another recent theoretical approach to restoration starts from the observation that people gain a sense of purpose and self-identity in life by feeling that they belong to the natural world. Based on this, it is predicted that feeling emotionally connected to nature is an important mechanism underlying beneficial effects of nature. Within this approach, several instruments have been developed to measure how connected an individual feels to nature, including the

Figure 7.1 *Examples of fractal patterns in nature.*
Source: Photo by Darren Kuropatwa (2008).

connectedness to nature scale (Mayer and Frantz 2004) and the nature relatedness scale (Zelenski and Nisbet 2014). Studies have shown that individuals who
are more connected to nature report higher well-being on psychological, emotional, and social dimensions (Olivos and Clayton 2017). In addition, it has
been found that temporary increases in nature connectedness can partly
explain restorative effects of exposure to nature (Mayer et al. 2009). These findings suggest that an experiential sense of belonging to the natural world plays
a role in restorative environment experiences, besides more unconscious,
automatic processes.

7.4.3 Micro-Restorative Experiences and Instorative Effects

A third approach has focused on **micro-restorative experiences** that result from brief sensory contact with nature, such as seeing nature through a window, in a book, on television, or in a painting (Kaplan 2001). Accumulated over time, such micro-restorative experiences may significantly improve people's sense of well-being and provide a buffer against the negative impacts of stressful events. A survey on nature-based coping strategies of elementary school teachers suggests that micro-restorative experiences are especially helpful when stress levels are low (Gulwadi 2006). Teachers who frequently suffered from vocational stress (having to teach in overcrowded classrooms, poor working conditions) preferred to actually go out and be in nature (such as taking a walk in the woods), whereas those with low levels of vocational stress found sufficient merit in brief sensory interactions with nearby nature, such as listening to a birdsong. Consistent with these findings, there is increasing evidence that exposure to nature may not only have restorative, but also **instorative effects** in individuals who are not stressed or fatigued (Hartig 2007). Studies among healthy, unstressed individuals have shown, among other things, that short-term exposure to nature may improve people's mood and ability to control their impulses (Beute and de Kort 2014) and increase subjective 'vitality' or energy levels (Ryan et al. 2010).

7.5 APPLICATIONS AND IMPLICATIONS

Findings from restorative environments research are increasingly being used to guide the design and management of natural and built environments. Given its emphasis on recovery, restorative design measures appear to be most suited for contexts in which stress and attentional fatigue are relatively acute and where such states hamper healing or developmental processes. This is one of the reasons why restorative elements have become an essential part of so-called **evidence-based design (EBD)** of healthcare settings (Ulrich et al. 2008; see also Chapter 11). However, as certain aspects of urban living constitute a significant and prolonged source of stress, nature-based or **biophilic design** is increasingly implemented on the scale of entire urban environments (Kellert et al. 2011; Van den Berg et al. 2007a). In particular, the findings on the micro-restorative and instorative effects of nature show that even in unstressed individuals, green interventions may have a vitalizing role and improve the appeal of the environmental context.

One challenge for applying restorative design measures involves the optimal amount of exposure to nature. Based on a large-scale survey, UK researchers have recommended a minimum threshold of 30 minutes visit to green space during the week to lower levels of high blood pressure and depression in the population (Shanahan et al. 2016). Quantity of neighbourhood greenspace cover was found to be unrelated to restorative outcomes, which suggests that green space design should focus on making green spaces more accessible and usable, instead of on increasing the amount of green space. However, more research is needed to determine the applicability of these guidelines to different cultural and geographical contexts.

Another question relevant to nature-based interventions is which modality of nature needs to be implemented. Research shows that not only exposure to actual nature, but also to visual simulations (e.g. videos, paintings) and to olfactory (smells) or auditory components can have restorative effects (Annerstedt et al. 2013; Kjellgren and Buhrkall 2010; Wooller et al. 2016). Restorative responses might even extend to geometric properties of nature, such as the fractal repetition of patterns at many scale levels of natural scenes. This extends the possible scope of restorative design measures from actual nature, to imitations of nature and nature's fractal geometry in architecture (Joye 2007).

7.6 SUMMARY

There is increasing empirical evidence that contact with nature can provide restoration from stress and mental fatigue. Two theoretical perspectives for the restorative effects of nature have dominated the restorative environments research agenda, namely the SRT and ART. While in both viewpoints it is commonly assumed that restorative responses are ancient relics of human evolution in natural environments, that view has become criticized. In recent years, theoretical developments relying on concepts such as 'fluency', 'connectedness to nature', and 'micro-restorative experiences' have aimed to deepen our understanding of restorative experiences. The empirical evidence for restorative effects of nature is increasingly applied in healthcare and in urban and landscape planning, but further research is needed to optimize these applications.

GLOSSARY

affective   Refers to responses and mechanisms that involve feelings and emotions.
arousal   A general state of psychological and / or physiological activation.
attention   The cognitive process of selectively concentrating on certain aspects of the environment while ignoring other things.
attention restoration theory (ART)   One of the main theories on restorative environments, according to which restoration implies the replenishment of attentional resources.

being away   A quality of restorative environments, as described by ART, indicating an environment that is free from reminders of daily hassles and obligations that overtax the capacity for directed attention.

biophilic design   A design approach that promotes the integration of natural shapes, forms, and processes in building design with the assumption that connecting people with nature is restorative because it emulates our species-long time spent in natural surroundings.

central executive   A brain system associated with the prefrontal cortex which is responsible for the control and regulation of cognitive processes.

cognitive   Refers to responses and mechanisms that involve beliefs, thoughts, ideas, judgements, perceptions, and other 'higher' mental processes.

compatibility   A quality of restorative environments, as described by ART, indicating a good fit between the individual's inclinations and the characteristics of the environment, so that no attentional resources need to be devoted to questioning how one should behave or act appropriately.

directed attentional fatigue (DAF)   A neurological symptom, also referred to as 'mental fatigue', which occurs when parts of the central executive brain system become fatigued.

evidence-based design (EBD)   An approach to designing buildings based on the best available evidence on the effectiveness of design measures.

extent   A quality of restorative environments, as described by ART, which is a function of scope and coherence. Scope refers to the scale of the environment, including the immediate surroundings and the areas that are out of sight or imagined. Coherence refers to a degree of relatedness between perceived features or elements in the environment, and the contribution of these elements to a larger whole.

fascination   A quality of restorative environments, as described by ART, indicating the capacity of an environment to automatically draw one's attention without cognitive effort, thereby relaxing the demand on the central executive and leaving room for the replenishment of directed attention.

fractal   A rough or fragmented geometric shape of which the parts are each (at least approximately) reduced-size copies of the whole. Most natural structures are fractal in form.

instorative effects   Improvements in psychological and/or physiological functioning that are triggered by particular environments and environmental configurations.

micro-restorative experiences   Brief sensory interactions with nature that promote a sense of well-being.

perceptual fluency   The subjective experience of the ease with which a certain stimulus is visually processed.

preferenda   Features of a setting or an object that are evaluated very rapidly on the basis of basic sensory information.

restoration   The physiological and psychological process of recovery from stress and mental fatigue.

restorative environment   An environment that promotes recovery from stress, mental fatigue, or other adverse conditions.

stress   A real or perceived threat or challenge to the integrity of the organism, which is often accompanied by fear or anxiety.

stress recovery theory (SRT)   One of the main theories on restorative environments, according to which restoration implies a recovery from stress.

SUGGESTIONS FOR FURTHER READING

Berto, R. (2014). The role of nature in coping with psycho-physiological stress: a literature review on restorativeness. *Behavioral Sciences* 4 (4): 394–409.

Collado, S., Staats, H., Corraliza, J.A., and Hartig, T. (2017). Restorative environments and health. In: *Handbook of Environmental Psychology and Quality of Life Research* (ed. G. Fleury-Bahi, E. Pol and O. Navarro), 127–148. Cham: Springer.

Von Lindern, E., Lymeus, F., and Hartig, T. (2017). The restorative environment: a complementary concept for salutogenesis studies. In: *The Handbook of Salutogenesis* (ed. M.B. Mittelmark, S. Sagy, M. Eriksson, et al.), 181–195. Cham: Springer.

REVIEW QUESTIONS

1. What are restorative environments and how can the restorativeness of an environment be measured?
2. Describe the four restorative qualities of people–environment interactions central to ART.
3. Explain why natural environments tend to be more restorative than built environments.
4. What is the relationship between restorative effects of nature and health benefits of nature?
5. To what extent can the use of imitations of nature or geometrical properties of nature in urban design compensate for restorative experiences with real nature?

8 Ambivalence Towards Nature and Natural Landscapes

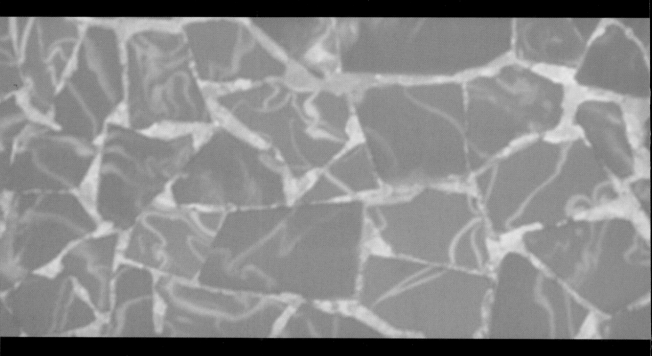

Agnes E. van den Berg
University of Groningen, The Netherlands

Cecil C. Konijnendijk
University of British Columbia, Canada

CHAPTER OUTLINE

8.1 INTRODUCTION

The previous chapters have featured evidence that **nature** and **landscapes** are generally considered beautiful and beneficial. Although this evidence is strong and compelling, there is reason to believe that people's reactions to nature are not always positive. Indeed, as we shall see in this chapter, at least some natural landscapes evoke a mixture of positive and negative feelings and thoughts. This **ambivalence** seems to be most pronounced for wild, untamed landscapes with a low degree of human influence. In what follows, we begin by providing a brief historical overview. We then present a review of contemporary empirical research and theorizing on ambivalence towards nature and natural landscapes. We conclude with suggestions on how this ambivalence can be dealt with in policy, planning, and design.

8.2 HISTORICAL OVERVIEW

Historically, ambivalence towards nature has been closely linked with the concept of **wilderness**. Although wilderness has been defined in many ways, the term is generally used as referring to those natural areas untouched (or unmanaged) by humans (Cronon 1996). For most of Western history, wilderness was viewed as a place to fear and avoid. It was associated with the deserted, savage, desolate, the barren, with places on the margin of civilization 'where it is all too easy to lose oneself in moral confusion and despair' (Cronon 1996, p. 8). Even after the Middle Ages, Europeans abhorred the wilderness so much that travellers sometimes insisted on being blindfolded so that they would not be confronted with the terror of untamed mountains and forests (Nash 1982).

The Enlightenment in Europe brought a first change in this negative perception of wilderness. Partly because of scientific discoveries, natural phenomena were seen by some (mostly intellectual and well-to-do city dwellers) as complex and marvellous manifestations of God's will. The dominant poor rural population, however, still had to deal with the dangers of untamed wild lands. This was also the case for pioneers settling North America, who were living too close to the wilderness for appreciation. During the era of Romanticism, however, wilderness became sacred and associated with the deepest core values of the culture that created and idealized it (Cronon 1996). It became the inspiration for the evolving concept of the **sublime**, i.e. a sense of awe and reverence, mixed with elements of fear (Burke 1757). In the United States, wilderness even became a source of national pride, with national wilderness parks compensating for the lack of cultural-historical monuments that could help define the nation state.

Environmental Psychology: An Introduction, Second Edition. Edited by Linda Steg and Judith I. M. de Groot.
© 2019 John Wiley & Sons Ltd. Published 2019 by John Wiley & Sons Ltd.

Since the late twentieth century, the dominant tendency in Western countries is towards **biophilia**, or love of nature (Wilson 1984; see also Chapter 5). However, negative perceptions of wilderness as a place that is useless, unsafe, and untidy have not vanished, and may quickly re-emerge in particular contexts and situations that heighten people's vulnerability to nature. Conversely, highly managed natural settings that are strongly controlled by humans may also evoke negative thoughts and feelings. Such settings are often perceived as overly formal and excessively tidy, and thereby, unnatural (Özgüner and Kendle 2006). In general, wild as well as managed natural settings appear to be imbued with ambivalent, positive and negative, meanings, which may create important variation between as well as within individuals in emotional and cognitive responses to these settings. In the following paragraphs, we will discuss empirical findings that testify to these ideas.

8.3 EMOTIONAL IMPACTS AND MEANINGS OF NATURAL ENVIRONMENT EXPERIENCE

A study among Dutch students provides some empirical evidence for the ambivalent meanings of wild nature (Koole and Van den Berg 2005). Among other things, participants were asked to report how often they were inclined to think about various specified topics, including death and freedom, when they were in a wilderness environment, relative to when they were in a managed natural environment. As many as 76.7% of the participants reported that they were more inclined to think about death in wild than in managed nature, while 81.1% of the participants reported that they were more inclined to think of freedom in wild than in managed nature. This double association between wilderness and thoughts about death and freedom fits with the idea that wilderness is laden with ambivalent meanings.

Wild nature is not only associated with ambivalent meanings, it may also evoke ambivalent emotional responses. Evaluations of outdoor wilderness and survival programmes have revealed that a stay in the wilderness can elicit strong fears and other negative emotions as well as strong positive emotions (Bixler and Floyd 1997; Kaplan and Talbot 1983). Fear responses to wilderness are generally assumed to be driven by **biophobia**, or a biological preparedness to quickly learn and retain fears of natural objects and situations that threatened the human species during the course of evolution (Seligman 1971; Ulrich 1993a). This assumption is supported by laboratory experiments which have shown that humans learn fear of snakes and other natural stimuli faster than fear of guns and other man-made stimuli (Öhman and Mineka 2003). Besides strong fears, participants of wilderness programs also report strong positive emotions from overcoming these fears, including an increase in psychological energy, a greater self-confidence and a sense of awe and wonder (Ewert 1986; Kaplan and Talbot 1983). These mixed emotions are reminiscent of so-called sublime or impressive nature experiences.

Qualitative analyses of people's personal experiences with nature have identified four clusters of situations that tend to evoke both fear and fascination in people: (i) close encounters with wild animals, (ii) confrontations with the forces of nature (e.g. a storm or an earthquake), (iii) overwhelming situations (e.g. being intimidated by the greatness of a forest), and (iv) disorienting situations (e.g. getting lost in the woods) (Van den Berg and Ter Heijne 2005). Most participants reported that they felt a mixture of fear and fascination when they were in these situations. However, there was substantial individual variation in responses in terms of gender and sensation seeking: women tended to respond primarily with fear, while sensation seekers responded primarily with fascination.

Not only wild untamed nature, but also more common urban green spaces and elements like trees tend to be associated with highly ambivalent meanings and emotions (Bonnes et al. 2011; Camacho-Cervantes et al. 2014). These spaces and elements are found to be associated with beauty, restoration, and oxygen supply as well as with crime, accidents, and lack of social safety. In particular, the presence of high levels of dense understory vegetation that offer potential attackers a place to hide are associated with a higher fear of crime and feelings of unsafety in urban parks (the so-called 'stranger danger') (Jorgensen et al. 2002; Jansson et al. 2013). These feelings of unsafety in urban parks tend to be highest among women and members of low income groups and ethnic communities (Sreetheran and Van den Bosch 2014; see also Chapter 5).

8.4 VIEWS OF NATURE AND LANDSCAPE PREFERENCES

Another domain which deals with ambivalence towards nature comprises studies of people's cognitive representations of the relationship between humans and nature. Much of this research has evolved around the long-standing philosophical issue of whether humans stand above nature – **anthropocentric view** – or whether they are part of or even subordinate to nature – **ecocentric view** (Flint et al. 2013; Zweers 2000). Four basic views of the relationship between humans and nature have been identified, ranging from anthropocentric to ecocentric: (i) master, (ii) steward (or guardian), (iii) partner, and (iv) participant (De Groot 2010; De Groot and Van den Born 2003; Keulartz et al. 2004: see Box 8.1).

Large-scale surveys have revealed that most people tend to endorse a more ecocentric view of nature (De Groot and De Groot 2009; Farjon et al. 2016; Hunka et al. 2009). An important finding is that respondents often agree with more than one view at the same time, which suggests that many people display

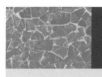

BOX 8.1   VIEWS OF HUMAN–NATURE RELATIONSHIPS

- *Master:* Humans stand above nature and may do with it as they want. Economic growth and technology are expected to solve environmental problems.

- *Steward/Guardian:* People have the responsibility to care for nature on behalf of God and/or future generations.

- *Partner:* Humans and nature are of equal value. They both have their own status and work together in a dynamic process of mutual development.

- *Participant:* Humans are part of nature, not just biologically, but also on a psychological level. Technological interventions in nature are not allowed.

a certain degree of ambivalence in their view of nature. This notion is corroborated by qualitative research showing that people's spontaneous descriptions of the relationship between humans and nature often contain a mixture of (opposing) ecocentric and anthropocentric elements (Van den Born 2008).

People's views of the relationship between humans and nature are closely related to their **images of nature** and aesthetic landscape preferences (Buijs 2009; De Groot and Van den Born 2003). An anthropocentric view is associated with a functional nature image, in which intensively managed settings that are useful for humans are considered beautiful and good examples of nature. An ecocentric view is associated with a wilderness image, in which natural settings that are untouched by humans are highly preferred and considered beautiful and good examples of nature.

A substantial body of research has investigated individual differences in views of nature, nature images, and landscape preferences (Özgüner and Kendle 2006; Sklenicka and Molnarova 2010; Van den Berg and Koole 2006). This research has consistently revealed that anthropocentrism, as indicated by people's views of nature, nature images, and landscape preferences, is strongest among people with a low income and education level, elderly, immigrants, and groups with functional ties to the landscape, such as farmers, hunters, and birdwatchers. For example, a Dutch survey revealed that 44% of first- and second-generation immigrants (mostly from Turkey or Morocco) adhered to a functional image of nature, whereas this image was held by only 15% of native Dutch respondents (Buijs et al. 2009).

8.5   THE ROLE OF BIODIVERSITY

Wild nature areas tend to be rich in species and other indicators of **biodiversity**. However, high levels of biodiversity can also be found in more managed areas. Urban parks, for example, have been found to constitute rich species 'hot-spots' in the cityscape (Alvey 2006; Nielsen et al. 2014). In general, biodiversity constitutes a distinctive component of natural areas that provides an indication of an ecosystem's health and resilience independent of its visual appearance as wild or managed. When studied independently of landscape type, high levels of biodiversity are mostly evaluated positively (Botzat et al. 2016; Carrus et al. 2015). Negative evaluations are rare, and usually mixed with positive results. For example, a study in small urban gardens in Paris found that visitors disliked insect diversity in gardens, but at the same time liked high plant diversity (Shwartz et al. 2014). Thus, biodiversity does not appear to play an important role in ambivalent responses towards nature and must therefore be considered separately from the concept of wilderness.

8.6   AN EXISTENTIAL-MOTIVATIONAL ACCOUNT

In the previous sections, we have seen that nature can evoke both positive and negative feelings and thoughts. What are the deeper causes of this ambivalence? According to the **existential-motivational account**, ambivalence towards nature is rooted in people's deep-seated existential concerns about their own mortality (Koole and Van den Berg 2004). As described in section 8.3 nature, particularly wilderness, is inherently associated with uncontrollability and death (Koole and Van den Berg 2005). Indeed, many children first learn about death by observing how animals die. Research on terror management theory has shown that people have a basic psychological need to protect themselves against existential anxiety that comes from the realization that their own death is ultimately uncontrollable and inescapable (Greenberg et al. 1997). Because of nature's close connection with death, terror management processes will often lead people to distance themselves from (wild) nature. For instance, individuals who have been experimentally reminded of death are especially likely to support beliefs that humans are distinct from animals and to report being disgusted by animals (Goldenberg et al. 2001). Additional experimental research has shown that visual preferences for wild over managed settings can be weakened by reminding people of their mortality (Koole and Van den Berg 2005, see Figure 8.1).

An important implication of the existential-motivational account is that negative reactions to wild nature do not derive from ignorance or lack of knowledge about nature's ecological significance and **intrinsic value**. This fits well with findings that negative reactions to wild nature are often found among farmers, hunters, birdwatchers, and other groups with profound and extensive knowledge of nature and ecosystems. Instead of a lack of knowledge, a common characteristic of individuals who display negative feelings and anthropocentric thoughts about nature and wilderness is that they are less able to buffer themselves against the existential anxiety evoked by the reminders of death that are present in nature.

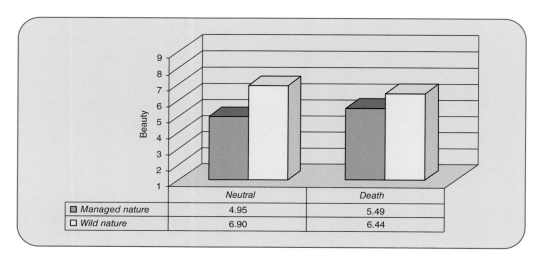

Figure 8.1 *An experiment among 48 university students showed that reminding participants of their own mortality weakened their aesthetic preference for wild over managed nature as compared to a neutral control group.*
Source: Adapted from Koole and Van den Berg (2005; Study 2).

This diminished buffer may be caused by a direct dependence on nature for existence (e.g. farmers), by a vulnerable and insecure position in life (e.g. people with a low income, older people), or by personality traits related to a desire for structure and stability (e.g. individuals low on sensation-seeking).

The existential-motivational account of ambivalence towards nature is also consistent with observations that the historical trend towards positive, ecocentric views of nature seems to go hand in hand with a growing separation and alienation from nature in Western countries (Cronon 1996). Indeed, for many urbanites, contact with nature is limited to what they see through the windshield on the daily commute along with some occasional visits to parks and countryside. From an existential-motivational perspective, this link between alienation from nature and ecocentricity may be explained by the fact that people who are more detached from nature are more capable to distance themselves, literally or psychologically, from the 'savage reality of nature' (Koole and Van den Berg 2004).

8.7   PRACTICAL IMPLICATIONS

The research and theorizing discussed in this chapter have important practical implications in many domains. In the domain of environmental education, for example, the research suggests that outdoor education programmes will be more effective if they focus on strengthening participants' self-confidence and sense of security. Indeed, evaluations of environmental education programmes have consistently revealed that the most successful programmes make use of hands-on learning as a way to help students master real-life skills and boost their self-confidence (Wheeler et al. 2007).

In the domain of nature policy and management the research is especially relevant for ecological restoration or 'rewilding' programmes, which are currently being developed or implemented in rural as well as urban areas in many countries. These programmes are aimed at restoring, and protecting wildlife and native vegetation in degraded, eroded, or disturbed sites and providing connectivity between these sites. Although such programmes will be supported by a large majority of populations in Western countries, some groups hold more critical/negative views (Van den Berg et al. 1998). The research and theorizing discussed in this chapter suggests that these views are rooted in deep-seated existential concerns, and should not be too easily discounted as the result of ignorance or 'resistance to change'.

In general, an important guideline that can be derived from this chapter is that nature education and management strategies should accommodate and match people's needs for existential security. **Participatory planning** trajectories are a widely used tool for identifying the needs and concerns of user groups. The knowledge presented in this chapter can contribute to such participatory discussions by providing insight into the deeper causes behind people's ambivalence towards nature which can facilitate understanding of one's own and others' position and ideas regarding nature.

8.8   SUMMARY

In this chapter we have reviewed research in environmental psychology that provides empirical support for the long-standing notion that nature, in particular wild nature, can evoke both positive and negative feelings and thoughts. We have argued that current knowledge on this ambivalence towards nature fits with an existential-motivational account, which states that nature is a reminder of people's existential insecurity because of the intrinsic link between nature and death. The chapter's main lesson is that ambivalence towards nature and natural landscapes is the result of deeply seated motivational concerns, and as such should be taken seriously and dealt with accordingly in nature education, management, and spatial planning.

GLOSSARY

ambivalence   The coexistence of opposing attitudes, thoughts, or feelings, such as love and hate, towards an object (i.e. a landscape), a concept (i.e. nature) or a person.

anthropocentric view   The view that humans stand above nature, leading to the assessment of nature through a human or functional perspective.

biodiversity   The variability within species, between species, and between ecosystems.

biophilia   People's innate tendency to seek connections with nature and other forms of life.

biophobia   People's innate tendency to quickly learn and slowly unlearn fearful responses to natural stimuli that have posed threats to human survival throughout evolution.

ecocentric view   The view that there are no existential divisions between humans and nature, leading to the assessment of nature as being valuable in itself, even if it has no (direct) use for humans.

existential-motivational account   A psychological theory that explains negative responses to wilderness and nature as the result of people's need to protect themselves against the anxieties evoked by the reminders of death that are present in nature.

image of nature   People's cognitive conception of what nature is.

intrinsic value   The value that a landscape has of itself, irrespective of its use or function for humans.

landscape   An area, as perceived by people, whose character is the result of the action and interaction of natural and/or human factors.

nature   A broad concept that encompasses natural areas such as forests as well as agricultural landscapes, urban greenery, and natural elements and features such as trees and lakes.

participatory planning   A paradigm that emphasizes involving urban or rural communities in the strategic and management processes of spatial planning.

sublime   A sense of awe and reverence, sometimes mixed with elements of fear.

wilderness   An area of land that is untouched (or unmanaged) by humans.

SUGGESTIONS FOR FURTHER READING

Jorgensen, A. and Tylecote, M. (2007). Ambivalent landscapes - wilderness in the urban interstices. *Landscape Research* 32 (4): 443–462.

Konijnendijk, C.C. (2008). *The Forest and the City: The Cultural Landscape of Urban Woodland.* London: Springer.

Nassauer, J.I. (1995). Messy ecosystems, orderly frames. *Landscape Journal* 14 (2): 161–170.

REVIEW QUESTIONS

1. Describe the four views of the relationship between humans and nature that have been identified in empirical research.
2. Which two kinds of landscapes typically evoke ambivalent (positive and negative) responses?
3. How can ambivalence in emotional and cognitive responses towards nature be explained?

9 Human Dimensions of Wildlife

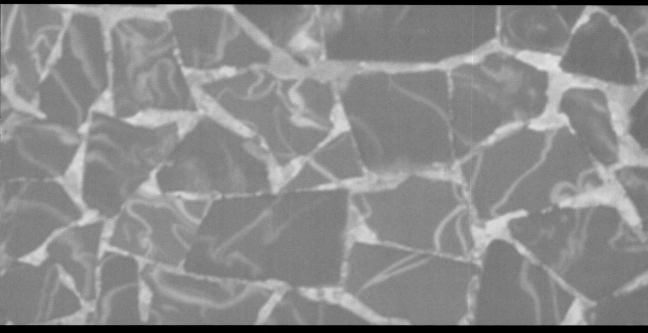

Maarten H. Jacobs
Wageningen University, The Netherlands

Jerry J. Vaske
Colorado State University, USA

Tara L. Teel
Colorado State University, USA

Michael J. Manfredo
Colorado State University, USA

CHAPTER OUTLINE

9.1   INTRODUCTION

Imagine walking in a forest and encountering a deer. You might remember this moment because it is special, perhaps the highlight of the trip. Humans are strongly attracted to **wildlife.** Wildlife-based tourism and recreation are increasingly popular (Newsome and Rodger 2013) and wildlife TV documentaries attract large audiences (Jacobs 2009). Negative relationships with wildlife (e.g. snake phobias), however, are also common (Öhman and Mineka 2003). In general, the relationships between humans and wildlife are complex, as they are closely tied to the evolution of humans in natural environments, and also are manifestations of socialization and past individual experiences. Because the human brain evolved in part to meet wildlife-related challenges, research into human thought, emotion, and action, can reveal insights into the general workings of the human mind. Research into human dimensions of wildlife is also of practical relevance as it helps to understand current opinions and public debates about wildlife-related issues such as the reintroduction of predators or the killing of species that cause harm to humans or damage crops.

In this chapter, we first briefly discuss a descriptive typology of **attitudes** towards wildlife that was quite influential in the pioneering years of research on human dimensions of wildlife (Kellert 1976). Subsequent sections describe a more recent theory-driven approach to understanding human relationships with wildlife, guided by the **cognitive hierarchy**. This theoretical framework differentiates among the various thought processes that form the basis for human behaviour (Manfredo et al. 2009; Teel and Manfredo 2010). While human dimensions research has predominantly focused on cognitive aspects, new avenues are beginning to emphasize the importance of emotional factors, which will be explored in the last section. To some extent, the research and theorizing discussed in this chapter overlaps with a broader research domain that focuses on people's responses to nature and landscapes and views of the relationship between humans and nature (see Chapters 6–8 and 17). As we will see, however, research on the human dimension of wildlife has increasingly generated its own network of experts and literature, and has become an independent field of research.

9.2   EARLY WORK: ATTITUDES TOWARDS WILDLIFE

Kellert (1976) presented a typology of attitudes towards wildlife that has received wide attention. Based on personal interviews and large scale surveys,

Environmental Psychology: An Introduction, Second Edition. Edited by Linda Steg and Judith I. M. de Groot.
© 2019 John Wiley & Sons Ltd. Published 2019 by John Wiley & Sons Ltd.

BOX 9.1   TYPOLOGY OF ATTITUDES TOWARDS WILDLIFE

Kellert (1976, 1996) has developed a typology consisting of nine basic attitudes towards wildlife, also referred to as 'values of wildlife':

Utilitarian. Practical and material exploitation of nature.

Naturalistic. Direct experience and exploration of nature.

Ecologistic-scientific. Systematic study of the structure, function, and relationships in nature.

Aesthetic. Physical appeal and beauty of nature.

Symbolic. Use of nature for language and thought.

Humanistic. Strong emotional attachment and 'love' for aspects of nature.

Moralistic. Spiritual reverence and ethical concern for nature.

Dominionistic. Mastery, physical control, and dominance of nature.

Negativistic. Fear, aversion, and alienation from nature.

Kellert distinguished nine basic attitudes (Kellert has also referred to these as **values**) towards wildlife (Box 9.1).

Kellert's typology has been mostly applied to describe the attitudes of different groups of people. For example, a large-scale survey in the United States showed that females had higher scores than males on humanistic, moralistic, and negativistic attitudes, while men scored higher on utilitarian, dominionistic, naturalistic, and ecologistic attitudes (Kellert and Berry 1987). Additional research has shown that favourable responses towards predators were positively related to naturalistic, moralistic, and ecologistic attitudes, but negatively related to negativistic and utilitarian attitudes (Kellert 1985).

By revealing this diversity in public responses to wildlife and wildlife-related issues, Kellert has opened up the study of human–wildlife relationships. Theoretically, however, his work is not informed by a clear conceptual foundation and conclusive evidence about the reliability and validity of the measurement instrument is lacking.

9.3   THE COGNITIVE HIERARCHY

Building on insights from social psychology (Homer and Kahle 1988), Manfredo and colleagues (Fulton et al. 1996; Manfredo 2008; Teel and Manfredo 2010; Whittaker et al. 2006) have developed a theory for studying human thought and behaviour towards wildlife, labelled the 'cognitive hierarchy'. This theory stresses that individual behaviour is guided by a hierarchy of interrelated **cognitions**

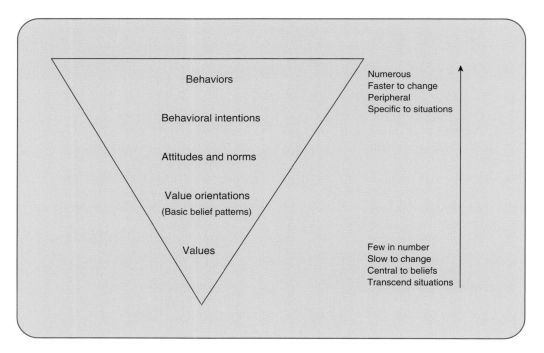

Figure 9.1 *The cognitive hierarchy framework.*
Source: Adapted from Manfredo (2008).

including values, **value orientations**, attitudes and **norms**, and behavioural intentions. In this hierarchy, values are the most abstract cognitions, while behavioural intentions are the most specific cognitions and immediate antecedents of actual behaviour (see Figure 9.1).

Because values are often formed early in life, are culturally constructed, transcend situations, and are tied to one's identity (Schwartz 2006), they are extremely resistant to change and are unlikely to explain much of the variability in specific behaviours within cultures. For example, two persons may both find the value 'freedom' important. In the context of wildlife, one person may project this value onto humans only and find hunting acceptable, while another person may project freedom onto both humans and wildlife and find hunting unacceptable. The fundamental value, then, does not directly explain specific thought and behaviour.

Manfredo and Teel (Manfredo et al. 2009; Teel and Manfredo 2010) have proposed that **ideologies** (e.g. egalitarianism) give direction and meaning to values in a given context. The resulting value orientations are reflected in a schematic network of **basic beliefs** that organize around fundamental values and provide contextual meaning to them within a given domain such as wildlife. Wildlife value orientations thus relate more directly to wildlife than general values and are therefore more useful in explaining individual variation in wildlife-related attitudes and behaviours. Wildlife value orientations mediate the relationship between general values and attitudes or norms in specific situations involving wildlife (Manfredo et al. 2009).

9.4   WILDLIFE VALUE ORIENTATIONS

Two predominant wildlife value orientations have been identified: **domination** (previously referred to as utilitarianism) and **mutualism** (e.g. Fulton et al. 1996; Manfredo 2008; Manfredo et al. 2009; Teel and Manfredo 2010). People with a domination wildlife value orientation believe that wildlife should be used and managed for human benefit and are more likely to prioritize human well-being over wildlife. Those with a mutualism wildlife value orientation see wildlife as part of an extended family, deserving of care and rights like humans. Teel and Manfredo (2010) argue that mutualism entails the belief that wildlife is capable of relationships of trust with humans, reflecting an egalitarian ideology, in which all living things are treated as having equal worth. A measurement instrument consisting of 19 survey items (Box 9.2) has been developed to assess these orientations. The domination value orientation is based on two basic belief dimensions: appropriate use beliefs and hunting beliefs. The mutualism value orientation is also based on two basic belief dimensions: social affiliation beliefs and caring beliefs. Composite indices are constructed from the basic belief items to reflect the extent to which a respondent holds a domination and/or mutualism orientation towards wildlife.

Research in various countries like the United States (Manfredo et al. 2009; Teel and Manfredo 2010), The Netherlands (Vaske et al. 2011), Germany (Hermann et al. 2013), Denmark (Gamborg and Jensen 2016), and Malaysia (Zainal Abidin and Jacobs 2016) has demonstrated the reliability of the Wildlife Value Orientations scales in different cultural contexts (see also Teel et al. 2010, for a comparative study in 10 European countries). These findings are further corroborated and expanded by qualitative analyses in The Netherlands, China, Estonia, Mongolia, and Thailand, all published in *Human Dimensions of Wildlife,* issue 12(5), 2007.

Studies using the Wildlife Value Orientation scales suggest that domination orientations are deeply engrained in the cultural transmission process and endure over generations. Data from a study in 19 states of the United States showed that domination is a prevalent American value orientation towards wildlife that can be traced to the dominant cultural orientation in countries from which their ancestors immigrated (Manfredo et al. 2016). At the same time, contemporary forces of modernization appear to be contributing to an intergenerational shift from domination to mutualism value orientations in the United States (Manfredo et al. 2009; Teel and Manfredo 2010). Data from the 19 US states revealed that the percentage of residents with a mutualism orientation was higher in states with a higher average state-level income, education, and urbanization, suggesting that ongoing demographic changes could be contributing to such a shift. Because the findings also revealed a strong relationship between wildlife value orientations and wildlife-related attitudes and behaviours (Teel and Manfredo 2010), these changes may additionally result in continued declines in public acceptance of traditional forms of wildlife management that are typically acceptable for those with a domination orientation (e.g. hunting, lethal control of wildlife).

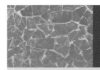

BOX 9.2   MEASUREMENT OF WILDLIFE VALUE ORIENTATIONS

Research has identified two predominant wildlife value orientations: domination and mutualism (Manfredo et al. 2009; Teel and Manfredo 2010). To measure these value orientations, an instrument has been developed that measures the degree to which individuals agree with the beliefs that are typical for the orientations. For each value orientation, two belief domains are distinguished. The items for each value orientation and belief domain are listed below. Response options range from 1 = strongly disagree to 7 = strongly agree.

Domination: Appropriate use beliefs

- Humans should manage fish and wildlife populations so that humans benefit.
- The needs of humans should take priority over fish and wildlife protection.
- It is acceptable for people to kill wildlife if they think it poses a threat to their life.
- It is acceptable for people to kill wildlife if they think it poses a threat to their property.
- It is acceptable to use fish and wildlife in research even if it may harm or kill some animals.
- Fish and wildlife are on earth primarily for people to use.

Domination: Hunting beliefs

- We should strive for a world where there's an abundance of fish and wildlife for hunting and fishing.
- Hunting is cruel and inhumane to the animals (reverse-coded).
- Hunting does not respect the lives of animals (reverse-coded).
- People who want to hunt should be provided the opportunity to do so.

Mutualism: Social affiliation beliefs

- We should strive for a world where humans and fish and wildlife can live side by side without fear.
- I view all living things as part of one big family.
- Animals should have rights similar to the rights of humans.
- Wildlife are like my family and I want to protect them.

Mutualism: Caring beliefs

- I care about animals as much as I do other people.
- It would be more rewarding for me to help animals rather than people.
- I take great comfort in the relationships I have with animals.
- I feel a strong emotional bond with animals.
- I value the sense of companionship I receive from animals.

9.5 PREDICTING NORMS AND ATTITUDES TOWARDS WILDLIFE

The usefulness of studying wildlife value orientations depends on the concept's predictive validity. Wildlife value orientations should predict people's attitudes, norms, and behaviours towards wildlife in specific situations. Research has shown that wildlife value orientations are effective in predicting reported behaviours such as participation in wildlife-related recreation activities (e.g. hunting, wildlife viewing) and support for wildlife management interventions across various issues and situations (e.g. Bright et al. 2000; Dougherty et al. 2003; Fulton et al. 1996; Hermann et al. 2013; Jacobs et al. 2014; Manfredo et al. 2016; Teel and Manfredo 2010; Whittaker et al. 2006). These studies have consistently revealed that mutualists are more likely to participate in wildlife viewing, whereas those with a domination orientation are more likely to be hunters and anglers. Those with a mutualism orientation are also less likely than individuals with a domination orientation to support management interventions that harm wildlife or favour human interests over wildlife protection (e.g. Jacobs et al. 2014, Vaske et al. 2011; Teel and Manfredo 2010). Overall, the two wildlife value orientations have been shown across studies to explain up to half of the variability in attitudes, norms, and behaviours (e.g. Fulton et al. 1996; Jacobs et al. 2014; Whittaker et al. 2006).

9.6 EMOTIONS TOWARDS WILDLIFE

The cognitive hierarchy does not explicitly consider emotions. The concepts and measurements may reflect emotional content (e.g. attitudes and values are often emotion-laden), but they are not intended to directly capture emotional dispositions or responses. While fear towards wildlife has occasionally been empirically addressed (Johansson and Karlsson 2011; Öhman and Mineka 2003), research on emotions towards wildlife is far less extensive than research on cognitions (Jacobs et al. 2012). Yet, emotions can play a key role in our experiences with, and responses to wildlife and reflect basic reactions to wildlife and the natural environment (Herzog and Burghardt 1988; Manfredo 2008; see also Chapter 8). Emotions influence other mental phenomena, such as perception, attitudes, and memories. For example, people who are afraid of wolves may think more positively about the shooting of wolves by humans (Jacobs et al. 2014). Also, most people can easily recall intense positive and negative emotional wildlife experiences (e.g. being delighted to see a deer in the wild, being afraid of snakes).

Emotional responses are characterized by valence (e.g. positive or negative, good or bad) and may comprise: (i) expressive reactions (e.g. smiling),

(ii) physiological reactions (e.g. increased heartbeat), (iii) behavioural tendencies or coping (e.g. approaching, avoiding), (iv) thoughts (e.g. interpreting the situation, identifying a supposed cause of the emotion), and (v) emotional experiences (e.g. feeling happy) (Cornelius 1996). These components of emotional responses can be influenced by biological factors as well as by cultural and individual learning (Jacobs 2009). In the course of biological evolution, emotional bodily reactions emerged as automatic adaptive responses to situations of life-importance, and facilitated the survival and well-being of animals and humans (Damasio 1999; LeDoux 1998). For example, an increased heartbeat as part of a fear reaction to a predator prepares a human for optimal fight-or-flight reactions (see also Chapter 4). Many bodily reactions are automatic; if the person had to think about increasing the heartbeat, the optimal bodily condition for an immediate adequate reaction would set in too late. How people interpret feedback from bodily reactions into an emotional experience is influenced by past experience and knowledge. The knowledge that a bear behind bars in a zoo cannot attack, for example, might block out an automatic fear response. Thus, knowledge can influence emotional experiences via feedback from the cognitive to the emotional system and can even suppress an initial emotional bodily fear reaction.

Different psychological mechanisms can cause emotional responses to wildlife (Jacobs 2009). First, humans have innate preferences for watching biological movement over non-biological movement, as demonstrated by experiments with newborn babies (Simion et al. 2008). Consequently, people are genetically inclined to attend to and respond to animals. Second, some emotional responses towards wildlife species relevant for survival (e.g. fear responses to snakes) are learned quickly and unlearned slowly because of innate quick learning programs (Öhman and Mineka 2003; see also Chapter 8). Third, people have mental dispositions to respond emotionally to wildlife that result from conditioning. Through conditioning, a previously neutral stimulus is associated with an emotional stimulus and then becomes an emotional stimulus as well. For example, scavengers such as crows and ravens tend to be seen in places associated with death and might thus become fear triggers for some people (Marzluff and Angell 2005). Fourth, we tend to react emotionally to the emotional expressions of wildlife; for example, animals that behave calmly tend to make us feel calm (Jacobs 2009). Fifth, knowledge about animals may reinforce or transform the way a bodily emotional reaction to an animal is interpreted into a conscious experience (Lazarus and Alfert 1964). For example, seeing a bear in the zoo and knowing that it can do no harm may convert an initial fear reaction into a positive fascination. Sixth, acquired knowledge about wildlife can prompt emotional reactions. For instance, birdwatchers enjoy encountering a bird that is rarely seen because they know it is a special event (McFarlane 1994). Different emotional responses to wildlife may be caused by various combinations of these mechanisms (Jacobs 2009). For example, many ancient and contemporary myths depict spiders and snakes as symbols of danger and evil (e.g. Shelob the spider in Lord of the Rings and Voldemort's snake Nagini in Harry Potter). Cultural learning thus reinforces our biologically constituted tendency to fear spiders and snakes.

9.7 SUMMARY

Wildlife can evoke strong positive and negative thoughts, feelings, and actions in people. In this chapter, we reviewed theories and corresponding empirical evidence on these human dimensions of wildlife. In particular, the cognitive hierarchy framework stresses that human cognitions exist on different levels of abstraction and are comprised of the concepts of values, value orientations, attitudes and norms, and behavioural intentions (values being the most abstract and behavioural intentions the most specific cognitions in the hierarchy). Wildlife value orientations are patterns of basic beliefs that give direction and meaning to fundamental values in the domain of wildlife. Research has revealed two primary wildlife value orientations: domination and mutualism. People with a domination wildlife value orientation believe that wildlife should be used and managed for human benefit and are more likely to prioritize human well-being over wildlife. Those with a mutualism wildlife value orientation see wildlife as part of an extended family, deserving of rights and care. These value orientations predict attitudes and norms towards wildlife-related activities and management issues, as well as wildlife-related behaviours. Along with cognitions, emotions are important components of human behaviour towards wildlife. Emotional responses to wildlife can be caused by general (e.g. conditioning) and specific (e.g. innate quick learning programs) psychological mechanisms. In general, future research on human dimensions of wildlife may benefit from the combined study of both cognitive and emotional responses to wildlife.

GLOSSARY

attitudes   Mental dispositions to evaluate an attitude object (i.e. a person, place, issue, thing, or event) with some degree of favour or disfavour.

basic beliefs   Thoughts about general classes of objects or issues within a given domain (e.g. wildlife).

cognitions   Mental dispositions that are used in perceiving, remembering, thinking, and understanding.

cognitive hierarchy   Theoretical framework that stresses that cognitions exist on different levels of abstraction that are causally related, including values (the most abstract), value orientations, attitudes, norms, and behavioural intentions (the most specific).

domination   A wildlife value orientation that comprises the beliefs that wildlife should be used and managed for human benefit and that human well-being is more important than wildlife.

emotional response   Response that is characterized by expressive reactions, physiological reactions, behavioural tendencies or coping, specific emotion-related thoughts, and emotional experiences.

ideologies   Consensually held beliefs that enable the people who share them to understand meaning, to know who they are, and to relate to one another.

mutualism   A wildlife value orientation that comprises the beliefs that wildlife is part of an extended family, deserving of care and rights like humans.

norms   Beliefs about how one ought to behave or think, often expressions of group-level influences.

values   Desirable trans-situational goals varying in importance, which serve as guiding principles in the life of a person or other social entity.

value orientations   Schematic networks of basic beliefs, reflective of cultural ideologies, that give direction and meaning to fundamental values in a particular domain (e.g. wildlife).

wildlife   Non-domesticated fauna.

SUGGESTIONS FOR FURTHER READING

Jacobs, M.H. (2009). Why do we like or dislike animals? *Human Dimensions of Wildlife* 14 (1): 1–11.

Manfredo, M.J. (2008). *Who Cares about Wildlife?* New York, NY: Springer.

Teel, T.L. and Manfredo, M.J. (2010). Understanding the diversity of public interests in wildlife conservation. *Conservation Biology* 24 (1): 128–139.

Vaske, J.J. and Manfredo, M.J. (2012). Social-psychological aspects of wildlife management. In: *Human Dimensions of Wildlife Management* (ed. D.J. Decker, S. Riley and W.F. Siemer), 43–57. Baltimore, MD: The Johns Hopkins University Press.

REVIEW QUESTIONS

1. Which core concepts are included in the cognitive hierarchy framework? How are they defined and differentiated?
2. Name and describe the two primary wildlife value orientations.
3. What are the components of emotional responses and can you give examples pertaining to responses to wildlife?
4. Some emotional dispositions towards wildlife are shared by all humans while other emotional dispositions vary across humans. Give examples of both kinds of dispositions.

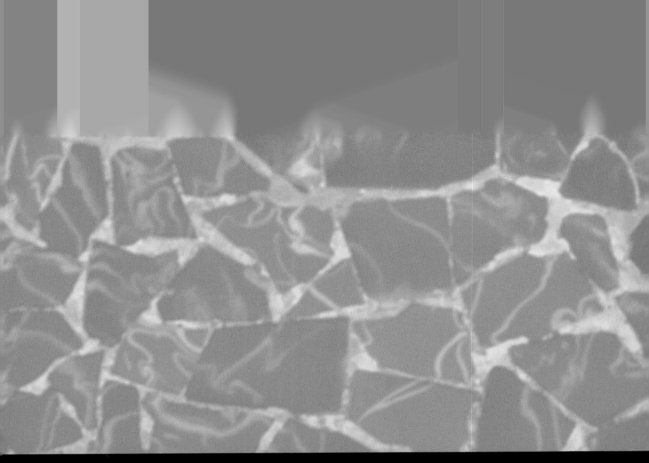

Karin Tanja-Dijkstra
Vrije Universiteit Amsterdam, The Netherlands

Jolanda Maas
Vrije Universiteit Amsterdam, The Netherlands

Janke van Dijk-Wesselius
Vrije Universiteit Amsterdam, The Netherlands

Agnes van den Berg
University of Groningen, The Netherlands

CHAPTER OUTLINE

10.1 INTRODUCTION

Television, computers, smartphone, tablets; these days, many children have access to a range of media and would rather spend their free time indoors behind a screen than outdoors playing in **nature** and **green space**. In addition, increasing urbanization has diminished opportunities for safe outdoor play, and many parents discourage children from going outdoors to protect them from the threats of traffic or **stranger danger** (Veitch et al. 2010). For these and other reasons more and more children are growing up disconnected from nature and the outdoors. A large UK survey showed that fewer than 10% of the interviewed children spend their time playing in natural places, such as woodlands and the countryside, compared with 40% of their parents and grandparents when they were young (Natural England 2009). There is growing concern that this disconnection may have negative consequences for children's development, health, and well-being. This concern has been captured in the term **nature deficit disorder,** reflecting the potential negative impacts of children's disconnection from the natural world (Louv 2005).

In this chapter, we give an overview of theory and research examining the importance of nature and nearby green space for children. We focus on children in the school age 6–12 years, with some reference to younger children and adolescents (13–18 years). We first discuss research on children's nature experiences, followed by a review of empirical evidence for positive impacts of nature on children's health and well-being. We also discuss emerging insights on the relationship between childhood nature experiences and adult environmentalism. We end with some implications and practical application of the growing body of knowledge on the importance of nature for children.

10.2 CHILDHOOD EXPERIENCES WITH NATURE

The first studies on children's experiences with nature consisted of **ethnographic studies** that rely on qualitative research methods (Hart 1979; Lynch 1977; Moore 1980). Children were for instance observed while playing, asked to tell about their experiences, keep a diary, take photographs, or make drawings of their favourite places. Content analysis of these data revealed that natural areas like riverbanks, forests, unmown grass, weedy waysides, water edges, and patches of woods are highly valued by children. What makes these places special is, among other things, that they contain many **affordances** or possibilities for

Environmental Psychology: An Introduction, Second Edition. Edited by Linda Steg and Judith I. M. de Groot.

action that 'challenge, engage, inspire and provoke' children to engage in active, diverse, and creative play experiences (Gibson 1979). In general, ethnographic studies reveal that experiencing nature during childhood gives children the opportunity to have meaningful experiences that contribute to their understanding of the world around them, developing a sense of self, imagination, and creativity, and affiliation with nature.

Much of the qualitative work on children's nature experiences has been conducted within the context of **environmental education** programmes. An important insight from this research is that **hands-on-learning** is an effective way of connecting children to nature. During hands-on-learning, children are encouraged to become actively engaged with the natural environment, and with all their senses and physical abilities interact, explore, modify, and take care of nature. In this nature-contact, children may have impressive nature experiences that have a long-lasting influence throughout their life-span. Different forms of impressive childhood nature experiences have been distinguished, namely peak experiences, significant life experiences, flow experiences, and magical moments (Verboom and De Vries 2006; see also Table 10.1). These concepts are clarified below.

A **peak experience** is a rare, exciting, deeply moving experience that stands out from everyday events (Maslow 1970). Peak experiences play an important role in self-actualization which represents the highest state of Maslow's pyramid of needs. Although peak experiences are more likely to occur in people with a

Table 10.1 *Typologies of impressive childhood nature experiences (Based on Verboom and De Vries 2006).*

	Peak & flow experiences	*Significant life experiences*	*Magical moments*
Examples	Building a dam at the beach, building a shelter or taking care of an animal	Getting lost in the forest or a confrontation with a (wild) animal	Intrigued by the beauty of a flower or animal or the growing process of a seed
Psychological state	Synergy of mind, senses and body. A deep focus and concentration	Conquer fears, feeling of mastery	Being grasped by something that you've never sensed before
Adult supervision	Alone, preferably without adult supervision	Alone or with adults, adults can function as a role model	Alone or with adults, adults can facilitate the experience by guiding attention
Availability of nature	Proximate and easily accessible nature	Access and accessibility to nature, preferable wild nature areas	A rich sensory natural environment, indoors or outdoors
Conditional: time and space	There needs to be time and space to emerge in the experience		

more mature personality, children and teens may also undergo peak experiences. For example, nature encounters, such as 'enjoying the sunshine as I sat at a windowsill' or 'exploring the forest near my neighborhood' were identified as distinct youth-peak experiences in various countries (Hoffman and Ortiz 2009).

Significant life experiences are deeply touching, forming experiences that often contain a component of anxiety, and may permanently change the vision on life (Tanner 1980). For an experience to qualify as a significant life experience, the experience should be challenging but not too much, evoking just the right amount of anxiety. An event that is too challenging will be negatively evaluated. What the right amount of anxiety is for a significant life experience to occur may differ from person to person. What is experienced as shocking for some children (e.g. letting a wood-louse crawl on your hand) can be too plain or boring for other children to make a lasting impression (Verboom and De Vries 2006).

A **flow experience** is an experience in which people are so involved in an activity that they forget everything around them (Csikszentmihalyi 1990). During this experience thoughts, intentions, feelings, and senses are aimed at the same goal. Flow experiences relatively often take place in nature because the variation in forms and materials that are present in nature environments challenge children to practise their sensorimotor coordination (Gibson 1979). An example of a flow experience is a child trying to cross a stream using a tree trunk. Such an experience can fully engage children, challenging them over and over again to try to smoothly reach the other side. To stimulate flow experiences children are best left on their own, and as a minimum a child has to feel that they are responsible for their actions and in control. Activities that evoke a sense of responsibility such as gardening, taking care of animals, or building huts or rafts can set the stage for flow experiences.

Magical moments appeal to children's need for the mystical and sense of wonder (Talbot and Frost 1989). Such moments may arise when a child is fascinated or intrigued by a certain natural phenomenon, like a butterfly going from flower to flower. These kind of nature experiences are characterized by rich sensory stimulation, that extends possibilities, expands awareness, transcends the common, and enhances opportunities for children to immerse in nature and to wonder, create, and experiment and thus to grow.

10.3 NATURE AND CHILDREN'S HEALTH AND WELL-BEING

Alongside qualitative studies, more rigorous quantitative and controlled studies provide further empirical evidence on the importance of nature for children's health and well-being. Results of these studies indicate that exposure to nature can have physical, emotional, and cognitive benefits for children. Below we give an overview of findings regarding these three types of benefits.

10.3.1 Physical Health Benefits

Exposure to neighbourhood green space has been found to be positively related to children's levels of moderate-to-vigorous physical activity (MVPA). For example, a study among American children aged 8–14 showed that children who experienced more than 20 minutes of daily exposure to green spaces in their neighbourhood engaged in nearly five times the daily rate of MVPA compared to children with nearly zero daily exposure to green spaces (Almanza et al. 2012). These positive impacts of green space on physical activity may result in lower levels of overweight and obesity among children in greener neighbourhoods (Wolch et al. 2011). Perhaps even more strikingly, green space can affect children's physical health even when they are still in the womb. A child's birth weight is an important predictor of its psychophysiological development into adulthood, with issues arising in particular for children with a very low birth weight. A meta-analysis pooling data of eight studies showed that more neighbourhood greenness was associated with higher birth weight, independent of socioeconomic status and other risk factors (Dzhambov et al. 2014). This association is assumed to arise from lower stress levels and other health advantages in the pregnant women living in green surroundings.

In line with observations from qualitative studies on the importance of natural environments for children's motor development, a study in Norway found that playing in nature, as compared to playing in a paved school ground, promoted the development of motor skills in pre-school children measured by standardized pre- and post- tests of motor fitness (Fjørtoft 2004). Also, controlled observational studies confirm that children display more diverse and creative play behaviour in natural than in non-natural environments (Dowdell et al. 2011).

10.3.2 Mental Health Benefits

A study in rural Austrian middle schools reported an increase in students' psychological well-being and a reduction in stress after greening of the school ground, compared to children in control schools (Kelz et al. 2015). Having nature nearby can also make children less vulnerable to negative impacts of stressful events, by helping them to cope better with adversities (Corraliza et al. 2012). Furthermore, several studies have revealed a relation between greenery in the school surroundings and a decrease of antisocial behaviours, such as bullying and aggressive behaviours (Cheskey 2001). In addition, at green playgrounds more prosocial behaviour occurs than at barren, paved playgrounds.

Further evidence for the importance of nature for children's mental health comes from evaluations of outdoor challenge programmes. In these programmes, children take part in various outdoor activities in the wilderness with the purpose of improving their mental well-being. Pre- and post-surveys among American youth who participated in a wilderness programme revealed an increased sense of personal autonomy, improved self-concept, a greater capacity for taking action and being decisive, and improved interpersonal skills (Kahn Jr. and Kellert 2002).

10.3.3   Cognitive Benefits

Interacting with nature can also improve cognitive functioning. As described in Chapter 6, natural environments support **restoration** from **directed attentional fatigue**. Among other things, natural environments tend to automatically draw attention without cognitive effort, thereby allowing central executive functions in the brain to rest and replenish. There is growing evidence that children may benefit from these restorative qualities of nature as much as adults do (Collado and Staats 2016; see Box 10.1). For example, children from low-income families demonstrated better ability to concentrate and other signs of improved cognitive functioning, as measured by a parents' rating scale, after moving to a house with greater accessibility to nature (Wells 2000). Girls aged 7–12 years scored better on tests of concentration, impulse inhibition, and delay of gratification when they had greener views from the home (Faber Taylor et al. 2002).

Children with attention deficit hyperactivity disorder (ADHD) suffer from deficits in their attentional functioning. Given nature's restorative qualities, natural environments might provide supportive settings for these children. In line with this notion, parents have reported a decrease in children's ADHD symptoms after their child played in a natural environment (Kuo and Faber Taylor 2004). In a large cross-sectional study, more green space in the living environment was related to the use of less ADHD medication (De Vries 2016). Children with ADHD also performed better on a concentration task after a visit to the woods, compared to a town visit (Van den Berg and Van den Berg 2011).

BOX 10.1   EFFECTS OF NATURE ON SCHOOL PERFORMANCE

Within the school environment, it has been found that children perform better on standardized tests of mathematics and English if there is more green space around their school (Wu et al. 2014). Furthermore, a study at five high schools showed that students who were randomly assigned to classrooms with views to green space, as compared to students in classrooms without green views, performed better on attention tests and recovered faster from a stressful experience (Li and Sullivan 2016). The greening of classrooms has similar benefits. Placement of a green wall in four classrooms of elementary schools, compared to control classrooms without green walls, resulted in better scores on a test for selective attention (Van den Berg et al. 2016b). Nature in and around schools thus has the potential to improve children's school performance, which may have a life-changing impact on career and future goals.

10.4 CHILDHOOD NATURE EXPERIENCES AND ADULT ENVIRONMENTALISM

While the short-term benefits of contact with nature for children are well documented, little is known about the long-term effects. As yet, no longitudinal studies have been conducted which follow children from a young age into adulthood to monitor the impacts of childhood interaction with nature through the life-course. However, several studies have retrospectively linked adults' recollections of their experiences with nature in childhood to various adult outcomes. Using this approach, a survey among 2000 adults living in the United States found that growing up in a home with natural surroundings, visiting parks, and gardening during childhood were associated with more positive adult attitudes towards trees and higher adult participation in gardening activities (Lohr and Pearson-Mims 2005). Another large-scale survey among adult residents of US cities showed that people who engaged in nature-based activities such as hiking or playing in the woods, camping, and hunting or fishing before the age of 11 were more likely to exhibit **pro-environmental behaviours** and attitudes as adults (Wells and Lekies 2006).

The pathway from childhood nature experiences to adult environmentalism is thought to reflect a stepwise process, in which children first become attached to specific natural places, and then later generalize these feelings of attachment to the natural environment more broadly. In adults, such general attachment or **connectedness to nature** has been found to correlate positively with biospheric values and pro-environmental behaviour (Schultz et al. 2004; see also Chapter 16). Connectedness to nature has not only been implicated in pro-environmentalism, individuals who feel strongly connected to nature also tend to feel happier than those who are less connected (see Chapter 7). These findings suggest that there may exist a 'happy path to sustainability' (Nisbet and Zelenski 2011). That is, if children spend more time in nature and develop a sense of connectedness to nature, they may become happier as adults and behave in more sustainable ways.

10.5 APPLICATIONS AND IMPLICATIONS

In response to the growing insights on how nature can promote children's development, health and well-being, there has been a surge of initiatives to (re)connect children with nature. Many of these initiatives have focused on 'bringing nature to children' by greening of places such as school grounds, classrooms, urban public spaces, and hospitals. Other initiatives have aimed at 'bringing children to nature' by encouraging and facilitating children to actively participate in nature-based programmes and activities, like nature experience programmes and gardening projects. These interventions may be especially relevant to children from deprived backgrounds, who have been found to have relatively limited access to natural spaces in their living environment (Strife and Downey 2009). As such, nature-based interventions may help to mitigate **health inequities** between children from families with a low and high socioeconomic status (see also Chapter 7).

10.6 SUMMARY

In this chapter, we have provided an overview of research on the relationship between children and the natural environment. This research shows that children are attracted to the rich sensory stimulation provided by nature, and derive pleasure from actively engaging with the natural environment with all their senses and physical abilities. While interacting with nature, children may have impressive experiences that strengthen their connectedness to nature and may lay a foundation for pro-environmental behaviour later in life. Furthermore, there is increasing evidence that exposure to natural environments can have physical, emotional, and cognitive health benefits for children. In general, childhood experiences with nature, or a lack of those experiences, can set in train developmental trajectories that may have life-long consequences for an individual's health and well-being. These research findings and insights provide a rationale for concerted efforts to reconnect children with nature, especially those children from deprived backgrounds who have limited access to nature in their daily living environment.

GLOSSARY

affordances   Attributes of a setting which provide potential for action.
connectedness to nature   The extent to which individuals feel emotionally connected to the natural world and consider nature as part of their identity.
directed attentional fatigue   A neurological symptom, also referred to as 'mental fatigue', which occurs when parts of the central executive brain system become fatigued.
environmental education   Organized efforts to raise sensitivity, awareness, and understanding of the linkages and interdependencies among humans and the natural environment.
ethnographic studies   A type of qualitative research where researchers observe and/or interact with a study's participants in their real-life environment.
flow experience   An experience in which people are so involved in an activity that they forget everything around them.
green space   A term mostly used by policymakers to refer to nature in and around urban areas.

hands-on-learning   A form of environmental education in which children are encouraged to become actively engaged with the natural environment, and experience it with all their senses.

health inequities   Disparities in health resulting from differences in social and economic status.

magical moments   Experiences with nature that appeal to children's need for the mystical and sense of wonder.

nature   A broad concept that encompasses natural areas such as forests as well as agricultural landscapes, urban greenery, and natural elements and features such as trees and lakes.

nature deficit disorder   The possible negative health consequences of the growing disconnection between children and nature.

peak experience   A rare, exciting, deeply moving experience that stands out from everyday events.

pro-environmental behaviour   Behaviour which harms the environment as little as possible or even benefits it.

restoration   The physiological and psychological process of recovery from stress and mental fatigue.

significant life experience   A deeply touching, forming experience which permanently changes one's vision on life.

stranger danger   The idea that strangers can potentially be dangerous to children or adults.

SUGGESTIONS FOR FURTHER READING

Chawla, L. (2015). Benefits of nature contact for children. *Journal of Planning Literature* 30 (4): 433–452.

Collado, S. and Staats, H. (2016). Contact with nature and children's restorative experiences: an eye to the future. *Frontiers in Psychology* 7: 1885.

Wood, C., Bragg, R., and Pretty, J. (2016). The benefits of green exercise for children. In: *Green Exercise: Linking Nature, Health and Well-Being* (ed. J. Barton, R. Bragg, C. Wood and J. Pretty), 46–52. London: Routledge.

REVIEW QUESTIONS

1. Describe what Louv means by 'nature-deficit disorder' and why this could be alarming for society.
2. Explain what 'hands-on-learning' is and how this can strengthen children's connectedness to nature.
3. Describe, if possible, an impressive experience with nature from your own childhood. Which type of experience was it? How did it affect you?
4. Give two examples of green interventions that may be used to reduce health inequities between children from families with a low and high socioeconomic status.

11 Appraising and Designing Built Environments that Promote Well-Being and Healthy Behaviour

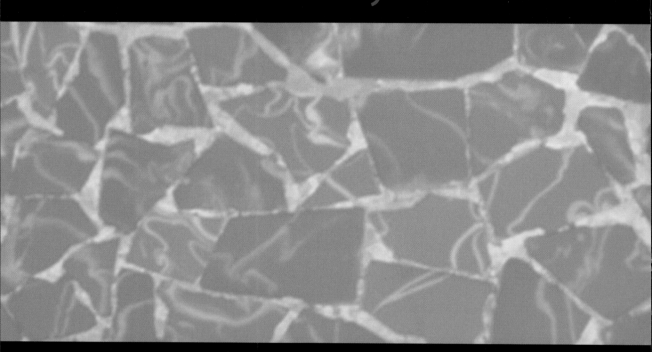

Robert Gifford
University of Victoria, Canada

Lindsay J. McCunn
University of Washington Tacoma, USA

CHAPTER OUTLINE

11.1   INTRODUCTION

Interactions between people and buildings are complex. People vary; built structures vary. Ask 10 people what they think of a particular building and you may hear 10 different answers. However, ask the 10 about another building and their answers may be quite uniform. The first part of this chapter is about the ways that people evaluate, or **appraise**, built environments around them. The second part describes insights and knowledge from environmental psychology for informing the design of built environments that enhance human welfare.

11.2   AESTHETIC APPRAISALS OF ARCHITECTURE

When is a building beautiful? The answer is that beauty is partly in the eye of the beholder and partly in the building itself (see Chapters 5 and 8 for a similar argument pertaining to natural stimuli and settings). For example, architects and laypersons sometimes disagree about whether a building is beautiful, but other times almost everyone thinks a building is beautiful or ugly (see Box 11.1). Environmental psychologists aim to discover which human differences and which design differences account for such variation and uniformity in environmental appraisals so they can usefully contribute to the design of buildings, neighbourhoods, and cities (e.g. Gifford 1980; Gifford et al. 2000, 2002). They also acknowledge the context in which built settings are appraised (e.g. high pollution, low crime) (Blaison and Hess 2016; Suls and Wheeler 2000, 2007). In this section, we first discuss uniformities in the appraisal of built settings based on the physical qualities of those settings. We then discuss variations in appraisals associated with differences in one's personal characteristics.

11.2.1   Uniformities in the Appraisal of Built Space

Environmental psychologists have spent much time identifying qualities of the built environment that lead to consistent appraisals across observers (Stamps and Nasar 1997). One such attribute is a building's exterior, or façade. Many people prefer facades that express a sense of the past, and that have detailed, decorated, grooved, or three-dimensional surfaces that appear to provide shelter and invite touch and exploration (Frewald 1990).

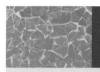

BOX 11.1 DECODING MODERN ARCHITECTURE

A set of 42 large, modern buildings was evaluated by groups of architects and laypersons (Gifford et al. 2000). The findings showed that some of the buildings were appraised positively by both architects and laypersons, some were appraised positively by one group and negatively by the other group, and some were disliked by both groups. The Bank of China Tower in Hong Kong was the #1 favourite of laypersons and the #2 choice of architects. This shows that it is possible to design a building that both experts and everyday people like. But the two groups can severely disagree too. Disney Headquarters in Los Angeles was hated by architects (#41) but loved by laypeople (#3). Yet Stockley Park Building (1987–1989) in England was #4 for the architects but #33 for laypersons. Some buildings were complete aesthetic failures according to both groups (e.g. the Chicago Bar Association building was #35 for architects and #34 for laypersons). Images of these buildings are easy to find using Google's images search engine, if you are curious. However, environmental psychologists are not merely poll-takers. The study compared all 42 buildings on 57 different aspects of their facades to learn what is associated with positive and negative appraisals for each group of observers. The results are complex but, in part, the two groups tended to focus on different aspects of the façade to reach their appraisals and value aspects differently. For example, buildings with more railings, more metal cladding and fewer arches elicited more pleasure for architects than for laypersons, and architects were more psychologically aroused than laypersons by buildings with numerous rounded edges and corners, and more triangular elements.

In general, three types of abstract, aesthetic qualities that elicit particular appraisals have been distinguished: **formal, symbolic**, and **schematic** (Nasar 1994). Formal qualities include abstract concepts such as complexity, order, and enclosure. Symbolic qualities are expressed through design style (e.g. art deco or postmodern). Schematic qualities refer to a design's goodness-of-example or typicality for its functional category (e.g. restaurants, shops). According to Nasar, combinations of these qualities evoke different appraisals. For example, buildings with a familiar design style that exhibit orderliness and moderate complexity are usually evaluated as 'pleasant', whereas buildings with a complex and atypical design style are usually evaluated as 'exciting'. The relation between complexity and preference usually takes an inverted U-shape: buildings with an intermediate level of complexity tend to be favoured over those with the most and least complexity (e.g. Imamoglu 2000); this is different from nature, for which greater complexity is generally associated with greater preference (see Chapter 5).

As for design style, both architects and laypersons rated farm and Tudor style buildings (houses with deeply pitched roofs and decorative timbering) as most desirable, Mediterranean and saltbox style buildings (wooden houses with sloping roofs) as least desirable, farm style as most friendly, colonial style as most unfriendly, colonial and Tudor style as highest in status, and saltbox and Mediterranean styles as lowest in status (Nasar 1989). Thus, sometimes building style preferences of architects and laypersons align well.

The influence of typicality on the aesthetic appraisal of built structures depends on the desirability of the structure. Perceived typicality influences preference positively (Purcell 1986) but more typicality increases preference for places that are already desirable, such as pastoral, grassland landscapes (Hagerhall 2001), and reduces preference for undesirable places, such as urban alleys (Herzog and Stark 2004).

11.2.2 *Observer Differences*

Despite these uniformities, appraisals also vary from person to person. Some people prefer new buildings, others prefer traditional buildings. Some appreciate the action of busy streets, while others despise it. In general, individual differences in goals, intentions, knowledge, moods, culture, and life experiences all interact with the physical characteristics of a built setting to determine appraisals of that setting (Amedeo and Golledge 2003; Canter 1985; Gifford 1980; Verderber and Moore 1977; Ward 1977). Sometimes a negative context surrounding a location can decrease how pleasant nearby locations are rated while, at other times, a negative spatial context can enhance appraisals of pleasantness for places that are farther away (Blaison and Hess 2016). Levels of education and income also influence the inferences that people draw from architectural styles. For example, as educational level and income increase, preference for colonial style houses decreases and preference for contemporary style houses increases (Nasar 1989).

One's training and occupation also influence environmental appraisal. For example, architects are socialized during their education to prefer certain designs over others (Wilson 1996) and to use specific schemes to judge buildings (Devlin 1990). This may be why architects are often unable to predict what non-architects will find desirable in a structure (Brown and Gifford 2001; Nasar 1989). In general, architects tend to prefer more unusual housing forms than non-architects, who tend to prefer conventional house styles (Nasar and Purcell 1990). Non-architects also differ from architects in that they often prefer square rooms over rectangular ones, with higher than average ceilings (Baird et al. 1978; Nasar 1981). These differences in preference seem to occur while architects are receiving their education: architecture students and non-architecture students sometimes differ in their preferences for building facades (Imamoglu 2000).

Other role differences influence preferences for the design or organization of buildings. For example, when nursing home administrators, designers, and residents were shown different nursing home design options, the administrators and designers favoured plans that supported social interaction for residents, while residents preferred plans that seemed to afford the most privacy (Duffy et al. 1986).

11.2.3 Meaning in Architecture

Given the marked differences in how people evaluate a setting, environmental psychologists search for reasons why. One idea is that architects and non-architects differ in their appraisals because they have a different sense of **architectural meaning**, that is, what sorts of associations from one's life the visual image of the building evokes in terms of historical events, styles, preferences, power relations, and so on. For example, architects sort modern and postmodern buildings according to design, quality, style, form, and possible historic significance, whereas accountants sort these buildings mostly according to their preferences and building type (e.g. residence, office) (Groat 1982). Remarkably, the accountants did not recognize postmodern buildings as being distinct from the other modern buildings, which suggests that some of the meanings that architects try to convey with their design styles do not exist for other people.

The goal of many architects is to design buildings that communicate meaning in the sense of typicality, or function: a library should look like a library and a hotel should look like a hotel, even if another goal is to accomplish this without making every building of a given type look the same (Genereux et al. 1983). Being able to discern the purpose of a structure is important for community residents (Groat and Canter 1979). In general, settings with multiple meanings (identities) are often disliked, whereas scenes in which the meaning of the building, and its use, is clear are preferred (Nasar 1983).

11.3 THREE BUILDING DESIGN APPROACHES THAT PROMOTE WELL-BEING AND HEALTHY BEHAVIOUR

Attempts to design buildings that promote human well-being and behaviour have been undertaken for many years (e.g. Dempsey 1914). Three modern approaches to this are **social design** – designing buildings to best serve human needs and wants; **biophilic design** – the integration of natural shapes, forms, and processes in architecture; and **evidence-based design** – designing buildings based on the best available evidence on the effectiveness of design measures.

11.3.1 Social Design

Unfortunately, in modern industrialized society, a gap often exists between building designers and building users. Architects generally do not discuss their project plans with those who will potentially use a space on a daily basis, except when they design a private residence. Instead, they communicate with boards of directors, owners, or facility managers who usually do not work in or visit the space after it is complete.

This gap means that specific behavioural needs of building users are not always included in the building design, and the rationales for the architect's decisions are not explained to most users. Social design (Sommer 1983; see also Box 11.2) aims to bridge the gap between building designers and users. It is distinguished from traditional (formal) design because it does not focus on large-scale, corporate, high-cost approaches. Instead, it favours a small-scale, human-oriented, democratic approach. Information from and about a building's potential occupants, meaning, and local context is used to help ensure that the design will enhance well-being and health-promoting behaviour.

Social designers investigate the attitudes and behaviours of future building occupants – even on large-scale projects. This is accomplished by interviewing potential occupants about their expected needs in various areas of the building, how much time they might spend at certain points within the floor plan, and whether any special requirements exist among them (e.g. different levels of lighting for people of different ages). This approach almost guarantees success because it combines the input of building users with the training and experience of an environmental psychologist, an architect, and other relevant expertise to create the best possible built space within local contexts and constraints.

Some examples of successful social design are in studies of hospital renovations (e.g. Becker and Poe 1980) and other health facilities (e.g. Gifford and Martin 1991). The healthcare and education sectors have been popular testbeds for the integrated design process (IDP) and the integrated project delivery (IPD) method (e.g. Ghassemi and Becerik-Gerber 2011). These are modern design processes formalized by organizations such as the American Institute of

BOX 11.2   SIX GOALS OF SOCIAL DESIGN

Social designers keep six goals in mind to facilitate communication between the principal players in the design process and remind them that the typical building user is a principal player (Gifford 2007).

Goal 1. Create a setting that matches or fits the needs and behaviours of its occupants. This goal is also referred to as **congruence**, habitability, or goodness of fit.

Goal 2. Satisfy the needs of building users, because occupants spend much time living and working in designed spaces.

Goal 3. Positively change behaviour in the setting. For example, increase productivity in an office building or enhance socialization in a community centre.

Goal 4. Enhance personal control of occupants. When users are able to change a setting to meet their needs, the setting tends to be less stressful.

Goal 5. Facilitate social support and encourage cooperation in the setting.

Goal 6. Employ **imageability** to help occupants and visitors find their way without the stress of becoming lost or confused.

Architects (AIA) to bring together key stakeholder groups throughout a project. Although these frameworks are similar to social design in that they encourage an understanding of the needs and preferences of building users, the focus is placed mainly on open, trusting collaborative relationships among building owners, designers, and constructors.

Not every principal player in the design process understands the advantages of social design. Some architects assume that if a space is structurally beautiful, the occupants will be so impressed with the aesthetics that functionality will 'take care of itself' over time. Some architects question why they ought to match a building to the needs and behaviours of a specific group of people when either the group, or the needs of that group, might change several times during the lifetime of the space. The response of environmental psychologists is that when a building's use changes, a new planning and design process can be undertaken.

11.3.2   *Biophilic Design*

Humans evolved in natural environments for millennia and have lived in cities for only about 10 000 years of our 230 000 years of existence as a species. Therefore, some argue that modern people still have **biophilia**, or an innate tendency to affiliate with nature and natural elements (e.g. Wilson 1984; see also Chapters 5, 7, and 8). If this tendency can be fulfilled in a building's design, then positive and restorative experiences are expected to follow from spending time in the building. Thus, built settings that integrate representations of the natural world into facades and interiors, as well as healthy attributes such as natural ventilation and daylight, would seem to benefit occupants' well-being and behaviour. This design approach strives to integrate biophilic experiences with sustainable building and landscape practice (Kellert et al. 2011).

Biophilic design is closely related to restorative design, an approach that focuses on the promotion of **restoration** from stress or mental fatigue as a key component of biophilic experience (Hartig et al. 2008; see also Chapters 6 and 7). Restoration may stem from the presence of plants and other natural elements, but it can also occur in restful places, such as museums, that do not have obvious natural elements (see also Chapter 12). Restorative design may be considered a more general form of biophilic design that aims to promote stress-reducing experiences that are characteristic of natural environments, but is not necessarily restricted to natural elements. After all, perhaps our most restorative activity is sleeping, which is almost always done indoors.

An important difference between biophilic design and social design is that in biophilic design, building users are not usually interviewed about specific building attributes. Instead, proponents of biophilic and restorative design make use of research evidence on the impacts of buildings on users. For example, a lack of exposure to nature leads to long-term stress and negative feelings about the built environment (Joye 2007; Parsons 1991; Ulrich 1984). However, if this is true, one may ask why buildings do not include more natural content. One reason is that buildings are often planned with cost efficiency in mind, instead of integrating natural forms (Salingaros 2004). Another reason might be rooted in the finding that productivity on a simple task can decrease when many plants are in an office (Larsen et al. 1998). Perhaps biophilic elements are good for workers' mental health, but less beneficial for their productivity.

11.3.3 Evidence-Based Design

According to this approach, all new buildings should be informed by the best available evidence on the effectiveness of each design decision. Proponents of this approach argue that designing by intuition, fashion, or solely on the basis of theory, precedent, or aesthetics is less likely to produce a positively habitable built setting than if design is solidly based on research.

The need for evidence-based design has been recognized for decades (e.g. Zeisel 1975). Environmental psychologists have documented the positive impact on well-being and functioning of building users of many design characteristics, such as reduced noise, enhanced lighting and ventilation, better ergonomic designs, supportive workplaces, the provision of personal control and improved layouts (Gifford 2014; Sommer 1983; Ulrich et al. 2004, see also Chapter 4). Especially in healthcare architecture, their findings are increasingly used in an effort to improve patient and staff well-being, patient healing, stress reduction, and safety.

11.4 SUMMARY

Even the most outdoors-oriented people spend a great deal of their lives in buildings, and the rest of us spend the vast majority of our time indoors. These structures are, therefore, of great importance to our well-being. In this chapter we have discussed some important similarities and differences in people's appraisal of built settings in relation to the physical qualities of those settings and personal characteristics. We have also discussed social design, biophilic design, and evidence-based design as three recent approaches that aim to translate insights from environmental psychology into building designs that satisfy users' needs and improve their well-being. In sum, this chapter shows that when empirical research successfully combines with architectural expertise, built spaces will mirror occupants' behavioural tendencies and enhance their daily experience. This will not only reduce stress and increase the satisfaction of occupants, but also save mistakes in future building designs.

GLOSSARY

appraisal One person's personal impression of a place or structure.
architectural meaning Associations from a person's life evoked by the visual image of a building, in terms of historical events, styles, preferences, power relations, etc.
biophilia People's innate tendency to seek connections with nature and other forms of life.

biophilic design   A design approach that promotes the integration of natural shapes, forms, and processes in building design with the assumption that bringing nature indoors is restorative because it emulates our species-long time spent in natural surroundings.

congruence   A match between a setting and the needs and behaviours of its occupants (also referred to as habitability or goodness of fit).

evidence-based design   An approach to designing buildings based on the best available evidence on the effectiveness of design measures.

formal quality   In Nasar's system, there are three formal qualities (or combinations of them): perceived enclosure, complexity, and order of a building.

imageability   A term defined by urban planner Kevin Lynch as the ease with which people understand the layout and meaning of a setting, or its physical attributes that afford clarity with which a place can be perceived and identified.

restoration   The physiological and psychological process of recovery from stress and mental fatigue.

schematic quality   A building design's typicality for a certain category (e.g. restaurants, shops).

social design   A small-scale, human-oriented, democratic approach to building design in which information about, and the views of, a building's potential occupants, local context, and meaning take precedence over formal design criteria.

symbolic quality   A type of abstract quality expressed through design style.

SUGGESTIONS FOR FURTHER READING

Gifford, R. (2014). *Environmental Psychology: Principles and Practice*, 5e. Colville, WA: Optimal Books.

Kellert, S.R., Heerwagen, J.H., and Mador, M.L. (eds.) (2008). *Biophilic Design*. Hoboken, NJ: Wiley.

Sommer, R. (1983). *Social Design: Creating Buildings with People in Mind*. Englewood Cliffs, NJ: Prentice-Hall.

REVIEW QUESTIONS

1. Mention two physical attributes and two observer characteristics that have consistently been found to influence the aesthetic appraisal of built settings.
2. Mention at least three differences between architects and laypersons in their appraisal of built settings.
3. How can differences in the appraisal of built settings between architects and laypersons be explained?
4. Describe the six goals of social design.
5. Besides social design, which other modern building design approaches have striven for the promotion of human well-being and behaviour?

12 Urban Environmental Quality

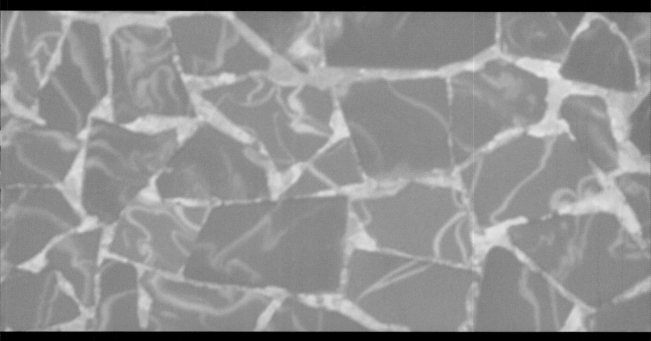

Mirilia Bonnes
Sapienza University of Rome, Italy

Massimiliano Scopelliti
LUMSA University, Italy

Ferdinando Fornara
University of Cagliari, Italy

Giuseppe Carrus
University of Roma Tre, Italy

CHAPTER OUTLINE

12.1 INTRODUCTION

The quality of the residential environment is fundamental to people's lives. Several environmental conditions such as noise, heat, air pollution, and **crowding** may constitute a source of discomfort and negatively impact **urban environmental quality** (see Chapters 4 and 13). Urban environments (from small towns to large and complex cities) also contain many conditions, such as infrastructure, green areas, and health and educational facilities that may positively influence urban environmental quality because they fit residents' needs. Urban environmental quality thus is a multidimensional concept that comprises both negative and positive influences.

The assessment of urban environmental quality has been a key topic in environmental psychology, since its beginning (e.g. see Bonnes and Carrus 2017; Craik and Feimer 1987) and it may be approached from either an expert or a lay-person perspective. The former involves expert judgements (based on a specific professional background) or formal (or quantitative) tools (see Poortinga et al. 2016), while the latter relies on 'soft' psychological responses (e.g. perceptions, appraisals, preferences, evaluations; see Bonaiuto and Fornara 2017). This chapter will focus in particular on the latter, more psychological, perspective. However, as pointed out in Chapter 5 on scenic beauty and Chapter 13 on quality of life, both the expert (objective) and lay-person (subjective) are important in urban environmental design and planning. Notably, the two perspectives may not always correspond, which is a topic of much research and debate in environmental psychology (see Bonnes et al. 2007).

Through an analysis of scientific contributions in the two most important journals about people–environment studies, urban environmental quality was identified as the 'hard core' of environmental psychology, encompassing the largest part of empirical studies (Giuliani and Scopelliti 2009). The potential sources of urban environmental stress, residential satisfaction, and place attachment (see Chapter 4), emerged as main research themes.

This chapter reviews psychological theories and research on urban environmental quality, through the analysis of **people–environment transactions** in residential environments. We first discuss negative influences of **environmental stressors** on urban residents' health and well-being along with theoretical explanations of these influences. Second, we discuss positive influences of urban infrastructure, green space, and other qualities of urban settings. We then introduce a multidimensional approach to studying environmental quality in terms of multicomponent constructs like residential satisfaction and affective quality of environments. We conclude with a multi-place approach, considering people-environment transactions with different places within the same urban environment.

Environmental Psychology: An Introduction, Second Edition. Edited by Linda Steg and Judith I. M. de Groot.
© 2019 John Wiley & Sons Ltd. Published 2019 by John Wiley & Sons Ltd.

12.2   URBAN SETTINGS AS A SOURCE OF STRESS AND DISCOMFORT

Urban settings have traditionally attracted many people because they offer a wide choice of positive stimulations, information, and opportunities for housing, work, and leisure. Negative – and potentially concurring – aspects of urban living can also be identified. Examples are road traffic noise, poor air quality, high temperature, and crowding. These sources of **environmental stress** have various physical and psychological consequences, including health-related problems, annoyance, negative emotions, diminished cognitive functioning and decreased prosocial behaviour (Lepore and Evans 1996; see also Chapter 4 for a detailed discussion).

Urban settings may be sources of stress when individuals *perceive* an imbalance between environmental demands and personal, social, or environmental coping resources. Individuals attribute meanings to environmental conditions, by evaluating the seriousness, necessity, and predictability of the threatening situation, and the perceived control over it, which may affect the extent to which environmental demands are perceived to be annoying or disturbing (Evans and Cohen 1987, 2004). For example, individuals who believe that the source of urban noise is unimportant, unnecessary, dangerous, and preventable, experience higher levels of annoyance than those with positive attitudes towards the noise source (Guski 1999).

Explanations of negative responses to urban environmental conditions have typically identified arousal and stimulus overload as key mechanisms. According to arousal theories, a person's task performance is to a large extent determined by his or her level of physical **arousal**. In general, the **Yerkes–Dodson law** (1908) states that the arousal–performance relationship can be represented through an inverted-U shaped curve, in which moderate levels of arousal are associated with optimal performances. Too low or too high levels of arousal can adversely affect performance, the former condition being too boring and the latter too exciting. Arousal theories predict that the impact of environmental stressors will depend on whether an individual's level of arousal is below, within the range, or above the optimal level. An urban resident with a high arousal level will experience more negative impacts from environmental stressors than a resident with a low arousal level.

In urban settings, the co-presence of multiple stressors can lead to **stimulus overload** (Evans and Cohen 1987). According to stimulus overload theories, continuous cognitive efforts are needed to cope with stressors, resulting in chronically increased arousal levels. As sustained attention depletes over time and turns into mental fatigue, cognitive functioning may be impaired (see also Chapters 6 and 7). People need to apply adequate coping strategies to compensate for their diminished capabilities. A common reaction to stimulus overload is a 'tunnel vision' in which people devote attention only to relevant information for the task at hand, while other inputs are ignored. Once attentional capacities have become depleted, even the smallest demands for attention, such as a neighbour wanting to chat about the weather, may become intolerable. In urban environments, demanding environmental conditions may thus lead to a need for privacy or social withdrawal, with a consequent reduction in social interaction, social support, and prosocial behaviour (Cohen 1980, see also Chapter 7).

12.3   URBAN SETTINGS AS A SOURCE OF WELL-BEING AND RESTORATION

Urban settings are not only sources of stress and illness, they may also offer possibilities for pleasant daily urban experiences for individual health and well-being (see also Chapters 5 and 6). For example, through pedestrian-friendly design and management, urban settings may support healthy and pleasant walking experiences (Wang et al. 2016). Several other urban features, often also linked to urban walkability, may offer support for enjoyable daily place experiences, such as greenery, nice views, interesting stores and buildings fronts (Brown and Werner 2012; Lee et al. 2016). In particular, various positive effects of greenery in urban settings have consistently been reported (see Chapter 6 and 7). Well-maintained green spaces and elements (e.g. urban parks and trees) can promote residents' health and well-being in several ways. They communicate the message that the place is cared for, thus promoting a sense of safety (Jansson et al. 2013). In addition, well-maintained green areas increase opportunities for social interaction and mutual acquaintance, thereby promoting **social cohesion** (Coley et al. 1997; Peters et al. 2010).

Urban settings can also provide psychological **restoration**, which refers to the reduction of stress and mental fatigue (Kaplan and Kaplan 1989, see also Chapter 7). For example, a study in a poor neighbourhood in Chicago, where buildings and apartments were architecturally similar but the amount of vegetation outside varied considerably, showed that residents in barren environments showed poorer attentional functioning than residents in greener environments, which led to higher levels of intra-family violence and aggression (Kuo and Sullivan 2001). Besides parks and green spaces, built settings such as museums and churches, characterized by adequate ambient conditions (e.g. lighting, space, layout, temperature, peace), can also provide restorative experiences (Herzog et al. 2010; Packer 2008). Furthermore, urban environments with mixed built and natural features (e.g. canals), can have stress-reducing and mood-enhancing potentials, especially if they are characterized by spacious and coherent designs (e.g. an intricate layout and landmarks providing opportunities for exploration and orientation), and attractive houses (e.g. with roof-terrace and patios) (Karmanov and Hamel 2008).

12.4 RESIDENTIAL SATISFACTION – A MULTICOMPONENT CONCEPT

As shown in the previous sections, urban settings are characterized by the simultaneous presence of environmental conditions providing either stress and discomfort or opportunities for well-being and restoration. A multidimensional assessment of urban residential environmental quality is thus crucial for environmental psychological research. To address this issue, the broad concept of **residential satisfaction**, encompassing cognitive, behavioural, and affective components, has been proposed.

Residential satisfaction refers to the experience of gratification deriving from living in a place (i.e. home, neighbourhood, or town). This concept has often been approached as a unidimensional variable by asking people to indicate how satisfied they are (e.g. on a Likert-type scale) with their overall residential environment, at a specified place-scale (e.g. neighbourhood, home, town). However, residential satisfaction can also be conceived as a multicomponent construct, by distinguishing its cognitive, behavioural, and affective components (Bonaiuto and Fornara 2017). We will elaborate on these components and their measurement below.

12.5 A MULTIDIMENSIONAL APPROACH TO URBAN ENVIRONMENTAL QUALITY

The cognitive component of residential satisfaction has been studied in terms of **perceived residential environmental quality**, by asking people to evaluate those aspects of their residential environment that are relevant for its overall quality (Bonaiuto and Fornara 2017). Various psychometric tools for measuring this multidimensional evaluation have been developed and used, such as the early perceived environmental quality indicators (PEQIs: Craik and Zube 1976), or the more recent perceived residential environment quality indicators (PREQIs: Fornara et al. 2010), that has been validated in several cultural contexts (Bonaiuto et al. 2015, see Box 12.1).

The behavioural component of residential satisfaction has mainly been studied in terms of **residential mobility**, interpreted as an indicator of residential dissatisfaction. Residential mobility refers to the change of one's residence, and has been studied in terms of mobility intention or actual mobility (e.g. Van Vugt et al. 2003). A longitudinal study involving 12 European Union countries found that room crowding exerted a direct influence on residential mobility, while other residential characteristics

BOX 12.1   PERCEIVED RESIDENTIAL ENVIRONMENT QUALITY INDICATORS

Since the 1990s Italian researchers have worked to develop a comprehensive set of PREQIs. Using factor analyses, 11 scales have been identified, reflecting four macrodimensions of residential quality: spatial (i.e. architectural and urban planning), human (i.e. people and social relationships), functional (i.e. services and facilities), and contextual (i.e. pace of life, environmental health/pollution and upkeep/care). Sample items are:

- Buildings are too tall in this neighbourhood (spatial)

- In this neighbourhood people are civil (human)

- Buses are too uncomfortable in this neighbourhood (functional)

- This neighbourhood is full of activity (contextual)

Among other PREQIs, buildings aesthetics and presence/maintenance of green areas (spatial), positive social relations (social), presence/access to facilities (functional), and a slow pace of life (contextual) were positively related to residential satisfaction (Fornara et al. 2010).

(i.e. housing inefficiencies, noise, pollution, and crime) affected residential mobility through their negative impact on overall residential satisfaction (Diaz-Serrano and Stoyanova 2010).

The affective component has been studied in terms of affective quality and place attachment (see Chapter 14). With respect to **affective quality**, Russell and Pratt (1980) proposed a circumplex model stating that places can elicit different affective responses, expressed through four main bipolar dimensions (pleasant–unpleasant, arousing–sleepy, relaxing–distressing, exciting–gloomy) that represent a combination of levels (high and/or low) of pleasure and arousal (see Figure 12.1). The authors developed a 40-item scale measuring the affective quality of places. Using this scale to study affective responses to suburban parks, one study found that tree density, presence of undergrowth and pathways increased user's pleasure and produced optimal levels of arousal (Hull and Harvey 1989). A Taiwanese study showed that open space, refined building texture, community signage, prominence of trees, and diverse street furniture were significant positive predictors of affective appraisal of urban streetscapes (Zhang and Lin 2011). Specifically, trees and openness were predictors of both pleasure and arousal, resulting in a positive emotion of high intensity.

Relevant aspects of **place attachment** are its support of personal, social, and place-based identity (the residential environment promotes distinctiveness, continuity of self, and local group membership), the positive feelings linked to being in a place (e.g. serenity, well-being), and the negative feelings of being away from it, like homesickness (Giuliani 2004; Lewicka 2011b; see also

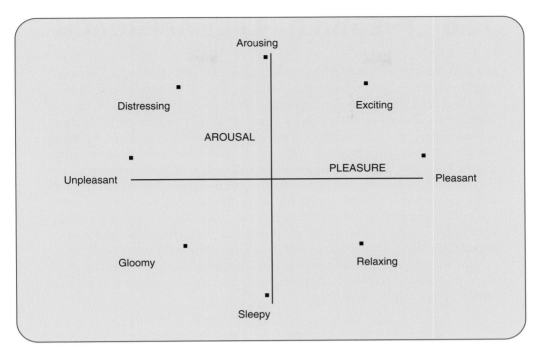

Figure 12.1 *Affective quality of places. Source: Adapted from Russell and Pratt (1980).*

Chapter 14). Many environmental factors have been found to predict attachment to residential neighbourhoods, such as buildings aesthetics and lower spatial density, presence and maintenance of greenery, and lack of pollution and of incivilities (Bonaiuto et al. 2003; Poortinga et al. 2016). Most of these environmental factors predicting place attachment are similar to the factors that influence overall residential satisfaction, although these two measures are only partially overlapping (e.g. Aiello et al. 2010).

The cognitive, behavioural, and affective components of residential satisfaction and place attachment are often studied separately. They have been considered together, in relation to neighbourhood physical features, using a comprehensive multidimensional approach in two neighbourhoods of Rome (Aiello et al. 2010). In this study, residential satisfaction was linked to perceived availability of commercial services and a positive pace of life, pleasant quality of places, and purchasing and leisure activities of residents. Physical features of the neighbourhood, namely number of shops and leisure facilities, in turn predicted the perceived availability of commercial services and a positive pace of life, respectively. Place attachment was linked to perceived building pleasantness, positive social relationships, and availability of commercial services, pleasant and arousing (and absence of gloomy) quality of places, and social and leisure activities of residents. Physical features of the neighbourhood, namely rate of green areas and building density, in turn predicted the perception of pleasant places and places for social activities, respectively.

12.6   THE MULTI-PLACE APPROACH

Physical features of urban environments may vary across different urban settings or places (i.e., home, neighbourhood, city-centre, suburbs) that tend to be used and perceived differently depending on its residents, and size of the city (Bonaiuto and Bonnes 1996; Bonnes et al. 1990). The perception of environmental quality of a specific urban place, such as the residential neighbourhood, can thus be related to residents' experiences and activities in all these urban places. Therefore, a more comprehensive and ecological understanding of the perception of urban environmental quality can be achieved through the **multi-place approach** that simultaneously considers the resident's experience in different urban settings (see Box 12.2). Hartig et al. (2003b) have proposed a similar approach in the field of housing–health research, through their **social ecological model**. This model considers the residential experience as the result of the transactions with several urban settings beyond the neighbourhood (e.g. the workplace and leisure places in other neighbourhoods), and analyses how these transactions can affect health.

BOX 12.2   THE MULTI-PLACE APPROACH TO STUDYING NEIGHBOURHOOD QUALITY

Using a multi-place approach, Bonaiuto et al. (2004) found that perceived neighbourhood quality is related to residents' experiences in different places of the same urban environment. They identified four different types of residents according to their multi-place urban activities, showing different levels of integration or confinement in the wider urban environment and also different perceptions of neighbourhood quality.

For example:

- the 'marginal escape group' (largely composed of long-term older residents, with a low to medium educational and socioeconomic level) engages mainly in home- and neighbourhood-confined urban activities, does not use the suburbs

and uses the city centre mainly to escape from daily routine. With regard to neighbourhood quality, this group perceives the highest insecurity, and expresses the lowest positive evaluations about its spatial and functional features, in comparison with the other groups.

- the 'quality users group' (largely composed of young and highly educated residents) carries out several cultural activities in the city centre, does not use the suburbs and uses the neighbourhood mainly for outdoor and sport activities. With regard to neighbourhood quality, this group perceives less insecurity and expresses higher positive evaluations about spatial and functional features, in comparison with the other groups.

12.7 SUMMARY

In this chapter we have reviewed the separate and combined influences of positive and negative environmental conditions on urban environmental quality, applying various theoretical models and research methods. We have shown that urban environmental quality can be studied within a multidimensional approach in terms of residential satisfaction and related concepts such as residential mobility, perceived residential environmental quality, affective quality of places, and place attachment. For all these concepts, valid and reliable psychometric tools have been developed that can be used in the design, management, and monitoring of urban environmental quality. However, for a comprehensive understanding of urban environmental quality, a multi-place approach is needed that takes into account residents' interactions with, and perceptions of, various urban places.

GLOSSARY

affective quality   The emotional meaning attributed to environments.

arousal   A state of psychological activation.

crowding   The subjective evaluation that the number of people in the environment exceeds the preferred or desired level. It differs from density, namely the objective ratio between number of people and size of environments.

environmental stress   The negative physiological and psychological effects of suboptimal environmental characteristics.

environmental stressors   Physical characteristics of environments that produce stress.

multi-place approach   The study of urban experience based on the analysis of residents' transactions with different urban settings.

people–environment transactions   The dynamic, reciprocal, interdependent, and temporally related process of interaction between an individual and the environment.

perceived residential environmental quality   The subjective evaluation of the quality of the residential environment.

place attachment   The emotional bond that individuals and groups have towards places of varying geographic scales.

residential mobility   The act of changing one's residence, either in the same community or between cities, states, or communities.

residential satisfaction   The feeling of gratification associated with living in a specific residential environment.

restoration   The physiological and psychological process of recovery from stress and mental fatigue.

social cohesion   The degree to which members of a community feel committed to the community and other members of the community.

social ecological model   A framework to examine the multiple influences of spatial, temporal, social, and behavioural levels of people–environment transactions.

stimulus overload   The condition of being overwhelmed by continuous environmental stimuli.

urban environmental quality   The quality of urban settings, encompassing physical, social, and psychological components.

Yerkes-Dodson law   The law that states a curvilinear relationship between arousal and performance.

SUGGESTIONS FOR FURTHER READING

Bonaiuto, M. and Fornara, F. (2017). Residential satisfaction and perceived urban quality. In: *Reference Module in Neuroscience and Biobehavioral Psychology* (ed. J. Stein), 1–5. Oxford, UK: Elsevier.

Francescato, G. (2002). Residential satisfaction research: the case for and against. In: *Residential environments. Choice satisfaction and behavior* (ed. J.I. Aragones, G. Francescato and T. Gärling), 15–34. Westport, CT: Bergin & Garvey.

Frick, D. (ed.) (1986). *The Quality of Urban Life: Social, Psychological and Physical Conditions.* New York, NY: Walter de Gruyter & Co.

REVIEW QUESTIONS

1. Which environmental conditions of urban settings tend to have a negative influence on urban environmental quality? What are the psychological processes implied?
2. Which features and conditions of urban environments can promote individual well-being? What are the psychological processes implied?
3. Which are the different measures of urban environmental quality? Briefly explain each of them.
4. Briefly discuss the multi-place approach to residential satisfaction.

Goda Perlaviciute
University of Groningen, The Netherlands

Linda Steg
University of Groningen, The Netherlands

CHAPTER OUTLINE

13.1   INTRODUCTION

Imagine a strict pro-environmental program going on. Meat and fish consumption is reduced to minimum, household energy use is severely restricted and biodiverse areas are prohibited for people to enter. From an ecological standpoint, this program would be considered sustainable, as it helps the natural world to remain intact and long-lasting. However, such a stringent initiative would threaten human well-being due to drastic behavioural changes and reduced comfort. Probably, people's quality of life would diminish and public resistance to the program would be strong. Could we still label the program as sustainable?

In this chapter, we argue that a purely ecological perspective on **sustainability** is too limited and that a human perspective should also be considered. We approach sustainability as well-balanced relationships between humans and their environments. Sustainability involves finding a balance between **environmental**, **social** and **economic sustainability** aspects (World Commission on Environment and Development 1987). For example, consider an initiative to increase fuel prices in order to reduce CO_2 emissions. The sustainability of such an initiative cannot be assessed without considering social and economic consequences. Some people, especially those with a lower income, might have to give up their car, which might increase social inequity. Household purchasing power might decrease, whereas cash flows to the fuel industry might increase. To achieve sustainable development, sustainability of any of the three aspects (environmental, social, economic) should not seriously impede sustainability of the other two.

To monitor the balance between the three aspects, sustainability criteria are needed for each of them. Adequate criteria have been developed for environmental and economic qualities (see Steg and Gifford 2005). Environmental sustainability criteria include, for instance, energy consumption rates and CO_2 emissions. Economic sustainability criteria cover, among others, levels of purchasing power and inflation rates. Social sustainability can be measured on a societal or individual level (see Table 13.1). On the societal level, well-being of a society is studied as a whole. On the individual level, well-being of individuals comes to the foreground. Social sustainability measures applied so far are typically grounded in the societal level, for example, average lifetime and public health.

In this chapter, we introduce a measure of **quality of life** (QoL) as a way to assess social sustainability on the individual level. We define QoL as the extent to which important needs and values of individuals are satisfied (Diener 2000), which depends on a person's physical, economic, and social environments. For example, being surrounded by nature may enhance your health (see Chapter 6).

Environmental Psychology: An Introduction, Second Edition. Edited by Linda Steg and Judith I. M. de Groot.
© 2019 John Wiley & Sons Ltd. Published 2019 by John Wiley & Sons Ltd.

Table 13.1 *Three types of sustainability criteria and examples of indicators.*

Environmental sustainability	Economic sustainability	Social sustainability	
		Societal level	*Individual level*
Gas, electricity, and water consumption	Production values	Average lifetime	Individual income level
CO_2 emissions	Inflation rates	Unemployment rates	Individual health status
Land use	Purchasing power	Service accessibility	
		Public health	

Or, a strong economy is more likely to satisfy people's needs for work and income than a weak economy. In a similar vein, being surrounded by people helps satisfy one's needs for social relationships. Therefore, a considerable part of individual QoL depends on environmental qualities. This environmentally determined individual QoL is a good sustainability criterion, as environmental, social, and economic development can only be considered sustainable if it supports individual QoL. In Chapter 12, Bonnes and colleagues discussed how various characteristics of urban environments may affect individual well-being. Similarly, the QoL approach allows the study of the effects of different environments on individual well-being, including physical as well as social and economic environments. Moreover, besides 'diagnosing' the effects of existing environments, the QoL measure can be used to assess how environmental changes affect individual QoL. This is important as continuous environmental changes are an inherent part of sustainable development.

In this chapter, we first elaborate on two important dimensions of QoL measures, namely objectivity–subjectivity and multidimensionality–unidimensionality. Next, we discuss how individual QoL measures have been applied in studies on human-environment relationships.

13.2 QoL: OBJECTIVE AND SUBJECTIVE MEASURES

To assess environmentally determined QoL, **objective** and **subjective measures** can be used (see also Chapter 5). Objective measures describe how well environmental characteristics meet the criteria that are believed to be necessary for a good life. These measures consist of technological measurements and expert judgements of environmental conditions (e.g. quality of tap water, sulphur dioxide in the air), that can be assessed at societal or individual level. Objective measures describe environmental qualities and their presumed effects on QoL, but have certain limitations (see also Diener et al. 2009a). To set objective criteria, someone (usually experts in the relevant fields) has to decide which life domains are most important to people and what levels of satisfaction with those domains are sufficient to sustain QoL. Although needs and values in life are generally universal, this does not hold for all indicators that are typically included in QoL measures. Also, people differ in how much value they ascribe to various life domains (see Chapter 17) and how satisfying they find different environments. People's QoL also depends on, among other things, individual expectations, values, and previous knowledge. Therefore, QoL cannot be derived from objective conditions alone.

To complement objective measures, subjective measures based on individual perceptions are used. Subjective measures allow studying how people appraise environmental characteristics and how well they think environments satisfy their important needs and values (see Chapter 17). For example, people can report how satisfied they are with their lives with regard to certain circumstances (e.g. Andrews and Withey 1976; Diener et al. 1985), or they express their positive or negative affect (e.g. Watson et al. 1988) or their optimism or pessimism (e.g. Scheier and Carver 1985) with regard to various life aspects in their current situation.

To conclude, objective as well as subjective measures can be used to study individual QoL and ideally they should complement each other. Later in this chapter, we focus on subjective QoL measures as they are more relevant for psychology due to their focus on people's experiences and perceptions.

13.3   QoL: UNIDIMENSIONAL AND MULTIDIMENSIONAL MEASURES

Scholars and practitioners tend to study the effects of specific environmental conditions on specific aspects of QoL. For instance, the effects of environmental stressors such as noise and pollution on people's (self-reported) health can be studied (see Chapter 4). **Unidimensional measures of QoL**, describing the relationship between one environmental factor and one **QoL aspect**, can be used for such purposes. For example, one might examine whether individual car use (e.g. weekly mileage) is related to personal freedom (e.g. 'How free or limited do you feel in deciding upon your daily activities?').

However, most often environmental conditions affect multiple aspects of QoL, just as most QoL aspects are influenced by multiple environmental conditions. Consider again individual car use. Car use not only affects one's freedom, but also various other needs and values, such as the need to be independent, enjoying life, and enhancing one's status (see Chapter 19 and 20). In a similar vein, freedom is not only determined by the level of car use, but also by other environmental conditions, such as accessibility of natural settings and availability of facilities (e.g. shops, hospitals). To study multiple relationships between environmental factors and QoL, **multidimensional measures of QoL** are needed. Multidimensional measures integrate various QoL aspects and allow the assessment of how and to what extent they are influenced by various environmental factors. For example, one can measure satisfaction with various QoL aspects in different environmental settings and examine how differences in environmental factors result in different levels of satisfaction with a range of QoL aspects. This can be done by comparing actual environments as well as hypothetical situations, as we will in Sections 13.4.3 and 13.4.4.

13.4 ENVIRONMENT AND QoL: RESEARCH OVERVIEW

Various empirical studies have examined relationships between environmental characteristics and individual QoL. Many of these studies have used a multidimensional instrument for assessing individual QoL (Poortinga et al. 2004). This instrument comprises 22 QoL aspects selected on the basis of an extensive literature review on needs and values and representing (very) important domains in people's lives (Steg and Gifford 2005; see Box 13.1). Which specific QoL aspects are studied may slightly vary for different environmental settings. For example, in studies on QoL in residential environments, the aspect *education* has been broadened into *personal development,* and the aspects *accessibility* and *participation in residential decision-making* have been added as important factors for QoL in residential environments (Tjoelker 2011).

In a typical study, individual QoL is studied by asking people how important they think the QoL aspects are and to what extent they are satisfied with the QoL aspects in their current situation, and (or) whether they think their satisfaction would change under different conditions. By doing so, four questions can be answered. First, one can identify which QoL aspects are most important to people. Second, one can assess QoL in specific situations. Third, variations in QoL across different environments can be identified and linked to particular environmental factors. Finally, changes in QoL due to environmental changes can be evaluated. We will elaborate on each of these questions.

13.4.1 *Which QoL Aspects Are Most Important?*

Environmental programs are not sustainable if they threaten important needs and values of individuals. To avoid that, one should know which QoL aspects are most important to people. Experts might misinterpret the preferences of people (e.g. Fawcett et al. 2008; see also Chapter 12). They tend to overestimate the importance of certain environmental characteristics (e.g. aesthetic and

BOX 13.1 DESCRIPTION OF 22 QUALITY OF LIFE (QoL) ASPECTS

Poortinga et al. (2004) have developed a multidimensional instrument for assessing individual QoL consisting of 22 QoL aspects. These aspects were selected on the basis of an extensive literature review on needs, values, and human well-being in relation to sustainable development (Steg and Gifford 2005), and are believed to represent (very) important domains in people's lives.

- *Health*. Being in good health. Having access to adequate health care.
- *Partner and family*. Having an intimate relationship. Having a stable family life and good family relationships.
- *Social justice*. Having equal opportunities and the same possibilities and rights as others. Being treated in a just manner.
- *Freedom*. Freedom and control over the course of one's life, being able to decide for yourself what you will do, when, and how.
- *Safety*. Being safe at home and in the streets. Being able to avoid accidents and being protected against criminality.
- *Education*. Having the opportunity to get a good education and to develop one's general knowledge.
- *Identity/self-respect*. Having sufficient self-respect and being able to develop one's own identity.
- *Privacy*. Having the opportunity to be yourself, to do your own things, and to have a place of your own.
- *Environmental quality*. Having access to clean air, water, and soil. Having and maintaining good environmental quality.

- *Social relations*. Having good relationships with friends, colleagues, and neighbours. Being able to maintain contacts and to make new ones.
- *Work*. Having or being able to find a job, and being able to fulfil it as pleasantly as possible.
- *Security*. Feeling attended to and cared for by others.
- *Nature/biodiversity*. Being able to enjoy natural landscapes, parks, and forests. Assurance of the continued existence of plants and animals and maintained biodiversity.
- *Leisure time*. Having enough time after work and household work, and being able to spend this time satisfactorily.
- *Money/income*. Having enough money to buy and to do things that are necessary and pleasing.
- *Comfort*. Having a comfortable and easy daily life.
- *Aesthetic beauty*. Being able to enjoy the beauty of nature and culture.
- *Change/variation*. Having a varied life. Experiencing as many things as possible.
- *Challenge/excitement*. Having challenges and experiencing pleasant and exciting things.
- *Status/recognition*. Being appreciated and respected by others.
- *Spirituality/religion*. Being able to live a life with the emphasis on spirituality and/or with your own religious persuasion.
- *Material beauty*. Having nice possessions in and around the house.

material beauty), while underestimating the importance of other characteristics (e.g. freedom of choice and privacy). The QoL measure involves individuals themselves rating how important (e.g. from 'not important' to 'very important' on a Likert scale) each QoL aspect is to them. The QoL aspects scoring highest on importance represent the priority needs and values of people, while the QoL aspects with lower importance ratings are less significant for individual QoL. For example, one study showed that Dutch respondents ascribed most importance to health, partner and family, social justice, and freedom in their lives, and they ascribed relatively little importance to status/recognition, spirituality/religion, and material beauty (Steg and Gifford 2005). Perlaviciute (2009) studied QoL in residential environments and found that residents evaluated safety, freedom, and privacy as the most important QoL aspects. Interestingly, residential factors often prioritized by housing experts, such as comfort and material beauty, were not among the most important QoL aspects for residents.

The relative importance of needs and values may vary across different groups. Indeed, research has shown that Dutch women value personal freedom and maturity more than men do, and unmarried persons rate family, health, and safety as less important than married people do (for a review, see Steg and Gifford 2005). Group differences should be considered when developing sustainability policies. Improving certain conditions may enhance QoL for one group but not for other groups.

13.4.2 To What Extent Is QoL Sustained in Certain Situations?

The QoL measure reveals how well certain conditions meet the needs and values of people, and which QoL aspects should be improved to promote QoL. This is useful for assessing the efficiency of policy-making and developing interventions. Respondents can be asked to report to what extent they are satisfied (e.g. from 'very dissatisfied' to 'very satisfied' on a Likert scale) with each QoL aspect in their current situation. Satisfaction judgments for the QoL aspects can be weighted with their importance ratings (explained in the previous section), as satisfaction with more important needs and values is more relevant to QoL than satisfaction with less important QoL aspects. Also, the QoL aspects can be plotted in a **Cartesian plane** according to their importance and satisfaction ratings (Steg et al. 2007, see also Figure 13.1). This Cartesian plane indicates which QoL aspects are satisfied and which are aspects are not sufficiently satisfied and require changes. The QoL aspects falling in the top right corner of the Cartesian plane are highly important to people and well satisfied under the given conditions. These are examples of good policy-making and require no changes. In the top left corner of the Cartesian plane, there are highly important but poorly satisfied QoL aspects. Urgent interventions are needed with regard to these aspects in order to sustain individual QoL. Satisfaction with less important QoL aspects (bottom part of the Cartesian plane) is less significant to QoL. Where there is poor satisfaction, improvements might be worthwhile but they are not

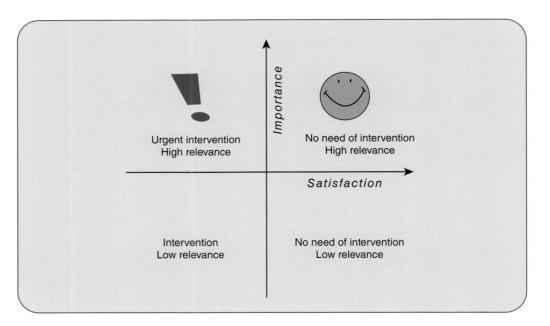

Figure 13.1 *Cartesian plane.*

urgent. In a study by Gatersleben (2000), Dutch respondents reported high satisfaction with many important needs and values, especially with their health and comfort. However, reported satisfaction with environmental quality was relatively low, suggesting that Dutch environmental policies and interventions should be improved to better meet this aspect.

13.4.3   How Does QoL Differ with Varying Environmental Conditions?

In **cross-sectional studies**, QoL can be measured in different environmental settings; observed variations in QoL can be linked to various environmental characteristics in those settings. So far, cross-sectional studies have mostly studied unidimensional QoL, for example, examining objective or subjective health across more versus less green environments (see Chapter 7) or measuring experienced stress across contexts differing in noise and crowding (see Chapter 4). Satisfaction with multiple QoL aspects was studied in a medium-size Dutch city (Perlaviciute 2009) and a small Dutch village (Tjoelker 2011). In both settings, residential characteristics turned out to satisfy many important needs and values of people. City residents, however, reported relatively poor satisfaction with nature and environmental quality which was not the case in the (greener) village. Village residents reported relatively low satisfaction with personal development and participation in residential decision-making. This is probably related to the limited social and political life in the sample village.

A disadvantage of cross-sectional studies is the lack of control over confounding factors such as social-economic characteristics (see also Chapter 4).

Therefore it is necessary to also conduct experiments in which participants are randomly assigned to different environmental settings. We elaborate more on this in section 13.4.4.

13.4.4   How Do Environmental Transformations Influence QoL?

Sustainability programs and interventions usually transform people's environments. It is important to clarify, among other things, how these transformations affect individual QoL. For that purpose, one can measure people's satisfaction with the QoL aspects before and after the intervention, and ideally, compare experimental groups with a control group. Steg and colleagues (as cited in Steg and Gifford 2005) found that, after an energy-saving intervention which required behavioural changes, participants reported higher satisfaction with environmental quality and nature than before the intervention, while satisfaction with the other QoL aspects did not change.

It is also useful to know how people evaluate interventions that are being planned but are not yet implemented. Here, respondents are presented with scenarios of future interventions and asked how these would affect their satisfaction with the QoL aspects and their overall QoL (e.g. from 'would decrease dramatically' to 'would increase dramatically' on a Likert scale). Studies on anticipated effects of environmental programmes typically found that people express mixed positive (e.g. increased satisfaction with environmental qualities) and negative (e.g. decreased satisfaction with comfort) effects on their QoL (see Box 13.2; for a review, see Steg and Gifford 2005). Perlaviciute (2009) examined how higher level of participation in residential decision-making would affect QoL. She found that Dutch respondents expected to be more satisfied with

BOX 13.2   EFFECTS OF ENVIRONMENTAL SUSTAINABILITY PROGRAMS ON QoL

De Groot and Steg (2006) studied the potential effects of doubling the costs of car use on QoL. Respondents expected negative changes in comfort, money/income, freedom, change/variation, leisure time, and work, while they expected positive changes in environmental quality, nature/biodiversity, and safety (see Figure 13.2). Interestingly, only a minor decrease in overall QoL was expected. Apparently, reductions in some QoL aspects were compensated by improvements in other aspects. Therefore, even such stringent environmental interventions might be publicly accepted if not only negative, but also positive outcomes are expected. When knowing for which QoL aspects people expect the strongest negative effects, additional interventions can be developed to enhance these QoL aspects. For example, people expect the strongest negative effects on comfort if the costs of car use were doubled, which can be reduced by making other transport modes more comfortable.

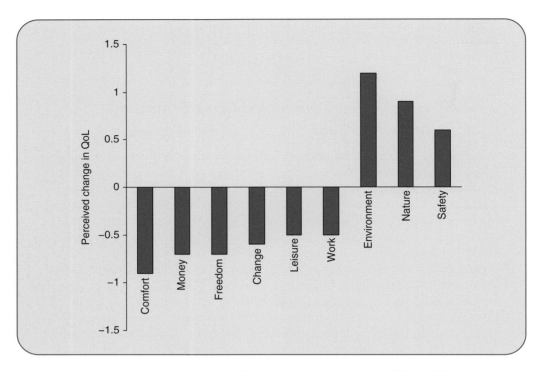

Figure 13.2 *Expected changes in QoL aspects if costs for car use were doubled (N = 490). Responses were given on a 7-point scale ranging from −3 'Would decrease dramatically' to 3 'Would increase dramatically'.* Source: Adapted from De Groot and Steg (2006).

participation-relevant QoL aspects, namely social justice, freedom and identity / self-respect, but also with other QoL aspects, including safety, privacy, leisure time, and accessibility (Perlaviciute 2009).

People's expectations about future events might differ from their actual experiences of those events. For example, people might be sceptical towards future environmental interventions and only expect reduced comfort and increased expenses. But after the interventions have taken place, they tend to report more positive changes in QoL than expected beforehand (e.g. better environmental quality: see Chapter 29). This discrepancy might be caused by cognitive biases in **affective forecasting** and by a psychological phenomenon called **hedonic treadmill**. Regarding affective forecasting, people tend to be biased when forecasting emotions caused by future events. They overestimate how long emotional effects will last (Wilson et al. 2000), or perceive future events as more pleasant (or unpleasant) than they actually are (Gilbert and Wilson 2000). Hedonic treadmill refers to the fact that people adapt to changing circumstances and report similar levels of well-being to before the changes took place (Diener et al. 2009a,b). For example, after a while, lottery winners are not particularly happier than before, and people with impaired motor or sensory functions are not as unhappy as expected beforehand (Brickman et al. 1978).

People's biased perceptions of future interventions shape public acceptance of these interventions. When knowing people's greatest concerns, policymakers can apply strategies to reduce these concerns (e.g. by providing information, or involving people in decision-making) and thus diminish public resistance to the implementation of interventions.

13.5 SUMMARY

We have presented a QoL measure to study individual perceptions of sustainable development. QoL reflects to what extent important needs and values are satisfied. Individual QoL can be measured objectively (observable environmental characteristics) or subjectively (people's perceptions of environmental characteristics). QoL measures can be unidimensional (relationship between a specific environmental factor and a specific QoL aspect) or multidimensional (relationship between multiple environmental factors and multiple QoL aspects). Measuring individual QoL serves four basic functions: identifying people's most important needs and values, assessing environmentally determined QoL, studying variations in QoL across different environments and evaluating effects of environmental transformations on QoL. Empirical studies have been carried out for each of these functions shedding more light on how, to what extent, and in which domains environmental characteristics affect individual QoL. These findings draw basic guidelines for moving towards sustainable human–environment relationships.

GLOSSARY

affective forecasting   Predictions of one's affect in the future.

cartesian plane   A coordinate system, in which the QoL aspects can be plotted according to their importance and satisfaction ratings.

cross-sectional study   A descriptive study which aims to describe the relationship (correlational rather than causal) between the measures of interest and other factors in a given population at a particular time.

economic sustainability   The extent to which welfare in a society remains sufficient over time.

environmental sustainability   The extent to which biological systems remain diverse and productive over time.

hedonic treadmill   People's tendency to adapt to improving or deteriorating circumstances to the point that these circumstances do not significantly affect their perceived QoL.

multidimensional measures of QoL   Indicators of multiple relationships between various environmental factors and various QoL aspects.

objective measures   QoL measures based on technological instruments or expert evaluations of environmental characteristics.

quality of life (QoL)   A psychological construct indicating the extent to which important needs and values of people are fulfilled.

QoL aspects   Aspects that significantly contribute to individual QoL, like family, social relations, and freedom.

social sustainability   The extent to which societal and individual psychosocial needs remain satisfied over time.

subjective measures   QoL measures based on individual perceptions of how well environmental characteristics satisfy one's important needs and values.

sustainability   Well-balanced human–environment relationships; an optimal balance between environmental, social, and economic qualities.

unidimensional measures of QoL   Indicators of relationship between a particular environmental factor and a specific QoL aspect.

SUGGESTIONS FOR FURTHER READING

Diener, E. and Diener, R.B. (2008). *Happiness: Unlocking the Mysteries of Psychological Wealth*. Malden, MA: Wiley Blackwell.

Eid, M. and Larsen, R.J. (eds.) (2008). *The Science of Subjective Well-Being*. New York, NY: Guilford Press.

Kahneman, D., Diener, E., and Schwarz, N. (eds.) (1999). *Well-Being: The Foundations of Hedonic Psychology*. New York, NY: Russell Sage Foundation.

REVIEW QUESTIONS

1. Explain the concept of sustainable development.
2. List one advantage and one disadvantage of subjective QoL measures.
3. Describe the difference between unidimensional and multidimensional QoL measures.
4. Explain briefly the four functions of measuring QoL.

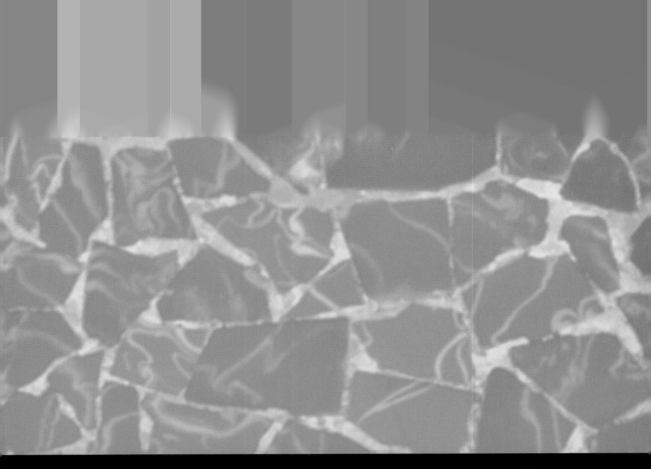

Lynne C. Manzo
University of Washington, Seattle, WA, USA

Patrick Devine-Wright
University of Exeter, UK

CHAPTER OUTLINE

14.1 INTRODUCTION

As people form emotional bonds to one another, so, too, do we form emotional bonds to the places that matter in our lives. These emotional bonds to places are what environmental psychologists call **place attachments**, Explorations of place attachments draw on the philosophy of meaning (especially **phenomenology**) and the notion of **topophilia** (love of place), and are concerned with how emotional bonds to place develop through people's experiences of the physical world. Place and our emotional bonds to it are relevant to us all, as they influence our well-being and quality of life.

Place attachments are as richly varied as people and places can be. For example, people can become attached to places at different geographical scales (from a tree fort to a country), and these places can evoke an array of emotions (from joy to sadness) in varying degrees of strength, either by the experiences that occur there, or by merely thinking of that place. Further, people may be attached to a place that they experience on a regular basis (e.g. a favourite hangout or home), or they may be attached to a place that they have never actually visited, but that represents an idea (e.g. the notion of homeland for immigrants). Additionally, people may be attached to a place that has been lost (either by physical destruction or by a change in place meaning), thus evoking a grief response.

Theory on place attachment has focused on what comprises place attachments, how they are formed, and how they relate to other similar concepts like place identity (see Chapter 20) or place dependence. Along with these theoretical developments, there emerged different methods to study place attachments (see Chapter 1 on research methods). For example, some researchers have taken a quantitative approach and seek to measure the strength of people's emotional bonds to place (Williams and Vaske 2003), or to identify the causal relationship between place attachment and variables such as length of residence. Others have taken a qualitative approach to capture the richness and nuances of people's emotional bonds to place. As research evolved, so did the study of the ways in which place attachments can be applied to real-world challenges such as pro-environmental behaviour, natural resource management, and climate change. This chapter will provide an overview of the key theoretical developments in the study of place attachments, and considers ways in which our understanding of place attachments can be applied to a variety of place-based subjects and problems.

Environmental Psychology: An Introduction, Second Edition. Edited by Linda Steg and Judith I. M. de Groot.
© 2019 John Wiley & Sons Ltd. Published 2019 by John Wiley & Sons Ltd.

14.2 THEORIES AND MODELS OF PLACE ATTACHMENT

Because place attachments have been explored from diverse perspectives, there are multiple avenues of research on the subject. Here, we identify four key theoretical developments in the research on place attachments: (i) the identification of components of place attachment; (ii) the identification of types of place attachments, and non-attachments; (iii) the recognition that place attachments involve an array of emotions, from positive to ambivalent to negative; and (iv) the exploration of place attachments as socially produced and therefore having a dynamic, social, and political nature. Each of these developments is explained in more detail in this chapter.

14.2.1 Components of Place Attachment

Several models have been developed to explain place attachment and identify its components. One popular model offers a three-dimensional framework of place attachment comprising person–process–place components (Scannell and Gifford 2010a). The *person* component refers to the fact that meaning is imparted on place by both individuals and groups and that this meaning emerges from people's particular histories, identities, and experiences. The *place* component focuses on the physical characteristics and qualities of place, including spatial scale and social/symbolic aspects, while the *process* component considers how place attachments form through a combination of feelings (affect), thoughts (cognitions), and behaviours.

Other models have identified additional components of place attachment. For example, one model identifies five components of place attachment: place identity, place dependence, nature bonding, family bonding, and friend bonding (Raymond et al. 2010). This model expounds on the general 'person' component described above by distinguishing between place-related bonds to family and place-related bonds to friends. It also expands on the 'Place' component by considering people's connections to both the natural and social environment in a given place. It is notable, however, that this specific model was built on research studies with particular populations – e.g. rural landholders in Australia – the question remains how widely this framework may be applied to other social and geographical contexts.

Efforts to refine the parameters of place attachment and identify its components have caused researchers to grapple with whether and how other phenomena like sense of place, place identity, or place dependence might relate to it. **Sense of place** is an experiential process created by a physical setting, combined with what a person brings to it in terms of their experiences, attitudes, values, beliefs, and meanings (Steele 1981). **Place identity** is understood to be those dimensions of the self that are related to the physical environment and our connections to it that define who we are (Proshansky et al. 1983), while

place dependence is the degree to which a place can support our needs and intended uses (Raymond et al. 2010). Several studies suggest that place attachment is the broader umbrella concept and that place identity and place dependence are components of place attachment (Jorgensen and Stedman 2006). However, there is no consensus about how the concepts are related and further research is warranted to clarify these relationships.

14.2.2   Types of Place Attachments

In addition to researchers identifying the elements that comprise place attachment, other researchers have sought to identify and classify different types of place attachments. For example, one study proposed two types of place attachment (traditional and active attachment) and three types of non-attachment (**alienation**, **place relativity**, and **placelessness**; Lewicka 2011a). Here, **traditional attachment** involves a taken-for-granted rootedness to one's neighbourhoods, town and/or region, while **active attachment** is defined by a high level of conscious attachment to physical settings from local to distant places. For example, people who have lived in a particular neighbourhood for many years report more traditional attachment than those who have lived in a neighbourhood for a short period of time. Similarly, people who are actively attached to a place tend to be more socially active in their neighbourhood (Lewicka 2011a).

Other studies identify civic and natural place attachment as two distinct types of attachment. **Civic place attachment** occurs at the neighbourhood or city/town level and tends to be social and symbolic in nature (Scannell and Gifford 2010b). That is, it tends to be associated with and symbolize one's association with a larger collective identity (such as feeling proud of your city). **Natural place attachment** is a type of emotional attachment directed towards the natural features of one's local area, as opposed to nature in general (Scannell and Gifford 2010b). The distinctions above are important when seeking to understand the role that place attachments might have in contemporary social and environmental issues. For example, research on place attachments that parses out natural place attachment indicates that those who are more attached to the natural aspects of their areas report engaging in more pro-environmental behaviours (Scannell and Gifford 2010b). Moreover, research has shown that those who are actively attached to a place are more likely to object to a local energy infrastructure proposal than those who are traditionally attached (Devine-Wright 2013).

14.2.3   Place Attachments Involve an Array of Emotions

Place attachments have been most frequently understood in terms of positive emotional bonds to place. Often explored in relation to one's place of residence – either the house or the neighbourhood – some studies revealed how the places to which we are attached evoke feelings of love and happiness, and create a sense of security, belonging, and comfort (Cooper Marcus 2006). Similarly, research on people's attachments to and ways of identifying with their favourite places in their everyday lives support a sense of positive self-esteem and a sense of pride about one's neighbourhood or hometown as a whole (Twigger-Ross and Uzzell 1996).

Place attachments may also involve negative or ambivalent feelings. Such attachments can develop through several circumstances: (i) when a loved place or place that has served as a positive presence in a person's life is lost or changed; or (ii) when important and meaningful places are a source of both joyful and painful experiences simultaneously. In the first type of case, unwanted and personally uncontrollable changes in or destruction of a place can cause a grief reaction, such as involuntary relocation of vulnerable people out of their homes (Fried 1963; Manzo 2014). A study investigating people who were forcibly removed from their village so it could be flooded to serve as a reservoir found grief and distress reactions even 40 years later (Nanistova 1998).

People can have mixed feelings about a place, and [yet] still experience it as a sense of attachment. More specifically, people qualify their feelings as attached, and report an emotional bond to a place, yet that bond is tinged with uncertainty or painful feelings. For example, young gay adults and people from socially marginalized groups have described simultaneously feeling a sense of inclusion and exclusion in places to which they describe being attached (Manzo 2003). Other studies show ambivalent attachments among residents of social housing estates as they grapple simultaneously with stigma and attachment to their home (Manzo 2014). In a world of increased mobility, environmental destruction, and change, understanding the complexities and nuances of our emotional response to place is important.

14.2.4   *Place Attachments as Dynamic and Socially Produced*

Place attachments demonstrate that our attachments to place are dynamic and socially produced. That is, both the physical places themselves and the meanings we give to those places that help us form attachments to them are a result of the sociocultural and political-economic context in which they appear. For example, the meaning of one's homeland can become more poignant when people are forced to flee from war or environmental destruction.

The dynamics of place attachments are well illustrated in studies of how socioculturally based place meanings influence attachments. This research examines how social relationships, and the language we use to communicate to each other about place, play a role in place attachments. This work demonstrates that place attachments are constructed by people who together formulate the everyday meanings of place (Di Masso et al. 2014). For example, one's attachment to a nearby city park may be influenced by culturally based celebrations that take place in a given part of the park each year.

14.3   APPLICATIONS OF PLACE ATTACHMENT

Place attachments contribute to our understanding and addressing of a variety of real-world issues. Key themes in the application of place attachment research include: mobility and relocation, environmental destruction, tensions across social groups in local communities, and challenges in urban design and planning projects. This section provide examples from each of these themes to illustrate the ways in which place attachment research can make a difference.

Research on place attachments in the context of mobility and relocation help us to understand the unintended consequences of place change, especially when such change is out of residents' control. For example, studies on the impacts of urban regeneration programs involving the demolition of housing for low-income families demonstrate the difficulties residents face when place attachments are severed (Manzo 2014; see Box 14.1). Research in this area can inform better policies around housing and relocation that take into account

BOX 14.1   DISPLACEMENT AND PLACE ATTACHMENTS

Urban regeneration programmes involve policymakers who make decisions about the demolition of existing housing and the resettlement of residents to other parts of the city. Although well intentioned, these decisions are typically based upon technical or physical assessments of the quality of housing stock, and desires to redevelop valuable urban land. Such programmes may overlook the importance of residents' emotional attachments to the places in which they live, and displace residents.

Displacement can evoke grief over the loss of an anchoring space that felt safe, and anxiety about where and how to set down roots elsewhere, as well as how to rebuild a sense of community in a new home (Fried 1963; Nanistova 1998). In addition, these negative impacts are worsened if social networks are disrupted by the move contributing to social isolation (Fullilove 2014).

Studies on the impacts of urban regeneration programmes involving the demolition of housing for low-income families in particular reveal that attachments are not only threatened by demolition, but by the stigma that policymakers and negative media reporting can create about people's homes in the redevelopment process (Manzo 2014). This research reveals a sharp contrast between residents' accounts of their lives in their housing communities as positive places to live and the rhetoric of 'severe distress' used by policymakers to justify demolition of the housing (Manzo 2014). Decision-makers should acknowledge such findings, for example, by developing urban regeneration policies with greater sensitivity to place attachment bonds, avoiding the stigmatization of communities, and ensuring that residents are co-housed following the move (Di Masso et al. 2014).

emotional dimensions of relocation and that attempt to maintain social ties with neighbours or family members.

Place attachment research can also be used to understand processes of migration and how immigrants adapt to their new neighbourhood. For example, research examining the meanings that immigrant residents attached to the everyday places in their adopted neighbourhoods showed that places which aided in the development of new transnational identities fostered place attachments (Rishbeth 2014). Such research provides important insights into processes of adaptation to relocation and place change, as immigrants bonded with places that held some characteristics reminiscent of valued places from their homeland, or that provided immigrants with enjoyable social experiences similar to those they enjoyed in their country of origin. This research has implications for immigrant support services, for example to make new migrants aware of these local places and resources that afford reminiscence of valued places in the homeland, thereby supporting resettlement efforts and enabling immigrants to be more invested in their new communities.

Place attachment research has shed light on the negative impacts of place change and environmental destruction on well-being. Early research on disruptions to place attachments described the consequences of several forms of place change in the home and local area, including burglaries and landslides, which led to feelings of distress and estrangement amongst local residents (Brown and Perkins 1992). Recent research has drawn on place attachment theory to shed light on community objections to the local siting of energy infrastructures (e.g. wind turbines and high voltage power lines), objections commonly and pejoratively labelled as 'NIMBYism' ('Not In My Back Yard', or a resistance to have certain land uses near one's home; Devine-Wright 2009). Such studies show that place attachments may lead either to support or protest, depending on whether technology and place-related meanings are seen as in harmony or conflict (e.g. Bailey et al. 2016). One application of this research is for developers to redesign consultation processes to discuss with local residents how new infrastructure can not only be beneficial for the country or planet, but also good for that particular place, without undermining its distinctive or historical character.

Place attachment has informed research into spatial aspects of social tensions and conflict between groups. Researchers have investigated residents' responses when urban areas change due to the influx of an 'out-group' or 'others'. For example, research on place meanings and attachments among residents in South Africa demonstrates that place attachments shifted after desegregation as white residents framed their opposition to desegregation in the language of environmental threat to obscure racial biases. Specifically, white residents recounted stories about a formerly segregated, now multiracial beach in terms of concern over a loss of a beloved place because integration undermined the beach's capacity to act as a restorative environment for them (Dixon and Durrheim 2004). This work addresses the social and political dimensions of place attachments as interactional processes that are collectively shared and deployed in relation to media accounts. One application of this research is for policy makers. Local governmental agencies, and decision makers would benefit from greater awareness of how insecurities of identity and belonging may strengthen discourses of nostalgia and threat, involving efforts to 'take back' control, to reinforce or rigidify physical boundaries and to exclude the 'other'. Policy makers can use insights from place attachment research to devise narratives describing local social change in ways that are more likely to be interpreted as an opportunity than a threat to the character of a specific place.

Finally, place attachment research has informed practitioners' work in enhancing the quality and social relevance of urban design projects by helping to save beloved places from demolition with the involvement of community members in the design process, thereby indicating the value and meaning of key local places (Hester 2014). Planning and design can benefit greatly from the consideration of place attachments as a way to guide sensitive, socially responsive design solutions. Practical applications of this include the need for planners to recognize that existing places have emotional significance to residents that should be taken account of when preparing new designs or projects; second, that the quality and significance of specific places may be evaluated differently by residents in comparison to design experts from outside of the area, necessitating a participatory approach to planning and design that is sensitive to local opinions.

14.4 SUMMARY

Place attachments, which represent the emotional bonds that people form with places that matter in their lives, are a fundamental aspect of environmental experiences. We discussed different components and types of place attachments, how place attachment relates to positive, negative, and mixed emotions, and how place attachments are dynamic and socially produced. Research in place attachment has helped to inform and resolve real-world problems, including mobility and relocation, migration and immigrant adaptation, environmental degradation, socio-spatial conflicts and planning and design processes that are socially responsive and participatory. In an era of increasing instability and place change, place attachments are likely to remain a significant topic of research for many years to come.

GLOSSARY

active attachment   A high level of conscious attachment to physical settings at all scales from local to distant places.

alienation   A condition of feeling unattached, separated or estranged from a place; feeling like an outsider in relation to a particular place.

civic place attachment   A type of place attachment that occurs at the neighbourhood or city/town level that tends to be social and symbolic in nature.

natural place attachment   A type of emotional attachment directed towards the natural aspects of a local place.

phenomenology   A branch of Western philosophy that considers the structure of consciousness, and therefore focuses largely on the nature of our lived experiences and the meaning that we attribute to those experiences.

place attachments   The emotional bonds that individuals and groups have towards places of varying geographic scales.

place dependence   The degree to which a place can support our needs and intended uses.

place identity   Those dimensions of our self-concept that are related to the physical environment and our connections to it that define who we are.

place relativity   An ambivalent and conditionally accepting attitude one holds towards a place.

placelessness   An attitude of indifference towards places, or the lack of a need to create emotional bonds with places.

sense of place   An experiential process created by a physical setting combined with what a person brings to it in terms of their experiences, attitudes, values, beliefs, and meanings.

topophilia   The affective bond between people and place or setting.

traditional attachment   The taken-for-granted sense of rootedness to one's neighbourhoods, town, and/or region.

SUGGESTIONS FOR FURTHER READING

Altman, I., and Low, S. (1992). *Place Attachment*. New York, NY: Plenum Press.

Lewicka, M. (2011). Place attachment: how far have we come in the last 40 years? *Journal of Environmental Psychology*, 31, 207–230.

Manzo, L.C., and Devine-Wright, P. (2014). *Place Attachment: Advances in Theory, Methods and Applications*. London: Routledge.

REVIEW QUESTIONS

1. Define place attachments. What are some of the components of place attachment?
2. Name and describe three types of place attachments identified in this chapter.
3. Provide three ways in which place attachments are relevant for understanding real-world problems.

15 How Cues in the Environment Affect Normative Behaviour

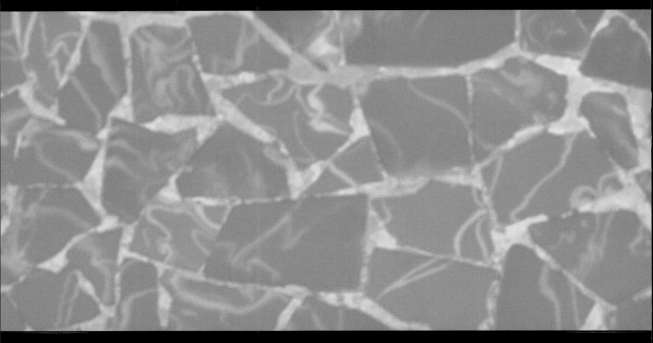

Siegwart Lindenberg
University of Groningen, The Netherlands

CHAPTER OUTLINE

15.1   INTRODUCTION

One important way in which **environments** influence behaviour is through **cues**. Cues are elements in the environment that convey important information or trigger an affective reaction. For example, for those walking by, litter on the sidewalk is an **environmental cue** that other people did not keep to the anti-litter norm. Seeing such a cue is likely to influence one's own behaviour. In this chapter, we will focus on the power environmental cues have on normative behaviour. In any society, it is essential that people endorse and keep to **social norms** and **legitimate rules** (see Sherif 1965; Cialdini et al. 1990). This is also essential for pro-environmental behaviour. But this attitudinal and behavioural respect for social norms cannot be taken for granted. We will explain how and why cues in the environment can have strong effects on the likelihood that people have norms on their minds and actually follow them.

Human behaviour always takes place in a certain environment: at home, in the schoolyard, in the city street, in the workplace, in the supermarket, etc. In each of these contexts, there are relevant social norms applicable. Quite generally, social norms can be defined as informally enforced rules about which there is at least some consensus (Horne 2001). If people don't follow the norms, or if they follow them only because it seems advantageous at the moment to do so, then both civic cooperation and the rule of law will suffer (Herrmann et al. 2008).

What elements in the environment exert influence on whether or not people respect social norms? Our general answer is that in each environment, there are cues that influence the relative strength of the **goal** to keep to social norms and to legitimate rules in general. Let us illustrate this with an example. The entrance of a parking lot is unexpectedly closed off (physically and with a sign from the police) and people have to walk for about 200 m to another entrance. They could squeeze through a narrow opening in the fence, disregarding the sign, or take the effort to walk the distance, conforming to the sign. What will they do? Keizer et al. (2008) found that 27% of the people who came for their car squeezed through the fence. However, when four bicycles were locked to the fence while a sign prohibited doing so, 82% disregarded the police sign about not using the entrance and squeezed through the fence. A cue in the environment that others were not keeping to one rule (concerning bicycles) made many people disregard another rule (concerning the detour). Why can environmental cues be so powerful? In the following paragraphs, we will elaborate the mechanisms that are likely to bring about this power of cues.

Environmental Psychology: An Introduction, Second Edition. Edited by Linda Steg and Judith I. M. de Groot.
© 2019 John Wiley & Sons Ltd. Published 2019 by John Wiley & Sons Ltd.

15.2 OVERARCHING GOALS AND THEIR RELATIVE STRENGTHS

According to **goal-framing theory**, the most important mechanism behind the effect of environmental cues on norm conformity is a shift in the relative strength of overarching goals (Lindenberg 2008; Lindenberg and Steg 2007, 2013; see also Chapter 22). Goals are mental representations of desired future states that are not purely cognitive, but they also mobilize certain kinds of motivations. Of particular interest with regard to the power of cues are **overarching goals,** i.e. abstract goals that, when **activated,** guide large sets of subgoals, and affect many different cognitive processes. Goal-framing theory deals particularly with these overarching goals.

Three overarching goals are distinguished.

Normative goal: to behave appropriately, conform to social norms and rules (subgoals are for example helping others, keeping the environment clean).

Gain goal: to maintain or improve one's resources (subgoals are for example making money, gaining status, saving for later).

Hedonic goal: to maintain or improve the way one feels right now (subgoals are, for example, economizing on effort, having fun).

Together, these three goals cover the most important aspects of human functioning: need fulfilment (hedonic), acquiring and maintaining the means for need fulfilment (gain), and fitting into the social context (normative). Goals can only guide behaviour to the degree they are activated (Kruglanski and Köpetz 2009). The salient (i.e. the most strongly activated) overarching goal is called **goal-frame** because it 'frames' a situation by governing what we attend to, what concepts and chunks of knowledge are being activated, what we like or dislike, what we expect other people to do, what alternatives we consider, what information we are most sensitive about, and how we process information (Bargh et al. 2001; Förster and Liberman 2007; Kay and Ross 2003; Kruglanski and Köpetz 2009). **Activation** can be due to a signal inside the person (e.g. a feeling of hunger activates the goal to eat) or a signal outside the person (e.g. the behaviour of others). To some degree, all three overarching goals are chronically activated and exert some influence at the same time. Hence, behaviour is almost always steered by multiple goals. But the influence of one of the three goals on behaviour depends on its salience, and it is this salience that can change due to cues in the environment.

The salience of the normative goal is also highly relevant for proenvironmental behaviours, because caring for the natural environment is most stable when it is based on normative concerns, rather than on mood, fear of punishment, and expectation of rewards. However, compared to the other two overarching goals, the normative goal needs the most support in order to influence behaviour (see Lindenberg and Steg 2007). If people's normative goal is salient, then they have respect for norms and their behaviour will reflect this respect. If the normative goal is weak, then respect is missing, and people will only follow the norm (if at all) if it happens to feel good or if they are rewarded for doing so or punished for failing to conform.

With regard to the salience of the three overarching goals, the most important environmental cues are the following: the presence or absence of people in the environment; cues about norm conformity of other people; objects that are strongly associated with a particular overarching goal (such as people wearing a business suit, which is associated with making money); and visceral cues (such as good or bad smells or appealingly decorated shop windows). Such cues can directly increase or decrease the salience of the normative goal. Alternatively, they can directly increase or decrease the salience of the hedonic or gain goal and thereby indirectly weaken the salience of the normative goal (see Figure 15.1). In the absence of cues that represent strong counter forces, hedonic or gain cues in the environment will typically lead to a weakening of the normative goal. In the following paragraph, we will illustrate and discuss these two basic mechanisms.

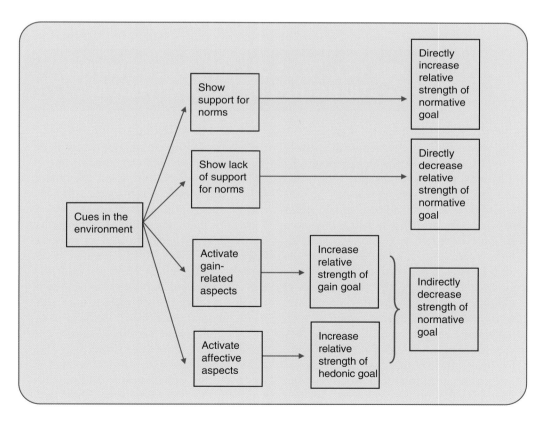

Figure 15.1 *The mechanisms by which cues in the environment affect the relative strength of the normative goal.*

15.3 ENVIRONMENTAL CUES THAT DIRECTLY STRENGTHEN THE NORMATIVE GOAL

Generally, other people and their behaviour are one of the strongest cues that influence the salience of one's own normative goal. Even the sheer presence of people in the environment will strengthen one's own normative goal, provided it is assumed that they have respect for the norms of the situation. For example, if a pedestrian on the pavement stumbles and falls, hurting himself badly, people are more inclined to follow the situational norm and help the pedestrian if there are other people present who presumably are willing to help (Rutkowski et al. 1983; see also Box 15.1). Conversely, the absence of people will have the opposite effect. Socially 'empty' environments, such as parking garages, office buildings at night, and empty streets, are in danger of leaving the activation of the normative goal at a low level, making room for considerations belonging to gain or hedonic goals. This can increase the chance of deviant behaviour or can make people feel unsafe.

The influence of others' presence (even if it is only an imagined presence) is even stronger if these others are 'significant' others, such as parents, teachers,

BOX 15.1 CUES OF CARE FOR EACH OTHER STRENGTHEN THE NORMATIVE GOAL

The effect of cues strengthening the normative goal is illustrated by an experiment by Rutkowski et al. (1983). At the time when the experiment was conducted it was already known that helping in public places shows a paradoxical regularity: the more people who watch a situation that calls for help, the less likely it is that any of them will help (Latané and Darley 1970). Rutkowski et al. (1983) showed that this 'bystander paradox' vanishes if the onlookers (who were strangers to each other when they initially met) had first sent out cues that they care for each other. The likelihood of helping by members of this 'care cue' group was three times as high as in a group of strangers, even though the person who needed help was not part of the care-cue group. In addition, Rutkowski and colleagues could show that the lack of willingness to help in the group of strangers was not the result of 'free-rider' behaviour. In fact, people in the strangers group did not expect the others to help and thus did also not expect to free-ride on their norm conforming behaviour. Rather, for them, the norm of helping was not sufficiently activated and so nobody helped. By contrast, for the people in the care-cue group, sharing personal information and showing that they care for each other activated the normative goal and made people more likely to help even though they expected others to do the same (which made their own help less rather than more necessary). Note that it was truly the activated norm and not the sympathy that had arisen among them during the period of sharing personal information: they helped a complete outsider (who had seemingly fallen in an adjacent room).

and religious leaders (Sentse et al. 2010). Thus, for example, youths who have mostly peers rather than parents or teachers in their physical environment can be expected to have less support for their normative goal-frame (and show more deviant behaviour) than youths whose environment clearly shows signs of the presence of norm-relevant significant others. Also, for children who come home from school and find no adult in their home environment, the likelihood is higher that they will fail to follow norms (Hay and Forrest 2008).

Cues in the environment related to norm-relevant significant others are still stronger when these others are not just present but also display additional cues that signal respect for norms (e.g. a teacher who throws paper into a trash can). Even entire neighbourhoods may differ in cues that signal the presence of norm-respecting significant others. Thereby they also differ in the salience of the normative goal of the adolescents living in this environment (Teasdale and Silver 2009).

This effect also holds for public officials. For example, if citizens perceive cues that indicate that the officials of their communities are committed to improve norm conformity, their own level of activation of norms in public places is likely to be higher. This can be illustrated with a study in England which found that improvement in the street lighting at night lowered crime rates not just during the night but also during the day, when lights were not on (Welsh and Farrington 2007). The authors suggest that the increased level of street lighting was interpreted as a clear sign that the community cares for norms. This cue then activated the normative goal in the citizens and thus boosted their own normative commitment, not just to deviate less but also by exerting social control, by reporting suspicious things to the police, and by spreading gossip about those who are thought to have violated important norms. In this way, the community official can also change the civic commitment of adolescents by creating cues that signal the presence of norm-relevant significant others throughout the neighbourhood.

It has also been found (Sonderskof and Dinesen 2016) that cues indicating that *institutional* significant others (i.e. politicians, the parliament, the judiciary, the police, and the public sector) are mainly acting with a salient normative goal, make people also confident that most people in their social environment are acting with a salient normative goal (measured in both cases with items that indicate trust).

15.4 ENVIRONMENTAL CUES THAT DIRECTLY WEAKEN THE NORMATIVE GOAL

The irony of the processes by which norms can be strengthened is that they can be reversed. People become less normative when cues in the environment signal disrespect for norms. For example, when one sees others dropping litter,

one's own level of activation of the no-litter norm also declines. As a consequence, one is more likely to litter oneself (Cialdini et al. 1990).

The negative effects of the power of environmental cues reach even further
than imitation. Cues that signal disrespect for one norm can lead to the transgression of other norms. This has been called **cross-norm inhibition effect** (Keizer
et al. 2008). Thus, if somebody is in an environment where there are signs that
others clearly deviate from a norm (such as graffiti on the walls, garbage on the
street), it is more difficult to keep to norms oneself and not to give in to hedonic
or gain goals. Normative disorder weakens the normative goal itself (see
Chapter 16 for more examples on this effect).

The cross-norm inhibition effect illustrates how the weakening of the normative goal can quickly spread from one person to another. Somebody sees
graffiti, interprets this as a sign of norm transgression, becomes themself more
hedonic and litters. Somebody else sees the litter and becomes more likely to
steal. A third person, seeing this, fails to inhibit their aggression towards their
neighbour, etc. Because the normative goal that is not well supported can be
pushed aside by hedonic or gain goals, disorder is likely to spread by itself. This
implies that people who live in a disorderly environment have a more difficult
time keeping to norms than people who live in an orderly environment.

Disorder as a collection of cues in the environment of disrespect for norms
can also increase the incidence of crime and fear of crime. For example, in a
correlational study, Armitage (2007) found that homes in whose vicinity there
were clear signs of disrepair or graffiti were more often victimized. People also
feel particularly unsafe in environments with such cues (Doran and Lees 2005).
Markowitz et al. (2001) found that it is particularly this increased fear of crime
generated by cues of physical disorder that mediates a vicious cycle of increasing crime. Ironically, cues of police presence can increase rather than decrease
people's fear of crime (Hinkle and Weisburd 2008).

15.5   INDIRECT WEAKENING OF THE NORMATIVE GOAL BY ENVIRONMENTAL CUES THAT STRENGTHEN THE GAIN GOAL

Some gain and hedonic aspects that stay in the cognitive background can support the normative goal, such as a small reward (gain) for helping somebody or
a warm glow and praise (hedonic) one gets for doing so. But when these aspects
become salient themselves they also make the gain or hedonic goal salient and
weaken the normative goal.

Not just the presence and behaviour of people are important cues, but also objects that emphasize one of the overarching goals. This effect of objects can be used to illustrate how the environment can directly increase the relative weight of the gain goal. Goal-framing theory holds that in most situations, strengthening hedonic or gain goals via cues in the environment means weakening the normative goal. The gain goal is mostly activated by cues that indicate that money or competition plays a central role in the environment. Such cues can be very subtle. Even just seeing typical objects that are used in business can activate a gain goal and thereby increase a competitive orientation. For example, an experiment with college students showed that when subjects were exposed to objects such as business suits, business cases, or boardroom tables, they were significantly more competitive and less normatively oriented than subjects exposed to neutral objects (such as kites, whales, sheet music; Kay et al. 2004). Also, just seeing or being reminded of money can increase the salience of the gain goal (Vohs 2015).

There is a well-known saying that opportunity makes thieves. Objects in the immediate environment can increase the relative weight of the gain goal to such a degree that people will even steal. For example, cues in the neighbourhood that people now living there are richer than the previous owners (such as an improved facade of the house, or a more expensive car in front of the house) attract extra crime (Covington and Taylor 1989). Such an effect is especially likely if, at the same time, there are also cues that other people have disrespect for norms. This has been demonstrated by Keizer et al. (2008) who showed in a field experiment that a sizable minority (13%) of passers-by is influenced by a letter with a €5 note visibly inside sticking out from a mailbox and steal the letter. Worse, if the mailbox is covered with graffiti, the percentage doubles. This is an illustration of a combined effect: a cue (the €5 note) that increases the relative weight of the gain goal and a cue (graffiti) that simultaneously decreases the relative weight of the normative goal.

15.6   INDIRECT WEAKENING OF THE NORMATIVE GOAL BY ENVIRONMENTAL CUES THAT STRENGTHEN THE HEDONIC GOAL

Visceral cues (i.e. very attractive or unattractive aspects in an environment) that create affective reactions and increase the salience of one or more basic needs easily strengthen the hedonic goal, thereby making people automatically more impatient and ready to act on impulse. They thus lower the possible guidance by the normative goal and the gain goal. For example, Li et al. (2007) showed that when people are exposed to an attractive ambient odour (such as freshly baked cookies), they will also become more impatient in financial transactions. The same holds for erotically explicit advertising (Van den Bergh et al. 2008).

With regard to the salience of the hedonic goal, objects can also play an important role. For example, visibility and convenient access to enticing food increases the salience of the hedonic goal and thus also consumption of this food (Painter et al. 2002).

15.7   SUMMARY

Environments are never neutral. Each environment sends out cues that influence both goals and behaviour. Importantly, environmental cues have a strong impact on normative behaviour, which, in turn, is crucial for social order. This influence of environmental cues runs via their impact on the salience of one of the three important overarching goals: the normative goal (to behave appropriately, conform to legitimate rules), the gain goal (to maintain or improve one's resources), and the hedonic goal (to maintain or improve the way one feels right now). All three goals are activated to some degree, but, due to environmental cues, their degree of activation (i.e. their salience) varies, as does the extent to which they influence behaviour. Cues do this by either directly strengthening or weakening the normative goal, or they do it indirectly by increasing the salience of the gain or hedonic goal. This simple insight on the power of environmental cues – that behaviour is mainly steered by the salience of goals which, in turn, depends on the activation by such cues – provides potentially new and powerful tools for interventions in favour of normative behaviour. But remember, cues only work if their meaning is related in a certain way to the overarching goals. For example, if litter in a public space is not a sign that people disrespect norms because everybody litters, the litter will not affect the normative goal. Meaning is also affected by who does something. For instance, littering in a public place by a member of an outgroup (say, a member of the Hells Angels) might increase rather than decrease the salience of the normative goal in the observer, because it focuses attention on what the ingroup would or would not do. Thus, the goal-framing theory of the power of cues is general on the higher level (e.g. cues of disrespect of norms lower the salience of the normative goal), and, on the more concrete lower level, needs specific information on the meaning of cues in this situation.

GLOSSARY

acitivate/activation   The extent to which a mental construct (and its motivational components) is cognitively accessible at a given moment.

cross-norm inhibition effect   The negative effect of observing other people's violation of norm A on one's own likelihood of following norm B.

cue   Element in the environment that conveys important information or triggers an affective reaction.

environment   The physical and symbolic conditions and circumstances that directly surround an individual.

environmental cue   Characteristic of the physical environment that conveys important information or triggers an affective reaction.

gain goal   The overarching goal to maintain and improve one's resources.

goal   Mental representation of a desired future state with both cognitive and motivational components.

goal-frame   Overarching goal that is more strongly activated than its rival overarching goals.

goal-framing theory   A theory about the workings of overarching goals with a special focus on the relative a priori strength of such goals and on factors that may change their salience.

hedonic goal   The overarching goal to maintain or improve the way one feels right now.

legitimate rule   A rule (such as a police ordinance, a prohibition, a federal law) that people accept as if it were a social norm.

normative goal   The overarching goal to behave appropriately, conforming to social norms and legitimate rules.

overarching goal   a high-level goal that 'captures' the mind by influencing many cognitive and motivational processes and which contains many different subgoals.

social norm   Informally enforced rule about which there is at least some consensus.

SUGGESTIONS FOR FURTHER READING

Keizer, K., Lindenberg, S., and Steg, L. (2008). The spreading of disorder. *Science, 322,* 1681–1685.

Lindenberg, S., and Steg, L. (2013). Goal-framing theory and norm-guided environmental behavior. In H. van Trijp (Ed.), *Encouraging Sustainable Behavior,* (pp. 37–54). New York, NY: Psychology Press

REVIEW QUESTIONS

1. Briefly explain how goal-framing theory can be applied to trace the influence of environmental cues on normative behaviour.
2. Give four examples of environmental cues that increase or decrease the relative strengths of the normative goal. Consider direct and indirect effects.
3. Describe in what ways physical disorder can make deviant behaviour spread.

Part II

Factors Influencing Environmental Behaviour

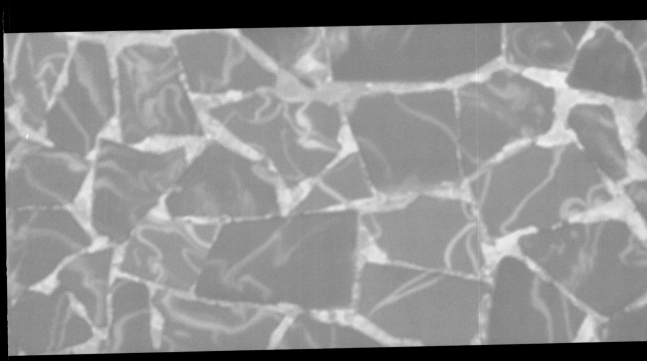

16 Measuring Environmental Behaviour

Birgitta Gatersleben
University of Surrey, UK

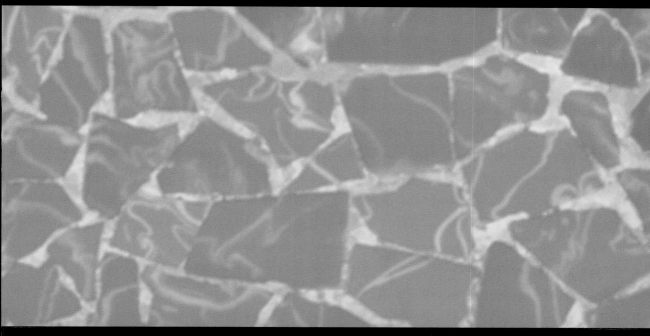

CHAPTER OUTLINE

16.1   INTRODUCTION

The goal of much environmental psychology research is to help understand and change **environmental behaviour**. In order to do this it is essential to develop robust measures of this behaviour. This chapter reviews some of the ways in which scholars have approached environmental behaviour and its measurement to date. It addresses three important issues: what to measure (behaviour or impact of behaviour), how to measure it (by means of self-reports or observation), and how to conceptualize it (unidimensional or multidimensional). Each of these three issues should be considered when developing a measure of environmental behaviour as decisions on them have theoretical, methodological, and practical implications.

16.2   WHAT TO MEASURE? BEHAVIOUR OR IMPACT

It is important to make a distinction between measures of behaviour and measures of environmental impact (Stern et al. 1997). Measuring impact is not the same as measuring behaviour and the two different types of measures may therefore not necessarily overlap.

16.2.1   Environmental Behaviour

Most research in environmental psychology focuses on studying **pro-environmental behaviour**, also referred to as environmentally friendly behaviour (Dolnicar and Grün 2009), ecological behaviour, or conservation behaviour (e.g. Scherbaum et al. 2008; Schultz et al. 2008). Pro-environmental behaviour has been defined as 'behaviour that consciously seeks to minimize the negative impact of one's actions on the natural and built world' (Kollmuss and Agyeman 2002, p. 240). This type of behaviour can therefore be labelled as **goal-directed pro-environmental behaviour** – behaviour which people adopt with the explicit goal of doing something beneficial for the environment. Some scholars suggest that environmental psychology can and should only be concerned with studying this type of goal-directed behaviour (Kaiser and Wilson 2004). Alternatively, pro-environmental behaviour has been defined as 'behaviour that harms the environment as little as possible, or even benefits the environment'

Environmental Psychology: An Introduction, Second Edition. Edited by Linda Steg and Judith I. M. de Groot.
© 2019 John Wiley & Sons Ltd. Published 2019 by John Wiley & Sons Ltd.

(Steg and Vlek 2009, p. 309). This is behaviour that is beneficial for the environment but is not necessarily (or exclusively) motivated by environmental goals. According to this definition people can act pro-environmentally without any intention to do so, for instance, because the behaviour is habitual (e.g. you always turn the tap off when brushing your teeth) or because the behaviour is motivated by other goals (e.g. not driving to work because cycling is cheaper and healthier).

Pro-environmental behaviour (whether goal-directed or not) differs from the broader term environmental behaviour. Environmental behaviour has been defined as 'all types of behaviour that change the availability of materials or energy from the environment or alter the structure and dynamics of ecosystems or the biosphere' (Steg and Vlek 2009, p. 309). This includes behaviours which are environmentally damaging as well as behaviours which are beneficial for the environment. Arguably this includes almost all kinds of behaviour as almost everything we do has some sort of impact on the environment. Measures of actual impact (see section 16.2.2) necessarily include both behaviours which are environmentally damaging and behaviours which are environmentally friendly.

Decisions on what to measure need to be informed by the theoretical and practical aims of a study. Goal-directed pro-environmental behaviour is by definition motivated by environmental goals, but may not necessarily reflect actual impact. A measure of goal-directed pro-environmental behaviour is likely to be suitable for a study that aims to understand the link between pro-environmental intentions and behaviour. However, a study that aims to test the actual environmental impact of an intervention may measure such impact through meter readings of electricity or gas use.

16.2.2   Environmental Impact

Environmental psychologists typically try to measure behaviours rather than the outcomes of such behaviours in terms of **environmental impact**. However, it has been argued that measuring environmental impact may be more relevant for environmental policy as it is more likely to help to attain the ultimate real-life objective of policies, which is to reduce the ecological footprint of individuals – their overall environmental impact (e.g. McKenzie-Mohr 2000; Oskamp 2000b).

There are several reasons why measures of behaviour may not necessarily reflect actual impact (Gatersleben et al. 2002; Stern et al. 1997). First, behaviour measures often rely on self-reports, which are sensitive to response biases (Schwarz 1999) and thus may not reliably reflect actual behaviour (Kormos and Gifford 2014) and consequently cannot accurately reflect environmental impact (e.g. energy use). Second, when scholars develop lists of behaviours to measure their constructs they rarely consider environmental impact. The most environmentally significant behaviours may therefore not be included in such measures. Also, when composite measures of pro-environmental behaviour are developed, variables are rarely weighted with their relative impact. A person conducting

BOX 16.1   BIASES IN ASSESSMENTS OF ENVIRONMENTAL IMPACT OF BEHAVIOURS

Gatersleben et al. (2002) investigated the environmental impact of various household activities (e.g. heating, washing) of more than 1200 Dutch households. Respondents estimated the average annual impact of the activities about the same (1.8–2.9 on a 5–point scale: 1 = very low, 5 = very high). However, the actual energy use related to the activities varied substantially from 7.2 GJ for washing to 47 GJ for home heating. Figure 16.1 shows that differences in the perceived environmental impact of the household activities do not correspond with differences in estimated actual impact (in energy use) of these activities, suggesting that individuals are not always aware of the relative environmental impact of their activities.

7 out of 10 behaviours is therefore labelled to be more environmentally friendly than a person adopting only three of these behaviours. But this may not be a valid conclusion if those three behaviours have a more significant environmental impact. This may be particularly important when people are unaware of the environmental impact of their behaviour (see Box 16.1 and Figure 16.1).

If the main focus of a study is to understand the variables that influence actual environmental impact, the outcome variable may be different than when the focus is on measuring goal-directed pro-environmental behaviour. One possibility could be to include only behaviours that are particularly significant in terms of environmental impact, such as car use (e.g. Stern 2000). Another option could be to directly measure outcome variables such as energy use (via meter readings: Schultz et al. 2007) or waste production (via bin weighing: Nigbur et al. 2010) instead of underlying behaviours. Finally, behaviours could be measured by means of self-reports or observations, and then weighted with assessments of the relative environmental impact of these behaviours before combining these variables into an overall measure of impact (e.g. Abrahamse et al. 2007; Gatersleben et al. 2002). Based on this last principle, environmental scientists have developed comprehensive measures to assess environmental impacts in various domains, such as measures of carbon footprints (e.g. Druckman and Jackson 2009) and measures of direct and indirect energy use that have been used in environmental psychology studies (Abrahamse et al. 2007; Gatersleben et al. 2002). The advantage of these measures is that they can provide a better understanding of psychological factors in tackling the environmental impact of lifestyles because they integrate measures of behaviour and impact.

It is important to note that measuring the actual environmental impact of behaviour is complex. The link between behaviour and impact may be easy to establish for some behaviours but not for others. Environmental problems are diverse and involve problems on local and global scales in many different areas, including pollution, resource depletion, and noise

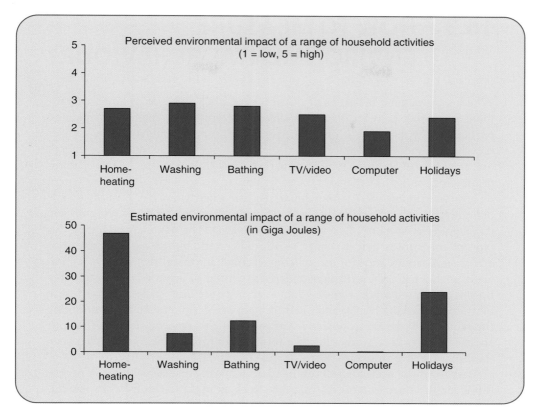

Figure 16.1 *Perceived (upper panel) and estimated (lower panel) environmental impact of household activities.*
Source: Adapted from Gatersleben et al. (2002); see Box 16.1 for an explanation.

(Vlek 2000). Therefore, behaviour may be beneficial for the environment at one level but harmful at another. For instance, organic food may be associated with reduced use of harmful pesticides but also with increased energy use, if this food is transported longer distances. When studying the variables that play a role in explaining or changing actual environmental impact, it is important to consider these potentially conflicting issues and to take advice from environmental scientists.

The question of whether to measure environmental behaviour or the impact of behaviour is a source of debate. As indicated, some argue that a focus on impact is useful when the goal of research is to provide clear policy insight (e.g. Gatersleben et al. 2002; McKenzie-Mohr 2000; Oskamp 2000b) whereas others argue that the aim of psychology should be to understand behaviour and not the impact of such behaviour (Kaiser and Wilson 2004), as impact is influenced by many other factors beyond the control of individuals, including technology. These fundamental issues need to be considered when determining which measure of environmental behaviour is most suitable for a study: a measure of behaviour, impact, or a combination of these.

16.3   HOW TO MEASURE ENVIRONMENTAL BEHAVIOUR?

Whether developing measures of environmental behaviour or of actual impact, there are further considerations that affect the validity and reliability of findings, particularly when relying on self-reports. Self-reported behaviours, such as recycling frequency, and self-reported outcomes, such as car mileage or energy use, are the most common type of data used in psychology research. Typical items of pro-environmental behaviour measures tend to ask for some sort of judgement on how often individuals (or households) perform a behaviour, e.g. 'I usually recycle old newspapers' (1 = totally disagree to 5 = totally agree) or 'How often do you recycle old newspapers?' (1 = never to 5 = always). The main advantage of this type of measure is that it is easy to administer and allows easy comparisons across behaviours and the use of conventional statistical techniques, such as factor analyses, in order to explore underlying clusters of behaviour. Unfortunately, however, such self-reports are also subject to response bias (such as social desirability or self-serving biases) and measurement error. A meta-analysis examining the relationship between objective measures of pro-environmental behaviour and self-reports in 15 studies found a positive but moderate correlation between these two types of measures (Kormos and Gifford 2014).

Perhaps more accurate self-report measures of actual behaviour ask people more detailed questions (or calculations), such as 'in the last week what percentage of your drink cans did you dispose of in a recycling bin?' One could also ask all individuals in a household to report on their behaviour. This type of questioning may elicit more detailed data, although it is still subject to measurement error and response biases. Moreover, it can result in complex questions that are not easy for people to understand (leading to more response bias) or which require calculation and a lot of detailed knowledge from respondents (e.g. exact times that lights are switched on and off or the exact volume of materials that is recycled). The latter is also the case for self-reports of outcomes of behaviour. For instance, it can be difficult for people to read their own gas and electricity meters or to reliably report on their car mileage. Moreover, more accurate measures can result in more complex questionnaires as different behaviours may need to be measured on different scales (e.g. frequency, volume, duration) making it less straightforward to subject the data to standard data analysis techniques and making responses more sensitive to errors.

The most accurate form of measurement may be the observation of actual behaviour (e.g. observing littering or recycling) or its immediate outcomes (e.g. weighing bins, reading meters). This, however, can be labour intensive and therefore require extra financial resources. Information technologies such as smart meters or smart plugs may reduce these problems, but these can raise issues around ethics due to potential privacy infringement (Bolderdijk et al. 2011). Observations are much less common in environmental psychology than self-reports, although there are exceptions (e.g. Bolderdijk et al. 2011; Nigbur et al. 2010; Schultz et al. 2007, 2008).

16.4   MULTIDIMENSIONAL OR UNIDIMENSIONAL MEASURES OF ENVIRONMENTAL BEHAVIOUR

Environmental behaviour is often conceptualized as multidimensional. Several studies have suggested that different behaviours are not necessarily correlated, and behavioural antecedents may vary between behaviours. For instance, when people recycle their glass bottles this does not necessarily mean that they also vote for a green party or refrain from driving a car. Kaiser and Wilson (2004), however, developed a unidimensional notion of goal-directed pro-environmental behaviour, which suggests that such behaviour can be conceptualized and measured as a one-dimensional construct. We now discuss the specifics of these multidimensional and unidimensional approaches to environmental behaviour.

16.4.1   *Multidimensional Measures of Environmental Behaviour*

Measures of environmental behaviour usually either focus on one type of behaviour, such as recycling (e.g. Carrus et al. 2008), transportation mode choice (e.g. Carrus et al. 2008; Matthies et al. 2002), or political activism (e.g. signing petitions, donating money; Berenguer 2007), or they include a range of different (types of) behaviours (Lee et al. 2013). When respondents are questioned about a range of behaviours, their responses are often subjected to some form of statistical exploration to examine whether different categories of behaviour can be distinguished empirically, for example, waste avoidance, recycling, consumerism, or political activism (Dolnicar and Grün 2009; Corraliza and Berenguer 2000; Milfont et al. 2006; Oreg and Katz-Gerro 2006). Based on statistical analyses of the bivariate correlations of various behaviours, most of this research suggests that pro-environmental behaviour is multidimensional. The precise number and type of dimensions that are distinguished varies between studies and depends on the number and types of questions that are included in the questionnaires (Lee et al. 2013).

These finding suggest that people do not appear to behave consistently pro-environmentally across different domains (i.e. some behaviours are not or weakly correlated) and that different behaviours are likely to be motivated by different factors. Moreover, the same motivational goal (doing something beneficial for the environment) may motivate one person to donate to charity, another to buy organic, and yet another to use a bicycle rather than a car. There is plenty of evidence to suggest that pro-environmental behaviours do not correlate reliably – sometimes even within but certainly not across – different domains, and that engagement in one pro-environmental behaviour does not necessarily spill over to another one (Truelove et al. 2014).

16.4.2   A Unidimensional Measure of Environmental Behaviour

A **unidimensional measure** of goal-directed pro-environmental behaviour was developed by Kaiser and Wilson (2004) based on what is called the **Campbell paradigm** (Kaiser et al. 2010). According to this paradigm, all behaviours regarding a specific goal (e.g. environmental conservation) can be ordered on one single dimension from easy to difficult with regards to reaching that goal. The idea is that someone with a strong motivation to achieve the goal will adopt all the easy behaviours as well as the more difficult ones, whereas those who are less committed to reaching the goal will only adopt the easier ones.

The Rasch model (Bond and Fox 2001) can be used as a construct validity tool to test this unidimensional model. It is commonly used to estimate performance or ability on a test. For instance, items on a knowledge test can be ordered from easy (answered correctly by most people) to difficult (answered correctly by only a few). A person's score on the scale then represents both the difficulty of the question and the person's knowledge of the topic. In a similar vein, the Rasch model has been used to order pro-environmental behaviours in a dataset from most frequently adopted (the easiest) to least frequently adopted (the most difficult; Kaiser and Wilson 2004). Behaviours that are adopted by the vast majority of people (even those with weak environmental goals) are presumed to be easy, whereas behaviours which are adopted by only a few people are presumed to be difficult and only those with strong pro-environmental attitudes (or goals) will adopt them.

Conceptualizing goal-directed pro-environmental behaviour of individuals in this manner implies that seemingly diverse behaviours, such as donating money to environmental organizations, recycling, and using public transport, form a uniform set of behaviours. These different behaviours are linked by one underlying goal (i.e. environmental conservation) and can be mapped onto one dimension from easy to difficult. Studies found that energy conservation, waste avoidance, recycling, vicarious acts toward conservation (e.g. political activism), and ecological transportation and consumer behaviour can indeed be mapped on one dimension (Kaiser et al. 2007; Kaiser and Wilson 2004).

This unidimensional measure has the advantage that it allows one to make a relatively simple distinction between more and less pro-environmental individuals and to include a wide variety of behaviours. However, it fundamentally rests on the assumption that behaviours are psychologically linked by one single underlying goal (doing something good for the environment). As such it assumes a shared understanding of what is pro-environmental or not. It also assumes that people behave relatively consistently and that difficulty of behaviour is the key factor that differentiates those with strong and weak environmental goals. Finally, this perspective departs from common views of attitude–behaviour relationships which perceive attitudes and behaviours as distinct psychological concepts because a higher score on the measure reflects not only the difficulty of a behaviour but also a person's commitment to achieving a goal – their attitude (Kaiser et al. 2007). This appears to conflict with the notion that environmental problems (and solutions) are multidimensional and that different behaviours may be motivated by different antecedents (see Chapter 22).

16.5   SUMMARY

Environmental behaviour has been defined, conceptualized, and measured in many different ways. This chapter gives an overview of these different approaches and their advantages and disadvantages. It distinguishes pro-environmental behaviour from the broader concept of environmental behaviour, which includes environmentally damaging as well as beneficial behaviours. Because the actual environmental impact of behaviour may differ from the intended impact, the chapter also discusses different measures of goal-directed pro-environmental behaviour and measures of environmental impact. The last parts of the chapter focused on multidimensional and unidimensional conceptualizations of environmental behaviour. The chapter demonstrates that the development of a measure of environmental behaviour requires consideration of three key issues: what to measure (impact or behaviour), how to measure it (self-report or observation), and how to conceptualize it (unidimensional or multidimensional). Answers to these questions will depend on the goal of the study and will have significant impact on the meaning and implications of the findings.

GLOSSARY

Campbell paradigm   A paradigm that explains the probability of a person to engage in a pro-environmental behaviour as a function of (i) that person's pro-environmental attitude and (ii) the difficulty of that behaviour. The Rasch model mathematically describes the Campbell paradigm.

environmental behaviour   Any behaviour that has an impact on the environment (good or bad).

environmental impact   The environmental outcomes of behaviours in terms of energy and materials use and waste production.

goal-directed pro-environmental behaviour   Behaviour which people adopt with the deliberate goal of doing something beneficial for the environment.

multidimensional measure of environmental behaviour.   A measure including behaviours from different domains that do not necessarily correlate.

pro-environmental behaviour Behaviour which harms the environment as little as possible or even benefits it.

unidimensional measure of goal-directed environmental behaviour A measure based on the Campbell paradigm which orders environmental behaviours along one dimension from easy to difficult.

SUGGESTIONS FOR FURTHER READING

Gatersleben, B., Steg, L., and Vlek, C. (2002). The measurement and determinants of environmentally significant consumer behaviour. *Environment and Behaviour* 34: 335–362.

Kaiser, F.G. and Wilson, M. (2004). Goal-directed conservation behaviour. The specific composition of a general performance. *Personality and Individual Differences* 36: 1531–1544.

Kormos, C. and Gifford, R. (2014). The validity of self-report measures of proenvironmental behavior: a meta-analytic review. *Journal of Environmental Psychology* 40: 359–371.

REVIEW QUESTIONS

1. Define environmental behaviour, pro-environmental behaviour, and goal-directed pro-environmental behaviour.
2. Why do measures of environmental behaviour not necessarily reflect environmental impact and how can this be resolved?
3. What are the advantages and disadvantages of self-reported behaviour measures?
4. Describe how the environmental attitude-behaviour relationship is defined following the Campbell paradigm.

17 Values and Pro-Environmental Behaviour

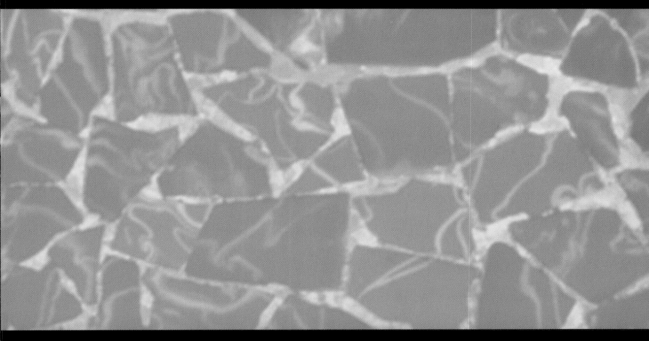

Judith I. M. de Groot
University of Groningen, The Netherlands

John Thøgersen
Aarhus University, Denmark

CHAPTER OUTLINE

17.1   INTRODUCTION

How important is protecting the environment for you? Most of you would probably respond that environmental protection is very important. Now, consider the following question: What actions do you take to protect the environment? You may be a member of an environmental organization, but you may not have chosen to take a cold or short shower this morning to save energy and water, or to commute by bus or bicycle instead of by car to reduce CO_2 emissions. To what extent do you act upon your environmental values consistently? When and how do you act or fail to act upon these values? In this chapter we try to answer these important questions. We provide a definition and discuss features of values, and discuss value theories. We also explain which values are important for environmental attitudes and behaviours, and how people can be encouraged to act upon their pro-environmental values. Finally, we describe how values differ from related concepts that are used in environmental psychological research and how value research can be used in interventions.

17.2   VALUES

Values are desirable trans-situational goals that vary in importance and serve as guiding principles in the life of a person or other social entities (Schwartz 1992). This definition includes three key features of values. First, values include beliefs about the desirability or undesirability of certain end-states. Second, values are rather abstract constructs and therefore transcend specific situations. This is the main difference from 'goals' (see Chapter 15). A goal refers to a target that an individual strives hard to reach in his or her life. It is thus understood that goals remain a target until they are reached or achieved while values are there to be adhered to on a longer term. Third, values serve as guiding principles for the evaluation of people and events and for behaviours. Values are ordered in a system of value priorities (i.e. they vary in importance), which implies that when competing values are activated in a situation, choices are based on the value that is considered most important.

There are important advantages to using values in environmental behaviour research. First, the total number of values is relatively small compared to the countless behaviour-specific beliefs, attitudes, and norms. Consequently, values provide an economically efficient instrument for describing and explaining similarities and differences between persons, groups, nations, and cultures. Second, the abstractness of values allows for predictions in almost all contexts. Values influence various specific attitudes and behaviours (Seligman and Katz 1996).

Environmental Psychology: An Introduction, Second Edition. Edited by Linda Steg and Judith I. M. de Groot.
© 2019 John Wiley & Sons Ltd. Published 2019 by John Wiley & Sons Ltd.

In the context of new or emergent attitude objects, which is very common in the environmental field, values are assumed to be even more important for predicting attitudes and behaviours because they provide a stable and relatively enduring basis for attitudes and behaviours (Stern et al. 1995). Furthermore, the causal influence of pro-environmental values on sustainable behaviours has been reliably documented (Thøgersen and Ölander 2002). This makes values a relevant starting point for changing behaviours. Through influencing or activating certain values, it is possible to influence a range of environmental behaviour-specific beliefs, norms, intentions, and behaviours (Thøgersen and Ölander 2006).

17.3   VALUE THEORIES

We first discuss two common value theories: the theory on **social value orientations** (Messick and McClintock 1968) and Schwartz's value theory (Schwartz 1992). We then give a brief overview of relevant values in an environmental context.

17.3.1   *Social Value Orientations*

Social value orientations (SVO), originating from social dilemma research (see Chapter 21), reflect the extent to which individuals care about own and others' payoffs in a social dilemma situation (Messick and McClintock 1968). Most studies only distinguish between a pro-self value orientation, in which case people are particularly concerned with their own outcomes, and a prosocial value orientation, in which people particularly care about the outcomes for other people or the community. A person's SVO is usually assessed by means of the **decomposed game technique** (Liebrand 1984) in which participants choose between options that offer points to themselves and another person.

Empirical evidence on relationships between SVO and environmental beliefs, norms, and behaviour is mixed. Some studies found that prosocial values are positively and pro-self values are negatively, often weakly, related to pro-environmental intentions and self-reported behaviours (e.g. Hilbig et al. 2013; Joireman et al. 2001), while SVO appeared not to be significantly related to preferences related to pro-environmental behaviours (e.g. Joireman et al. 2004).

17.3.2   *Schwartz's Value Theory*

In Schwartz 's value theory (1992, 1994), a general and comprehensive taxonomy of 56 values is proposed. Respondents taking Schwartz's value survey rate each value item on a 9-point scale measuring their importance as 'a guiding principle in their life'. Based on survey data from 44 countries, Schwartz identifies 10 motivational types of values (see Table 17.1 for examples of four of the types). These 'types' of values include a variety of values closely related to each other. For example, the value type 'universalism' includes values such as 'social justice', 'broadminded', 'protecting the environment', and 'equality'. The 56 values can be plotted in a two-dimensional space in which the 10 motivational value types are identified as separate clusters of values, which together form a **circumplex** structure (see Figure 17.1). The closer value types or individual values are to each other in this structure, the more compatible they are; the further away, the more incompatible they are. For example, universalism values (e.g. broadminded, equality) are closely related to benevolence values, such as helpful or honest, but are likely to conflict (i.e. negative correlation or no correlation at all) with values that express achievement values (e.g. successful, capable). In Schwartz's theory, scores on the importance of values have little meaning on their own, particularly the relative priorities of values compared with other values is important.

The first dimension in Schwartz's value structure is openness to change versus conservatism, which distinguishes values that stress openness to new things and ideas, such as self-direction and stimulation, from values that emphasize tradition and conformity. The second dimension distinguishes values that stress the interests of others, society, and nature, such as universalism and benevolence, from those that emphasize self-interest (e.g. power, achievement). This self-transcendence versus self-enhancement dimension is comparable to

Table 17.1 *Examples of definitions of four motivational types expressed in Schwartz's (1994) value theory.*

Motivational type	Definition	Examples of values
Power	Social status and prestige, control, or dominance over people and resources	• Social power • Wealth • Authority
Universalism	Understanding, appreciation, tolerance, and protection for the welfare of all people and for nature	• Social justice • Broadminded • Protecting the environment • Equality
Benevolence	Preservation and enhancement of the welfare of people with whom one is in frequent personal contact	• Helpful • Forgiving • Honest
Tradition	Respect, commitment, and acceptance of the customs and ideas that traditional culture or religion impose on the self	• Accepting my portion in life • Devout • Respect for tradition

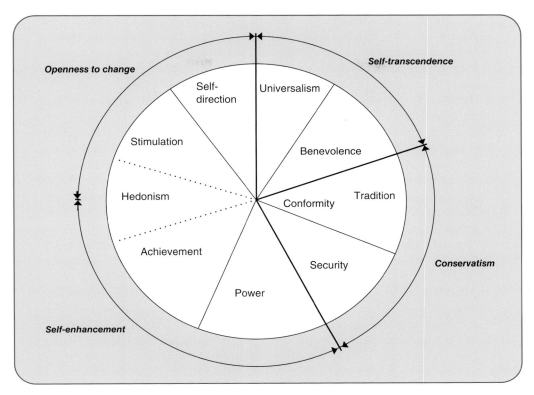

Figure 17.1 *The motivational types of values placed into a two-dimensional space (Bilsky and Schwartz 1994).* Source: Reproduced by permission of [Academic Press, Inc].

the distinction between prosocial (or **altruistic**) and pro-self (or **egoistic**) value orientations discussed in the section 17.3.1.

The postulated value clusters are universally found across countries and cultures (Schwartz 1994).

Especially, the self-enhancement versus self-transcendence dimension appears to be important when explaining environmental beliefs, norms, and behaviours (e.g. De Groot et al. 2016), probably because many pro-environmental behaviours require individuals to restrain egoistic tendencies. Research shows that, generally, individuals who strongly endorse self-transcendent values are likely to show more positive attitudes, norms, and behaviour in favour of the environment, while the opposite is true for people who strongly endorse self-enhancement values (De Groot et al. 2016; Steg and De Groot 2012).

17.3.3 *Four Key Values for Pro-Environmental Behaviour*

In the environmental domain, two types of self-transcendence (altruistic and biospheric) and two types of self-enhancement (egoistic and hedonic) values appear to be particularly relevant in relation to attitudes, norms, and behaviour.

It appears to be important to make a distinction between biospheric and altruistic values within Schwartz' self-transcendent value dimension (Stern, 200; see also De Groot and Steg 2008). **Biospheric values** reflect a concern for the quality of nature and the environment for its own sake, while altruistic values reflect a concern with the welfare of other human beings.

Biospheric and altruistic values are positively correlated, which is in line with Schwartz's value theory, as both reflect self-transcendence values. Yet, biospheric and altruistic values can be distinguished empirically (De Groot and Steg 2008). Moreover, when pro-environmental choices reflect both values differently, they may contribute to the prediction of pro-environmental behaviours in a unique way, and sometimes even in an opposite direction (see Box 17.1). In most cases, biospheric values are more predictive of pro-environmental attitudes, norms, and behaviours than are altruistic values (De Groot et al. 2016; Schuitema and De Groot 2015; Van Doorn and Verhoef 2015).

Second, scholars have argued that both egoistic and **hedonic value** types included in Schwartz' self-enhancement dimension are important for predicting attitudes, norms, and behaviour in the environmental domain (Steg et al. 2014b). While egoistic values reflect costs and benefits affecting individual resources (such as money and power), hedonic values reflect a concern with improving one's feelings and reducing effort. Indeed, studies have shown that hedonic values can be distinguished from egoistic values; like egoistic values, hedonic values are typically negatively related to a range of environmentally

BOX 17.1   BIOSPHERIC VALUES

De Groot and Steg (2008) examined whether egoistic, altruistic, and biospheric values could be distinguished empirically by using an adapted value instrument based on Schwartz's (1994) value survey. They included a selection of values that belonged to the self-transcendence versus self-enhancement dimension of Schwartz's value theory, and included extra biospheric value items because these values were underrepresented in Schwartz's original value instrument.

Results of three studies provided support for the reliability and validity of the value instrument. Egoistic, altruistic, and biospheric values could be distinguished empirically and the scales had sufficient internal consistency. In most cases, egoistic values were negatively related to environmental beliefs and intentions, while biospheric and, to a lesser extent, altruistic values were positively related to environmental beliefs and intentions. As expected, altruistic and biospheric values were correlated, but predicted choices differed when participants were forced to choose between donating to an environmental or a humanitarian organization: altruistically oriented people intended to donate more often to humanitarian organizations, while biospherically oriented people intended to donate more often to environmental organizations. Thus, altruistic and biospheric values seem to be differently related to intention when these values conflict.

relevant attitudes, preferences, and behaviours. This seems hardly surprising as people seem to take a lot of pleasure in behaviours that are environmentally harmful (e.g. driving a car, taking long showers).

17.4   HOW VALUES AFFECT ENVIRONMENTAL BEHAVIOUR

How should one act upon a value, such as 'biospheric values'? The abstractness of values allows for a great deal of individual interpretation. A person valuing the environment may go on a holiday to the Galapagos to enjoy its magnificent nature and scenic views, but may also decide to not go on such a trip if they believe it will harm the local or global environment. Thus, people can decide to do the exact opposite based on the same value. As a consequence, behaviour-specific attitudes and norms are generally better predictors of behaviour than are values (Eagly and Chaiken 1993). Indeed, various studies showed that values mostly influence behaviour indirectly, via behaviour-specific beliefs, attitudes, and norms (see Chapter 22; e.g. De Groot et al. 2016; Thøgersen et al. 2016).

The value that is prioritized in a specific situation will be most influential for beliefs, attitudes, and norms (hence, behaviour). For example, when choosing between restaurants with different hedonic, egoistic, altruistic, and biospheric features, individuals who prioritized biospheric values over other values considered the biospheric aspects of the restaurants (i.e. whether organic food was served), while those who strongly endorsed altruistic values particularly considered altruistic aspects (i.e. working conditions), and those prioritizing hedonic values mostly considered hedonic aspects (i.e. whether the food was tasty; Steg and De Groot 2012). Although values mostly influence behaviour indirectly, some studies have also reported direct relationships between values and behaviour (e.g. De Groot et al. 2013).

It is possible to focus attention towards specific values and thereby increase their saliency, which can affect the way one's values direct attention to value-congruent information (which affects beliefs and behaviour; e.g. De Groot and Steg 2009a, b). One way to increase a value's saliency is by enhancing one's self-focus (Verplanken and Holland 2002). People care about maintaining a favourable view of themselves. Consequently, they may prefer to see themselves as people who actually care for the environment rather than as people who only care about themselves. Indeed, two studies showed that making biospheric values more salient by focusing on environmental reasons ('Want to protect the environment? Check your car's tire pressure') rather than making egoistic values salient with economic reasons ('Want to save money? Check your car's tire pressure') helped people to keep a more positive self-concept, which also resulted in more pro-environmental actions (i.e. taking up the offer of coupons for free tyre checks; Bolderdijk et al. 2013b).

Another way to make (especially biospheric) values salient to promote value-congruent actions is by providing cognitive support for one's values, that is, by making sure that people can provide reasons for their values (Tapper et al. 2012). Without cognitive support, people have difficulty generating counterarguments against messages attacking an endorsed value, which may result in value-incongruent behaviour. Hence, especially making salient biospheric values by linking these values to someone's self-concept and providing cognitive support for these values seem to be effective ways to promote pro-environmental behaviours.

17.5   RELATED CONCEPTS

In addition to values, a number of related psychological determinants of environmental behaviour have been distinguished in the environmental psychology literature, notably environmental concern, ecological worldviews, and myths of nature.

Environmental concern reflects a general attitude towards the environment (Fransson and Gärling 1999), reflecting a personal evaluation of environmental issues. Some widely used instruments are multiple-topic, multiple-expression instruments based on the classical tripartite conceptualization of attitude as consisting of affective, cognitive, and conative dimensions (e.g. Weigel and Weigel's (1978) Environmental Concern Scale). Other measures aim at uncovering the salience of environmental problems in the population, often in comparison with other social problems (e.g. Dunlap and Jones 2002). Irrespective of the measure used, environmental concern is typically found to be positively related to pro-environmental intentions and behaviour, although relationships are often weak (e.g. Mcdonald et al. 2015).

Ecological worldviews reflect fundamental beliefs on the relationship between humans and the natural environment (Dunlap et al. 2000, see also Chapter 22). A popular measure of ecological worldviews is the New Environmental (or Ecological) Paradigm (NEP): individuals who endorse the NEP believe that humanity can easily upset the balance of nature, that there are limits to growth for human societies, and that humanity does not have the right to rule over the rest of nature. The NEP has been found to be positively (although weakly) related to pro-environmental intentions and behaviour (Dunlap and Jones 2002).

Myths of nature reflect perceptions of environmental risks and preferred management strategies to control these risks (Steg and Vlek 2009). Four myths of nature are distinguished: nature capricious, nature perverse/tolerant, nature benign, and nature ephemeral. Figure 17.2 provides a graphical representation of how environmental risks are perceived in the different myths of nature and lists the main differences in beliefs in environmental concern and preferred risk management strategy between the myths of nature. The propositions of the theory, including the relationships with pro-environmental behaviour, were supported in empirical research (see Steg and Vlek 2009, for an overview).

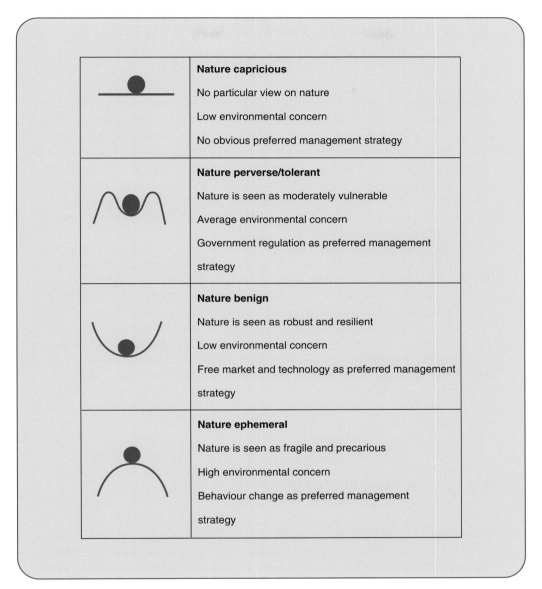

Figure 17.2 *Myths of nature. The line symbolizes the landscape and the vulnerability of nature; the ball symbolizes environmentally risky behaviour. See Steg and Vlek (2009) for a full description of the myths of nature and how they are applied in research.*

Environmental concerns, worldviews, and myths of nature are more specific than are values, because they focus on environmental issues only, while values focus on general overarching goals in life, including environmental and non-environmental (e.g. egoistic, hedonic) concerns. Empirical evidence shows that values are often more predictive of environmental behaviours than these related concepts (Steg et al. 2011), perhaps because most people do not act environmentally due to environmental reasons only (but also due to altruistic, and sometimes even egoistic or hedonic, reasons).

17.6 PRACTICAL RELEVANCE OF VALUE RESEARCH

Practitioners, such as those who design social marketing campaigns, often use the knowledge of value research to promote pro-environmental behaviour. For example, the Danish bus company Midttrafik released a campaign in 2010, 'be a World saver', emphasizing the positive climate consequences of taking the bus instead of the car. This consequence is typically regarded as important for someone who endorses biospheric values. By focusing on these biospheric consequences, it is assumed that biospheric values will be activated and become more salient relative to other values, thus strengthening an argument, or a justification, for taking the bus.

Because individuals differ in their value priorities, values are also used to segment the population into relatively homogeneous groups that can be targeted by tailored messages or other forms of interventions (Kamakura and Mazzon 1991; see also Chapter 26). Indeed, research suggests that campaigns highlighting biospheric values particularly motivate behaviour change among those who strongly endorse biospheric values (see Bolderdijk et al. 2013a). From this perspective, Midttrafik's campaign may be perceived as a campaign targeting a particular segment: those giving high priority to biospheric values. In order also to persuade a segment of travellers with an egoistic value orientation to take the bus, Midttrafik might run other campaigns emphasizing attributes on which the bus compares favourably to the car, such as the possibility to relax or read, or meet interesting people.

17.7 SUMMARY

In this chapter we have discussed the role of values in pro-environmental behaviour. Values are abstract, overarching goals that vary in importance and serve as guiding principles in someone's life. We have argued that values provide a useful tool in research on the psychological determinants of environmental behaviour, because they are stable and widely applicable. In the second part of this chapter, we have reviewed different value theories and typologies along with empirical research that studied how different value types affect pro-environmental beliefs and behaviour. An important conclusion from this review is that self-transcendent values (including biospheric and altruistic values) and self-enhancement values (including egoistic and hedonic values) are especially relevant in relation to pro-environmental beliefs, attitudes, norms, and behaviours. Self-transcendent values tend to be positively related to these concepts, whereas self-enhancement values tend to be negatively related to them. In general, people will be more inclined to act upon biospheric and altruistic values when these values are prioritized and made salient in a specific context, for exampling making biospheric values more salient by linking them to one's self-concept, or by supporting them with cognitive reasons. Finally, we have discussed how values differ from related concepts such as environmental concern, worldviews, and myths of nature, and have illustrated how values may be used in applied settings to design value-tailored interventions.

GLOSSARY

altruistic values   A value type reflecting the concern for society and other people.

biospheric values   A value type reflecting the concern with the quality of nature and the environment for its own sake.

circumplex   A set of variables which, when plotted as vectors in a two-dimensional space, fall in a circular pattern.

decomposed game technique   An experimental instrument to assess one's social value orientation.

ecological worldviews   Beliefs regarding humanity's ability to upset the balance of nature, the existence of limits to growth, and rejecting humanity's right to rule over the rest of nature.

egoistic values   A value type reflecting a concern for your own resources.

environmental concern   The extent to which an individual is concerned about environmental problems.

hedonic values   A value type reflecting a concern for improving one's feelings and reducing effort.

myths of nature   Perceptions of environmental risks and preferred management strategies to control these risks.

social value orientations (SVO)   Value orientations reflecting the extent to which individuals care about own payoffs and payoffs of others in a social dilemma situation.

value   A desirable trans-situational goal that varies in importance and serves as a guiding principle in the life of a person or other social entity.

SUGGESTIONS FOR FURTHER READING

Maio, G.R. (2010). Mental representations of social values. In: *Advances in Experimental Social Psychology* (ed. M.P. Zanna), 1–43. San Diego, CA: Academic Press.

Schwartz, S.H. (1992). Universals in the content and structure of values: theoretical advances and empirical tests in 20 countries. In: *Advances in Experimental Social Psychology* (ed. M. Zanna), 1–65. Orlando, FL: Academic Press.

Seligman, C. and Katz, A.N. (1996). The dynamics of value systems. In: *The Psychology of Values: The Ontario Symposium*, vol. 8 (ed. C. Seligman, J.M. Olson and M.P. Zanna), 53–75. Hillsdale, NJ: Lawrence Erlbaum Associates.

Steg, L. and De Groot, J.I.M. (2012). Environmental values. In: *The Oxford Handbook of Environmental and Conservation Psychology* (ed. S. Clayton), 81–92. New York, NY: Oxford University Press.

REVIEW QUESTIONS

1. Explain the advantages and disadvantages of focusing on values in environmental psychological research.
2. Describe which values are important when explaining pro-environmental behaviours.
3. How can we use our current knowledge about values in applied research?
4. How do values differ from related determinants of environmental behaviour, such as environmental concerns or myths of nature?

18 Social Norms and Pro-Environmental Behaviour

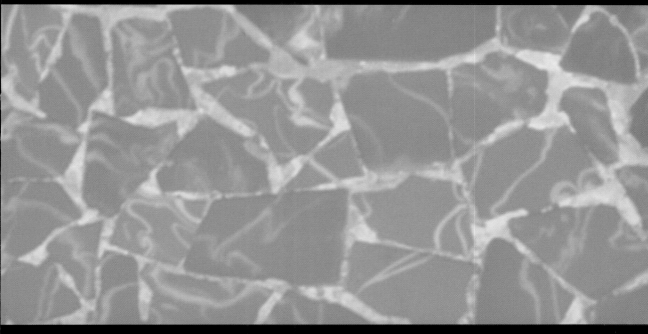

Kees Keizer
University of Groningen, The Netherlands

P. Wesley Schultz
California State University, USA

CHAPTER OUTLINE

18.1   INTRODUCTION

Many of the environmental problems we face today are the consequence of human behaviour, and as a result these problems can be solved by changing our behaviour. Consider the following environmental decisions:

- Buying a traditional washing machine, or spending more money to purchase the energy-efficient version;
- Riding a bicycle to work, rather than travelling by car;
- Dropping a piece of paper on the ground as litter, rather than carrying it to a recycling bin.

In each of these situations, there is a clear environmental choice. In many instances, the pro-environmental option requires more effort or inconvenience, or costs more money. Other chapters of this book have examined personal and contextual factors that explain when a person will make the environmental choice. This chapter focuses on **social norms** and people's tendency to conform to them. We will explain what social norms are, how they influence (environmental) behaviour, and when.

18.2   WHAT IS A SOCIAL NORM?

Social norms are 'rules and standards that are understood by members of a group, and that guide and/or constrain human behaviour without the force of laws' (Cialdini and Trost 1998, p. 152). In a general sense, social norms *are* what is commonly done or (dis)approved. They refer to what *other people* think or do. This sets them apart from **personal norms**, which are rules or standards for one's own behaviour (Kallgren et al. 2000; see also Chapter 22). It is useful to distinguish between two types of social norms: **injunctive norms** which refer to the behaviour commonly approved or disapproved, and **descriptive norms** which refer to the behaviour shown by most group members. Littering or pouring used paint down a storm drain are both socially disapproved behaviours, and there is an injunctive norm against doing so. A newspaper article stating that the majority of people in the Netherlands use a bicycle to cover short distances, or donate annually to environmental organizations, gives descriptive norm information. It tells which behaviour is common (using a bicycle), or the extent to which a certain behaviour is common (donating money).

Environmental Psychology: An Introduction, Second Edition. Edited by Linda Steg and Judith I. M. de Groot.
© 2019 John Wiley & Sons Ltd. Published 2019 by John Wiley & Sons Ltd.

When psychologists talk about social norms, they are typically referring to an individual's *beliefs* about the behaviours and evaluations of group members. Consider Jan who takes the train to work every day. He might think, based on the crowds in the train station, that the majority of people take the train instead of travelling by car. While, for Jan, commuting by train might be perceived as the descriptive norm, it may be that in reality most people travel by car.

18.3   HOW INFLUENTIAL ARE NORMS ON BEHAVIOUR?

Social psychologists have studied social norms for many years. An early study by Sherif (1936) showed that individuals used the responses given by others as a reference point for their own answer. Participants in this study were asked to estimate the movement of a light dot in an otherwise dark room (this basic perceptual task is called the autokinetic effect, and in the absence of any contextual information, the light will normally appear to move). In Sherif's studies, the sessions were conducted in groups of three, and each person gave their answers out loud. The results showed that over multiple trials, the answers given by the participants became closer together. In essence, hearing the responses of others led to the development of a norm. In these studies the situation was highly ambiguous for the participants. However other studies have shown that the influence of norms is not limited to such situations.

In a study by Asch (1951), participants had to indicate which of three lines was similar in length to a fourth line. When seated alone, 100% of the participants gave the correct answer. This number however dropped to 68% when the participant was seated in a group where the other members all gave the same but wrong answer. So 32% of the participants went along with the descriptive norm and gave what was clearly a false answer on at least one occasion. Norms not only influence stated opinions but also (private) behaviour. In one study, residents who learned that most of their neighbours engaged in specific behaviours to reduce their energy at home used subsequently less energy themselves (Schultz et al. 2007).

Although norms can exert a powerful influence on (environmental) behaviour, people tend to underestimate their own susceptibility to social pressure. This tendency was illustrated in study by Nolan et al. (2008) on individuals' willingness to conserve energy in their homes. The study showed that providing normative information about the (better) conservation behaviours of other households in the same neighbourhood was more effective then receiving information about conserving energy for reasons of environmental protection, social responsibility, saving money, or just tips on ways to reduce their energy use. However, when asked how much the normative information motivated them to conserve energy, residents rated it as much less influential than messages about saving money or environmental protection.

18.4   WHY DO PEOPLE CONFORM TO NORMS?

Injunctive social norms tell us which behaviour is approved or disapproved. Conforming to such norms is often associated with social acceptance or rewards, whereas violating them often entails disapproval and social sanctions. People conform to injunctive norms to gain social approval or to avoid social sanctions. In essence, we want people to like us. Deutsch and Gerard (1955) termed this type of motivation **normative social influence**. Conforming to descriptive norms typically has a different motivation, namely the desire to be correct. In many instances, following the group will lead to a correct outcome. For example, following the crowd after arriving by train to an unfamiliar station will likely lead you to the exit. Deutsch and Gerard (1955) termed this type of motivation **informational social influence**.

18.5   WHEN DO NORMS INFLUENCE BEHAVIOUR?

As described in section 18.4, social norms can exert a powerful influence on our behaviour. But subsequent studies have shown a number of important moderator variables. **Moderators** are variables that increase or decrease the strength of an effect. In this section, we examine several moderators that have been found to affect the strength of normative social influence. We focus specifically on pro-environmental behaviour, and illustrate the effects with examples from recent studies.

18.5.1   *Salience*

In thinking about social norms, it is important to point out that norms are generally specific to a context. That is, norms refer to beliefs about the common or appropriate behaviour in a specific setting. Thus, while you might think that it is appropriate to reuse a bath towel at home for six or seven times before washing it, when staying in a hotel you might believe it is appropriate to use the towel only once. In addition, in most contexts there are multiple norms that are relevant, like for example, norms about social behaviour such as eye contact or interpersonal distance, norms about personal attire, or norms about environmental behaviour, to name just a few.

The extent to which a (specific) social norm is (made) salient determines the degree to which it is activated. The **focus theory of normative conduct** proposes that norms will motivate behaviour primarily when they are activated

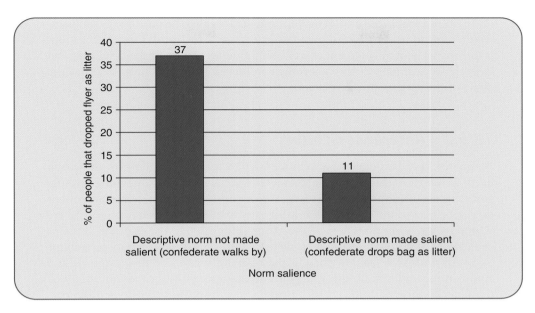

Figure 18.1 *Percentage of participants littering a clean environment as a function of descriptive norm salience.* Source: Adapted from Reno et al. (1993).

(Cialdini et al. 1990). A study designed to test the effects of norm salience examined whether people littered a handbill placed on the windshield of their parked car in a litter-free parking structure at a public library (Reno et al. 1993). The litter-free state of the environment revealed descriptive norm information, namely: 'it is common not to litter in this setting'. Upon approaching their car, the participants saw an experimental confederate who carried a bag from a fast food restaurant. In the control condition this confederate just walked by. However, in the experimental 'salience' condition, the confederate dropped the bag onto the ground (in the otherwise litter-free setting). The authors argued that the act of littering served to make salient the descriptive norm (i.e. 'it is common not to litter in this setting'). The results indeed showed that participants who observed the confederate dropping the bag into the litter-free environment were less likely to litter the handbill on their car (11%) than those who saw the confederate just walking by (37%; see Figure 18.1).

18.5.2   *Group Size*

A second variable found to moderate the influence of social norms is group size. Cialdini et al. (1990) showed that the more pieces of litter in a setting, which is an indication of the number of people littering, the more likely people are to litter. The classic studies described earlier by Asch (1951) showed a similar moderating influence of group size. In the initial studies – which found that individuals conformed to a group norm even when they knew their responses were incorrect – groups ranged in size from 8 to 10. In subsequent studies, Asch

(1956) found that groups of 4 (with 3 confederates plus the one true participant) resulted in more conformity than did groups of size 2 or 3. However, groups larger than 4 generally did not exert more influence. These findings suggest that larger groups tend to exert a stronger influence on individuals, but that the effect of group size quickly plateaus.

18.5.3 Reference Groups

Normative social influence is also moderated by the characteristics of the group itself. Research in this area often draws on a social identity framework and suggests that social influence results largely from categorizing oneself as a member of a specific group, and then adopting the attitudes and behaviours that are shared by the other members of the group (Hogg 2003). For example, Abrams et al. (1990) reported a series of studies using the classic conformity paradigms of Sherif and Asch (as described in the opening section of this chapter). In a study on the autokinetic effect, they found that estimates for the movement of the light became particularly more similar over repeated trials when the participants were led to believe that they were part of single group, rather than acting individually. Furthermore, using the Asch line paradigm, Abrams et al. (1990) showed that when confederates were other psychology students (i.e. an in-group) the normative influence of this group was higher than when confederates were described as ancient history majors (i.e. an out-group).

Similar results have been reported in other studies. For example, Smith and Louis (2008) found that participants were more influenced by normative information about the opinions and behaviours of other students at their university (i.e. an in-group) than when the same normative information was described as from students at another university. In essence, when normative information is provided about an out-group, it exerts little (if any) influence on behaviour.

18.5.4 Personal Norms

The preceding examples illustrate the general power of normative information, and describe several aspects of the social context that can moderate the effect. But what about a person's existing personal norms about a topic; can they override the normative pressure to conform? The results from a study by Schultz et al. (2016) suggest that (the strength of) personal norms can moderate normative social influence. Personal norms refer to an individual's belief about their moral obligation to engage in the behaviour. The results from this study showed that normative social influence is strongest among individuals who are generally ambivalent about the behavioural topic. Consider a person who feels passionately about the importance of conserving water. This person regularly does things to conserve, and in fact, they even admonish other people for not conserving. Such a person is less likely to be swayed either by messages indicating that other people are (also) doing things to conserve or by cues that other people are not conserving, than someone who does not have strong feelings about energy conservation.

18.5.5 *Norm Conflict and the Importance of Aligned Messages*

Our final consideration in understanding moderators of normative social influence pertains to conflicting norms. The research on littering by Cialdini et al. (1990) shows that people are more likely to litter in a littered setting than in a litter-free setting. It also makes clear that a descriptive norm can conflict with an injunctive norm. In a littered setting, the presence of signals that many people litter (the descriptive norm) conflicts with the general (injunctive) norm that one should not litter. The results of the study indicate that the injunctive anti-litter norm is not as influential in this 'conflicting' setting as it is in a setting where the descriptive norm supports the injunctive norm (i.e. a clean environment). Research reveals that a descriptive norm showing a lack of respect for an injunctive norm not only inhibits the influence of this norm but also the influence of other injunctive norms in that setting, suggesting a **cross-norm inhibition effect** (Keizer et al. 2008; see Box 18.1 and Figure 18.2). This spreading effect is explained by goal framing theory which states that observing cues that signal a specific norm-violating behaviour weakens people's goal to act appropriately (Steg et al. 2016; also see Chapters 15 and 22).

In crafting messages to promote pro-environmental behaviour, developers often incorporate images or wording that depict the undesirable behaviour (Cialdini 2003). Such messages are designed to 'raise awareness' about the severity of an issue or to underscore the importance of adopting the new behaviour. But lurking in this awareness message is a descriptive norm – other people are not doing the desired behaviour.

In a series of studies at the Petrified Forest National Park, Cialdini et al. (2006) showed a possible resolution of such an awareness message. The park features ancient pieces of wood, turned to stone (i.e. petrified wood) over the

BOX 18.1   THE CROSS-NORM INHIBITION EFFECT

A series of field experiments by Keizer et al. (2008) showed that the influence of an injunctive norm is inhibited when violations of another injunctive norm are observed (i.e. a cross-norm inhibition effect). Individuals who came to retrieve their parked bicycle were more likely to drop a flyer as litter that was attached to the handlebar when the setting (an alley) had been sprayed with graffiti (69%) than in the same setting without graffiti (32%). In turn, a littered environment sparked other norm violating behaviours. In another study, for example, people were more likely to steal an envelope (visibly) containing money that was hanging from a mailbox when the mailbox was surrounded with litter (in which case 25% stole the envelope) than when the setting was clean (where 13% stole the envelope).

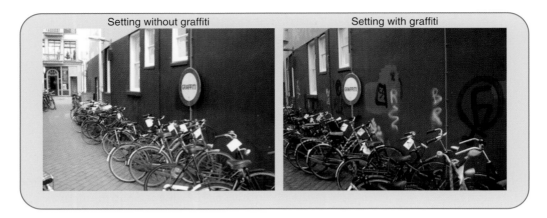

Figure 18.2 *Impressions of the experimental conditions for testing the cross-norm inhibition effect (See Box 18.1).*
Source: Photos by Kees Keizer.

course of thousands of years. The often small pieces of wood are strewn about the floor of the park making them an easy target for visitors looking for a souvenir. In an effort to curb the loss of wood, the researchers conducted a study of signage encouraging visitors to leave the wood undisturbed. In one of the conditions, the sign provided a strong injunctive norm against taking the wood:

Please don't remove the petrified wood from the park.

The sign was accompanied by a picture of a lone visitor taking a piece of wood, with a red circle-and-bar admonishing this behaviour. In a second condition, the sign provided a descriptive norm message about the severity of the problem.

Many past visitors have removed the petrified wood from the park, changing the state of the Petrified Forest.

The sign was accompanied by pictures of visitors taking wood from the park. To test the effectiveness of the signs, the researchers placed marked pieces of wood along several of the trails in the park. The dependent variable was the percentage of marked pieces that were stolen. The results showed that the message focusing attention on the injunctive norm produced the lowest rate of theft (1.67%) compared to the sign that made focal the (negative) descriptive norm (7.92%). However when comparing these results to the theft rate when no sign was present (2.92%; Cialdini 2003), it becomes clear that awareness campaigns that highlight the large number of people who behave in undesirable ways can produce boomerang effects.

The petrified wood study shows that the impact of an injunctive norm can be seriously threatened by a conflicting descriptive norm. However, when the descriptive norm is aligned with the injunctive norm, a combination of both norms can make an effective intervention (Schultz et al. 2008; see Box 18.2).

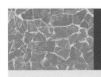

BOX 18.2   ALIGNED NORMS MAKE AN EFFECTIVE INTERVENTION

In a study on the usage of social norms Schultz et al. (2008) developed messages placed in hotel rooms encouraging guests to reuse their bath towels. In one of the studies, the descriptive and injunctive messages were *aligned*. The message read:

> Many of our resort guests have expressed to us the importance of conserving energy. When given the opportunity, nearly 75% of our guests choose to reuse their towels each day. Because so many guests value conservation and want to conserve, this resort has initiated a conservation program. ….
> PLEASE REUSE YOUR TOWELS.

Results over a six-month period showed that 62% of guests who stayed in a room with the aligned norm message reused at least one towel on the first opportunity to do so, and the average room replaced 1.74 towels on the first cleaning day. By comparison, 57% guests who stayed in rooms with a control message about the environmental benefits of reusing towels chose to reuse at least one towel, and the average room replaced 2.32 towels. See Smith et al. 2012 for a study showing the importance of aligned norm messages when stimulating energy conservation.

The positive influence of observing other people's respect rather than disrespect for an injunctive norm also increases conformity to other injunctive norms in that setting (Keizer et al. 2013). More specifically, people were more likely to help a stranger in a setting that was relatively clean rather than littered. The study also showed that helping increased even more in the clean setting when a confederate was observed showing clear respect for the 'anti-litter' injunctive norm by removing their own or other people's litter. The latter suggests that when it comes to stimulating pro-environmental behaviour in others, even one person can make a difference.

18.6   SUMMARY

In this chapter, we discussed the role of social norms in understanding and changing pro-environmental behaviour. We distinguished two types of social norms: injunctive and descriptive norms. Next, we described research showing that social norms can exert a powerful influence on (pro-environmental) behaviour through normative and informational influence. This influence is moderated by the salience of the norm, the size of the reference group, the extent to which this group is considered an in-group, one's personal norms, and the extent to which injunctive and descriptive norms are aligned. When designing messages to promote pro-environmental behaviour, it is essential that information regarding corresponding descriptive norms is in line with the targeted behaviour.

GLOSSARY

cross-norm inhibition effect   The negative effect of observing other people's violation of one norm on one's own likelihood of following another norm.

descriptive norm   The behaviour shown by most group members.

focus theory of normative conduct   Theory that proposes that norms will motivate behaviour primarily when they are activated.

informational social influence   The influence of norms on behaviour that is the result of a person's desire to be correct.

injunctive norm   The behaviour commonly approved or disapproved.

moderators   Variables that increase or decrease the strength of an effect.

normative social influence   The influence of norms on behaviour that is the result of a person's desire to gain social approval or to avoid social sanctions.

personal norms   An individual's belief about their moral obligation to engage in certain behaviour.

social norm   What is commonly done or (dis)approved.

SUGGESTIONS FOR FURTHER READING

Keizer, K., Lindenberg, S., and Steg, L. (2008). The spreading of disorder. *Science* 322: 1681–1685.

Nolan, J., Schultz, P.W., Cialdini, R.B. et al. (2008). Normative social influence is underdetected. *Personality and Social Psychology Bulletin* 34: 913–923.

Schultz, P.W., Tabanico, J., and Rendón, T. (2008). Normative beliefs as agents of influence: basic processes and real-world applications. In: *Attitudes and Attitude Change* (ed. R. Prislin and W. Crano), 385–409. New York, NY: Psychology Press.

REVIEW QUESTIONS

1. Define social norms, and describe the distinction between descriptive and injunctive social norms. Give two unique (i.e. not from the readings) examples of each.
2. Name and describe the two types of motivations behind normative social influence.
3. Name and describe three moderators of normative social influence.
4. Imagine that you are asked by your university to develop a campaign to reduce the number of cigarette butts littering the ground. Identify two strategies that you think would be effective, and two strategies that would be ineffective.

19 Emotions and Pro-Environmental Behaviour

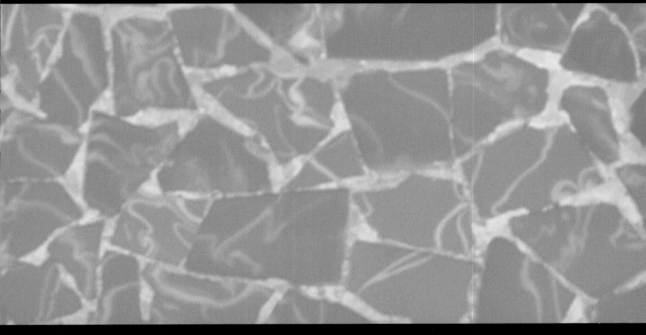

Danny Taufik
Wageningen University & Research, The Netherlands

Leonie Venhoeven
University of Groningen, The Netherlands

CHAPTER OUTLINE

19.1   INTRODUCTION

Think of all the things that you have done so far today (assuming reading this chapter is not your way of starting the day). Maybe you took a nice warm shower this morning, you attended a lecture which you went to by bike, bus, or car, and you may have been thinking ahead about whether you would like a vegetarian dinner. Every day, people make many decisions that can have important implications for the quality of the environment. From an environmental standpoint, it matters how long you showered and how warm the water was, what type of transport you chose for your travels to university, and whether you will cook a vegetarian meal or a meal with meat tonight. Various considerations may affect which choices you make (see Part II of this book). For example, you could have travelled by car rather than cycle to your lecture, as you believe it saves you time and allows you to arrive without a sweaty shirt, although travelling by car is more polluting and would cost you more money than a bicycle ride would. Aspects such as time, comfort, environmental impact, and money are referred to as **instrumental consequences** of one's behaviour (Dittmar 1992). It is often assumed that people make rational choices, weighing the (instrumental) costs and benefits of a product or behaviour and engaging in behaviour that has the most positive and least negative instrumental consequences.

Yet, people do not always act in such a rational manner when it comes to environmental behaviour. Notably, people may also engage in certain types of behaviour because it feels good, or refrain from behaviour that makes them feel bad. In the current chapter, we describe the significant role emotions can play in people's engagement in environmental behaviour. In the first section we will discuss empirical research that shows how emotions can be a motive for environmental behaviour. We then discuss a so-called hedonic and eudaimonic view of environmental behaviour, to gain more clarity into why pro-environmental behaviour can be associated with negative as well as positive emotions. While it is often presumed that pro-environmental behaviour is associated with the former (for instance, because it can be a hassle to act pro-environmentally), we will explain why it can also be associated with positive emotions. Finally, we elaborate on conditions under which acting pro-environmentally elicits positive emotions.

Environmental Psychology: An Introduction, Second Edition. Edited by Linda Steg and Judith I. M. de Groot.
© 2019 John Wiley & Sons Ltd. Published 2019 by John Wiley & Sons Ltd.

19.2   EMOTIONS AS A MOTIVE FOR ACTION

Emotions are elicited by something, are reactions to something, and are generally about something – namely a specific object or behaviour (Ekkekakis 2012). This distinguishes emotions from core affect and mood. Core affect is defined as the most elementary consciously accessible feeling, like feeling pleasure or displeasure (Russell and Feldman Barrett 1999). Core affect itself is not consciously directed at anything. When it becomes directed at something, core affect becomes part of an emotion. Similarly, moods are defined as 'affective states that are about nothing specific or about everything – about the world in general' (Frijda 2009, p. 258). Moods could thus be seen as a longer-lasting version of core affect. In this chapter, we focus on core affect in relation to environmental behaviour; in other words, the emotions that environmentally friendly behaviour elicits.

Research shows that the extent to which people believe engaging in behaviour will elicit positive or negative emotions, so-called, **anticipated emotions**, can be an important predictor of whether they will act accordingly. This can lead people to engage in environmentally harmful behaviour, such as commuting by car more often because they associate car use with bringing pleasure (Steg 2005). However, anticipated emotions can also lead people to engage in pro-environmental behaviour. For example, the less boring and more pleasant people expect recycling to be, the higher their intention to recycle is (Kraft et al. 2005). In a similar manner, people's intention to use public transport is stronger when they anticipate positive emotions coming from using it and when they anticipate negative emotions when not using it (Carrus et al. 2008). People can thus be motivated to engage in a particular behaviour because they believe it will make them feel good (i.e. experience positive emotions), or because they believe it will help them to avoid feeling bad (i.e. experience negative emotions). The emotions that an object or behaviour is expected to elicit can thereby serve as a motive for (further) engagement in that behaviour. These reasons to engage in behaviour are referred to as **emotional motives**.

When it comes to explaining why people decide to do something that benefits the environment, emotional motives can in some cases even outweigh anticipated instrumental consequences of pro-environmental behaviour. Anticipating experiencing positive emotions about reducing one's energy consumption, for instance, has been shown to be a stronger predictor of people's intention to conserve energy, than how much instrumental gain people anticipate getting from energy conservation (Taufik et al. 2016). Even though saving energy often results in relatively small monetary savings, people might still be inclined to take energy-saving measures if they anticipate that such actions will elicit positive emotions. As many pro-environmental behaviours might have little positive and more negative instrumental consequences, for instance because they are more expensive and/or more time-consuming and effortful than less pro-environmental options (Bolderdijk and Steg 2015), emotional motives may be highly important. For instance, walking for a few minutes to the recycling bin to throw away your used paper takes more time and effort than putting it in your trash bin at home. Furthermore, there are often few positive instrumental consequences of recycling paper, as recycling paper in most municipalities will not lead to monetary savings for the individual. However, when people expect to experience positive emotions as a result of recycling, these emotional motives may still lead them to act recycle, even when few or no positive instrumental consequences are present.

In sum, the extent to which people anticipate experiencing certain emotions as a result of environmental behaviour can have an important influence on whether or not they intend to engage in this behaviour. If anticipated emotions have an important influence on whether or not people will act pro-environmentally, an important question is where these anticipated emotions come from – what leads people to anticipate either positive or negative emotions about pro-environmental behaviour? Not surprisingly, an important source for the emotions people anticipate experiencing in the future, is the emotions they actually experienced when they engaged in behaviour (**experienced emotions**; Carver and Scheier 1990). An interesting question is therefore what leads people to feel good or bad about engaging in pro-environmental behaviour.

19.3   HEDONIC AND EUDAIMONIC VIEW ON EMOTIONS

Two different views have been provided to explain why pro-environmental behaviour elicits positive or negative emotions. To illustrate the first view, imagine it rained very heavily this morning and you decided to travel to the university by car. Although driving by car is not a very pro-environmental thing to do, the weather conditions may still have made it a pleasurable experience. On a sunny day, however, you may decide to cycle to work, and experience this as a very pleasurable thing to do.

Emotions having their roots in a pleasurable (or unpleasurable) experience are part of the **hedonic view** on which emotions are elicited by pro-environmental behaviour (Venhoeven et al. 2013). Some environmentally friendly behaviours can be inherently pleasurable, and from a hedonic viewpoint lead to positive emotions. For example, organic food is perceived by some to be better tasting than non-organic food (Zanoli and Naspetti 2002), and cycling to work on a nice, sunny spring day can be perceived as more inherently pleasurable than driving a car. However, environmentally harmful behaviour may often be perceived as more pleasant or less unpleasant than its pro-environmental counterpart. For example, taking a long hot shower will often be perceived as a more pleasurable experience than taking a short, colder shower, while the latter is more pro-environmental. It seems to be the lack of pleasure that leads people to see environmentally friendly behaviour as 'requiring personal sacrifice of the highest order' (De Young 1990–1991, p. 216), and a need to assure voters that 'the American way of life is not up for negotiations' (by former U.S. president George H.W. Bush prior to the Earth Summit in Rio de Janeiro). Consequently, from a hedonic viewpoint, many pro-environmental actions may be associated with negative feelings. If pro-environmental behaviour is indeed seen as less pleasant or even as unpleasant behaviour, this may inhibit pro-environmental action.

The question, however, is whether we need to make all pro-environmental behaviour pleasant, in order for this behaviour to feel good. In fact, viewing pro-environmental behaviour as merely unpleasant and somewhat of a sacrifice overlooks the fact that there is a positive side to this behaviour as well: Pro-environmental behaviour contributes to improved environmental quality and can therefore be seen as moral and meaningful behaviour.

To illustrate the second view on the positive and negative emotions environmental behaviour elicits, think of a different example: you took a short shower in the morning, and realize that taking shorter showers is a helpful way to protect the environment. When looking at it like this, taking a short shower may feel good, as you did something meaningful and contributed to a good cause: improved environmental quality.

Emotions having their roots in a meaningful (or meaningless) experience are part of the **eudaimonic view** on which emotions are elicited by pro-environmental behaviour. Pro-environmental behaviour is often regarded as **moral behaviour**, as acting pro-environmentally can benefit the quality of nature and the well-being of other people (Van der Werff et al. 2013a; see Chapter 22). Specific moral emotions have also been connected to the likelihood that people will act pro-environmentally. For instance, the more guilt people anticipate as a result of *not* buying pro-environmental products, the higher their intention to buy these products (Onwezen et al. 2013). Also, the more pride people anticipate as a result of buying pro-environmental products, the higher their intention to buy environmentally friendly products (Onwezen et al. 2013; see also Chapter 22).

Because of its moral connotation, acting pro-environmentally may feel meaningful to those engaging in it, because they are making a contribution to the greater good. Consequently, because of its benefits for the quality of nature, taking a shorter shower may elicit positive emotions (Venhoeven et al. 2013). In support of this reasoning, Venhoeven (2016) showed that the more people perceived behaviour to be pro-environmental, the more meaningful they deemed this behaviour to be. In turn, the more meaningful people deemed the behaviour to be, the better they expected to feel and actually felt about engaging in this behaviour. Furthermore, people who attribute more personal meaning to pro-environmental behaviour (i.e. value the environment more strongly and feel more moral obligation to engage in pro-environmental behaviour) anticipate feeling more positive emotions when acting accordingly. The meaning people attribute to this behaviour may thus indeed be partly responsible for the positive emotions elicited by pro-environmental behaviour.

19.4 WHY PRO-ENVIRONMENTAL BEHAVIOUR ELICITS POSITIVE EMOTIONS: A CLOSER LOOK AT THE EUDAIMONIC VIEW

Based on the specific pro-environmental behaviour at hand, acting pro-environmentally may be pleasant or unpleasant to engage in, eliciting positive or negative emotions (the hedonic view). As we suggested in section 19.3, however, doing something good for the environment in general may elicit positive emotions, as this behaviour can be seen as moral behaviour (the eudaimonic view). In the current section, we discuss in more depth why this latter link may exist: why engaging in moral behaviour may elicit positive emotions.

An important explanation for this link may be that by engaging in moral behaviour such as acting pro-environmentally, you show yourself that you are a good person. As such, engaging in pro-environmental behaviour sends a positive **self-signal**. People's self-image can be seen as a collection of different components that together form a person's view of who they are (see also Chapter 20). For instance, you can consider yourself a diligent student, the joker of your group of friends, and as someone who acts pro-environmentally. All of these components together form your self-image. One of the pillars on which people base their self-image is the behaviour they show (Bem 1972). As Bem (1972) proposes 'individuals come to "know" their own attitudes, emotions, and other internal states partially by inferring them from observations of their own overt behaviour and/or the circumstances in which this behaviour occurs' (p. 2). Indeed, acting pro-environmentally leads people to view themselves subsequently as a more pro-environmental person (van der Werff et al. 2014b; see Chapter 20). Moreover, when they engage in pro-environmental behaviour, people conclude they must be a good person (Venhoeven et al. 2016). How positively people think of themselves is an important determinant of how good they feel (Baumeister 1993). When perceiving one's actions to be environmentally friendly leads to a positive self-image, this in turn elicits positive emotions (Venhoeven et al. 2016). Such a positive feeling as a result of helping others or benefiting the environment is also referred to as a **warm glow** (see Box 19.1; Taufik et al. 2015).

The circumstances under which behaviour occurs can affect how the behaviour is interpreted. The motives behind *why* you are taking a shorter shower, for instance, can influence how you feel about your actions. Is it some external factor (e.g. time constraints) that makes you stay in the shower for only a few minutes, or do you choose to do so because you think taking shorter showers contributes to an improved environmental quality? While the behaviour in both cases is equally (un)pleasant (the hedonic view), the behaviour may be seen meaningful when engaged in for the second reason (the eudaimonic view).

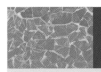

BOX 19.1   WARM GLOW FEELINGS OF PRO-ENVIRONMENTAL ACTIONS

Anticipated positive affect might explain why people choose to make decisions that benefit the environment. As discussed, pro-environmental behaviour may be seen as meaningful behaviour, and thereby feel good to engage in. It has been proposed that engaging in meaningful actions elicits a warm glow feeling (Andreoni 1990), a positive feeling as a result of helping others. Interestingly, this warm glow feeling may be interpreted quite literally (Taufik et al. 2015).

In two studies, participants completed a carbon footprint calculator to indicate how large the impact of their behaviour was on the environment. This calculator included questions on travel, energy, and eating behaviour. In the experimental conditions, participants received their own carbon footprint combined with information that the average carbon footprint of other students (who had ostensibly calculated their carbon footprint in a previous experiment) was either 49% lower, reflecting that other students were more pro-environmental, or 49% higher, reflecting that others students were less pro-environmental than the participant. Thus, this information made it salient that

one's own behaviour was either very pro-environmental or environmentally harmful. This was communicated explicitly by stating 'Compared to the average student, your carbon footprint is 49% better (worse)', to make it salient to participants that their own behaviour was relatively pro-environmental or relatively environmentally harmful.

In Study 1 participants who learned that their behaviour was relatively pro-environmental, on average perceived the ambient temperature to be higher (20.76 °C), than participants who learned that their behaviour was relatively environmentally harmful (19.86 °C). The same pattern was found in Study 2 (20.23 °C versus 19.49 °C, respectively), which was conducted in a climate-controlled room where the actual ambient temperature was held constant at 20 °C. In addition, Study 2 showed that the more the carbon footprint feedback contributed to a positive self-image, the higher participants perceived the temperature to be. Together these studies suggest that people can indeed get a literal warm glow out of doing something good for the environment, as these actions can send a positive self-signal.

Whether situational constraints or personal choice are perceived to be the cause of behaviour may thus influence how people interpret their behaviour, which in turn influences the self-signal behaviour sends. When people engage in certain behaviour voluntarily, they are more likely to attribute the choice to engage to internal instead of external causes (Van der Werff et al. 2014b). Especially when people (feel they) make the decision to behave in a certain way because they wanted to, they reveal something of their inner traits or dispositions – not only to others, but also to themselves (Bodner and Prelec 2003). Acting pro-environmentally because you chose and wanted to do so may particularly send a positive self-signal: it shows more strongly that you are a good person, and acting this way thereby elicits positive emotions (Venhoeven et al. 2016). Hence, taking a shorter shower may particularly elicit more positive emotions when one voluntarily and purposely decides to engage in the behaviour to protect the environment.

When designing marketing campaigns in an attempt to promote pro-environmental behaviour, it is thus important to take into account why and under which conditions this behaviour may elicit positive emotions. For instance, such campaigns may be more effective when they stress how the behaviour contributes to the greater goal of improving environmental quality, and when people have the impression that they engage in the targeted behaviour out of one's own choice, thereby sending a positive self-signal. An example would be placing a poster at a bus-stop that shows a mirror where people waiting for the bus see their own reflection. Under this reflection, they read 'I chose to take the bus to help tackle climate change'. As one's choice to contribute to a cleaner environment is made explicit, the following bus ride may send a positive self-signal. The positive emotions the bus ride elicits because of this framing, may in turn lead people to take the bus more often, setting in motion a virtuous loop.

19.5   SUMMARY

This chapter aimed to provide an overview of research and theory developments on the role of emotional motives in environmental behaviour. We showed that pro-environmental behaviour is not only influenced by instrumental consequences such as costs or time investments, but also (and sometimes more strongly) by the extent to which behaviour is anticipated to elicit emotions (emotional motives). Next, we discussed one source of these anticipated emotions: the emotions actually elicited by previous pro-environmental behaviour. We provided two different views on why pro-environmental behaviour can elicit emotions. First, acting pro-environmentally can be pleasurable or unpleasurable (the hedonic view). Second, acting pro-environmentally can be meaningful (the eudaimonic view). While both pleasure and meaning may play a role in the emotions specific pro-environmental behaviour elicits, the latter is more broadly applicable to pro-environmental behaviour in general. As all pro-environmental behaviour can contribute to the quality of nature and the environment, and the well-being of other people, this type of behaviour is likely to be seen as moral and meaningful behaviour. Engaging in such behaviour may therefore send a positive self-signal: it shows you that you are a good person, and may therefore elicit positive emotions.

GLOSSARY

anticipated emotion   The expectation that engaging in a particular behaviour makes us experience positive or negative emotions.
emotional motives   Motivation for specific behaviour based on emotions.

eudaimonic view   The view that positive and negative emotions related to environmental behaviour have their roots in the behaviour being a meaningful experience.

experienced emotion   The extent to which engagement in behaviour actually makes us feel good or bad.

hedonic view   The view that emotions related to environmental behaviour have their roots in the behaviour being a pleasurable or unpleasurable experience.

instrumental consequences   The perceived functional consequences of a product or behaviour, such as costs or time.

moral behaviour   Behaviour that benefits the well-being of others in both present and future generations – sometimes also extended to benefiting nature and the environment.

self-signal   People's interpretation of what their actions or behaviour reveal about their inner traits or dispositions.

warm glow   A good feeling elicited as a result of helping others or benefiting the environment.

SUGGESTIONS FOR FURTHER READING

Taufik, D., Bolderdijk, J.W., and Steg, L. (2015). Acting green elicits a literal warm glow. *Nature Climate Change* 5 (1): 37–40.

Venhoeven, L.A., Bolderdijk, J.W., and Steg, L. (2013). Explaining the paradox: how pro-environmental behaviour can both thwart and foster well-being. *Sustainability* 5 (4): 1372–1386.

REVIEW QUESTIONS

1. Describe how anticipated emotions may be a motivator or a barrier to adopting pro-environmental behaviour.
2. Think of pro-environmental behaviour that can elicit positive emotions according to both the hedonic and eudaimonic view, and explain how.
3. Explain why acting pro-environmentally may elicit positive emotions, even if it is somewhat unpleasant.
4. Describe a situation in which separating waste sends a strong, positive self-signal, and a situation in which separating waste does not send a strong, positive self-signal.

20 Symbolic Aspects of Environmental Behaviour

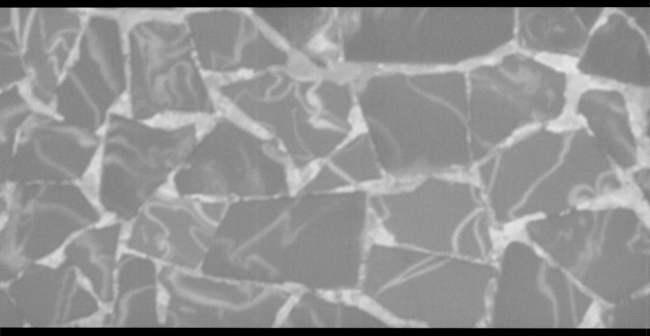

Birgitta Gatersleben
University of Surrey, UK

Ellen van der Werff
University of Groningen, The Netherlands

CHAPTER OUTLINE

20.1   INTRODUCTION

People adopt behaviours for many different reasons. Often these are functional instrumental reasons. For instance, people eat when they are hungry and drive their car to get from A to B. Sometimes, however, people do things because of their **symbolic meaning** – because this behaviour signifies something to the actor or to others about who they are, would like to be, or think they ought to be. For instance, some people may proudly drive a big 4-wheel drive car, others may proudly drive an electric car, and this may have little to do with the price of the car, whether it can get them from A to B, or their fuel consumption. Instead people may own and drive these cars because they signify their unique human qualities (e.g. successful, environmentally friendly) and group membership (e.g. a businessman, an environmental activist). As such these cars have self-expressive (signifying unique human qualities) and categorical (signifying group member-ship) symbolic functions (Dittmar 1992). The role of such symbolic aspects has been extensively studied in consumer psychology but only more recently in environmental psychology. However, as we will show in this chapter, environ-mental behaviour can have strong symbolic value. In this chapter we will discuss two areas of research that have examined the symbolic value of environmental behaviour: environmental self-identity and impression management. These related but distinct research areas demonstrate that environmental behaviour is influenced by the way people see themselves (their identity) and how they would like to be seen by others (impression management).

20.2   IDENTITY

Self-identity refers to the labels people use to describe themselves (Cook et al. 2002). People hold many different (sometimes even conflicting) identities that become salient at different points in time depending on the context (Stryker and Burke 2000). These include social identities (Chapter 23), consumer identities and many others.

One particular identity that has important implications for environmental behaviour and has received significant attention in the environmental psychol-ogy literature is **environmental self-identity** – the extent to which people see themselves as an environmentally friendly person. Environmental self-identity has been conceptualized in different ways, focusing primarily on pro-environ-mental behaviour ('I see myself as an environmentally friendly person'; Van der Werff et al. 2013a) or consumer identities ('I am a green consumer'; Gatersleben et al. 2012). Others have included in their measures both reflections of how

Environmental Psychology: An Introduction, Second Edition. Edited by Linda Steg and Judith I. M. de Groot.
© 2019 John Wiley & Sons Ltd. Published 2019 by John Wiley & Sons Ltd.

people see themselves as well as reflections on how they would like to be seen by others (see Section 20.3). For instance, when measuring environmental self-identity, Whitmarsh and O'Neill (2010) asked respondents to reflect on their behaviour ('I am an environmentally-friendly consumer'), their own values ('I am someone who is very concerned with environmental issues') as well as how others may see them ('I would be embarrassed to be seen as having an environmentally-friendly lifestyle').

A different conceptualization of identity is **identity similarity,** that is, the correspondence between the perceived characteristics (such as fashionable, socially accepted, easy-going) a person attributes to him or herself and to a particular stereotype such as the typical recycler or the typical owner of a sports car (Manetti et al. 2002, 2004).

20.2.1   *Environmental Self-Identity and Behaviour*

The salience of identities is often context dependent. However, identities that are more central to one's sense of self (more important) are more chronically salient and will influence a wide range of behaviours across a variety of contexts (Burke 2006). The more important an environmental self-identity is to a person, therefore, the more likely it is that they will adopt a wide range of pro-environmental behaviours. Indeed environmental identity importance has been shown to influence a variety of environmental behaviours including green shopping, reducing waste, saving water and energy (Whitmarsh and O'Neill 2010), refraining from flying, separating waste, buying fair trade products (Gatersleben et al. 2012), energy use, sustainable product choice, using green energy (Van der Werff et al. 2013a, b), and green talk and reducing car use (Kashima et al. 2014).

Environmental self-identity has been shown to predict behaviours over and above other variables such as attitudes, perceived behavioural control, and subjective norms, demonstrating that understanding identities can provide unique insights into understanding such behaviour that cannot be explained by other variables (Gatersleben et al. 2012; Manetti et al. 2002, 2004; Van der Werff et al. 2013a, b).

People's desire to maintain a positive and consistent sense of self can help explain the link between environmental self-identity and environmental behaviour. **Self-discrepancy** theory (Higgins 1989) suggests that people strive for **self-consistency**, that is, consistency between their actual self (what they do), the valued self (their values and aspirations), and the ought self (perceived norms). People will try to resolve any discrepancy they experience between these different aspects of the self, for instance by changing their behaviour. Similarly **self-perception** theory (Bem 1972) suggests that people know who they are by looking at what they do. When people perceive a discrepancy between what they do and what (they say) is important to them, they will experience psychological discomfort: **cognitive dissonance** (Festinger 1957), which is a powerful motivator for behaviour or attitude change. As such, people with a strong environmental self-identity are more likely to adopt environmental behaviours in particular when those behaviours are perceived to be consistent with an environmental self-identity (Kashima et al. 2014). This desire to be self-consistent also influences moral obligations. People with a strong environmental self-identity have been shown to experience a stronger moral obligation to engage in pro-environmental behaviour, which in turn influences their behaviour (Van der Werff et al. 2013a, b).

20.2.2   Factors Influencing Identity

Environmental self-identities are associated with a range of other psychological variables such as values, attitudes, and behaviours. Environmental self-identity is particularly strongly associated with people's values, in particular their biospheric values (see Chapter 17). After all, if protecting the environment is a guiding principle in someone's life, they are more likely to think they should act upon their values and they will be more likely to see themselves as a person who acts in an environmentally friendly manner. Biospheric values are associated with environmental self-identity even when values are measured months before environmental self-identity, supporting the stability of these concepts (Van der Werff et al. 2013a, b). Environmental self-identity mediates the relationship between values and behaviour suggesting that identities are indeed broader concepts, which are stable over time (Gatersleben et al. 2012; Van der Werff et al. 2013a, b).

Although identities are relatively stable there is evidence that they can be influenced by behaviour changes and reminders of past behaviour (Cornelissen et al. 2008; Poortinga et al. 2013; Van der Werff et al. 2014a). For instance, the introduction of a 5 pence plastic bag charge in Wales resulted in a significant reduction of plastic bag use as well as an increase in environmental self-identity (Poortinga et al. 2013). This is in line with self-perception theory (Bem 1972), discussed in section 20.2.1. Reminding people of their past pro-environmental behaviours has also been shown to strengthen environmental self-identity (Van der Werff et al. 2014a). However, not all reminders of past behaviour can strengthen identity (see Box 20.1 and Table 20.1). In line with **attribution theory,** past behaviour is more likely to influence how people see themselves when the behaviour strongly signals that they are a pro-environmental person (see Kelley 1973). This was found to be the case when it concerned a range of different past pro-environmental actions, or difficult and unique environmental behaviours (Van der Werff et al. 2014a). It should be noted it can also work the other way around: when people realize that they often do not engage in pro-environmental behaviour, their environmental self-identity is weakened which in turn reduces subsequent environmentally friendly actions (Cornelissen et al. 2008; Van der Werff et al. 2014a).

It is clear that environmental self-identity is important for understanding environmental behaviour. Research in this area demonstrates that people do not only adopt such behaviour because of functional or instrumental reasons but also because this behaviour is a symbol of a person's sense of self about their unique human qualities. But people are not only motivated to act in line with how they see themselves, they also care what others think of them. Their behaviour is also influenced by impressions they would like to make on others.

BOX 20.1   HOW CAN INITIAL PRO-ENVIRONMENTAL ACTIONS STRENGTHEN ENVIRONMENTAL SELF-IDENTITY AND SPILL-OVER?

A study tested under which circumstances initial pro-environmental actions can strengthen environmental self-identity and spill-over to other pro-environmental behaviours (Van der Werff et al. 2014a). Participants were assigned into one of four experimental groups in which they were reminded of different past behaviours. One quarter of participants was reminded of eight past behaviours reflecting different types of pro-environmental behaviour (e.g. transport, recycling), one quarter was reminded of eight behaviours reflecting one basic type of behaviour (switching off appliances), one quarter – the control group – was reminded of one pro-environmental behaviour (i.e. buying organic products), and finally one quarter was reminded of eight behaviours not related to the environment (e.g. reading the newspaper). Participants who were reminded of eight behaviours reflecting different types of behaviour indeed had a significantly stronger environmental self-identity than participants in the control group (see Table 20.1). Environmental self-identity of participants who were reminded of eight behaviours reflecting one basic type of

behaviour and of one behaviour did not differ significantly from the control group. Furthermore, results showed that participants who were reminded of eight behaviours reflecting different types of behaviour also had a stronger environmental self-identity than participants who were reminded of one behaviour.

Environmental self-identity was in turn related to pro-environmental product choices. The stronger one's environmental self-identity, the more pro-environmental products participants preferred. Also, environmental self-identity mediated the relationship between the manipulation of past behaviour (comparing the group reminded of eight different environmental behaviours to the control group). These results show that reminding people of eight different environmental behaviours can strengthen environmental self-identity, which in turn increases pro-environmental product choices. However, reminding people of eight similar environmental behaviours or of one environmental behaviour is not enough to strengthen environmental self-identity and thereby promote subsequent pro-environmental behaviour.

Table 20.1 *Environmental self-identity (means) for participants reminded of different types of behaviour.*

	Environmental self-identity
Different types of environmental behaviour	4.53
One basic type of environmental behaviour	4.24
One environmental behaviour	3.80
Control group	4.08

20.3   IMPRESSION MANAGEMENT

Impression management refers to the idea that people tend to try to control the image others form of them (Baumeister 1982; Schlenker and Leary 1982) in order to create an impression that is in line with how they would like to be seen. For instance, someone may be more likely to purchase and display a consumer product if they believe this product will show others they are a successful person or a moral person. Impression management has been extensively studied in consumer and marketing psychology (Christopher and Schlenker 2000) because consumer goods can be particularly useful for communicating to others (non-verbally) who people are, what they have achieved, and what they believe in (Dittmar 1992). Impression management also plays an important role in explaining the purchase of environmental products and engaging in environmental behaviour.

Similar to the finding that not all past behaviours may strengthen one's identity, not all products or behaviours may be useful for communicating unique human qualities to others. In line with attribution theory, some products and behaviours are more likely to signal something about a person to others (see Kelley 1973). More specifically, the symbolic value of consumer goods has been associated with product conspicuousness (visibility), uniqueness and cost (Sirgy and Johar 1999). After all, products or behaviours that cannot easily be seen by others (loft insulation), that are owned or adopted by almost everybody (recycling), and that are of little (monetary) value and therefore require little voluntary investment (washing up liquid) are less likely to signal to others that a person cares about the environment. Purchasing and displaying a solar panel or electric car on the other hand, can help demonstrate to others that no expense or effort is spared to do something that is beneficial for the environment. Experimental studies among US students showed that participants were more likely to choose a green product rather than its non-green alternative (e.g. a hybrid versus a normal car) after manipulating status concerns (Griskevicius et al. 2010). Notably, this was only the case when behavioural decisions were made in public rather than in private (in a regular versus an online store), and only when they were more expensive than the non-green alternatives. This work suggests that people may buy green products if they believe that it will enhance their status by showing others that they have sufficient resources to make sacrifices for the environment.

The influence of impression management on reported environmental behaviour can also be found in a very different area of research; that of socially desirable responding. **Socially desirable responding** refers to the tendency to respond to survey questions in a way that people believe will present themselves favourably to others. When people are asked to report their environmental behaviour they often overestimate how often the engage in pro-environmental behaviour. For instance, a study comparing self-reports of pro-environmental behaviour with independent records of that behaviour by trained observers found that self-reports were consistently higher (Chao and Lam 2011). Such (overly) positive presentations of one's own pro-environmental behaviours have been associated with impression management as well as self-deception (Ewert and Galloway 2009). For example, scores on a standard impression management scale were found to be stronger correlates of self-reports of environmental behaviour than environmental concern (Bratt et al. 2015). These findings suggest that people with a stronger desire to make a good impression may report more pro-environmental behaviour, supporting the idea that such behaviours have positive symbolic value for these people.

The impact of the symbolic value of environmental behaviours depends on people's acknowledgement of this symbolic value. Environmental behaviours can only have expressive symbolic or status functions if actors and observers attach the same symbolic meaning to this behaviour. For instance, 'a Porsche cannot function as a symbol of virile, masculine identity unless at least the owner's reference group shares the belief that the car is indeed masculine' (Dittmar and Pepper 1994, p. 235). Owning a sports car might not impress everyone, nor does a solar panel. For instance, a study conducted in the UK showed that those with stronger biospheric and altruistic values were more likely to believe they could impress others by adopting different environmental behaviours, whereas those with stronger egoistic values were more likely to believe they could impress others by purchasing luxuries (see Box 20.2), presumably because those people compare themselves with different reference groups.

BOX 20.2   THE SYMBOLIC VALUE OF DIFFERENT GOODS AND VALUE ORIENTATIONS

The study examined whether the status value assigned to different behaviours was associated with the extent to which people endorse different value orientations. Participants ($n = 138$) of a longitudinal study on household energy use were asked to what extent they believed other people would be impressed if they adopted 16 behaviours (1 = not at all, 7 = very impressed). A factor analysis demonstrated that the behaviours could be captured in four clusters: adopting pro-environmental behaviour (eating free range, eating less meat, using public transport, avoid using a plane for holiday travel), investing in green technology (solar panel, wind turbine, green roof, green car), buying luxuries (sports car, mobile phone, games console, expensive holiday), and not using a car (getting rid of the car, cycling). Four reliable scales could be computed on the basis of these findings. Respondents also completed a values questionnaire measuring egoistic, altruistic, and biospheric values (see Chapter 17).

As expected, those with stronger egoistic value orientations were more likely to think others would be impressed if they bought expensive luxuries, whereas those with stronger altruistic values were more likely to think other people would be impressed if they adopted pro-environmental behaviours (Table 20.2). Those with stronger biospheric values were more likely to think that investing in green technology would impress others and they were less likely to think that buying luxuries would impress others. They did not believe adopting pro-environmental behaviours would impress other people; perhaps such behaviour had lost its status value for those people as it was not unique anymore. Values were not related to the perceived status value of not driving a car. Altogether these findings support the idea that the symbolic value of different behaviours varies between people depending on their values.

Table 20.2 *Correlations between values and perceived status value of different behaviours.*

	Mean	Standard deviation	Egoistic values	Altruistic values	Biospheric values
Pro-environmental behaviour	3.84	0.89	0.08	0.23 ($p < 0.001$)	0.03
Green technology	4.70	1.02	−0.09	0.13	0.18 ($p < 0.01$)
No car	4.21	1.24	0.01	0.15	0.08
Buy luxuries	3.58	1.14	0.23 ($p < 0.001$)	−0.14	−0.22 ($p < 0.001$)

20.4   SUMMARY

People adopt environmental behaviours not only for instrumental, functional reasons but also because of the symbolic meaning of those behaviours. Environmental behaviours can say something about oneself and can communicate something to others. First, people's self-identity, in particular their environmental self-identity, plays a significant role in understanding environmental behaviour. People are motivated to act in line with how they see themselves (self-consistency). Second, people are motivated to manage the impression others form of them (impression management). Relatively visible, unique, and costly environmental behaviours in particular are likely to be strongly influenced by people's desire to be consistent with how they see themselves and to make a good impression on others.

GLOSSARY

attribution theory   This theory suggests that behaviour is more likely to be attributed to a personal internal characteristic of the actor when it is distinct and consistent and consensus is low.

cognitive dissonance   The tension that arises when individuals become aware of inconsistencies between their attitudes and their behaviour, or inconsistencies between different beliefs.

environmental self-identity   The extent to which people see themselves as an environmentally friendly person.

identity similarity   The correspondence between characteristics a person attributes to him or herself and to a particular stereotype.

impression management   The idea that people tend to try to control the image others form of them in order to create an impression that is positive and in line with their self-image.

self-consistency   The idea that people are motivated to act in line with how they see themselves.

self-discrepancy   The idea that people are motivated to strive for consistency between three different elements of the self: the actual self, the valued self, and the ought self.

self-identity　The label people use to describe themselves.
self-perception　The idea that people know who they are by looking at what they do.
socially desirable responding　The tendency to respond to survey questions in a way that people believe will present them favourably to others.
symbolic meaning of behaviour　The extent to which a behaviour signifies something (to the actor and to others) about who people are.

SUGGESTIONS FOR FURTHER READING

Griskevicius, V., Tybur, J., and Van den Bergh, B. (2010). Going green to be seen: Status, reputation, and conspicuous conservation. *Journal of Personality and Social Psychology* 98: 392–404.

Van der Werff, E., Steg, L., and Keizer, K. (2013). The value of environmental self-identity: the relationship between biospheric values, environmental self-identity and environmental preferences, intentions and behaviour. *Journal of Environmental Psychology* 34: 55–63.

Whitmarsh, L. and O'Neill, S. (2010). Green identity, green living? The role of pro-environmental self-identity in determining consistency across diverse pro-environmental behaviours. *Journal of Environmental Psychology* 30: 305–314.

REVIEW QUESTIONS

1. How can environmental self-identity be strengthened?
2. How are values associated with environmental self-identity?
3. How does the way people see themselves (their self-identity) influence their environmental behaviour?

21 Social Dilemmas: Motivational, Individual, and Structural Aspects Influencing Cooperation

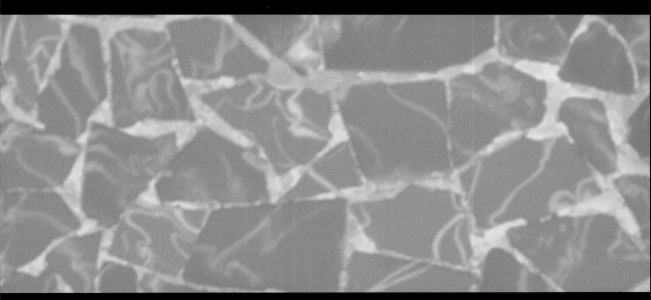

Chris von Borgstede
University of Gothenburg, Sweden

Lars-Olof Johansson
University of Gothenburg, Sweden

Andreas Nilsson
University of Gothenburg, Sweden

CHAPTER OUTLINE

21.1   INTRODUCTION

Imagine that you live on the outskirts of a densely populated area. Every day you commute to your university situated in the town centre. On a normal day, you also work two hours after school at a call centre, situated about 10 km from the university, to earn some extra cash. The average time it takes you to commute by bus, including the stop at work, is about one and a half hours. However, if you instead chose to go by car, the average time would be less than 35 minutes. Obviously, you are better off individually if you take the car. It is quicker and you will probably find it more comfortable. However, if everybody chose to commute by car the effects on congestion and emissions would be appalling, leading to a worse situation than if everybody chose to commute by public transport.

The above example is just one of many situations that can be characterized as **social dilemmas**. Modern social dilemma research started with Hardin's (1968) widely cited article 'The tragedy of the commons'. Hardin describes a group of herders who have open access to a common parcel of land where their cattle graze. It is in each herder's interest to let as many animals as possible graze the land, since each herder receives the benefits and the damage is shared by the entire group. Yet, if all herders make this individually rational decision, the commons is quickly depleted and all will suffer. According to Hardin, if each individual is driven by self-interest and benefits from consuming the common resource, they will continue to do so until use of the resource is restricted or destroyed. To use Hardin's words, 'freedom in a commons brings ruin to all'.

In this chapter we will first give a brief overview of different types of social dilemmas. Then we describe motives that are important for choices in social dilemmas. Finally, we discuss factors influencing people's choices to act in their self-interest or in the interest of the collective.

21.2   DEFINING SOCIAL DILEMMAS

As noted, social dilemmas are situations in which individual interests are in conflict with collective interests. Two criteria have been set up to define social dilemmas: (i) the payoff for each individual to act in their self-interest (called **defection**) is higher than the payoff for acting in the collective interest (called **cooperation**), regardless of what others do; but (ii) all individuals receive a lower payoff if all defect than if all cooperate. Put another way, each selfish decision creates a negative outcome (or cost) for other people involved. When a large number of people make selfish choices, negative outcomes accumulate, creating a situation in which everybody would have been better off if they had not acted in their own interest (Dawes 1980).

21.3   TYPES OF SOCIAL DILEMMAS

21.3.1   *Large-Scale Dilemmas*

A **large-scale dilemma** refers to situations where many people interdependently act under conditions that represent high anonymity, a low degree of communication, where choices to cooperate or defect are made by people in a collective that is weakly united, and where individuals are geographically separated. Such social dilemmas usually imply short-term (e.g. immediate economic benefits) as well as long-term consequences (e.g. global consequences such as climate change). When someone acts according to individual interest in a large-scale social dilemma this often means positive short-term consequences for that person, while if many people behave in this way the negative long-term consequences will stand out. In large-scale social dilemmas, selfish choices will be favoured due to the burdens being spread among a vast number of others.

To act in accordance with collective interest or to pay attention to outcomes for others requires at least some knowledge about the interdependency in the situation (Dawes 1980). It is important that people grasp that they are acting within a social dilemma and understand that their behaviour affects other people and that the behaviours of others affect themselves. This is not a perspective that is easily taken, especially not when there is little or no information about the problems caused by individual behaviour. Furthermore, uncertainty is often very high in large-scale dilemmas, both in terms of the actual state of the resource (**environmental uncertainty**) and in terms of other people's behaviours (**social uncertainty**). Therefore, it is difficult to know how much withdrawal one can make without depleting the resource and whether other people will act selfishly or cooperate. We elaborate on uncertainty in the section 'Factors promoting cooperation'.

21.3.2   *Resource Dilemmas*

A **resource dilemma** arises when multiple individuals share a limited resource with free access, where each group member decides how much to withdraw from the common resource. Examples are common forests, rivers, fisheries, or grazing land. Resource dilemmas are also often named common pool resource (CPR) dilemmas (Ostrom et al. 1994).

21.3.3 *Public Good Dilemmas*

In a **public good dilemma** the common goods depends on individual contributions but is accessible to all group members. An example is paying taxes: others benefit when I pay my taxes regardless of whether they contributed as well. For instance, others may enjoy the city parks regardless of whether they contributed to their maintenance through local taxes. In a short-term perspective, it is costly for me to contribute to the common good, but we are all better off doing so in the long-term, resisting the temptation to free-ride on the contributions of others (Messick and Brewer 1983). As public goods are non-excludable (once these goods are provided, nobody can be excluded from using them), people can be tempted to enjoy the good without making a contribution. The cost of contributing is a negative short-term consequence for the individual, while the long-term consequences are positive for the whole group or society. However, the benefits are distributed equally among members in the group regardless of each member's own contribution (e.g. Van de Kragt et al. 1983). Examples include financing public radio or TV stations, or donating to research funds or environmental organizations.

21.4 MOTIVES IN SOCIAL DILEMMAS

People are not only driven by maximizing their own interests when making choices in social dilemmas. The Greed Efficiency Fairness (GEF) hypothesis (Wilke 1991; see Box 21.1) predicts that people's greed (G) is constrained by a desire to use the resource efficiently (E) and a desire to have a fair allocation of the resource (F). When individuals experience an ever-decreasing resource and large inequities, efficiency and fairness motives can be intensified. We now give a more detailed account of the three motives.

21.4.1 *Greed*

Traditionally it has been assumed in economic theory that individuals always act in their own best interest ('Homo economicus'). Since the reward structure in a social dilemma is such that the defecting choice gives the individual a higher payoff than cooperation, defection is predicted to always be the dominating choice (see Dawes 1980). This choice corresponds to what is labelled the greed motive, that is, to maximize own outcome. In social dilemmas, **greed** can vary from egoism or self-enhancement types of motives close to the individual's survival instincts, to social comparison motives like trying to avoid being worse off than others (see Chapter 1). The effect of greed, however, depends on the decision context. Some research has found that if the stakes are raised, self-interest

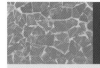

BOX 21.1   GREED EFFICIENCY FAIRNESS HYPOTHESIS

The GEF Hypothesis proposed by Wilke (1991) predicts that there are three conflicting motives in social dilemmas: greed, efficiency, and fairness.

- Greed
  The competitive or defecting choice in a social dilemma corresponds to the greed motive to maximize own outcomes. Greed can be based on survival instincts or social comparison motives like trying to avoid being worse off than others.

- Efficiency
  The cooperative choice in a social dilemma corresponds to the efficiency motive to maximize collective outcomes. In productivity- and performance-oriented groups it is often linked to the distribution principle of equity (see below). Efficiency is assumed to restrain greed.

- Fairness
  The fairness motive reflects a desire to distribute outcomes according to one of three principles: equity (distributing a resource in proportion to input, which is common when productivity is a primary goal), equality (to split resources equally, which is common when group harmony is a primary goal), and need (helping others in need or jeopardy, which is common when well-being and personal development are primary goals). Fairness is assumed to restrain greed.

becomes more important (Bethwaite and Tompkinson 1993; Boyes 1996). Also, with high environmental uncertainty, people harvest somewhat more than their equal shares (De Vries and Wilke 1992). Moreover, people seem to be driven by the greed motive despite being recommended by an outside adviser to restrain their harvest. According to these results, environmental uncertainty enforces greed on behalf of other motives.

21.4.2 Efficiency

Efficiency is reached when total outcomes are maximized, while safeguarding the common resource. But, if we aim to maximize long-term outcomes, how should we choose when the future state of a resource is uncertain? It seems intuitive that one should act cautiously in cases of high uncertainty and minimize resource use in order not to risk depleting a resource that our survival depends on. Yet, people typically overharvest in such situations (De Vries and Wilke 1992). However, the impact of the efficiency motive on behaviour depends largely on which type of goal dominates in a group in a particular situation, which in turn affects how distributive fairness is defined (see section 21.5). The efficiency motive is assumed to be most strongly linked to fairness as equity, that is, proportionality between input and output (Deutsch 1975).

21.4.3 *Fairness*

Fairness exerts a strong influence on behaviour in social dilemmas (Tyler and Dawes 1993). People find it hard to accept unfairness, both in terms of procedures and distributions of resources. Deciding what is a fair share of a particular resource is often done by a process of social comparison, where people commonly use other people's outcomes as a reference point for judgement of their own outcomes. It is assumed that an individual's utility depends not only on his or her own outcomes, but also on the outcomes of other people (Fehr and Schmidt 1999; see also Chapter 29).

What is perceived as a fair distribution will not be the same for different types of good or harm (e.g. work, education, medical care, property, power; Walzer 1983). For instance, at work we commonly expect to be rewarded in proportion to our skills and efforts, but when we are sick we expect to get the proper treatment regardless of economy or social status. Deutsch (1975) proposes that the three distributional fairness principles – equity, equality, and need – are linked to different collective goals and underlying values, and the type of situation in which a resource is distributed. The **equity principle** reflects distributing a resource across individuals according to merit and in proportion to their input. Equity is assumed to be associated with efficiency and to be dominant in competitive situations where productivity is a primary goal. The **equality principle**, splitting resources equally among group members, is assumed to dominate when the common group goal is enjoyable social relations, since this principle does not emphasize differences between people. The **need principle**, that is helping other people in need or jeopardy, is assumed to dominate when well-being and personal development of individuals are primary common goals. These three fairness principles are in practice often combined in an overall judgement of fairness. For example, when one knows about group members' needs and contributions, one may care for someone in need (i.e. need) and still want to reward someone who made an extra effort (i.e. equity), but when lacking good information about group members' needs and contributions, one may revert to using equality as a heuristic (Messick 1993; Messick and Schell 1992; distributional fairness principles are further discussed in Chapter 29).

21.5 FACTORS PROMOTING COOPERATION

The lion's share of all social dilemma research has been concerned with the crucial question of what motivates people to act more (un)selfishly. Below, we discuss factors that affect the degree of cooperation in social dilemmas (see Box 21.2; for reviews, see Suggestions for Further Reading).

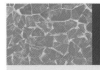

BOX 21.2   FACTORS INFLUENCING COOPERATION IN SOCIAL DILEMMAS

- Group size
- Communication
- Response-efficacy

- Environmental uncertainty
- Social uncertainty
- Social norms

21.5.1   *Group Size*

The degree of cooperation increases when group size decreases (e.g. Brewer and Kramer 1986; Van Lange et al. 1992). It should be kept in mind, though, that an effect of group size was observed when groups of three to five members were compared to groups of around 10 members (Kerr 1983). This result is difficult to generalize to real-life settings where many more persons are involved. The size of a group is, however, linked to other factors that promote cooperative action, such as communication, environmental and social uncertainty, and group identification. It is likely that communication will increase as group size decreases. If people are able to communicate with each other, they will have more opportunities to make strategic and coordinated choices; members in a group can decide how to act in order not to deplete or reduce a common resource, resulting in a decrease in environmental and social uncertainty.

21.5.2   *Communication*

People make fewer defecting choices when they discuss the dilemma in advance than when there is no prior discussion (Dawes et al. 1977). Discussing the dilemma offers information about which option others in the group will choose (defect or cooperate), which establishes a group norm about proper behaviour, thus reducing social uncertainty. Overall, the opportunity of face-to-face communication raises the cooperation rate, on average, by more than 45% (Sally 1995). However, communication is not essential or even necessary to produce cooperative behaviour within a group (Buchan et al. 1999). Consequently, communication is important, but mostly for small collectives.

21.5.3   *Response Efficacy*

Response efficacy reflects the extent to which people feel that their cooperative actions are crucial in order to maintain or create a common resource. Obviously, response efficacy is linked to group size: members in large groups tend to believe that their efforts will be insignificant (Kerr 1989). People are less likely to act for the common good if they feel that a cooperative act will be wasted.

21.5.4   Environmental Uncertainty

The level of cooperation depends on group members' knowledge about the size of the common resource (Messick et al. 1983). Quite often, however, there is no or incomplete environmental information, giving rise to so-called environmental uncertainty (Wit and Wilke 1998). Environmental or resource uncertainty increases subjects' estimation of the size of the resource (the big-pool illusion), resulting in a higher request from the resource (Messick and McClelland 1983).

21.5.5   Social Uncertainty

Social uncertainty reflects the uncertainty about other members' choices in a social dilemma. It has been found that when participants were unaware of how others in a group would act, they were less cooperative (Rapaport et al. 1992). Social uncertainty is reduced, for example, by the principle of equal share (De Vries and Wilke 1992). It seems rather straightforward to apply a principle of equal share in social dilemmas where the size of the resource and the number of 'harvesters' are well-known. However, people often do not know what others do; when there is incomplete information about the resource size, equality principles are difficult to implement (e.g. how much water to consume during a spell of drought).

21.5.6   Norms in Large-Scale Dilemmas

In social dilemmas, the conflict between selfish and cooperative behaviour is sometimes difficult to spot, because of few communication possibilities and high anonymity. When this is the case, a guideline for appropriate behaviour may be how others in the social group behave or think one ought to behave. In such situations, **social norms** could guide behaviour; with no clear information about how to act, people may simply do what other people do or regard as appropriate. A social norm is defined as an expectation held by an individual about how he or she should or ought to act in a particular social situation (Schwartz 1977; see also Chapters 18 and 22). Social norms and internalized personal norms limit egoistic behaviour in favour of collective behaviour, such as different pro-environmental activities (see Biel and Thøgersen 2007, for a review). Furthermore, Kerr (1995) suggested norms that regulate and coordinate social interactions, such as commitment, reciprocity, and equity, increase cooperation in social dilemmas. Yet, it is unclear which types of norms are most significant when choosing to cooperate or to defect in large-scale social dilemmas.

21.6   SUMMARY

Managing scarce resources is a major challenge in most societies. Social dilemmas differ as to what kind of decision individuals or groups need to make; whether they should restrict the use of (resource dilemma) or contribute to a common good (public good dilemma). We reviewed the most important factors explaining why individuals choose to act selfishly or to cooperate in social dilemmas. Greed, efficiency, and fairness are three basic motives that promote either cooperation or defection. Furthermore, communication, group size, and uncertainty are well established factors that influence behaviour in social dilemmas. However, when people act in large-scale social dilemmas, acting under large anonymity and uncertainty, norms guide people's behaviours in favour of the collective, given that members in the group are aware of the norms and approve of them as guidance for managing the commons.

GLOSSARY

cooperation   Acting in the collective interest.

defection   Acting in the individual interest.

efficiency   A motive in social dilemmas reflecting the aim to maximize total collective outcomes.

environmental uncertainty   The state of being uncertain about the size of the common resource.

equality principle   The principle of distributing resources in a social dilemma equally among group members.

equity principle   The principle of distributing resources in a social dilemma to individuals according to merit and in proportion to their input.

fairness   A motive in social dilemmas reflecting the aim to distribute resources according to a particular distribution principle (i.e. equity, equality, or need).

greed   A motive in social dilemmas reflecting the aim to maximize one's self-interest.

large-scale dilemmas   Situations where large groups of people act under conditions of high anonymity, low degree of communication, low collective unity, and high geographical separation.

need principle   The principle of distributing resources in a social dilemma to help other people in need or jeopardy.

public good dilemma   A specific class of social dilemma in which the people need to contribute to create or maintain a common resource.

resource dilemma   A specific class of social dilemma in which people have to share a common resource.

response efficacy   The extent that people feel that their cooperative actions are crucial in order to maintain or create a common resource.

social dilemmas   Situations in which short-term personal gain is at odds with the long-term good of the collective.

social norms   What is commonly done or (dis)approved.

social uncertainty   The state of being uncertain about other members' choices in a social dilemma.

SUGGESTIONS FOR FURTHER READING

Komorita, S.S. and Parks, C.D. (1996). *Social Dilemmas*. Boulder, CO: Westview Press.

Van Lange, P.A.M., Balliet, D.P., Parks, C.D., and Van Vugt, M. (2014). *Understanding Social Dilemmas*. New York, NY: Oxford University Press.

Van Lange, P.A.M., Joireman, J., Parks, C.D., and Van Dijk, E. (2013). The psychology of social dilemmas: a review. *Organizational Behavior and Human Decision Processes* 120: 125–141.

REVIEW QUESTIONS

1. What are the defining characteristics of a social dilemma? Briefly explain each of them.
2. Communication has been shown to have a positive effect on levels of cooperation in social dilemmas. Explain why that is so.
3. Describe how the three distributional fairness principles – equity, equality, and need – are linked to different collective goals and underlying values, and the type of situation in which a resource is distributed.

22 Theories to Explain Environmental Behaviour

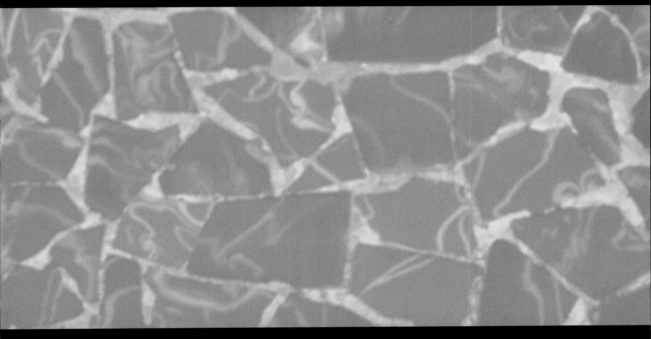

Linda Steg
University of Groningen, The Netherlands

Annika Nordlund
Umeå University, Sweden

CHAPTER OUTLINE

22.1   INTRODUCTION

In this chapter, we discuss theories to explain environmental behaviour. We focus on theories that typically assume that people make reasoned choices; theories on habitual behaviour are discussed in Chapter 24. We first discuss the theory of planned behaviour (TPB) that focuses on the role of individual costs and benefits. Subsequently, we discuss the protection motivation theory (PMT) that assumes people consider individual and collective costs and benefits of behaviour. Next, we explain two theories that focus on morality: the norm activation model (NAM) and the value-belief-norm (VBN) theory of environmentalism. Finally, we discuss goal-framing theory, which provides an integrated framework for understanding factors influencing environmental behaviour.

22.2   THEORY OF PLANNED BEHAVIOUR

The **theory of planned behaviour** (TPB; Ajzen 1985; Figure 22.1) assumes that behaviour results from the **intention** to engage in specific behaviour (i.e. whether people plan to do so). The stronger your intention, the more likely it is that you engage in the behaviour. The intention depends on **attitudes** towards the behaviour, **subjective norms** related to the behaviour, and **perceived behavioural control**.

Attitudes reflect the extent to which engaging in a behaviour is evaluated positively or negatively. Attitudes are based on beliefs about the likely costs and benefits of behaviour, weighted with the perceived importance of these costs and benefits. For example, a person may believe that the car is fast, comfortable, reliable, and enjoyable, and consider these aspects as highly important. Furthermore, this person may think the car is expensive and not environmentally friendly, and consider these aspects as less important. This will result in an overall positive attitude towards car use, as the weighted benefits are higher than the weighted costs.

Subjective norms reflect the extent to which a person believes that important others would approve or disapprove of the behaviour (similar to injunctive norms; see Chapter 18), reflecting social costs and benefits of behaviour. Subjective norms are based on beliefs about the expectations of relevant reference groups concerning the behaviour, weighted by one's motivation to comply with these expectations. For instance, your classmates and friends may expect you to cycle to university and you may be strongly motivated to comply with

Environmental Psychology: An Introduction, Second Edition. Edited by Linda Steg and Judith I. M. de Groot.
© 2019 John Wiley & Sons Ltd. Published 2019 by John Wiley & Sons Ltd.

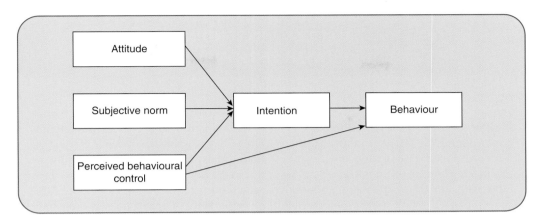

Figure 22.1 *A schematic representation of the TPB.*

their expectation, while your neighbour, whose opinion you value less, may approve of you driving to work. In this case, you will experience a stronger subjective norm in favour of cycling than of driving.

Perceived behavioural control refers to the perceived ability to perform the behaviour, which depends on beliefs about the presence of factors that may facilitate or hinder that behaviour. For example, you may believe that you are not fit enough to cycle to work, resulting in a low perceived behavioural control to cycle. Perceived behavioural control can influence behaviour via intention, as explained in the examples above, but may also influence behaviour directly. For example, when you intend to take the bus to work, and learn that the bus drivers are on strike, perceived behavioural control will directly affect your behaviour.

The TPB assumes that all other factors, such as socio-demographics and values, influence behaviour indirectly, via attitudes, subjective norms, and perceived behavioural control. For instance, strong **biospheric values** (see Chapter 17) may result in positive attitudes towards cycling and a negative attitude towards driving, as people with strong biospheric values will particularly consider the environmental impact of behaviour. Also, due to poor public transport services, people living in the countryside may have a lower perceived behavioural control to take the bus than urbanites.

The TPB has been successful in explaining various types of environmental behaviour, including the intention to use transport forms other than the car, the use of unbleached paper, reductions in meat consumption, and the use of energy-saving light bulbs (Bamberg and Schmidt 2003; Harland et al. 1999). Particularly attitudes and perceived behavioural control appeared to predict these behaviours. The predictive power of the TPB increases when other motivational predictors are included in the model. For example, **personal norms**, reflecting feelings of moral obligation to engage in pro-environmental actions, predicted different pro-environmental intentions and behaviours over and above the TPB variables (Bamberg and Schmidt 2003; see Box 22.1). Personal norms are a key factor in two prominent theories in environmental psychology that we will discuss later: the NAM and the VBN theory of environmentalism.

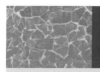

BOX 22.1   EXTENDING THE TPB WITH PERSONAL NORMS

Harland et al. (1999) asked respondents to indicate how often they used unbleached paper during the last six months. Furthermore, respondents indicated (i) how they evaluated the use of unbleached paper (attitudes), (ii) to what extent important others expect them to use unbleached paper (subjective norms), (iii) whether they could in most instances use unbleached paper when they wanted to do so (perceived behaviour control), and (iv) to what extent they felt personally obliged to use unbleached paper (personal norms). The TPB variables explained 28% of the variance in the behaviour: positive attitudes towards using unbleached paper and a higher perceived behavioural control resulted in a higher use of unbleached paper. Subjective norms did not significantly contribute to this regression model. When adding personal norms to this regression model, 34% of the variance in behaviour was explained. Personal norms appeared to be the strongest predictor: participants used unbleached paper more often when they felt morally obliged to do so. Attitudes and perceived behavioural control were still significant predictors as well. Similar results were found for other types of pro-environmental intentions and behaviour included in this study.

22.3   PROTECTION MOTIVATION THEORY

The **protection motivation theory** (PMT; Rogers 1983) assumes that people consider costs and benefits of pro-environmental and environmentally harmful behaviour when making choices. PMT proposes that people are more likely to act pro-environmentally when both **threat appraisal** and **coping appraisal** are high (Rogers 1983). Threat appraisal involves evaluating the perceived benefits of environmentally harmful actions, the perceived severity of risks caused by such actions, and one's perceived vulnerability to these risks. Coping appraisal reflects the extent to which people think they can engage in pro-environmental actions that will reduce the threat, which is based on perceived self-efficacy (similar to perceived behavioural control in the TPB), perceived outcome efficacy (the extent to which people think their pro-environmental actions will reduce environmental problems), and the perceived costs of pro-environmental behaviour (Bockarjova and Steg 2014; see Figure 22.2).

The PMT was successful in explaining the adoption of electric vehicles (Bockarjova and Steg 2014). Adoption of electric vehicles is more likely the more people perceive problems caused by conventional fossil fuel vehicles as severe, the more they feel vulnerable to these problems, and the less favourably they evaluate the advantages of fossil fuel cars (reflecting high threat

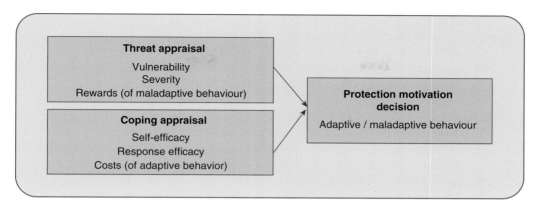

Figure 22.2 *Protection-motivation theory.*

appraisal). Moreover, the more people think electric vehicles can solve the problems caused by conventional vehicles, the more they feel capable of driving an electric vehicle, and the less negatively they evaluate the disadvantages of electric vehicles to be (reflecting high coping appraisal), the more likely they are to adopt an electric vehicle.

22.4   THE NORM ACTIVATION MODEL

Many pro-environmental actions involve higher costs and effort for individuals. In such cases, people will be more likely to act pro-environmentally when they feel it is the moral or right thing to do. The **norm activation model** (NAM; Schwartz 1977; Schwartz and Howard 1981) proposes that pro-environmental actions follow from the activation of personal norms, reflecting feelings of moral obligation to perform or refrain from actions. Personal norms are activated by four factors: **problem awareness** (or awareness of need), **ascription of responsibility**, **outcome efficacy**, and **self-efficacy**. Notably, personal norms are stronger when people are aware of the environmental problems caused by their behaviour, and when they feel personally responsible for these problems and do not attribute these problems to the actions of others, industry, or the government. Moreover, personal norms are stronger when people believe that their actions will help to reduce the relevant problems (outcome efficacy). Yet, many environmental problems, such as global climate change, will only be solved when many people cooperate. Hence, outcome efficacy depends on the extent to which people expect that others will engage in pro-environmental actions too. Finally, personal norms are stronger when people feel able to engage in the actions needed to reduce environmental problems (self-efficacy); this is comparable to perceived behavioural control in the TPB.

The NAM has been successful in explaining various types of pro-environmental intentions and behaviours, such as car use (Eriksson et al. 2006) and general pro-environmental behaviour (Nordlund and Garvill 2002). However, many studies did not include self-efficacy and either included ascription of responsibility or outcome efficacy. The main constructs of the NAM have been conceptualized on a general level (such as general awareness of environmental problems, e.g. Stern et al. 1999), as well as on a behaviour-specific level (such as awareness of problems caused by car use, e.g. Nordlund and Garvill 2003). Behaviour-specific variables are generally more strongly related to intentions and behaviours than are general beliefs (Ajzen 1985).

Experimental studies have shown that the NAM variables are causally related. Notably, people first need to be aware of the problems caused by their behaviour before they consider their own responsibility for these problems, and before considering whether they can help to reduce these problems (see Box 22.2). This makes sense theoretically, because it is not likely that people will think about whether they can engage in actions to reduce environmental problems when they are not aware of adverse environmental consequences caused by their behaviour.

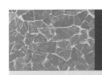

BOX 22.2   TESTING CAUSAL RELATIONSHIPS IN THE NAM

In an experimental study, problem awareness was manipulated by presenting half of the respondents with a text in which the problems of particulate matters were stressed, whereas the other respondents read a text in which these problems were trivialized (Steg and De Groot 2010). After establishing that the manipulation was successful, the researchers examined to what extent this manipulation influenced feelings of responsibility to take action to reduce emissions of particulate matters (e.g. I believe that I am co-responsible for the reduction of particulate matters in the city), personal norms towards doing so (e.g. I feel morally obliged to demonstrate against particulate matters), and intention to participate in such actions (e.g. to what extent are you prepared to collect signatures to reduce the emissions of particulate matters). As expected, higher problem awareness resulted in stronger ascription of responsibility, personal norms, and intention to participate in actions to reduce the emission of particulate matters. As this was an experimental study, in which problem awareness was manipulated while all other variables were kept constant, we can conclude that problem awareness influences responsibility feelings, personal norms, and pro-environmental intentions.

22.5   THE VALUE-BELIEF-NORM THEORY OF ENVIRONMENTALISM

The **value-belief-norm theory of environmentalism** (VBN theory; Stern 2000) is an extension of the NAM. The VBN theory proposes that problem awareness depends on **values** (i.e. general goals that serve as guiding principles in your life; see Chapter 17) and **ecological worldviews** (i.e. beliefs on relationships between humans and the environment; see Chapter 17). The VBN theory proposes that egoistic values are negatively related, and altruistic and biospheric values are positively related to ecological worldviews. In turn, ecological worldviews predict problem awareness, which next influences one's beliefs on whether one can act to reduce the environmental threat, personal norms, and subsequently behaviour (see Figure 22.3). Each variable in the causal chain is assumed to be related to the next variable, but may also be directly related to variables further down the chain, although these relationships are likely to be weaker. Personal norms may influence all kinds of behaviours taken with pro-environmental intent, including environmental activism (e.g. active involvement in environmental organizations or demonstrations), non-activist behaviours in the public sphere (e.g. acceptability of environmental policies), private-sphere environmentalism (e.g. the purchase, use, and disposal of products with environmental impact) and organizational actions (e.g. designing environmentally benign products; see Figure 22.3).

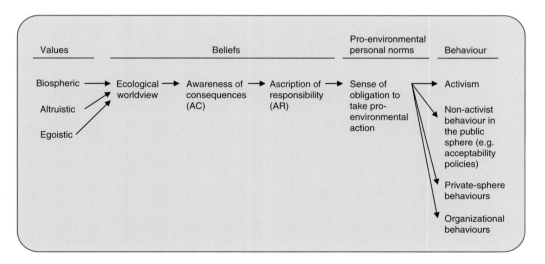

Figure 22.3 *A schematic representation of the VBN theory of environmentalism.*
Source: Adapted from Stern (2000).

The VBN theory appeared to be successful in explaining behaviour (e.g. Eriksson et al. 2006; Stern et al. 1999). Also, support was found for the causal structure proposed in the VBN theory in different cultures: all variables were significantly related to the next variable in the causal chain, and in most cases, the explanatory power of the model hardly increased when predictor variables further up the causal chain were entered into the regression model as well (Jakovcevic and Steg 2013; Steg et al. 2005). Yet, biospheric values were also significantly related to feelings of moral obligation when intermediate variables were controlled for, suggesting that biospheric values can directly activate personal norms.

Studies revealed that the NAM and VBN theory are particularly successful in explaining low-cost pro-environmental behaviours and 'good intentions' such as willingness to change behaviour, political behaviour, and policy acceptability (as explained above), but have less explanatory power in situations characterized by high behavioural costs, such as reducing energy use (e.g. Abrahamse and Steg 2009). The TPB can be more powerful in explaining high-cost environmental behaviour (Bamberg and Schmidt 2003), probably because the TPB includes a wider range of non-environmental motivations. It is not clear yet which theoretical model is most useful in which situation because systematic research on the range of application of each theory is lacking.

When acting pro-environmentally is costly, people can be tempted to reduce feelings of moral obligation via self-serving denial (Lindenberg and Steg 2007). They can do so by denying the seriousness of environmental problems, rejecting their liability for these problems, or identifying others such as industry as responsible for environmental problems. Also, they can indicate that individual actions are not effective in reducing environmental problems, or that they are not able to perform the necessary actions.

22.6   GOAL-FRAMING THEORY

Goal-framing theory (Lindenberg and Steg 2007; see Chapter 15) proposes that three general goals govern or 'frame' the way people process information and act upon it: the **hedonic goal** 'to feel better right now', the **gain goal** 'to guard and improve one's resources', and the **normative goal** 'to act appropriately'. The strength of different goals influences what people think of at the moment, what information they are sensitive to, what alternatives they perceive, and how they will act. According to goal-framing theory, one goal is focal (i.e. the **goal-frame**) and influences information processing the most, while other goals are in the background and increase or decrease the strength of the focal goal. Normative goals provide the most stable basis for pro-environmental actions, as acting pro-environmentally is the appropriate way to act. If people act pro-environmentally based on gain or hedonic goals, they will only do so as long as doing so is profitable and comfortable.

The a priori strength of goals depends on the values people endorse (Steg et al. 2014a): hedonic goals are likely to be stronger among people who strongly endorse hedonic values, strong egoistic values increase the strength of gain goals, while strong altruistic and biospheric values will strengthen normative goals. Indeed, people with strong hedonic values were more likely to consider hedonic aspects of choices, while people who strongly endorse biospheric values were more likely to consider the environmental consequences of their choices (Steg et al. 2014b). Besides, situational factors can affect the strength of goals (Steg et al. 2014a). For example, signs of norm-violating behaviour of others convey that others do not respect norms (see Chapter 18) and may weaken the normative goal, while situational factors that signal that others respect norms can strengthen the normative goal. Furthermore, normative goals may be weaker in situations where pro-environmental actions are very costly, making people focus on costs, and strengthening gain goals.

The three goal-frames coincide with the three theoretical frameworks commonly used in environmental psychology: theories and models on affect (see Chapter 19) focus on hedonic goals, the TPB focuses on gain goals, the NAM and VBN theory focus on normative goals, while PMT focuses on gain and normative goals. As such, goal-framing theory offers an integrative framework for understanding environmental behaviour.

22.7 SUMMARY

We discussed prominent theories explaining environmental behaviour. The TPB assumes that behaviour results from the intention to engage in specific behaviour. Pro-environmental intentions and behaviours are more likely when people have a positive attitude towards the relevant behaviour, when subjective norms support this behaviour, and when one feels in control over the behaviour. The PMT describes how threat and coping appraisal relate to cost and benefit considerations for environmentally related behavioural choices. The NAM and the VBN theory of environmentalism focus on the relation between morality and environmental behaviour. The NAM proposes that pro-environmental actions follow from the activation of personal norms, reflecting feelings of moral obligation to perform or refrain from specific actions. Personal norms are activated when people are aware of environmental problems caused by their behaviour, feel personally responsible for these problems, have the feeling that their actions help to reduce the relevant problems, and feel able to engage in relevant pro-environmental actions. The VBN theory extends the NAM and assumes that problem awareness depends on ecological worldviews and value orientations. Goal-framing theory provides an integrated framework for understanding factors influencing environmental behaviour, and assumes that multiple goals – notably hedonic goals, gain goals, and normative goals – are active at any given time.

GLOSSARY

ascription of responsibility   Feelings of responsibility for negative consequences of not acting pro-environmentally.

attitudes   Mental dispositions to evaluate an attitude object (i.e. a person, place, thing, or event) with some degree of favour or disfavour.

biospheric values   A value type reflecting concern with the quality of nature and the environment for its own sake.

coping appraisal   Evaluation of the likelihood that one's action will reduce a threat, which depends on perceived self-efficacy, perceived outcome efficacy, and perceived costs of pro-environmental actions.

ecological worldviews   Beliefs regarding humanity's ability to upset the balance of nature, the existence of limits to growth, and rejecting humanity's right to rule over the rest of nature.

gain goal   The goal to maintain and improve one's resources.

goal-frame   The focal goal in a particular situation.

goal-framing theory   Integrated framework for understanding factors influencing environmental behaviour, with an emphasis on the relative strength of hedonic, gain, and normative goals.

hedonic goal   The goal to feel good right now.

intention   A person's specific purpose to engage in a particular action.

norm activation model   A model proposing that pro-environmental action follows from the activation of personal norms.

normative goal   The goal to behave appropriately, conforming to social norms and legitimate rules.

outcome efficacy   The extent to which a person thinks one's actions will be effective in reducing environmental problems.

perceived behavioural control   The perceived abiltiy to perform behaviour in light of present facilitating or hindering factors.

personal norm   Feelings of moral obligation to perform or refrain from specific actions.

problem awareness   The extent to which one is aware of the adverse consequences of not acting pro-environmentally.

protection motivation theory   A theoretical framework focusing on how costs and benefits of pro-environmental and environmentally harmful behaviour are considered when making choices.

self-efficacy   The extent to which one recognizes one's own ability to provide relief to environmental threats.

subjective norm   Perceived social pressure to engage in behaviour.

theory of planned behaviour   A model assuming that individuals make reasoned choices and that behaviour results from the intention to engage in specific behaviour.

threat appraisal   Evaluation of the degree of a threat, which depends on the evaluation of the severity of and vulnerability to environmental problems, and the perceived benefits of behaviour that causes these problems.

value-belief-norm theory of environmentalism   An extension of the NAM, proposing that problem awareness depends on ecological worldviews and value orientations.

values   Desirable trans-situational goals varying in importance, which serve as a guiding principle in the life of a person or other social entity.

SUGGESTIONS FOR FURTHER READING

Bamberg, S. and Möser, G. (2007). Twenty years after Hines, Hungerford, and Tomera: a new meta-analysis of psycho-social determinants of pro-environmental behaviour. *Journal of Environmental Psychology* 27: 14–25.

Steg, L. and Vlek, C. (2009). Encouraging pro-environmental behaviour: an integrative review and research agenda. *Journal of Environmental Psychology* 29: 309–317.

Vining, J. and Ebreo, A. (2002). Emerging theoretical and methodological perspectives on conservation behaviour. In: *Handbook of Environmental Psychology* (ed. R.B. Bechtel and A. Churchman), 551–558. New York, NY: Wiley.

REVIEW QUESTIONS

1. Describe the TPB.
2. Describe the protection-motivation theory.
3. What is the main difference between the NAM and the VBN theory of environmentalism?
4. Which four factors influence the strength of personal norms?
5. Which goals steer behaviour according to goal-framing theory?

Environmental Issues, Attitudes, and Behaviours

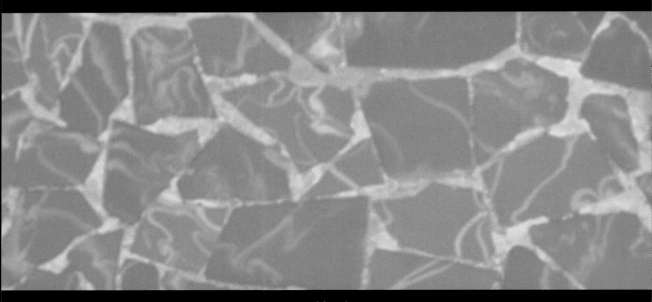

Lise Jans
University of Groningen, The Netherlands

Kelly Fielding
University of Queensland, Australia

CHAPTER OUTLINE

23.1   INTRODUCTION

Who do you think are more concerned with the environment: students today or students in 1960? Questions such as this do not just assess knowledge about whether environmental concern has changed over time. Questions that ask us to compare ourselves to other groups – in this case previous generations – make salient specific group identities that can influence our environmental attitudes and behaviours (Ferguson et al. 2011). In this chapter we address the important role of group processes in the context of environmental issues, attitudes, and actions. We will discuss why environmental attitudes and behaviours are not solely the product of individual attributes but are also affected by group memberships and the group processes associated with these memberships.

23.2   WHY SHOULD ENVIRONMENTAL PSYCHOLOGISTS BE INTERESTED IN GROUP PROCESSES?

There are at least four reasons why it is important for environmental psychologists to understand how group memberships and associated group processes are related to environmental issues, attitudes, and behaviours.

First, environmental issues can accentuate differences between groups and this can lead to conflict. Conflicts can arise between groups (e.g. between citizens and businesses,) because they differ in their environmental attitudes and behaviours. For example, some groups may support whereas others may oppose plans to build new energy infrastructure. Second, group memberships can influence individuals' environmental attitudes and behaviours because group members are guided by their group's environmental norms (see Fielding and Hornsey 2016, for a review). Third, many environmental problems reflect social dilemmas, in which groups play a key role. Social dilemmas require individuals to cooperate as a group, and for groups, such as different nations, to cooperate to prevent pollution and depletion of collective resources (see Chapter 21). Finally, environmental issues can strengthen existing group memberships and provide the impetus for new groups to form. For example, people may form or join groups to foster pro-environmental behaviour within their community (Sloot et al. 2017a) or to oppose a development that is harmful for the environment. These new group memberships will then guide their environmental attitudes and behaviours.

In the following sections, we outline the social identity approach (Tajfel and Turner 1979; Turner et al. 1987) which provides a theoretical lens to understand (i) why conflicts between groups can emerge in the context of environmental issues, (ii) why group memberships influence individuals' environmental attitudes and behaviours, (iii) why group membership can foster cooperation to advance the interests of the group in relation to environmental issues, and (iv) how environmental issues can foster greater group identification with existing groups or generate new group memberships. In doing so, we provide evidence for the important role of group membership and associated group processes in environmental attitudes and behaviours, and illustrate how environmental psychologists can use these insights to encourage pro-environmental attitudes and behaviours.

23.3   HOW THE SOCIAL IDENTITY APPROACH EXPLAINS ENVIRONMENTAL CONFLICT

The social identity approach is an account of how group memberships influence individuals' attitudes and behaviours. It incorporates two interrelated theories – social identity theory (SIT) and self-categorization theory (SCT). Social identity theory (SIT; Tajfel and Turner 1979) proposes that individuals derive part of their self-concept – their **social identity** – from their knowledge of, and emotional attachment to group(s). For example, an individual's self-concept may be made up, in part, of the social identities of being a woman, a student, and a vegetarian. According to SIT, these social identities are defined and evaluated through comparisons with other relevant groups (i.e. intergroup comparisons) made salient by the particular social context. People are motivated to see themselves positively, which is more likely when they see the group they are a member of as positively distinct from relevant outgroups (e.g. vegetarians versus meat lovers).

According to SIT, this desire to positively differentiate one's own group from other relevant groups can, under certain contextual conditions (e.g. unstable status differences between groups that are seen as illegitimate), motivate behaviour in which group members favour their ingroup over the outgroup (**intergroup behaviour**), and this can potentially result in conflicts between these groups. Examples include conflict that arises between different groups over environmental and natural resource management (Colvin et al. 2015a), such as between environmental groups and farmers over species protection laws that could affect farmers' property rights. In these types of situations group members seek to positively distinguish their group from other groups through stereotyping themselves in ways favouring their own group (e.g. 'We are the defenders of the environment') and denigrating and morally excluding out-group members from the scope of justice ('They are the destroyers'; Opotow and Weiss 2000). In this way, the differences between groups become entrenched and the negative relations between the groups can undermine the enactment of conservation laws. In the context of environmental issues, though, some level of intergroup conflict is probably inevitable and may even be productive, such as when groups take action to protect the environment in the face of opposition groups whose actions may be environmentally destructive (Colvin et al. 2015b).

23.4   WHY SOCIAL IDENTITY GUIDES ENVIRONMENTAL ATTITUDES AND BEHAVIOURS

While SIT was originally developed as a theory to explain intergroup conflict, the relevance of the social identity approach is not limited to understanding conflicts associated with environmental issues. The second theoretical perspective incorporated into the social identity approach is self-categorisation theory (SCT; Turner et al. 1987) which is an extension of SIT. SCT proposes that individuals can either define themselves in terms of personal identity or in terms of social identity. When personal identity becomes salient, individuals distinguish themselves from others on the basis of distinctive attributes; behaviour is driven by individual motives, and social identities become less salient. In contrast, when a social identity becomes salient, group members are defined by their shared group membership and they behave in line with internalized group norms and motives. Hence, individuals' self-perceptions become 'depersonalized' and personal identity is pushed to the background and thus becomes less salient. This process of **depersonalization** is what, according to SCT, promotes group behaviour, group influence, and cooperation.

The relevance of SCT for environmental psychology lies in the proposal that when a particular group membership is salient, environmental attitudes, and behaviours are not guided by personal identity and associated individual motives (see Chapter 20) but instead by social identity motives, leading to the following propositions: (i) group norms influence group members' environmental attitudes and behaviour, and the content of the group's norms depend – at least in part – on which group you are comparing your group with (i.e. the particular intergroup context), (ii) people we see as belonging to our group will more strongly influence our environmental attitudes and behaviours than people who do not belong to our group, and (iii) the more salient a particular group membership is, i.e. the more a particular group membership is self-defining, the more influential this group membership is on group members' environmental attitudes and behaviours.

23.4.1 Group Norms Guide Environmental Attitudes and Behaviours

Whether or not a specific group membership is associated with more or less pro-environmental attitudes and behaviours depends on the content of social identity (**social identity content**) as expressed through group norms. Chapter 18 has already discussed the influence of social norms. **Group norms** are social norms associated with a particular group identity. When a particular group membership is salient, group members internalize the norms of the group, which then guide their environmental attitudes and behaviours. The social identity approach suggests that identity content is fluid, and can change depending on the particular outgroup with which group members are comparing their group.

Evidence for the influence of group norms on environmental attitudes comes from studies of the relationship between political identity (a particular type of social identity) and climate change beliefs: Americans who identify as Republican and conservative (social identities that have group norms that do not endorse anthropogenic climate change) tend to be more sceptical about climate change and less supportive of taking action to mitigate climate change than Americans who identify as Democrat and liberal (social identities that have group norms that endorse anthropogenic climate change) (Hornsey et al. 2016). An experimental study showed that when political identity is made salient, people's environmental attitudes align with the norms associated with their political identity (Unsworth and Fielding 2014; see Box 23.1 and Figure 23.1).

BOX 23.1   POLITICAL IDENTITY AND CLIMATE CHANGE

In an experimental study by Unsworth and Fielding (2014), the salience of Australian students' political identity was primed through describing the study as a comparison of left- and right-aligned political parties and getting participants to generate characteristics of people who support left- and right-aligned parties. When the political identity of right-aligned participants was made salient (i.e. primed), they judged the percentage of human contribution to climate change as less than when their political identity was not primed (see Figure 23.1). A follow-up experiment also showed that when right-aligned political identity was made salient, these participants thought the government was doing too much to address climate change, compared to when their identity was not primed. These findings suggest that right-aligned people are more likely to express attitudes that align with their political identity when this social identity is salient, than when it is not. Interestingly in left-aligned participants, the priming of political identity did not influence beliefs and attitudes, potentially because the prevailing political context already satisfied their need for group distinctiveness.

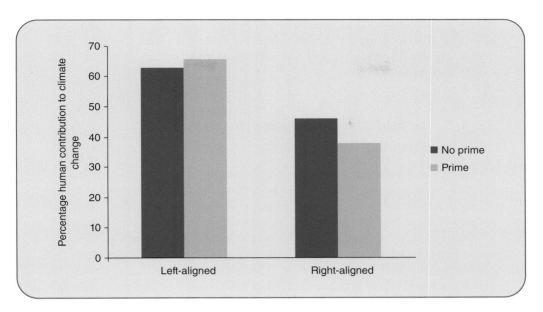

Figure 23.1 *Interaction between political identity salience manipulation and political orientation on perceptions of human contribution to climate change.*

The content of a social identity can change depending on the comparison group. For example, a study revealed that British participants (the ingroup) who compared themselves to Americans (i.e. a stereotypically less pro-environmental outgroup) judged their group to be more pro-environmental than Americans and this shift in norms was accompanied by a shift in biospheric values and pro-environmental behavioural intentions. In contrast, British participants judged their ingroup as less pro-environmental, and shifted their values and behavioural intentions accordingly, when the comparison group was Swedish (i.e. the stereotypically more pro-environmental outgroup; Rabinovich et al. 2012). This research highlights that whether group membership can foster or hamper pro-environmental attitudes and behaviours depends on the specific identity content that is elicited through group comparisons.

23.4.2   *Group Members Influence Environmental Attitudes and Behaviours*

Another key outcome of thinking of oneself in terms of a particular social identity is that people are more likely to be influenced by people they see as belonging to their group. For example, people who identified with a particular region were more likely to support the use of recycled water when a scientist who endorsed the use of recycled water highlighted their shared regional identity than when she did not emphasize her regional identity (Schultz and Fielding 2014). This suggests that environmental attitudes and behaviours are more likely to be changed by someone who is considered an ingroup member.

Another study showed that leaders who advocated for renewable energy and highlighted shared group membership (e.g. using we and us) influenced people's renewable energy intentions more than leaders who did not use such language (Seyranian 2014).

23.4.3   Group Identification Influences Environmental Attitudes and Behaviours

The more salient a particular group membership is, the more it will influence people's environmental attitudes and behaviours. SCT proposes that if a particular group membership is relatively more accessible to a person, this social identity is more likely to be salient in a particular situation (i.e. Oakes et al. 1994). Social identity salience depends on the level of **group identification**, that is, the extent to which an individual evaluates and emotionally experiences the relationship to the group as positive. The higher the identification with the group, the more salient group membership is, and the more likely a person is to act in accordance with the group's norms (Turner 1991). Indeed, research has shown that people who strongly identify with pro-environmental groups are more likely to recycle (White et al. 2009), to engage in sustainable agricultural practices (Fielding et al. 2008), and to reduce carbon emissions (Masson and Fritsche 2014).

23.5   WHY SOCIAL IDENTITY CAN AFFECT COOPERATION ON ENVIRONMENTAL ISSUES

SCT assumes that when a social identity is salient, the self is depersonalized and people do not behave in line with their individual motives, but instead in accordance with the needs, goals, and motives associated with their shared group membership. People are also more likely to cooperate with other group members to advance group interests and concerns when their social identity is salient (Turner et al. 1987). This implies that social identity salience can foster cooperation among group members on environmental issues. Indeed, identification with the local community is related to the willingness to engage in community-based collective climate action (Bamberg et al. 2015b). Furthermore, membership of, and identification with, community energy groups can foster cooperation to advance the sustainable energy goals of the group as a whole (Sloot et al. 2017b). As environmental issues can be seen as social dilemmas, which can only be solved when people act in line with the collective rather than individual interests in mind (see Chapter 21), stressing shared social identity and pro-environmental group norms, may be one way to overcome such social dilemmas.

Although social identity salience can enhance cooperation among group members, it can at the same time make it more difficult for different groups to cooperate on environmental issues. Indeed, strong national identities (a particular type of social identity) may underlie the difficult negotiations between the United Nations to mitigate climate change, as people focus on what is in the interest of their nation, rather than on what is in interest of all nations (Batalha and Reynolds 2012).

23.6   HOW THE SOCIAL IDENTITY APPROACH EXPLAINS ENVIRONMENTAL GROUP FORMATION

The social identity approach addresses the important question of how particular group memberships become salient and how new social identities are formed. SCT proposes that social identity salience depends on both the person and the situation. A particular social identity is more likely to become salient to the extent that between-group differences are larger than differences within the group (**principle of meta-contrast**; Turner et al. 1987). This suggests that an existing identity will increase in salience and people are more likely to form a new shared identity when the social context makes them stand out as a distinctive group. We have discussed how political identity salience influenced climate change attitudes. The principle also explains how debates around climate change have resulted in the formation of new social identities: climate change believers and climate change sceptics defining themselves as opposing groups, with the content of their respective new social identities informing their climate-related actions (Bliuc et al. 2015). Thus, environmental issues can give rise to the emergence of new social identities, when the issues highlight the distinction between different groups.

Interactions between group members can also foster social identity salience, as it allows group members to induce a shared social identity from the contributions of group members (Postmes et al. 2005). For example, research suggests that interaction can increase levels of identification with the group (Jans et al. 2015), and foster consensus on group norms (Smith and Postmes 2009). This can help promote pro-environmental action, as long as the emergent content of the social identity is pro-environmental.

Interactions between group members may be particularly important for the formation of new social identities (Jans et al. 2015; Thomas et al. 2016). For example, interactions among community members may facilitate setting up or getting engaged in community pro-environmental groups and thereby developing a new social identity (Sloot et al. 2017a). Furthermore, interactions between members of different groups can help people to integrate different subgroup identities into a new overarching social identity (Haslam et al. 2003). To illustrate in the context of climate change debates, interactions at different levels may be vital for establishing a superordinate United Nations identity in support of climate change mitigation (Batalha and Reynolds 2012). First, interactions are needed within individual nations to define the most relevant aspects of their national identity in the context of global climate change. Then, interactions are needed between like-minded nations to induce a shared social identity among them. Finally, at the higher-order level of the United Nations, interactions are needed to form an overarching identity that encapsulates the diverse interests and needs of (subgroups of) nations in the context of climate change. This new social identity allows nations to put the United Nation's interest above their nations' interests, and to cooperate with other nations to mitigate climate change.

23.7 SUMMARY

We discussed how and why group membership and associated group processes influence environmental issues, attitudes, and behaviours. We have outlined how a social identity approach can help to understand these influences. When a social identity is salient, people's individual interests are pushed to the background (depersonalization), and people's environmental attitudes and behaviours are guided by the content of that identity, as expressed by group norms – which may support or undermine pro-environmental attitudes and behaviours. Social identity salience may result in conflicts between groups over environmental issues, but can also promote cooperation among group members in the service of the environment. The influence of group membership is particularly strong for people who highly identify with their group. Furthermore, people are more likely to define themselves in terms of a shared group membership when the social context makes them stand out as a distinctive group. Interactions between people can contribute to the experience of shared group membership and may particularly underlie the formation of new groups around environmental issues (either supporting or opposing pro-environmental action). The social identity approach provides new insights into the important role of group processes in the context of environmental issues, which can provide suggestions for strategies to encourage pro-environmental attitudes and behaviours.

GLOSSARY

depersonalization   The shift from thinking of oneself as an individual (i.e. personal identity) to thinking of oneself as a group member (i.e. social identity).

group identification   The positive emotional value placed on the relationship between self and the group.

group norms   Social norms associated with a particular group membership that are internalized by group members and guide their attitudes and behaviours when social identity is salient.

intergroup behaviour   When individuals belonging to one group interact with another group or its members in terms of their group membership.

principle of meta-contrast   Any subset of people is more likely to be 'grouped' the smaller the perceived differences between those people, relative to the perceived differences between those people and others on relevant dimensions of comparison.

social identity   The part of an individual's self-concept that is derived from their knowledge of, and emotional attachment to, group(s).

social identity content   The content of social identity, such as group values and norms, in a particular context and situation.

SUGGESTIONS FOR FURTHER READING

Fielding, K.S. and Hornsey, M.J. (2016). A social identity analysis of climate change and environmental attitudes and behaviors: insights and opportunities. *Frontiers in Psychology* 7: 121.

REVIEW QUESTIONS

1. Why should environmental psychologists be interested in group processes?
2. Briefly describe the social identity approach, i.e. SIT and SCT.
3. What are the consequences of salient group membership for environmental attitudes and behaviours?
4. Give an example of how groups may be formed in the context of environmental issues.

24 Yesterday's Habits Preventing Change for Tomorrow? About the Influence of Automaticity on Environmental Behaviour

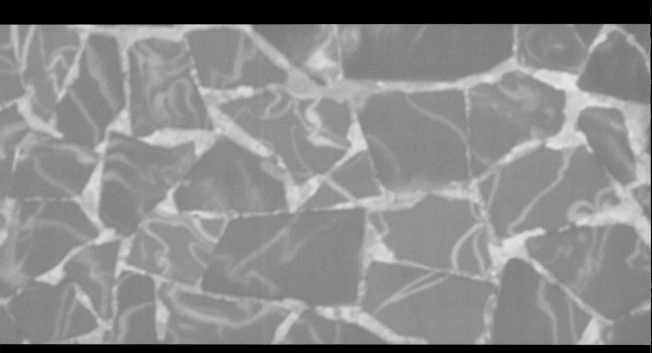

Christian A. Klöckner
Norwegian University of Science and Technology, Norway

Bas Verplanken
University of Bath, UK

CHAPTER OUTLINE

24.1 INTRODUCTION

Imagine you want to buy a new refrigerator. Your decision for one type or the other has an impact on the environment and reading several chapters of this book gives you a good impression of predictors of such a decision (e.g. Chapters 17, 18, and 20, and 22). Now consider your everyday life. Small things like switching off the lights when you leave the room, not leaving your TV on stand-by, and deciding how you want to travel to the university in the morning, have a significant cumulated impact on the environment. Does the same set of predictors apply to such behaviours as to buying a refrigerator? Do you really weigh up all your attitudes, values, norms, etc. every time before you switch the light off? The answer is probably no. Most likely, you will simply automatically repeat behaviour you have shown before. A closer analysis of everyday behaviour shows that many things we do during the day qualify as potentially automatic behaviours (Wood et al. 2002; see Box 24.1). This chapter will introduce habits as an important predictor of such behaviours. **Habits** are defined as cognitive structures that automatically determine future behaviour by linking specific situational **cues** to (chains of) behavioural patterns. We will first discuss the theoretical background of habits and outline how habits influence information processing. We follow with a discussion of different approaches to measure habits and conclude with an overview of intervention strategies to change highly habitual behaviour.

BOX 24.1 HABITS

Wood et al. (2002) asked participants to keep a diary for one or two days and to report what they were doing, thinking, and feeling once every hour they were awake (prompted by a wristwatch signal). Furthermore, they reported the frequency of each behaviour in the past month and if it was usually performed at the same physical location. Between 35% (Study 1) and 53% (Study 2) of all reported behaviours were classified as habits, because they were performed frequently (almost every day) and at the same location every time which indicates a high stability of situational circumstances. Whereas for non-habitual behaviours thoughts and behaviour usually corresponded (the participants thought about what they were doing), while performing habitual behaviours people's thoughts wandered off.

Environmental Psychology: An Introduction, Second Edition. Edited by Linda Steg and Judith I. M. de Groot.
© 2019 John Wiley & Sons Ltd. Published 2019 by John Wiley & Sons Ltd.

24.2   THEORETICAL BACKGROUND: HOW HABITS ARE ACQUIRED

The study presented in Box 24.1 introduces two of the four key features of habitual behaviour: **frequency** and **stability**. Two other features are **success** and **automaticity**. Every time a behavioural pattern is successfully performed in stable situational circumstances – which means the intended **goals** are reached and the behaviour leads to the intended outcomes – the likelihood increases that the behaviour is automatically repeated the next time the situation is encountered. This process described by Triandis (1977) should over time lead to a trade-off between intentional behaviour and habitual behaviour. The first time behaviour is performed, intention is likely to be a strong predictor. The more often the same behaviour is repeated and yields desired outcomes, the stronger becomes the influence of habits, until it is stronger than that of intentions. A reanalysis of 64 studies on various types of behaviour (Ouellette and Wood 1998) demonstrated the predicted effect: behaviour that is performed annually or biannually in unstable contexts is strongly predicted by intentions and only weakly by past behaviour which was used as an indicator of habit, whereas behaviour performed daily or weekly in stable contexts is predicted strongly by past behaviour and the intention–behaviour link is significantly weaker. However, it is important to note that not all behaviours performed successfully, frequently, and in stable contexts are habits. Medical doctors for example often make the same decisions, with success in stable contexts, but they do it – hopefully – not automatically. This is why automaticity is an important fourth characteristic of habits.

In the environmental domain, habits appear to be important predictors of many different behaviours, such as travel mode choice (e.g. Friedrichsmeier et al. 2013; Verplanken et al. 1998), energy use (e.g. Maréchal 2010), and organic food purchase (e.g. Biel et al. 2005). Habits are usually considered as *barriers* against pro-environmental behaviour, which interfere with pro-environmental intentions or norms. A strong habit to use the car for your daily trips for example makes it very difficult to change your behaviour, even if you formed an intention to use the bus more often. Indeed, habits moderate the impact of both intentions and personal norms on environmental behaviour, meaning that both your pro-environmental intentions and your personal norms are less relevant for your behaviour if you have strong habits (Klöckner and Matthies 2004; Verplanken et al. 1998).

How can the strong effect of habits on everyday behaviour be explained theoretically? Repeating behavioural patterns over and over again in stable contexts links behaviour to situational cues. If this linkage becomes strong enough, execution of a behavioural pattern is elicited just by encountering the relevant cues. Processes of deliberate decision-making are bypassed. The cues can be both external (e.g. setup of your bathroom) and internal (e.g. activation of the goal to travel to university). Different approaches have been put forward to explain how situational cues and behavioural patterns are linked, the two most prominent are the **connectionist approach** (e.g. Neal et al. 2006, see Box 24.2) and the **script-based approach** (e.g. Aarts and Dijksterhuis 2000; Verplanken et al. 1994, see Box 24.3). The approaches are not mutually exclusive but propose different perspectives on

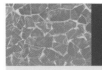

BOX 24.2   THE CONNECTIONIST APPROACH

The connectionist approach of habits assumes that simultaneous activation of neuronal structures, responsible for processing situational cues, and other structures, responsible for performing behaviour, creates a neuronal connection between the two structures. Repeatedly co-activating these structures strengthens this connection over time. The stronger the connection between the structures, the easier and faster an activation of the cue processing structures leads to a co-activation of the behaviour structures. Neal et al. (2006) describe this approach as **direct-context-cuing** which means that via associative learning, a direct connection between the context as a cue and distinct behaviour is established without the need for any other mediating structure.

BOX 24.3   SCRIPT-BASED APPROACH

The script-based approach to habits assumes that the consistent pairing of situational cues and behaviour leads to the development of behavioural **scripts**, which are memory structures storing a blueprint of the relevant behaviour. A script contains the sequence of acts that is usually performed when relevant situational cues are detected, and that has led to successfully obtaining the respective goal before (Verplanken and Aarts 1999). This perspective considers habits as principally goal-directed, which means that a goal is usually initially activated deliberately (e.g. 'I want to take a trip to the university now'); then automaticity – in the form of a script – partly or completely takes over by defining the substeps to reach this goal. Habits are considered to be automatic links between goals and actions (Aarts and Dijksterhuis 2000).

analysing habits. There has been empirical support for the connectionist approach in the domain of travel mode choice (Friedrichsmeier et al. 2013).

24.3   NARROWING DOWN DECISION-MAKING: HOW HABITS AFFECT INFORMATION USE

If we accept that large portions of our everyday behaviour are under control of automatic processes and further consider that this deprives us of control over what we do, we might ask what the benefit of automaticity in behaviour is.

The study described in Box 24.1 already gives a hint: people who perform habitual behaviour are able to think about something else whereas people performing non-habitual behaviour have to focus on what they do. Not needing to think about everything we do enables us to allocate our scarce cognitive resources efficiently. The key features of this dualism of deliberate behaviour and automatic behaviour are outlined in Table 24.1 (Chaiken and Trope 1999). Although the boundary between automatic and deliberate processes is not always clear-cut, generally deliberate decision-making is characterized by high demands for cognitive resources, which makes it almost impossible to go through several deliberate decision-making processes in parallel. Also, a large proportion of the available information is taken into account, which makes strategy highly flexible and sensitive to changes. Consider you need to find your way in a city you have never been to. You will focus on signs, landmarks, your map, or your navigation system and constantly monitor your progress. You will adjust whenever you find new information indicating that you are going the wrong way. However, this will require so much cognitive effort that you will hardly be able to, for example, have a conversation at the same time or listen to an audiobook. In contrast, automatic decision-making is characterized by high speed and a low level of mental resources needed. Parallel processing is possible but relevant information might not be considered. The awareness about the process and its controllability is low. Now consider you are on your way from your home to the university. You know the way and you do not continuously think about where to turn. You can comfortably listen to your audiobook and still find your way. But what happens if there is an unexpected road blockage? It is quite likely that you miss the informing signs and just take the same way as every day, ending up at a dead end.

Table 24.1 *Characteristics of deliberate and automatic decision-making.*

	Deliberate decision-making	Automatic decision-making
Level of mental resources needed	High	Low
Parallel processing	Not possible	Possible
Flexibility	High	Low
Sensitivity for change	High	Low
Efficiency	Low	High
Controllability	High	Low
Awareness	High	Low
Attention needed	High	Low
Decisional involvement	High	Low
Speed	Low	High
Accuracy	High	High if situation is the same Low if situation changed

BOX 24.4 HABITS AND INFORMATION PROCESSING

A series of experiments analysed the impact of strong bike use habits on information acquisition and information use for a simulated trip to a shop in the city centre (Verplanken et al. 1997). Information about certain aspects of the trip (e.g. physical effort, probability of delay) was offered for four different travel modes (walking, bus, train, bicycle), but had to be activated by a mouse-click before it was displayed. Then the participants had to choose one of the travel modes. Participants with a strong habit inspected significantly less information before making a choice. Furthermore, they were more selective in the information they inspected, indicating that some travel alternatives were ruled out early in the decision process. Enhancing decisional involvement by telling participants that they would have to justify their decision to the researcher increased information use. However, this increased information search lasted only for a relatively short period if the participants held strong habits. As Figure 24.1 shows, participants with strong habits initially inspected as many pieces of information as participants with weak habits when they were told that they would be asked for a justification (see 'enhanced attention condition' in Figure 24.1) but returned to a significantly lower level of information use after approximately 20 trials.

Strong habits lead to less interest in information about alternative behaviours (see Box 24.4). Another study demonstrated that participants with strong habits not only inspect fewer pieces of information but also implement fewer pieces of information in the actual decision-making process (Aarts et al. 1997). These two studies show the limiting effect strong habits have on the acquisition and use of information. This effect may have serious implications for people's environmental behaviour in changing situations. Consider a person who is strongly habituated to use the car for their frequent trips. Introducing a new, very comfortable bus lane that could substitute for the car on the trip to their workplace might not affect them at all, because the relevant information about this new bus route will most likely not be perceived or included in their decision-making.

24.4 MEASURING HABITS: A CHALLENGE FOR RESEARCH

As habits are by definition unconscious, the measurement of habits is a challenge, because the validity of people's self-reports is questionable. However, if habits are acquired by repeating the same behaviour over and over again, the frequency of the respective behaviour in the past seems at first glance a valid measure of habit strength. This approach – utilized by, among others, Ouellette and Wood (1998) – is problematic though because it neglects both some of the

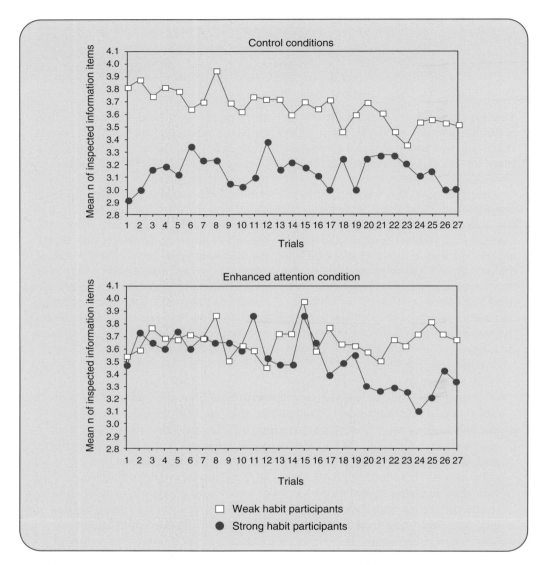

Figure 24.1 *Mean number of inspected information items across 27 trials for the control conditions (top panel), and the enhanced attention condition (in which participants had to justify their decision afterwards; bottom panel). Source: From Verplanken et al. 1997, p. 554 (with permission from the publisher).*

important components of habit development (e.g. the stable situation) and other possible sources of stable behaviour (e.g. stable intentions or situational conditions). Various alternative measures have been proposed. First, a script-based measure, referred to as the response frequency measure (RFM; see Box 24.5), which is linked to the script-based approach (see Box 24.3). Second, a self-report measure of habit that includes theoretically derived key characteristics of habitual behaviour and is consequently referred to as self-report habit index (SRHI; see Box 24.6). Third, the compound measure of habit measures both the frequency of the respective behaviour in the past and the stability of the context as two

BOX 24.5   THE RESPONSE FREQUENCY MEASURE (RFM)

The RFM of habit strength (Verplanken et al. 1994) builds on the assumption that people need to make use of existing scripts to make a decision when they are provided with insufficient information and are put under time pressure. Measuring the consistency of the scripts is treated as a measure of general habit strength. The original version of the measure was developed to measure travel mode habits and confronts participants with a selection of five to 15 imaginary travel goals (e.g. visiting a friend in a nearby city, shopping to buy daily needs, taking a trip to the beach). Only the goal of the trip is described and people are asked to name the first travel mode they associate with each goal as quickly as possible. Habit strength corresponds to the frequency by which a single travel mode (e.g. the car) is named across situations. Habits measured with the RFM reflect general habits because it generalizes over different travel goals and is not specific to one destination or goal.

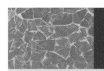

BOX 24.6   SELF-REPORT HABIT INDEX (SRHI)

The SRHI (Verplanken and Orbell 2006) measures if a target behaviour is characterized by basic features of a habit: a history of repetition, lack of control and awareness, efficiency, and expressing one's identity (the latter aspect was added by Verplanken and Orbell and was not included in the original concept discussed so far). This measure has the advantage of not relying on a behavioural measure to assess habit strength. Habit measures based on behaviour often are confounded with other sources of stability and overestimate the relation between habit and future behaviour. Furthermore, the SRHI acknowledges that habit strength might vary independently from behavioural frequency (Verplanken 2006). The standardized items used for accessing habit strength are:

Behaviour X is something…
1. I do frequently.
2. I do automatically.
3. I do without having to consciously remember.
4. that makes me feel weird if I do not do it.
5. I do without thinking.
6. that would require effort not to do it.
7. that belongs to my (daily, weekly monthly) routine.
8. I start doing before I realize I'm doing it.
9. I would find hard not to do.
10. I have no need to think about doing.
11. that's typically 'me'.
12. I have been doing for a long time.

BOX 24.7   THE COMPOUND MEASURE OF HABIT

Wood et al. (2005) proposed a measure of habit strength that combines two main components of establishing a habit (frequency and stability of the context), which is linked to the connectionist approach (see Box 24.2) because it tries to capture the frequent co-activation of cue processing and behaviour triggering structures by measuring both the stability of the behavioural context and the frequency of performance. Frequency is assessed by measuring how often a particular behaviour is performed in a given time period (for example a month). Context stability is assessed by asking participants how much selected features of the context (e.g. location, other peoples' behaviour) varied whenever they performed the behaviour (e.g. very little). These single measures of variation of context features are then averaged. The final habit strength score is computed by multiplying frequency with stability, resulting in the highest scores for frequent behaviour in stable circumstances, medium scores for frequent behaviour in unstable circumstances and infrequent behaviour in stable contexts, and the lowest scores for infrequent behaviour in unstable contexts. This measure is challenging to include in a study because both past behaviour and relevant aspects of context stability have to be captured; no standardized measures of situational stability are available.

compounds of a habit (see Box 24.7). All three measures have been used in environmental psychological research with promising results. Whereas the RFM is restricted to computer-based studies where the aspect of induced time pressure can be controlled, the SRHI and the compound measure of habit are applicable also in questionnaire studies.

24.5   BREAKING BAD HABITS, CREATING GOOD HABITS: INTERVENTIONS CHANGING ROUTINE BEHAVIOUR

Many environmental behaviours can be considered habitual because they are deeply implemented into our everyday routines. Not all habits in the environmental domain are necessarily 'bad habits'. We could for example also have a habit to switch off the light whenever we leave a room. However, if people form pro-environmental intentions, habits are often acting against them and are therefore **counterintentional habits**. Changing habitual behaviour is extremely difficult evidenced because many well-established intervention techniques (see Chapter 26) often fail. Information on the negative impact of behaviour or procedural information on how to perform the positive alternative may not be perceived or processed if the old behaviour is habitualized. Strategies targeting social or personal norms may succeed in changing norms but strong old habits can still interfere with the behaviour, as norms are less influential when a person holds strong habits (Klöckner and Matthies 2004). Thus, an intervention strategy aiming at changing habitual behaviour has to address the issue of deactivating old habits; while new habits are being created, old habit traces still exist, and carry the risk of relapses (Walker et al. 2015). Two main strategies can be identified that have been shown to successfully deactivate old habits: (i) a substantial change of the situational conditions and (ii) encouraging the target group to form implementation intentions.

The first strategy builds on the theoretical background of habits. If habits are a direct and automatic link between situational cues and specific behavioural patterns, a change or removal of relevant cues could result in deactivation of the habit. As habits react rather inflexibly to situational change, the cue alteration has to be substantial enough to be recognized. For example, the introduction of a free one-month travel card for public transportation to deactivate car use habits succeeded in the short run, but people returned to their old behavioural patterns after the intervention (Thøgersen and Møller 2008). This means that habit deactivation is a necessary but not sufficient condition to change habitual behaviour; it has to be combined with other strategies. Indeed, a time-limited free ticket combined with a subsequent written commitment to try public transportation had better effects in the long run than the two strategies alone (Matthies et al. 2006; see also Chapter 26 for a discussion of commitment). Such combinations of strategies have been called **downstream-plus-context-change** interventions (Verplanken and Wood 2006). Fujii and Kitamura (2003) found that a time-limited bus ticket induced more bus use one month after the free-ticket intervention only for participants who strengthened their bus use habit during the intervention. This indicates that a free ticket might be an opportunity to try alternative travel modes. If positive experiences occur in this trial period and behaviour is implemented consistently enough into everyday life, new habits might be established that lead to a sustaining intervention effect.

However, fundamental situational change is difficult to achieve in an intervention setting. Thus, several authors examined the impact of naturally occurring changes in people's lives on habit strength caused by for example moving to another place, taking up a new job, being retired, or becoming a parent. Such life events open a window of opportunity, which may reduce habit strength. Such life events appeared to have a significant impact on changes in travel mode choice and reduced habit strength for a limited period after a life event (Klöckner 2004). Also, a residential relocation deactivated existing car use habits and made people more receptive to interventions that fostered the use of public transportation (Bamberg 2006; Davidov 2007). Indeed, in a large field experiment, it was found that an intervention to promote 25 sustainable behaviours was more effective among residents who had relocated during the previous three months, compared with a matched control group who had not relocated (Verplanken and Roy 2016). A variation of the first strategy to deactivate habits is to prevent the habitual behaviour from being performed. For example, former car drivers who changed to public transportation during an eight-day freeway closure, which made performance of habitual driving behaviour impossible, continued to use public transportation more frequently even after a year (Fujii and Gärling 2003). Also, especially high-frequency car drivers who overestimated travel time by public transport corrected their estimation of travel time during the freeway closure when they had first-hand experiences with public transportation (Fujii et al. 2001), suggesting that time-limited periods of forced behavioural change might pose an opportunity to correct misconceptions and thereby promote sustainable change in behaviour.

Another strategy to deactivate habits is the use of implementation intentions. Whereas **goal intentions** just describe people wanting to achieve a certain goal ('I intend to recycle paper'), **implementation intentions** includes a concrete plan on when and where to perform the intended behaviour ('Next time I have read my newspaper I will put it directly into the recycling bin'; Gollwitzer 1999). By forming an implementation intention, an association between situational cues (reading the newspaper) and the relevant behaviour is formed in a single act of will. This association is then supposed to act automatically once the cues are encountered. Thus, implementation intentions can be conceived of as an antagonist of habits because they act at the same level of automaticity. Implementation intentions appeared to effectively reduce the importance of habit strength for participation in paper recycling in an office setting (Holland et al. 2006).

24.6   SUMMARY

In this chapter, we demonstrated that many types of environmental behaviours are under the control of automatic processes. By successfully repeating the same behavioural patterns, under stable contextual conditions, people establish an automatic link between selected situational cues and performance of behaviour. In such circumstances, deliberate decision-making is less likely and behaviour is less under conscious control. This implies that traditional intervention techniques will most likely fail for such types of behaviour and a combination of habit deactivation either by situational changes or implementation intentions and traditional techniques has to be considered. With the connectionist and the script-based approach, we discussed two theoretical concepts of habit, key features of a habit, and three measures for habit strength in environmental domains.

GLOSSARY

automaticity   Performance of behaviour or cognitive processes without conscious control; a key feature of habit.

connectionist approach   A theoretical perspective that understands habits as a strengthened neuronal connection between neuronal units processing situational cues and units triggering behavioural patterns.

counterintentional habit   A habit that acts against your intentions after intentions have changed.

cue   A distinct situational characteristic that conveys important information or triggers an affective reaction.

direct-context-cuing   A direct connection between the context as a cue and distinct behaviour without mediating structures that is established by associative learning.

downstream-plus-context-change interventions   Intervention techniques designed to change habitual behaviour that combine habit deactivation by changes in the context with traditional intervention techniques such as providing information.

frequency   How often a behaviour is performed in a given time period. High frequency of performance is a key feature of habit.

goal   Mental representation of a desired future state.

goal intention   The will to achieve a goal without a concrete procedural plan of how to achieve it.

habit   Cognitive structure that automatically determines future behaviour by linking specific situational cues to (chains of) behavioural patterns.

implementation intention   A concrete procedural plan on how, when, and where to act to reach an intended goal.

script   Mental representation of a stereotypical sequence of acts associated with a goal that is based on previous experience.

script-based approach   A theoretical perspective that understands habits as behavioural scripts that link triggering cues to stereotypical sequences of behaviour.

stability   The degree of constancy in the context in which a specific behaviour is performed. Stability of the context is a key feature of habit.

success   A state where a goal has been reached by performing a certain behaviour and the outcome is satisfactory. Success of a behaviour is a key feature of habit.

SUGGESTIONS FOR FURTHER READING

Aarts, H. and Custers, R. (2009). Habit, action, and consciousness. In: *Encyclopedia of Consciousness*, vol. 1 (ed. W.P. Banks), 315–328. Oxford: Elsevier.

Dahlstrand, U. and Biel, A. (1997). Pro-environmental habits: propensity levels in behavioural change. *Journal of Applied Social Psychology* 27 (7): 588–601.

Neal, D.T., Wood, W., and Quinn, J.M. (2006). Habits – a repeat performance. *Current Directions in Psychological Science* 15 (4): 198–202.

Verplanken, B. and Aarts, H. (1999). Habit, attitude, and planned behaviour: is habit an empty construct or an interesting case of automaticity? *European Review of Social Psychology* 10: 101–134.

Verplanken, B. and Wood, W. (2006). Interventions to break and create consumer habits. *American Marketing Association* 25 (1): 90–103.

REVIEW QUESTIONS

1. What characterizes habitual behaviour? Find examples for positive and negative environmental behaviours that are most likely habitual.
2. Why is habitual behaviour different from non-habitual behaviour?
3. How can habits be described theoretically?
4. How can habits be measured? What challenges are there in measuring habits?
5. What strategies are there for changing habitual behaviour?

25 Environmental Psychology in Latin America

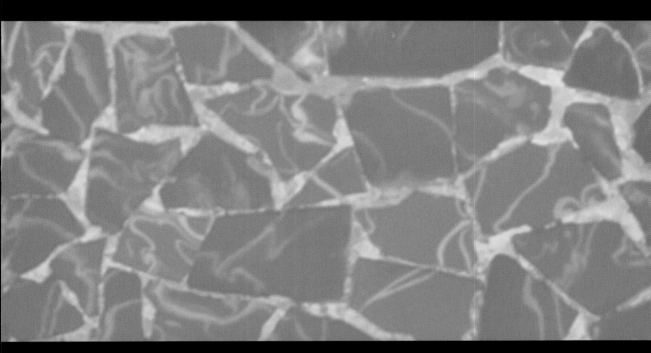

Javier Urbina-Soria
National Autonomous University of Mexico, Mexico

Emilio Moyano-Díaz
Talca University, Chile

CHAPTER OUTLINE

25.1   INTRODUCTION

Environmental psychology has gradually gained relevance in Latin America, as a response to the increased significance of environmental issues and their effects on human behaviour, health, and well-being, and due to social demands for better environmental conditions. Its relevance, however, has not risen uniformly throughout the region. This chapter contains a contextual analysis and literature review to describe the main topics and key characteristics of environmental psychology research in **Latin America**. We aim to provide an overview of these characteristics for future development of environmental psychology within this region.

25.2   LATIN AMERICAN BACKGROUND

The Latin American continental region comprises 20 countries in North, Central, and South America, spanning 20 million square kilometres, with over 600 million inhabitants. Geographically, Latin America extends from Mexico (part of North America) across seven Central American countries and 12 South American countries as well as 20 island nations located in the Caribbean Sea.

Latin American countries have heterogeneous economic growth (low per capita income levels opposed to considerable growth of others), huge inequities ('in 2014 the richest 10% of people in Latin America had amassed 71% of the region's wealth'; Barcena Ibarra and Byanyima, 2016), and low economic development levels (high poverty levels, low education quality, high unemployment, and a shortage and deterioration of housing). However, the levels of happiness and satisfaction of the population are high, especially in Costa Rica and Colombia (Diener 2011).

Latin America has a wide and rich variety of ecosystems (Antarctic zones, deserts, and coastlines) with vast natural resources and the greatest biological diversity on the planet. But there are also two large metropolitan areas with more than 20 million inhabitants: Mexico City and Sao Paulo, and two cities with more than 10 million inhabitants: Rio de Janeiro and Buenos Aires. These densely populated areas result in high migration from the countryside to the cities, and problems such as minimal sanitary services and poor means of communication in small communities.

One of the most important issues is the multi-ethnic and plurilinguistic context (192 languages in Brazil alone, 69 in México, and so on). Subsequently there is a variety of **values** derived from the region's indigenous past and its European background, shaping a hybrid culture that presents strong native features. At the same time, fundamental changes occur due to the process of globalization. Religion, community, and especially family, and a collectivist tradition are still core values for the majority of population, while an increased number of others are moving away from them to a more individualistic way of life. These contradictory values have a powerful influence on psychological processes and environmental behaviour (see also Chapter 17).

The variety of values also results in a variety of ideologies and these in turn generate differences, for example, in environmental beliefs (Moyano-Díaz et al. 2015). Therefore, a first relevant aspect is that, in Latin America, ideological differences should be taken into account when designing studies and programmes in relation to environmental behaviour, for two reasons. First, established psychological constructs of the kind found for the population of Northern or Mediterranean Europe might not be applicable to the Latin American world. Second, it is not easy to translate instruments developed in other languages into Spanish, Portuguese, or any of the hundreds of languages within the Latin-American region. It is, therefore, essential to meet the requirements of **ethno-psychometrics** (Reyes 2010) to strengthen the reliability and validity of instruments employed in measuring commonly used psychological constructs, such as attitudes, norms, and perceptions.

Only a few Latin American psychologists publish in English and most of the work is not indexed, due to language barriers. Many books in the field are published entirely in Spanish (Corral-Verdugo 2010; Granada 2002; Guevara and Mercado 2002; Ortega-Andeane et al. 2005; Urbina-Soria and Martínez 2006), or Portuguese languages (Pinheiro 2003). In addition, most sponsored research for public and private institutions is not disseminated outside those institutions (e.g. Moreno and Urbina-Soria 2008; Urbina-Soria et al. 2010). For these reasons, this chapter integrates an analysis of such research to provide an inclusive view of the research work carried out in the region from its beginnings to recent years.

25.3 PAST REVIEWS ON ENVIRONMENTAL PSYCHOLOGY IN LATIN AMERICA

Although there are other reviews available on the importance of environmental psychology in Latin America – such as environmental psychology in Mexico (Montero y López Lena 1997; Urbina-Soria and Ortega-Andeane 1991), and environmental psychology in Brazil (Pinheiro 2003) – there are only two reviews that deal with environmental psychology in Latin America as a whole.

Thirty years ago, the first description of environmental psychology from a Latin American perspective came to light (Sánchez et al. 1987). Ten years later, the very first review of studies in Latin America came out. It was a review included as a special issue of *Environment and Behavior*, under the title 'Environmental psychology in Latin America: Efforts in critical situations' (Corral-Verdugo 1997). Some of the topics included post-occupancy evaluation in elementary and high schools in São Paulo), the relationship between reuse and recycling beliefs and recycling behaviours in a Mexican community, and construction of the meaning of a barrio house in Caracas.

Later, in 2009, a second review came out, identifying main themes in Latin American studies (Corral-Verdugo and Pinheiro 2009). Rather than focusing only on concrete topics, this review identified basic psychological processes related to the environment and environmental behaviour (change), including emotion, values, perception, and cognition, alongside more 'classical' themes in environmental psychology, such as housing and urban stressors (noise, traffic accidents). In comparing these basic reviews of environmental psychology in Latin America, we notice two major developments. First, comparing the number of themes identified in the reviews published in 1987 and 2009 shows that environmental psychology is growing in Latin America, and that a wider range of themes is studied. Second, we observe a growing emphasis on global issues related to sustainability, in addition to local issues specific to the region.

25.4   RECENT DEVELOPMENTS IN ENVIRONMENTAL PSYCHOLOGY IN LATIN AMERICA

To analyse developments in the field of environmental psychology in Latin America, we searched for publications related to environmental psychology by one or more Latin American authors, in journals indexed on the ISI Web of Science for the period 1971–2015. In addition, to obtain a representative selection of publications, dissertations, and other non-indexed literature, we asked members of the Latin American Environmental Psychology Network (Spanish acronym:+ REPALA) and members of the Environmental Psychology Working Group of the Inter American Society of Psychology to send short descriptions of their most representative works in environmental psychology. We obtained more than 150 papers and articles, mostly empirical, providing data or confirming specific or more universal hypotheses regarding environments or populations. Box 25.1 provides a summary of the main research topics that we found based on this search. Although the results provide a good exploration of recent developments in the field, it is not clear to what

BOX 25.1   OVERVIEW OF TOPICS STUDIED IN ENVIRONMENTAL PSYCHOLOGY IN LATIN AMERICA

Environmental quality: Assessment of environmental quality, optimism, responsibility, environmental impact, healthy environments, assessment of environmental quality of forest reserve, landscape quality, environmental stress, perception of environmental design, quality of life, quality of water, restorative environments, space organization, space syntax, pro-environmental behaviour, climate change, environmental education and its effects.

Cognitive processes: Environmental meaning, environmental preference and motivation, environmental evaluation, environmental perception, environmental risk perception, representational content about environment in the media, perception of water quality, occupation space.

Feelings, emotions, and attributions: Affection, guilt, happiness, identity, perceived responsibility, perceived vulnerability, perception of environmental threats.

Housing: Place attachment, habitability, 'alive' neighbourhoods, residential aesthetics, residential environments, residential furniture, residential satisfaction.

Attitudes and beliefs: Environmental attitudes, environmental beliefs, causal attribution, environmental norms, theory of planned behaviour and conservation, personal norms, value orientations, ideology, attitudes, and pro-environmental behaviour.

Specific behaviours: Child play, environment behaviour in children, space appropriation in preschool, adaptation to Antarctic environment, anti-social behaviour, conservation behaviour, environmental risks coping, environmental behaviour, environmentally harmful behaviour, norms violation, pro-environmental competency, recycling, residential water consumption, residential water uses, reuse, sustainable behaviour, traffic violation behaviour, use of bicycle as mean of transportation.

Specific environments: Classrooms, schools, urban parks, squares, residential units, forest reserves, cities.

Local environmental concerns: Air quality, waste control, environmental risks, waste generation, waste management, water conservation, water consumption, weather pessimism.

Global environmental concerns: Global environmental change, climate change and motivation, sustainability.

Miscellaneous: Environmental education, community consciousness, health, post-occupancy evaluation, time perspective, traffic accidents.

extent the results of such studies can be generalized to other groups or to the general population. What *is* clear is that it is necessary to work with broader, more representative, and diverse samples in the future, since many of the studies were limited to samples of university students.

In the early years (1985–2000), emphasis was placed on interactions between humans and the built environment, addressing issues such as residential satisfaction, environmental assessment, environmental impact, and environmental stressors. In recent years, while interest in cognitive and affective processes related to environmental meaning, orientation, perception, and evaluation has been maintained, the specific themes have been extended, for example, to long-term stay in extreme environments such as the Antarctic region (Zimmer et al. 2013), the design of 'living' neighbourhoods (Mattos and Pinheiro 2013), and place attachment (Felippe and Kuhnen 2012; see Chapter 14).

In the last years (2005–present), the emphasis has shifted from the study of interactions with the built environment towards themes related to the natural environment, such as the perception, use, and management of natural resources (Bustos et al. 2005; Corral-Verdugo et al. 2002; Mocelin Polli and Vizeu Camargo 2015), psychological dimensions of global environmental change (Urbina-Soria and Martínez 2006), ecological behaviour (Pato et al. 2005), sustainability (Corral-Verdugo et al. 2010; Páramo et al. 2015), environmental preference (Sánchez Miranda et al. 2012), evaluation of environmental quality of nature reserves (Granada and Molina Cortés 2015), impacts of disasters such as landslides (Landeros-Mugica et al. 2015), and earthquakes and tsunamis (Díaz et al. 2012). Urban mobility and traffic are also topics of increasing interest, including traffic systematization (Günther and Neto 2015), intentions to violate traffic rules (Moyano-Díaz 2002), the evaluation of eight modes of motorized urban mobility (Urbina-Soria and Flores-Cano 2010), comparative risks of pedestrian behaviour between Chilean and Brazilian citizens (Moyano Díaz et al. 2014), and the use of bicycles in urban spaces (Olekszechen et al. 2016).

In addition, we found studies concerning healthcare and restorative environments (Ortega-Andeane and Estrada-Rodríguez 2010), and environmental health (Valadez and Landa 2007). Although this topic was also important in the earlier years, the focus has changed from the negative influence of environmental conditions on well-being to the positive effects of environmental conditions and on the comprehension and change of environmental behaviour. The focus on the positive impacts of environmental conditions is evidenced in topics such as restorative environments (see Chapter 7) and the sense of gratification when performing pro-environmental behaviours.

25.5 KEY ISSUES FOR THE DEVELOPMENT OF RESEARCH IN LATIN AMERICA

Among the factors that limit the development of environmental psychology in Latin America, three stand out: (i) Lack of collaboration between Latin American researchers and with those from other countries. (ii) Difficulties of publishing in Spanish or Portuguese languages. (iii) Limited opportunities for postgraduate studies.

25.5.1 *Lack of Collaboration*

Although the collaboration between Latin American environmental psychologists and colleagues from other latitudes has been increasing, this collaboration is still at a minimal level. For instance, relatively few studies have been published jointly by researchers from Latin America and other regions, considering the search in Scopus, Scielo, and ISI index journals. This is a large area of opportunity to evaluate the relevance and applicability of the underlying psychological constructs in each and every one of the subfields of environmental psychology in a context of cultural, economic, ideological, and social diversity. The accomplishment of joint work would be very valuable in creating knowledge about where results and perspectives converge and diverge. This collaboration could be an important element giving great impetus to the research work between researchers from different Latin American countries, as well as those from other regions and continents.

25.5.2   Few Possibilities to Publish in Spanish or Portuguese

Increasing numbers of Latin American environmental psychologists publish in international journals whose language is English, but many do not do so entirely for language reasons. Clearly, if the engagement of Latin American psychologists with English-speaking countries increases, there will also be a greater presence in books and journals. Another possibility for promoting the publication of international collaborations is the creation of Latin American academic journals focused on the field of environmental psychology, which would help to establish similarities and differences in Latin American regional contexts in environmental psychological issues. A publication worth highlighting here is the environmental psychology journal *Psico* (De Campos and Bonfim 2014), which contains a good collection of Brazilian, Argentine, Venezuelan, and Spanish papers in the field.

25.5.3   Academic Training in Environmental Psychology

Compared with countries outside Latin America, most researchers who study environment–behaviour interactions have not been trained as environmental psychologists. For example, currently only the National University of Mexico has a specific environmental psychology Master's degree and a PhD programme focused on environmental psychology research (both are recognized for excellence in postgraduate studies, which ensures that all applicants accepted receive scholarships). No other Latin American university has established a Bachelor, Master, or PhD programme: environmental psychology postgraduate courses, seminars, or workshops are offered in isolation. Of course, it is desirable for universities in other countries to establish formal postgraduate courses in environmental psychology in general, or in one of the subfields. As long as there are no opportunities for this, the field will not be fully developed. Unfortunately, for the creation of such courses it is necessary first to convince university and government authorities of the potential benefits of training specialists in environmental psychology to help contribute to the analysis and solution of the multiple problems of environment–behaviour interactions. It should be remembered here that although environmental problems are not going to be solved by psychology or the social sciences, without psychology and without the social sciences these problems will not be solved.

25.6 SUMMARY

Latin America is an extremely rich and diverse region, both in natural resources and in cultural elements that combine the legacies of the original peoples with those of the European countries, forming a valuable mix. Like other regions of the world, it is currently undergoing environmental changes (overuse and depletion of natural resources), as well as socio-demographic (migration, lifestyles) changes. This underscores the need for environmental psychologists to focus their professional and research work on the conservation of natural resources, the improvement of built environments, and the psychological processes that contribute to an environmentally friendly lifestyle.

From the analysis in the chapter, it follows that: (i) research work in environmental psychology has had considerable growth since its inception in the 1980s; (ii) the issues originally addressed were mainly focused on the built environment, while at present most of the work has to do with natural environments and sustainability; (iii) a systematic look at the research carried out shows that initial work focused mainly on the negative effects of environmental conditions on behaviour and well-being, while recent work focuses more strongly on a combination of positive effects; (iv) the issues of interest were originally limited to aspects of local order, and now also include global problems.

Factors limiting the development of environmental psychology in the region are: (i) a low contribution between environmental psychologists in the region and those of other countries; (ii) the research work that is done is not always published, mainly for reasons of language; (iii) there are few opportunities to undertake postgraduate studies in environmental psychology in Latin American universities. It is clear, then, that initiatives should be taken to strengthen collaboration between Latin American and other environmental psychologists, to have more options for publication in trilingual journals or to create Latin American journals in the field, and to establish formal postgraduate programmes in environmental psychology.

GLOSSARY

ethno-psychometrics   Construction of psychological measuring instruments taking into account the specific cultural features of a population.

Latin America   The region comprising the group of countries on the American continent in which languages derived from Latin (Spanish, Portuguese, and French) are spoken.

values   Desirable trans-situational goals, varying in importance, that serve as guiding principles in the life of a person or other social entity.

SUGGESTIONS FOR FURTHER READING

Corral-Verdugo, V., & Pinheiro, J. (2009). Environmental psychology with a Latin American taste. *Journal of Environmental Psychology*, 29, 366–374.

Díaz-Loving, R. (2000). An historic psycho-socio-cultural look at the self in Mexico. In: *Indigenous and Cultural Psychology. Understanding People in Context* (ed. U. Kim, K. Yang and K. Hwang), 315—325. New York, NY: Springer.

REVIEW QUESTIONS

1. What have been the thematic changes throughout the development of environmental psychology in Latin America?
2. Select three topics from Box 25.1 that you think should be studied in a comparative way between a Latin American city and a European city. Explain your reasons for that selection.
3. Compare the number of inhabitants of the conurbation zone of Mexico City (about 20 million people) with the total population of Sweden, the Netherlands, Greece, Austria, or Portugal, and propose a conclusion about the environmental implications for the quality of life.
4. There are three key issues for the development of environmental psychology in Latin America. Which one do you consider most important? Why?

Part III
Encouraging Pro-Environmental Behaviour

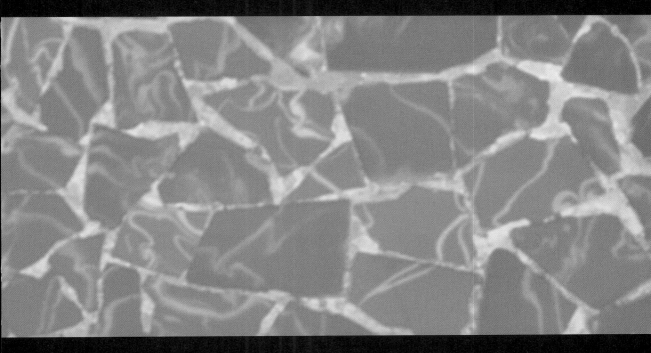

26 Informational Strategies to Promote Pro-Environmental Behaviour: Changing Knowledge, Awareness, and Attitudes

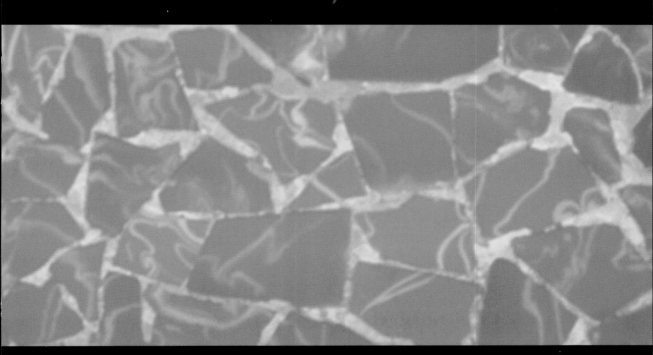

Wokje Abrahamse
Victoria University of Wellington, New Zealand

Ellen Matthies
Otto-von-Guericke University, Germany

CHAPTER OUTLINE

26.1   INTRODUCTION

Since the 1970s, social and environmental psychologists have examined different ways to encourage people to adopt pro-environmental behaviours in order to alleviate the effects of human behaviour on the environment, such as the depletion of fossil fuels and climate change. Current global trends however, indicate that our impact on the environment is still considerable: carbon dioxide emissions through the combustion of fossil fuels have steadily increased over the past decade (Field et al. 2014). Earlier chapters in this volume have discussed various approaches and models to describe and explain pro-environmental behaviour and environmental impact of behaviour. In this chapter we will focus on strategies for behavioural change, as they have been studied in the past three decades. The question is: What has this research taught us, and, perhaps more importantly, how can the research base be improved in order to foster pro-environmental behaviour change?

Interventions to promote behaviour change can be divided into two categories (Steg and Vlek 2009). **Informational strategies** are aimed at changing knowledge, awareness, norms, and attitudes (such as information campaigns to raise awareness about recycling). **Structural strategies** are aimed at changing the circumstances in which behavioural decisions are made (such as the provision of recycling facilities). In this chapter, we focus on informational strategies, which are also sometimes referred to as 'soft measures' and can be distinguished from so-called 'hard measures', that is, strategies that use incentives or technical alterations (see Chapters 27 and 28). To start, we will outline some basic principles of intervention research, followed by an overview of research into the following informational strategies: provision of information, goal setting, commitment, prompting, and feedback. Lastly, we will give recommendations and avenues for future research.

26.2   INTERVENTIONS: FROM RESEARCH TO IMPLEMENTATION

Interventions need to be carefully planned before they are implemented (Gardner and Stern 2002; Steg and Vlek 2009). A few points are noteworthy in this respect to increase the effectiveness of interventions.

Environmental Psychology: An Introduction, Second Edition. Edited by Linda Steg and Judith I. M. de Groot.
© 2019 John Wiley & Sons Ltd. Published 2019 by John Wiley & Sons Ltd.

Firstly, it is important to target behaviours that can significantly improve environmental conditions. To illustrate, while refusing plastic bags in shops is well-intentioned, its impact is relatively small compared to for instance the impact of buying food that has been produced locally instead of food flown in from abroad. Ideally then, interventions should focus on behaviours with relatively high environmental impacts.

Secondly, interventions should be rooted in theory. Using a theory-driven approach is important as it will provide a good basis not only for understanding and changing environmentally significant behaviours but also for developing sound evaluations. For each of the five informational strategies presented here, the theoretical assumptions underlying the intervention will be discussed.

Thirdly, it is essential that the effect of the intervention is assessed properly. Ideally, intervention studies include measurements of the target behaviour before and after implementation of the intervention, a so-called pre-test/post-test design, and include a control group that has not been exposed to the intervention. This way, changes in the outcome measure can be monitored and compared to a 'business as usual' situation. Also, including measurements of factors related to behavioural decisions (e.g. knowledge, attitudes) is important, as this will provide insight into the reasons why an intervention was effective (or not). For instance, failure of an energy conservation campaign to change behaviour may be attributable to the fact that people already have sufficient knowledge about how to save energy.

26.3   INFORMATIONAL STRATEGIES

In this section, we will discuss the following informational strategies: information provision, goal setting, commitment, prompting, and feedback. They were chosen because they are most frequently used in the literature (for systematic reviews and meta-analyses, see Abrahamse and Steg 2013; Abrahamse et al. 2005; Möser and Bamberg 2008; Osbaldiston and Schott 2012).

26.3.1   *Provision of Information*

Information provision is probably the most widely used intervention to promote behaviour change. Generally, two types of information are distinguished: information about environmental problems and information that helps people to take action to alleviate these problems. Information provision has its roots in the so-called **knowledge-deficit model**, the assumption being that people do not know about a specific environmental problem, or they do not know in detail what to do about it (Schultz 2002). Information provision aims to overcome this knowledge deficit.

The research to date indicates that information alone is not very effective (e.g. Schultz 1998; Staats et al. 1996). A study (Staats et al. 1996) evaluated a Dutch mass media campaign aimed at raising awareness of global warming and things people could do to take action. A pre-test/post-test survey revealed an increase in knowledge about global warming, but no behavioural changes occurred.

A more effective strategy to encourage behaviour change is **tailored information** (Abrahamse et al. 2007; Daamen et al. 2001). Tailored information is designed to reach a specific person or group(s) of people on the basis of characteristics unique to those individuals (Kreuter et al. 1999). A study conducted in the workplace (Daamen et al. 2001) found that tailored information was more effective at encouraging employees to engage in behaviours to reduce oil pollution (e.g. checking for leaks in oil pipes), compared to information that was not tailored.

Information that is conveyed via 'models', i.e. other persons carrying out the recommended behaviours, can be another effective informational strategy (e.g. Sussman and Gifford 2013). This strategy is based on Bandura's **social learning theory** (1977) and assumes that people make inferences about how to behave in a given situation by observing the behaviour of others.

Normative information, that is, information on the opinion or behaviour of others can be effective in encouraging pro-environmental behaviour (Cialdini 2003). Such interventions are based on insights from social norm theories (Cialdini et al. 1991; see Chapter 18). For example, a study found that towels were reused more frequently when hotel guests were provided with descriptive norm information (about how many other guests were reusing towels) compared to the standard environmental message often used in hotels (Goldstein et al. 2008).

It would appear that information alone is not very effective in encouraging behaviour change and it is essential to combine it with other interventions (Gardner and Stern 2002). When information is tailored, when it is conveyed through **modelling**, or when information is provided on the behaviour of others, it can be more effective (see Abrahamse et al. 2005).

26.3.2 Goal Setting

This intervention technique is based on goal setting theory, which states that individual behaviour is goal-directed and that the anticipation of reaching an attractive goal motivates respective behaviour (see also Chapter 22). **Goal setting** is most effective when goals are high but, at the same time, realistic (Locke and Latham 1990). Moreover, goals should be clearly formulated and achievable within a short period of time.

A study (Becker 1978) examined the effect of goal setting and feedback (see Section 26.3.5) to encourage households to reduce their energy consumption. Reduction goals were assigned that differed in difficulty (savings of 20% versus savings of 2%), and were either combined with feedback or no feedback. Goal setting was only effective in combination with feedback and only for the high reduction goal (20%) group (who in fact achieved a reduction of 15%).

Goal setting appears to be more effective when combined with other informational strategies. Whereas early research primarily focused on the assignment of individual goals, more recent intervention programs have effectively included the assignment of group goals (see Box 26.1).

BOX 26.1 A SUCCESSFUL INTERVENTION PROGRAM USING A COMBINATION OF GROUP GOALS AND INCENTIVES

The strategy of group goal assignment was applied in the European intervention program 'Energy Neighbourhoods' (Merziger and Neumann 2010). Groups of households (so-called 'Energy Neighbourhoods') were asked to collectively reduce their energy consumption by 8% or more (the goal was linked to the overall EU CO_2-reduction goal of 8%, to be reached by 2010). The neighbourhoods were supported by so-called 'Energy Masters' – volunteers from the participating households who were specially trained to support other households in achieving savings. Neighbourhoods who attained the 8% group goal during the six-month competition were given prizes (e.g. fleece blankets, light bulbs). In total, around 600 neighbourhoods in nine EU countries took part. About 60% of the neighbourhoods were able to meet or exceed the 8% reduction goal, with an average saving per household of 1%.

The effect of goal setting could be enhanced by so-called **implementation intentions**. 'Implementation intentions are if-then plans that spell out when, where, and how a set goal has to be put into action' (Schweiger Gallo and Gollwitzer 2007, p. 37). A series of studies indicates that implementation intentions can be effective to encourage a range of environmentally friendly behaviours (e.g. Bamberg 2003; see also Chapter 30).

26.3.3 Commitment

In a **commitment** intervention, individuals, or groups are asked to sign a pledge (commitment) to change their behaviour. It can be assumed that a commitment affects behaviour change via reduction of **cognitive dissonance** (Festinger 1957), i.e. the tension that arises when one's beliefs or attitudes do not align with one's behaviour (e.g. I promised to do this, but I am not acting accordingly). Commitment techniques are regularly combined with other informational strategies (e.g. goal setting) as well as incentives (Bachmann and Katzev 1982; Matthies et al. 2006).

A German study (Matthies et al. 2006) used a combination of commitment and incentives to encourage habitual car users to try out public transport. Participants in the incentive-only group received a free public transport ticket. Participants in the commitment-only group were asked to commit themselves to try out at least one activity of their choice (out of a list of 10 suggested activities, including using public transport). In a third group, the commitment was combined with the free public transport ticket. A fourth group did not receive any intervention. All intervention groups showed an increase in use of public transport compared to baseline levels, while the control group showed no increase.

In a follow-up measure (12 weeks later), only the commitment groups (commitment only and commitment combined with a ticket) had more frequently tried out public transport.

Commitments require relatively high amounts of time and resources, e.g. when people need to be contacted individually. Also, not everyone who is approached with the request to sign a commitment as part of such studies may actually do this. These participants were then often excluded from the study. It may well be that those participants were less willing to change their behaviour anyway, which may have resulted in an overestimation of the effects of commitment (for an exception of a study where those participants were not excluded, see Matthies et al. 2006).

26.3.4   Prompting

The technique of **prompting** has been used to encourage pro-environmental behaviour since the early years of intervention research. It entails a short written message or sign, which draws attention to a specific behaviour in a given situation. Prompts are simple reminders that can encourage people to behave in an appropriate way, e.g. to avoid littering or to switch off the lights when leaving a room (e.g. Sussman and Gifford 2012). By using prompts one assumes that the target group already has a positive attitude or has the intention to carry out the behaviour in question, but lacks a cue in the situation where the behaviour is required. Thus, prompts can be assumed to overrule the automatic elicitation of a problematic behaviour (see Chapter 24). Depending on the content of a prompt, they can be assumed to directly convey sanctions or incentives (e.g. 'Thank you for not littering'), which can be linked to behaviourist approaches (Bell et al. 2001; see also Chapter 27).

A study (Austin et al. 1993) used prompts (pictograms) to encourage recycling and proper disposal of trash. Prompting resulted in an improvement of correct disposal of both recyclables and trash by 54% and 29%, when posted directly above the receptacles. In a variation, the prompts were posted 4 m from the receptacles, which resulted in an increase of only 19%, suggesting that prompts can be especially effective if placed directly where the requested behaviour is going to be carried out.

Prompting techniques have been criticized for having only weak, short-term effects (Bell et al. 2001). Prompting is mainly effective with less complex and easy behaviours, if formulated politely and if well placed and timed (see Geller et al. 1982).

26.3.5   Feedback

Feedback consists of giving people information about their performance, for instance, energy savings, or amount of recycled materials. According to feedback intervention theory (Kluger and DeNisi 1996), feedback influences behaviour because it gives insight into the links between certain outcomes (e.g. saving energy) and the behaviour changes necessary to reach that outcome (e.g. switching off lights). The more frequently feedback is given, the more effective it tends to be (Abrahamse et al. 2005). For instance, studies that have used in-home energy displays have found this type of continuous feedback to be more effective than less frequent (monthly) feedback (Van Houwelingen and Van Raaij 1989).

Studies also examine how feedback can be more effectively conveyed to households. Households in Los Angeles were provided with feedback about their energy consumption (Asensio and Delmas 2015). The feedback was framed either in terms of financial savings ('Last week, you used 66% more electricity […]. In one year, this will cost you $34 dollars extra'.), or, in terms of public health ('Last week, you used 66% more electricity […] You are adding 610 pounds of air pollutants which contribute to health impacts such as childhood asthma and cancer'.). The study found that, compared to a control group, the public health feedback resulted in average savings of about 8%, whereas the financial savings feedback resulted in increased energy consumption of about 4%. This suggests that financial savings are not always the main motivator for behaviour change. Also, an appeal to public health effects may be more effective – particularly in places where this is a serious problem (such as in Los Angeles).

Feedback appears to be an effective way to encourage behaviour change (Abrahamse et al. 2005). However, as feedback is often used in combination with other strategies (e.g. information, goal setting), it is not always clear what the unique contribution of feedback is (e.g. Abrahamse et al. 2007; Staats et al. 2004; for a meta-analysis on the effectiveness of feedback, see Karlin et al. 2015).

26.4 INTERVENTION RESEARCH: SOME GENERAL ISSUES

Several issues concerning intervention research and the application of informational strategies are noteworthy here. In the following section, we would like to focus on three central issues.

Firstly, as has been mentioned elsewhere (Abrahamse et al. 2005), relatively little is known about the long-term effects of interventions and their cost effectiveness. Due to time, resource, or other constraints, many studies have not monitored the effects of the interventions over longer periods of time. However, it is important to establish whether behavioural changes are maintained once an intervention has been discontinued.

Secondly, intervention research is often action-based and seems to lack a coherent theory underlying the promotion of pro-environmental behaviour. In order to further enhance our understanding of informational strategies and behaviour change, it is important to clarify the underlying theoretical assumptions about how interventions work, in which contexts they work, and for which types of behaviour they are most suitable. These factors should be systematically recorded as part of an evaluation (e.g. Matthies et al. 2006; Staats et al. 2004).

Thirdly, collaboration with other disciplines is important and necessary to help inform (future) research on the effectiveness of informational strategies. For instance, environmental scientists may indicate where behaviour change would be more, or less, effective in terms of reducing environmental impacts (e.g. reducing thermostat settings versus switching off lights).

Lastly, informational strategies to encourage behaviour change can often only be part of a solution to environmental problems. In most of the contexts where behavioural change is needed a more effective approach might be to combine informational strategies with structural strategies (such as pricing strategies, see also Chapter 27), and pro-environmental actions may be encouraged by different approaches.

26.5   SUMMARY

In this chapter we have discussed five informational strategies to promote pro-environmental behaviours: provision of information, goal setting, commitment, prompting, and feedback. These strategies have been employed with varying degrees of success. The provision of information results in increased awareness, but not necessarily in behaviour change. However, when information is tailored, when it is conveyed through modelling, or when it is provided on the behaviour of others, it can be more effective. Goal setting and commitment have generally been successful in encouraging behaviour change, especially when used in combination with other interventions. Prompting also appears to be effective, though mainly for relatively easy behaviours. Providing feedback, and especially frequent feedback, is an effective intervention for encouraging behaviour change. In the last part of the chapter, we have discussed three issues that are of central importance to intervention research. First, insight into the long-term effect of interventions is crucial in order to encourage behaviour change that is sustained over longer periods of time. Second, theoretical insights are essential for (better) understanding and changing environmentally significant behaviours. Finally, given that environmental issues are multifaceted, informational strategies need to be combined with structural intervention strategies to encourage people to adopt a more environmentally-friendly lifestyle.

GLOSSARY

cognitive dissonance   The tension that arises when individuals become aware of inconsistencies between their attitudes and their behaviour, or inconsistencies between different beliefs.

commitment   A technique where individuals or groups are asked to sign a pledge (commitment) to change behaviour.

feedback   An intervention which consists of giving people information about their performance, which makes the consequences of a certain behaviour salient.

goal setting   An informational strategy which entails setting clear performance targets, often combined with feedback or commitment.

implementation intentions   If-then plans that spell out when, where, and how a set goal has to be put into action.

information provision   An intervention where people are provided with information about environmental problems, information on the opinions or behaviour of others, or information that can help them to take action.

informational strategies   Interventions aimed at changing perceptions, knowledge, awareness, norms, and attitudes, which are in turn assumed to lead to behaviour change.

knowledge-deficit model   An assumption which underlies information provision, that is, the reason people do not change behaviour is that they do not know about a specific environmental problem, or they do not know in detail what they can do about it.

modelling   A strategy which entails the use of examples ('models') who display recommended behaviours and serve as a guide for people to change their own behaviour.

normative information   Information about the opinion or behaviour of other people, thereby making a social norm salient.

prompting   An intervention technique that uses reminders to draw attention to a specific desirable or undesirable behaviour.

social learning theory   A theory positing that people learn from one another via observation, imitation, and modelling.

structural strategies   Interventions aimed at changing the circumstances in which behavioural decisions are made (such as financial incentives, the provision of facilities).

tailored information   Information designed to reach a specific person or group(s) of people on the basis of characteristics unique to those individuals.

SUGGESTIONS FOR FURTHER READING

Gardner, G.T. and Stern, P.C. (2002). *Environmental Problems and Human Behavior*. Boston: Allyn & Bacon.

Geller, E.S. (2002). The challenge of increasing proenvironment behavior. In: *Handbook of Environmental Psychology* (ed. R.G. Bechtel and A. Churchman), 525–540. New York, NY: Wiley.

Lee, N.R., Lee, N., Schultz, P.W., and Kotler, P. (2011). *Social Marketing to Protect the Environment: What Works*. London: Sage.

REVIEW QUESTIONS

1. Imagine a university or other large organization that wants to implement a recycling scheme to collect paper, glass, and tin cans. Which informational strategies would you recommend to the university or organization in order to encourage the uptake of recycling, and why?
2. How would you design an evaluation study that examines the effectiveness of the intervention(s) you suggested to the university or organization to encourage recycling?
3. Why is it important that intervention research is informed by theory?
4. Name three important elements of intervention planning that policymakers should take into consideration when they plan an intervention aimed at encouraging behaviour change.

27 Encouraging Pro-Environmental Behaviour with Rewards and Penalties

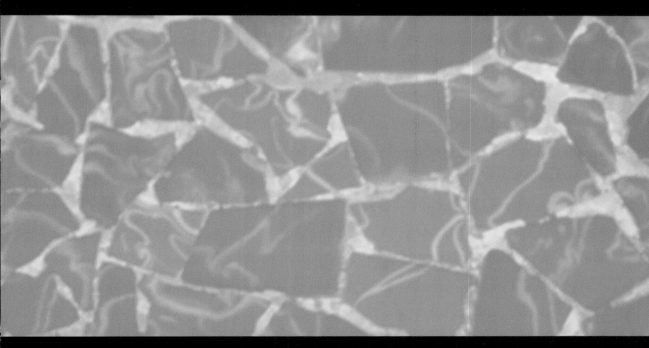

Jan Willem Bolderdijk
Rijksuniversiteit Groningen, The Netherlands

Philip K. Lehman
Salem VA Medical Center, USA

E. Scott Geller
Virginia Tech, USA

CHAPTER OUTLINE

27.1 INTRODUCTION

Chapter 26 of this volume discussed how informational strategies can encourage pro-environmental behaviour, but providing information alone is seldom enough to promote behaviour change (Bolderdijk et al. 2013a). People often persist with old patterns of behaviour despite awareness of the negative consequences for the environment and the presence of viable alternatives (e.g. organically grown products, public transport). So why do people maintain their environmentally harmful behaviour? How can we decrease the occurrence of such undesirable behaviour and increase the frequency of pro-environmental behaviour? According to **applied behaviour analysis** (see also Geller 2016), in order to change behaviour, one has to analyse and alter the **consequences** of behaviour.

27.2 ANALYSIS OF CONSEQUENCES

Consider your current behaviour. What motivated you to open this book, turn its pages, scan its sometimes hard-to-understand content and try to make sense of it all? We suspect your behaviour was motivated to some extent by one or more consequences. For some of you, a consequence might be gathering information to use in writing a paper or performing well on an exam. Others may be reading for nobler consequences – to gain knowledge for solving an environmental problem or simply to learn more about environmental psychology. We hope you are not reading the book for soporific effects. (If you don't know what the word 'soporific' means, and choose to look it up, you may be doing so for the consequence of reducing an arousal state called curiosity.)

As you may realize by now, almost all behaviour is determined by its consequences. As proposed by B. F. Skinner (1974), founder of the field of experimental and applied behaviour analysis, people are motivated to do things for the promise of what follows. In other words, we do what we do to obtain positive consequences or to escape or avoid negative consequences. Moreover, we repeat behaviours that lead to positive consequences and avoid behaviours that result in negative consequences. This elegantly simple idea is the theoretical basis for interventions that aim to improve environmental behaviour by offering **rewards** and **penalties**.

While research in applied behavioural science shows behaviour is controlled by consequences, it also demonstrates the importance of stimuli in the environment that announce the availability of consequences, thereby directing behaviour towards a desired outcome. Because these stimuli precede behaviour, they are referred to as **antecedents** or activators. The Antecedent Behaviour Consequence sequence is known as the three-term contingency or ABC model, and is the theoretical basis for many interventions designed to improve environmental behaviour.

The three-term contingency suggests two behaviour-based approaches for encouraging pro-environmental behaviour. One strategy is to introduce or add antecedents that announce the availability of pleasant consequences for pro-environmental behaviours or unpleasant consequences for environmentally harmful behaviours. Alternatively (or in addition) interventions can introduce new positive consequences (i.e. rewards) for pro-environmental behaviours, or negative consequences (i.e. penalties) for environmentally harmful behaviours.

Programmes that offer refunds for beverage containers provide a real-world example of the three-term contingency. In this case, the antecedent is the message on the container announcing the availability of a rebate. When individuals perform the desired behaviour (i.e. turn in the bottles or cans at a designated location instead of throwing them in the trash), they receive the consequence of a small financial reward (see Box 27.1).

The example of bottle rebates provides an opportunity to introduce additional terms. Antecedents that promise pleasant consequences or rewards for a desired behaviour are termed **incentives**. In contrast, antecedents such as rules and policies which announce unpleasant consequences or penalties for undesired behaviours are referred to as **disincentives**. A recent example of a disincentive is the introduction of a charge for plastic bags in supermarkets, which was found to reduce consumer request for plastic bags (Jakovcevic et al. 2014).

When a consequence results in an increase in the frequency, duration, or intensity of a behaviour, the consequence is termed a **reinforcer**. Research has shown rebates reinforce the behaviour of taking the bottles to a recycling centre (Levitt and Leventhal 1986). In contrast, consequences that result in a decrease in the occurrence of a behaviour are termed **punishers**. An example is to charge for garbage collection by weight. This strategy might punish the behaviour of throwing bottles in the trash, and increase recycling behaviour.

BOX 27.1   REFUNDS FOR BEVERAGE CONTAINERS

In 1971, Oregon was the first US state to enact a 'bottle bill'. This bill mandated a five-cent rebate for the return of cans, bottles, and other beverage containers. After the bill was implemented, 90% of containers were returned, resulting in a significant reduction of levels of litter (Oregon Department of Environmental Quality 2004) and improved recycling rates, and thus helped to improve resource conservation. It is now considered one of the success stories in environmental management. Unfortunately, only 10 of the 50 US states followed in Oregon's footsteps.

Before we continue our discussion of how consequences should be presented, it is important to note that not all consequences are created equal. As a rule, pleasant consequences that appear soon and are certain are more powerful than consequences that are distant and uncertain to occur (Geller 2016). Many of the pleasant consequences of environmentally harmful behaviours fall into the soon and certain category. For example, consider your food consumption. While environmentally responsible food choices often entail purchasing locally produced food, the immediately available consequence of a cheeseburger at a fast-food drive-through may be more alluring than the time-consuming and effortful prospect of shopping at the local farmer's market and preparing a meal at home. Likewise, when we choose to drive to work in our gas-guzzling vehicle instead of cycling or taking the bus, the soon and certain consequences of comfort, efficiency, and convenience can overpower our concern over the impact of our behaviour on the distant and uncertain prospect of global warming (Van der Linden et al. 2015).

27.3   NATURAL VERSUS EXTRA CONSEQUENCES

Although we have made the case for all behaviour being determined by consequences, you probably realize reinforcers do not drop from the sky. You do not have a person following you around daily doling out rewards each time you do the right thing. In fact, for some behaviours the consequences may not be readily apparent. Consider the example of participating in sports. Only a miniscule percentage of the world's population is paid for athletic performance, but millions regularly engage in sports-related activities such as jogging, hiking, cycling, soccer, golf, tennis, and basketball. Sports and many other activities we frequently perform are motivated by **natural or intrinsic consequences**.

Consider, for example, a basketball player practising free throws. On a well-executed shot, the graceful arc of the ball through the air and the satisfying swish sound as the ball drops through the net provide rewarding feedback, encouraging the player to repeat the same sequence of behaviours. On the not-so-well executed shot, the flat trajectory of the ball and the discordant clang off the front of the rim provide corrective feedback which directs the player to refine and repeat the sequence of behaviours until she once again sees the graceful arc and hears the gratifying swishing sound. In other words, the built-in consequences that follow naturally from a task itself can reinforce behaviour.

Our discussion of natural or intrinsic reinforcement is extremely important for pro-environmental behaviours, because many of these behaviours do not offer immediate natural rewards. In fact, behaviours like recycling, cycling instead of driving, or turning down the thermostat in the winter can be inconvenient, time-consuming, and uncomfortable (Venhoeven et al. 2013). In order to motivate the occurrence of pro-environmental behaviours which lack natural reinforcers, it may be beneficial to add **extra consequences** (see Box 27.2). In

BOX 27.2   EFFECTS OF A TEMPORARY FREE BUS TICKET

The adverse effects of automotive transportation on the environment are well understood (e.g. emission of pollutants and greenhouse gasses). Policymakers have therefore been looking for ways to convince drivers to switch to public transport instead. This is however easier said than done, as attitudes towards public transport are much more negative than they are towards car travel (Steg 2003). Still, as a study by Fujii and Kitamura (2003) showed, it is not impossible.

In a field experiment, drivers were given a one-month free bus ticket and bus route map of Kyoto, and completed questionnaires on their attitudes towards car use and public transport. The researchers found the intervention worked: a free bus ticket increased bus use by 20%. Moreover, they found that one month later, when drivers had to pay for the fares again, many persisted in using public transport. How can these results be explained?

Initially, drivers expressed an overly negative attitude towards public transport. The experience of a bus ride may have corrected this perception: riding the bus was experienced as more pleasant than anticipated. In other words, an extra consequence (a temporary reduction in travelling expenses) motivated drivers to experience an unanticipated natural consequence (e.g. riding the bus allows you to read a book or relax while travelling).

the next section, we discuss how such extra consequences – rewards and penalties – can aid in promoting pro-environmental behaviour. We discuss situations where extra consequences are effective, as well as situations in which applying penalties and rewards can actually be counterproductive.

27.4   WHEN IS IT APPROPRIATE TO APPLY EXTRA CONSEQUENCES?

Determining *when* to use extra consequences to increase occurrences of pro-environmental behaviour requires a careful analysis of the behaviour in question, using the ABC model to evaluate the context in which the behaviour occurs. This analysis focuses on the antecedents and consequences of the relevant environmental behaviour.

There are many cases when people know that actively caring for the environment is the right thing but are not doing it (see also Chapter 24 about habits). In this situation providing information and instructions will not help, since people are already intentionally performing the behaviour despite the knowledge that it is environmentally harmful. The natural consequences of environmentally harmful behaviour are more often positive and motivating than the natural consequences of pro-environmental behaviour. Using a bicycle to commute

BOX 27.3   CHANGING DRIVING STYLE VIA MOTIVATIONAL INTERVENTIONS

Considering the safety risk and negative environmental impact of speeding, one would think drivers would complete the relatively effortless behaviour of easing up on the gas pedal. Most drivers neverthe-less continue speeding. This is a situation in which a motivational intervention is needed to improve behaviour, as many governments seem to realize. When mobile radar and fixed cameras are employed to catch and fine speed violators, the percent-age of drivers exceeding the posted speed limits is often reduced. However, these disincentive or penalty strategies have some limitations. Speeding is typically only reduced in areas where the correct driving speed is being enforced (Hauer et al. 1982) and driv-ers have been observed increasing their speed after leaving a speed-enforcement area to compensate for lost time. Safe driving could alternatively be promoted through incentive or reward strategies. A study offered young drivers a discount on their insurance premium when sticking to the speed limit. Analyses of participants' GPS data showed that speeding – across all roads – was reduced by 14% (Bolderdijk et al. 2011).

typically involves much more effort and tolerance for discomfort than enjoying the speed and comfort of one's car. As the problem lies with a lack of motiva-tion, a **motivational intervention** is called for (Geller 2002). Motivational inter-ventions (i) encourage pro-environmental behaviour through incentives and rewards, or (ii) discourage environmentally harmful behaviours via disincen-tives and penalties (both options are illustrated in Box 27.3).

In sum, before applying a motivational intervention it is crucial to realize *why* people are failing to perform the desired behaviour. Specifically, adding consequences may be an appropriate means to encourage pro-environmental behaviour when people have the resources, time, knowledge, and ability to per-form the particular pro-environmental behaviour, believe that performing the behaviour will actually result in environmental benefits, but do not perceive those natural consequences as sufficiently motivating (see also Geller 2016).

27.5   HOW SHOULD EXTRA CONSEQUENCES BE ANNOUNCED AND DELIVERED?

Once you have established that a motivational intervention is required to promote behaviour change, some additional decisions are needed. Should you introduce positive (incentives and rewards) or negative consequences (disincentives and penalties)? Will you use tangible (e.g. monetary) or non-tangible consequences (e.g. feedback)? These choices are important, as they determine whether motivational interventions will ultimately be successful in promoting pro-environmental behaviours.

27.5.1 Negative Versus Positive Consequences

When applying extra consequences, psychologists generally prefer rewards over penalties because of the undesirable side-effects associated with negative consequences (see also Box 27.3). Penalties typically make specific undesired behaviours more costly to perform, thereby limiting people's freedom to behave as they choose. This perceived loss of freedom can influence people to act in ways counter to what the intervention intended, a process called **psychological reactance** (Brehm 1966) or countercontrol (Sidman 1989). In the Netherlands, for instance, speed enforcement devices are frequently vandalized by angry motorists. Similarly, people may try to escape penalties: when rubbish collection is charged by weight, people may be inclined to illegally dump their rubbish, rather than reducing their waste.

Moreover, penalty strategies can result in a negative attitude towards the agent administering the consequence. Speeding tickets, for instance, may annoy drivers who are fined for an unintentional violation of the speed limit: 'The police are only fining me to make money'. Citizens' appreciation and trust in governments could be undermined if policymakers rely exclusively on negative consequences to promote sustainability. So why do governments rely on penalties to control behaviour?

First and probably foremost, rewards cost money, whereas penalties generate revenue. Second, rewards differ from penalties in that they signal that behaviour is voluntary, whereas penalties communicate mandatory behaviour (Mulder 2008). Financially rewarding people for observing the speed limit, for instance, could unintentionally send out the signal that respecting the speed limit is optional, not obligatory.

27.5.2 Monetary Versus Non-Monetary Consequences

Extra consequences come in a wide range of tangible (e.g. dollars, stickers) and intangible (e.g. praise, privileges) varieties. Still, policymakers mostly rely on *financial* consequences such as subsidies, rebates, fines, and taxes to encourage pro-environmental behaviour and to discourage environmentally harmful behaviours. The reason for this is obvious: financial consequences are relatively easy to administer on a large scale.

Although the introduction of monetary rewards and penalties can certainly change behaviour for the better (Van Vugt 2001), there is an important risk to this particular approach. Specifically, merely thinking about money can induce a mindset in which the influence of personal norms or moral obligations is suppressed (see Chapter 22). When money enters the picture, people start seeing the decision whether or not to act morally as a business decision, rather than as an ethical or a moral issue (Lindenberg and Steg 2007; Tenbrunsel and

BOX 27.4   A FINE IS A LICENCE TO MISBEHAVE

Energy savings typically results in both environmental (reduced carbon emissions) and monetary (lower bills) savings. A study compared which of three arguments – stressing monetary benefits, environmental benefits, or a combination of monetary and environmental benefits – would be most effective in getting households interested in enrolling in an energy-savings programme.

By now, you would perhaps predict that stressing the monetary benefits, in isolation or in combination with environmental benefits, would be most effective, as monetary consequences are more immediate, noticeable, and certain than the potential and intangible reductions in carbon emissions that may ensue from enrolling. However, it turns out that many consumers already spontaneously realize energy savings would save money. Stressing this fact adds little persuasive power. Moreover, messages that highlight monetary consequences can have a psychological impact: they draw consumers' attention away from normative considerations (the fact that enrolling could also result in reduced carbon emissions). This is important, because some consumers are willing to enrol knowing this could help to reduce carbon emissions. In sum, both the monetary and combined arguments backfired because it made consumers neglect the environmental benefits that follow from enrolling (Schwartz et al. 2015).

Messick 1999). As a result, financial rewards and penalties can make people 'forget' about the moral aspects of pro-environmental behaviour and thereby paradoxically lead to *less* rather than *more* desired behaviour (Gneezy and Rustichini 2000; Heyman and Ariely 2004; see Box 27.4).

This means there is a risk in providing monetary consequences for behaviours people perform for ethical or environmentally conscious considerations. Since many pro-environmental behaviours are motivated by a sense of moral obligation (e.g. De Groot and Steg 2009b), policymakers should be careful that their environmental taxes and subsidies do not cancel out people's moral motivation to act pro-environmentally, and thereby do more harm than good (Frey and Jegen 2001). But how can this be accomplished?

Firstly, it seems important to pay attention to the way monetary consequences for pro-environmental behaviour are communicated. Policymakers could attempt to prevent the onset of a business (rather than an ethical) mindset by positioning monetary rewards and penalties as support for – rather than the ultimate goal of – pro-environmental action. So rather than presenting subsidies for fuel-efficient cars as being in the economic self-interest of consumers, subsidies could alternatively be presented as recognition and appreciation for the environmentally conscious consumer.

Secondly, policymakers could attempt to promote behaviour change through non-monetary consequences. Praise, compliments, candy, toys, privileges, and public recognition can reinforce pro-environmental behaviour, but are less likely to induce a business mindset (Heyman and Ariely 2004). But how might one efficiently present non-monetary consequences for pro-environmental behaviour on a large scale? Praise seems to be a powerful non-monetary reward, but requires the presence and attention of a teacher, parent, or peer. With electronic communication, however, praise can also be applied on a large scale. For example, 'emoticons' such as smiley faces can be used to signal both praise (•‿•) and disappointment (•⌒•) via online media. A field experiment found that emoticons posted on doorhangers increased energy-conservation behaviour among neighbourhood residents (Schultz et al. 2007; see also Chapter 18).

There are many more ways non-monetary consequences can be employed to encourage pro-environmental behaviour. Consider for instance the promotion of ride-sharing through the introduction of separate lanes for vehicles that have more than one occupant (Golob et al. 1990). To this day, however, non-monetary consequences remain an underused consequence strategy for encouraging pro-environmental action and discouraging environmentally harmful behaviour.

27.6 SUMMARY

In this chapter, we explained how behaviour is motivated by natural and extra consequences. Many pro-environmental behaviours lack natural rewards, and their regular occurrence may require the addition of extra consequences through incentive or reward strategies, or disincentive or penalty strategies. Extra consequences are particularly effective in situations where people are aware their actions are harmful to the environment, have the ability to change their behaviour, but are lacking sufficient motivation to change.

The beneficial impact of extra consequences depends on how they are announced and delivered. Soon and certain rewards have more impact than uncertain distant rewards. Whereas penalties can result in countercontrol or psychological reactance, rewards can foster a positive attitude. The application of monetary, instead of non-monetary consequences bears some risks, but the potentially negative effects may be curbed by ensuring monetary consequences are perceived to support, rather than undermine, people's moral obligation to preserve the environment.

GLOSSARY

antecedent   A stimulus that announces the availability of a certain consequence if the target behaviour is performed.

applied behaviour analysis   An intervention approach that targets observable behaviours and alters antecedents and consequences to influence beneficial change.

consequence   An event that follows a behaviour and may determine its recurrence.

disincentive   An antecedent that announces the availability of a behaviour–penalty contingency.

extra consequence   A consequence that is added to a task, usually in an attempt to influence its recurrence.

incentive   An antecedent that announces the availability of a behaviour–reward contingency.

intrinsic consequence   A natural behavioural consequence that may or may not influence behaviour.

motivational intervention   A program that motivates behaviour by providing extra consequences.

natural consequence   A consequence that follows inherently from engaging in a task.

penalty   An unpleasant consequence, implemented to discourage recurrence of some target behaviour.

psychological reactance   A process in which people act in the opposite way to the intention of persuasion attempts, in order to restore their lost sense of freedom.

punisher   A consequence that results in a decrease in the frequency, duration, or intensity of the behaviour it follows.

reinforcer   A consequence that results in an increase in the frequency, duration, or intensity of the behaviour it follows.

reward   A pleasant consequence delivered to encourage recurrence of a target behaviour.

SUGGESTIONS FOR FURTHER READING

Bolderdijk, J.W. and Steg, L. (2014). Promoting sustainable consumption: the risks of using financial incentives. In: *Handbook of Research on Sustainable Consumption* (ed. L.A. Reisch and J. Thøgersen), 328–342. Cheltenham, UK: Edward Elgar Publishing.

Geller, E.S. (ed.) (2016). *Applied Psychology: Actively Caring for People*. New York, NY: Cambridge University Press.

Lehman, P.K. and Geller, E.S. (2004). Behavior analysis and environmental protection: accomplishments and potential for more. *Behavior and Social Issues* 13: 13–32.

REVIEW QUESTIONS

1. Some behaviours offer natural or intrinsic consequences, while others do not. Provide an example of both, and explain the presence or absence of a natural consequence that might be a reinforcer.

2. Pro-environmental behaviour often lacks natural reinforcers. Explain the meaning of this statement with a practical example.

3. Why does most research favour incentive and reward interventions over disincentive and penalty strategies?

4. Monetary incentives and disincentives may not always work as intended. Explain why this is the case.

5. Provide an example of the antecedents and consequences of a pro-environmental behaviour, along with potential ways to alter the antecedents and consequences in order to increase the occurrence of that behaviour.

28 Persuasive Technology to Promote Pro-Environmental Behaviour

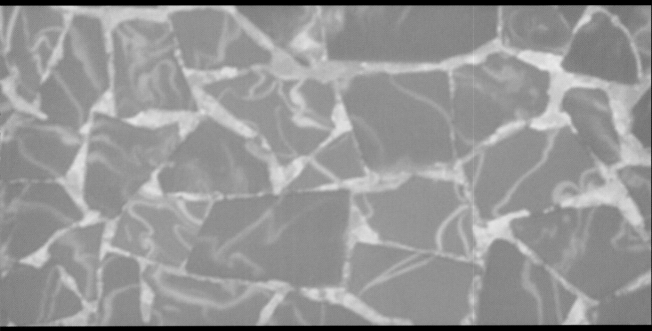

Cees Midden
Eindhoven University of Technology, The Netherlands

Jaap Ham
Eindhoven University of Technology, The Netherlands

CHAPTER OUTLINE

28.1   INTRODUCTION

From the earliest times humans have used technology as a means to make life easier. Unfortunately, the use of technology has often led to unwanted side-effects and by-products such as pollution and industrial waste. However technology can also be used to support pro-environmental behaviour and to promote sustainable living. Chapters 26 and 27 have described how various interventions and incentives have been introduced to persuade people to act in a more pro-environmental way. In this chapter we will discuss the dimensions and scope of **persuasive technology** and its potential to promote sustainable use of the environment surrounding us. Persuasive technology aims to bridge the gap between technological and psychological contributions to solving environmental problems by intervening in user–system interactions that have environmental consequences. Various approaches to persuasive technology will be introduced including the use of persuasive agents, the provision of new experiences, the use of persuasive ambient technology, and persuasive technology at the group level that acknowledges the social nature of environmental behaviour.

28.2   TECHNOLOGY AND BEHAVIOUR

Environmental policy and scientific research usually approach technology by emphasizing either technological innovation to reduce environmental impact or the need to change human use of technology and resources. However, each approach has its limitations, because technology and behaviour often appear closely interwoven. For example, to become successful, technological innovation must be accepted by consumers. Furthermore, while better engineering undeniably has improved the resource-efficiency of many technical appliances such as lighting systems and cars, technical improvements do not necessarily lead to less environmental impact. For example, despite remarkably improved car technology, car use still remains a major source of air pollution in many countries. While this is mostly due to the absolute increase in vehicle numbers, part of it results from adaptive consumer reactions that are referred to as **rebound effects**. These effects suggest that consumers intensify car use (e.g. take longer trips, drive larger car), as a result of the increased fuel efficiency (Midden et al. 2007).

Environmental Psychology: An Introduction, Second Edition. Edited by Linda Steg and Judith I. M. de Groot.

Not only does behaviour influence the acceptance and impacts of technology, technology may in turn influence human behaviour. Behaviour, to a large extent, results from its interaction with the context (see also Chapter 15), including technological products and systems that increasingly shape the behavioural context of people. For example, our mobility choices are as much dependent on our goals and preferences for destinations and comfort as on available systems of public transport, cycling lanes, and parking facilities. However, the influence of technology on behaviour is often unintended and unknown. From this perspective designing technological environments that sparsely strain resources, but also foster sustainable human use, could contribute significantly to the pursuit of sustainable living. We use the term 'persuasive technology' to refer to systems and environments that are designed to change human cognitive processing, attitudes, and behaviours (see Fogg 2003).

28.3   PERSUASIVE TECHNOLOGY

Persuasion can be argued to be a typical human activity. In particular, humans are capable of applying persuasive mechanisms like argumentation, praise, reciprocity, norm activation, or authority. Research on persuasion has almost exclusively focused on human–human persuasive interactions (see e.g. Petty and Wegener 1998, for an overview). This research has identified many persuasion factors that are related to source features (e.g. trustworthiness), message factors (e.g. argument strength), and receiver factors (e.g. involvement). One may wonder whether similar processes would occur if the persuader were technological in nature instead of human.

Technology has always played an important role in facilitating the delivery of persuasive messages using traditional channels (e.g. billboards) to modern interactive systems that pervade human lives (e.g. Google internet search outcomes). Due to their sometimes human-like communication features (e.g. use of speech) these interactive systems can take over the role of persuasive agents, at least at the perceptual level of the receiver. Technological persuaders have specific advantages over human persuaders (Fogg 2003). They can be more persistent (although this can be annoying as well), they allow anonymity (which is useful for example when sensitive issues are at stake), they can employ virtually unlimited amounts of data (to retrieve the right information at the right time) and they can use many modalities of interaction (e.g. audio, video, virtual environments, games) to convey messages and provide experiences that are convincing. Moreover, technological interventions can easily be distributed and, with computers becoming increasingly ubiquitous, persuasive technology may gain access to areas where human persuaders would not be welcomed (e.g. bedroom) or are physically unable to go (e.g. inside clothing). In the next section we will identify three ways persuasive technology can be used to change user behaviour.

28.4   APPROACHES TO APPLYING PERSUASIVE TECHNOLOGY

Persuasive technology can have various functions: it can work as a social actor capable of establishing a social relationship that forms the basis of social influence, it can it can be a medium that allows for persuasive experiences, and it can provide tools that guide or support behaviour (Fogg 2003).

As a social actor, persuasive technology applies principles that humans use to influence others through social mechanisms like social approval, norm activation, or social comparison. Research has demonstrated that people react to intelligent systems similarly to the way they react to other human beings (Reeves and Nass 1996). For example, people showed gratitude to a technological system after it provided a service just as when appreciating other humans. These effects suggest that 'smart systems' can affect people through social influence.

As a medium, persuasive technology can provide novel experiences. Technology mediates many of our experiences of the world, for example, when we see a piece of nature through binoculars. These mediations transform our perceptions, thereby emphasizing certain elements and ignoring others (see Verbeek and Slob 2006). Multimedia technologies can add persuasive significance by inducing direct sensory experiences such as sounds, images, scent, and touch that create 'presence' (the feeling of 'being there' in a mediated environment). Technological media may for example call attention to issues that are temporally and spatially distant (e.g. climate change, which takes place in the future or in faraway countries) through direct sensory experiences instead of indirect information. In the section 'Providing Persuasive Experiences' we discuss the use of mediated experiences in more detail.

As a tool, persuasive technology can help in various ways to promote change. First, it can make new behaviours easier and thereby more attractive and controllable for a person. An example is buying organic products on a website that supports one-click shopping. Second, persuasive technology can help to tailor information, making the message more personal and context-specific and therefore more persuasive. For example, a food advisor may use technology to take account of the user's mood. Third, persuasive systems may be used to implement learning schemes that systematically reinforce desired behaviours. For example, persons can get engaged in simulation games that contain these learning mechanisms. Fourth, persuasive technology can help people to monitor the consequences of their behaviours by providing feedback about those consequences (see the discussion of ambient light feedback in Section 28.7). Fifth, persuasive technology can activate social norms, for example by providing performance information in a group (see the discussion of group interventions as a way to strengthen social norms in Section 28.7). In the following sections we will take a closer look at the three functions of persuasive technology.

28.5   SOCIAL INFLUENCE THROUGH SMART SYSTEMS

Basically, humans employ three types of strategies to influence others (Cialdini and Trost 1998): social norms (see also Chapter 18), conformity (e.g. Moscovici 1985), and compliance (e.g. Milgram 1974; see also Chapter 23). Intelligent systems seem capable of employing these social influence strategies, particularly since people's interactions with these kinds of systems are similar to those with real people (Reeves and Nass 1996). For example, people are comparably sensitive to praise from a computer as to praise from humans. However, it remains unclear what the underlying cognitive mechanisms are of social human–artificial agent interaction, to what extent these social interactions lead to real social influence, and which agent and interaction features are relevant.

Research indicates that persuasive technology that employs social influence strategies has stronger persuasive effects than persuasive technology that employs non-social influence strategies (Midden and Ham 2009). For example, in a lab setting, experiments investigated whether social norm information provided by persuasive technology was effective in reducing energy consumption. Participants could conserve energy while carrying out washing tasks with a simulated washing machine. During this task, some participants received (positive or negative) **social feedback** about their energy consumption from a robot (the iCat; developed by Philips Corporation: see Figure 28.1) that is able to show human-like facial expressions, can talk, and has lights on its ears and paws. The iCat told participants for example 'Your energy consumption is terrible' when they set the temperature of the washing machine to 90 °C, indicating social disapproval. Other participants received (positive or negative) feedback of a non-social, more factual nature: an energy-bar indicator was included in the washing machine interface that indicated energy consumption. Results showed that social feedback had stronger persuasive effects than factual feedback. Furthermore, one of the experiments suggested that even when factual feedback comprised an evaluation (a lamp indicating energy consumption through colour changes indicating high or low consumption), social feedback led to the lowest energy consumption thereby supporting the notion that social feedback caused the effect. In addition, the studies suggested that negative feedback (especially social but also factual) leads to more conservation actions than positive feedback. This finding fits earlier research indicating that negative (social) events more strongly draw attention and are processed more intensely than positive events (Baumeister et al. 2001), although this depends on the specific situation (see Chapter 27).

28.5.1   *The Role of Social Cues*

If social influence is typical for human actors, should effective persuasive technology have humanoid features that suggest its capability of social interaction?

Figure 28.1 *The iCat, an animated robot capable of expressing emotions and providing spoken factual and social feedback.*

In other words, which and how many social cues are needed to make systems capable of exerting social influence? Research indicates that a humanoid body and humanoid speech are important social cues, and that the presence of either of these enhances the persuasiveness of technology (Vossen et al. 2010). Interestingly, using a single social cue, speech, or a humanoid embodiment, was equally effective in activating a social mode of interaction with a persuasive agent as using a combination of both cues. This suggests that artificial agents need not necessarily be extremely human-like to be effective in social influence. Intriguingly, when an artificial agent has social cues similar to the user (e.g. looks like you), it is trusted more easily (Verberne et al. 2015). These social responses are difficult to control, and happen especially when people are distracted (Ham et al. 2012). Research (Roubroeks 2014) suggested that only participants who were continuously reminded to focus on the artificiality of an agent (e.g. that it was not really crying) showed fewer social responses to it (e.g. feel empathy for it).

28.5.2 Reactance

People may experience persuasive messages, including those coming from technology, as a threat to their autonomy, which can lead to **psychological reactance** (Brehm 1966; Roubroeks et al. 2010). Indeed, participants experienced more psychological reactance (anger and negative thoughts about the iCat) when the iCat gave advice that threatened a participant's freedom ('You have to set the temperature to 30 °C') compared to advice that was less threatening ('You can set the temperature to 30 °C'). Psychological reactance might even lead to unintended behavioural responses (e.g. increasing washing temperature).

28.6 PROVIDING PERSUASIVE EXPERIENCES

Many governments launch mass-media campaigns to raise awareness about environmental issues, risks, and the urgency of significant behaviour change, often with disappointing results (see Bartels and Nelissen 2001, for an overview). It appeared difficult to raise awareness for issues that are abstract, distant, or hard to imagine, like climate change. New technological media, though, may add persuasive significance to the traditional communication (e.g. text or speech) by inducing direct sensory experiences (e.g. scent, touch) that create 'presence'. These technologies may enable people to better conceptualize the effects of climate change. New media technologies employ for example user-initiated simulation control, 3D- presentation, and haptic (through touch) feedback (see IJsselsteijn 2004, for an overview).

Technical media can use the effects of sensory experiences for increasing message persuasiveness. Studies show that video images with emotionally charged content stimulate attention and information search for climate risks and coping options (Meijnders et al. 2001). Research on flooding experiences indicated that an immersive 3D virtual environment was more effective than traditional video in stimulating the processing of coping information and enhancing the willingness to buy additional flooding insurance (Zaalberg and Midden 2010). Also, room lighting (e.g. warmer white lighting) can influence people's experiences of room temperature (e.g. perceiving it to be warmer than it actually is) potentially influencing heating energy consumption (Lu et al. 2015).

28.7 PERSUASIVE TECHNOLOGY AS A TOOL TO PROMOTE BEHAVIOUR CHANGE

In this section, we will discuss two ways in which persuasive technology can be used as a tool to promote behaviour change: ambient persuasion and group interventions.

28.7.1 *Ambient Persuasion*

Most types of persuasive communication are only effective if the user pays attention to them. However, in many situations people might not be motivated or lack the cognitive capacity to consciously process relatively complex information (see also Chapter 26) like factual feedback. Could we design a form of persuasive technology that does not need the user's conscious attention to be effective?

One possibility is **ambient intelligence**: the pervasion of everyday life with information technology (Riva et al. 2004). This allows new forms of influencing through subtle cues in the environment (see also Chapter 15) or prompting (see Chapter 26) reflecting changes in form, movement, sound, colour, smell, or light. For example, a device called WaterBot aims to reduce water consumption by tracking and displaying information about water consumption at the sink itself (Arroyo et al. 2005).

A crucial advantage of **ambient persuasive technology** is that it can continue influencing people, even in daily situations in which cognitive resources are taxed and where interventions that need cognitive attention would not be influential (Ham and Midden 2010). Interactive feedback using lighting can function as ambient persuasive technology as it might be simpler to process than factual feedback: It can directly express evaluative meaning whereas factual feedback still needs to be processed and evaluated by the user. Ham and Midden (2010) found that participants who processed interactive lighting feedback about their energy consumption in a certain task could easily perform a second task at the same time, whereas participants who processed factual energy consumption feedback could not. What makes this type of feedback so fast and easy? In Box 28.1 we discuss the role of colour associations.

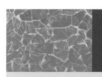

BOX 28.1   AMBIENT PERSUASIVE TECHNOLOGY: THE ROLE OF COLOUR ASSOCIATIONS

Research (Lu et al. 2016) demonstrated that using strong and association-consistent colours in relation to the task eases the processing of the feedback information, while information that is inconsistent with pre-existing associations will inhibit processing. Colours may have strong associations. For example, red indicates 'alertness' or 'danger', in the context of green, and 'hot' in the context of blue. Coloured light-glow feedback with high association strength like red for high energy consumption and green for low worked better than a colour pair with weaker associations like yellow for high and purple for low energy consumption. Lighting-mediated information, possibly in combination with ambient sound offers great opportunities to support individual or groups of users to achieve their goals while keeping cognitive efforts and disturbance at a minimum.

28.7.2 Group Interventions

Most interventions encouraging energy savings (and pro-environmental behaviour in general) treat individuals as the decision-making unit. However, energy conservation usually happens in social systems and is the result of actions by group members. The social dynamics that occur within these groups may influence energy consumption behaviours to a large extent. So, technological interventions should also address the group level.

The most important group levels, like the household and groups in offices, seem to be largely ignored by researchers. A potential reason for why household dynamics have received little attention is that behaviours are often private and hence difficult to observe. In addition, consumption measures are available only at the aggregate household level making it difficult to understand the group behaviour. Persuasive technology may offer options to better observe the behaviour of group members and facilitate communication in the group, thereby allowing more effective interventions. For example, technology that makes group members identifiable can make the feedback given to the group more specific and accurate.

Research investigating persuasive technology (Midden et al. 2011) tested the persuasive power of group and **individual comparison feedback** within households in two identical studies in the Netherlands and Japan. Subjects participated in a simulated household in which they could conduct various types of energy-consuming tasks (e.g. set the climate control). Feedback was provided using an interface based on the Eco-Island application (Shiraishi et al. 2009). This interface showed four (identifiable) participants as avatars on an island (see Figure 28.2). Half of the participants received **group feedback** (about the total group performance) while the other half did not: A higher water level indicated higher group energy consumption. Furthermore, half of the participants received individual comparison feedback (about the relative member contribution) while the other half did not: Shirt-colour indicated the relative amount of energy consumed by each group member. The study in the Netherlands indicated that individual comparison feedback especially lowered energy consumption. Group feedback only reduced energy consumption when individual comparison feedback was also given.

In contrast, in the collectivistic Japanese context, group feedback especially was effective in reducing energy consumption, while individual comparison feedback did not produce significant effects. So, the effectiveness of group and individual comparison feedback seems to differ across cultures (Midden et al. 2011). In sum, interventions at the group level, like group and individual comparison feedback, are promising for the reduction of energy consumption. The type of intervention, the combination of interventions, and the cultural context are important factors to consider in the design of persuasive technology.

Finally, research indicates that artificial agents may also be able to exert group pressure. Two studies were conducted to investigate the conformity effect of group pressure on participants' comparative judgements of lengths of lines, based on the classic Asch paradigm (Midden et al. 2015). Group pressure by human majorities was compared with pressure by majorities of boxed PCs

Figure 28.2 *Eco-Island providing group and individual comparison feedback.*

and of artificial virtual agents. Results indicated that normative pressure is limited to human majorities, while informational pressure can also be exerted by artificial majorities. Thus, artificial agents seem able to exert group pressure, although the extent of these effects needs further clarification.

28.8   SUMMARY

Persuasive technology aims to bridge the gap between technological and psychological contributions to solving environmental problems by intervening in user–system interactions that have environmental consequences. Technology and behaviour are closely interwoven: the environmental impact of technical innovations depends to a large extent on people's acceptance and reactions; while, the technological environment increasingly shapes human behaviour. There are three functions of persuasive technology. First, persuasive technology can function as a social actor or 'smart system' that applies principles that humans use to influence others through social mechanisms such as social approval, norm activation, or social comparison. Smart persuasive technology offers novel capabilities to make information more interactive and context specific. It can offer users advice and feedback at the right time and place and with precision and consistency that cannot be achieved by human agents. Second, persuasive technology can provide a medium that filters our experience of the world. In particular, interactive virtual environments can provide persuasive sensory experiences that are not achievable in the physical world. Third, persuasive technology can provide tools for promoting behaviour change by making desirable behaviours easier and more controllable. For example, the use of ambient intelligence decreases the use of cognitive resources which helps to ease behaviour change. Furthermore, technology that provides feedback about group and individual behaviour may influence the group dynamics that are crucial for understanding energy consumption behaviour.

GLOSSARY

ambient intelligence   The pervasive presence of information technology in everyday life that is sensitive and responsive to the presence of people.

ambient persuasive technology   Technological systems and environments that are designed to change human cognitive processing, attitudes, and behaviours without the need for the user's conscious attention.

group feedback   Information about group performance.

individual comparison feedback   Information that compares the individual performance of a group member to the performance of the other group members.

persuasive technology   Technological systems and environments that are designed to change human cognitive processing, attitudes, and behaviours.

psychological reactance   A process in which people act in an opposite way to the intention of persuasion attempts, in order to restore their lost sense of freedom.

rebound effects   Responses to the introduction of new technologies, or other measures taken to reduce specific effects of technology (e.g. resource consumption), that tend to offset the beneficial effects of these technologies or measures.

social feedback   Social approval or disapproval of individual or group performance, coming from an (artificial) social actor.

SUGGESTIONS FOR FURTHER READING

Fogg, B.J. (2003). *Persuasive Technology: Using Computers to Change What We Think and Do*. Amsterdam: Morgan Kaufmann.

IJsselsteijn, W., de Kort, Y., Midden, C.J.H. et al. (2006). *Persuasive Technology*. Heidelberg: Springer.

Spahn, A. (2011). And lead us (not) into persuasion…? Persuasive technology and the ethics of communication. *Science and Engineering Ethics* doi: 10.1007/s11948-011-9278-y.

REVIEW QUESTIONS

1. How can persuasive technology contribute to the promotion of pro-environmental behaviour? Name and describe three functions of persuasive technology.
2. Why would people be sensitive to the social approval or disapproval of artificial persuasive agents?
3. Why might ambient persuasive technology be effective in daily life?

29 Acceptability of Environmental Policies

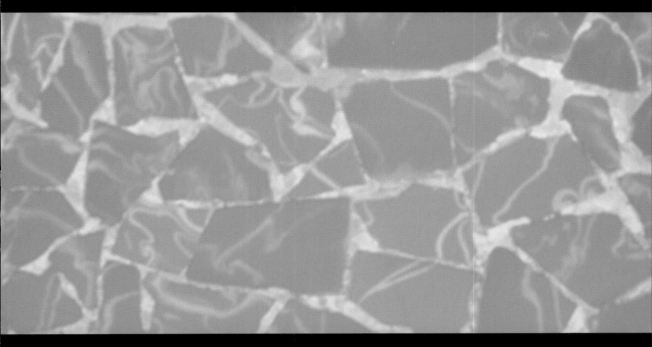

Geertje Schuitema
University College Dublin, Ireland

Cecilia J. Bergstad
University of Gothenburg, Sweden

CHAPTER OUTLINE

29.1   INTRODUCTION

The introduction of a congestion charge in London in 2003 effectively reduced car travel and improved the local environmental quality, traffic safety, and the accessibility of locations. In the slipstream of London's road user charge, similar road pricing schemes were proposed in other cities in the UK, as well as in other countries. On multiple occasions, the public strongly opposed the introduction of these road pricing schemes, for example in Manchester (2005), Edinburgh (2007), New York City (2008), the Netherlands (2010), and Copenhagen (2012). As a result, the road pricing schemes were rejected, sometimes through local referendums, sometimes as a result of national debate. To date road pricing schemes have not been implemented in these places. Hence, public **acceptability** can have a strong influence on the decision-making process around implementing environmental policies. Earlier chapters in this volume have explained how behaviour can be changed by various types of environmental policies and interventions; this chapter focuses on the factors that influence the public acceptability of such policies and interventions.

Environmental policies are implemented at all levels in society. Some are directed towards groups of people, whereas others specifically aim to influence large companies or planners at the municipal level. We focus on a specific type of environmental policy, that is: policies that target individuals, including taxes on energy, water, car use, and flying; bans on energy-inefficient appliances, such as light bulbs; use of renewable energy sources (e.g. wind or solar energy); implementation of fishing and agricultural quotas; wildlife protection ordinances; and information campaigns or social marketing strategies to stimulate sustainable consumption patterns.

The outline of the chapter is as follows. Firstly, we explain the concept of acceptability and present a theoretical framework to explain which individual factors affect the acceptability of environmental policies. Next, we explain the role of perceived **procedural fairness** and **trust** in authorities for judgements of acceptability. Finally, we illustrate how all these factors affect the acceptability of environmental policies in a real-life example.

29.2   ACCEPTABILITY AS A SOCIAL DILEMMA

The concept of acceptability of environmental policies is usually approached in two different ways. Acceptability can be defined as a specific type of pro-environmental behaviour (Stern 2000), that is, it reflects a type of non-activist

Environmental Psychology: An Introduction, Second Edition. Edited by Linda Steg and Judith I. M. de Groot.
© 2019 John Wiley & Sons Ltd. Published 2019 by John Wiley & Sons Ltd.

behaviour in the public sphere. Non-activist behaviour, such as voting in referendums or signing petitions, can affect the decision-making process around the implementation of public policies (see Chapter 22).

On the other hand, acceptability of policy measures can be defined as an **attitude** towards these policies (Eriksson et al. 2006), that is, an evaluation of environmental policies with some degree of favour or disfavour (Eagly and Chaiken 1993). Attitudes are generally considered to be an important determinant of behaviour and can influence the implementation of environmental policies, for example, by influencing actions such as protesting. In addition, attitudes also influence how people change their behaviour when policies are implemented. If they have a strong negative attitude towards a policy, they might refuse to comply with the policy.

In both approaches, it is assumed that acceptability is determined by specific beliefs about the policy outcomes. Environmental policies can have positive and negative consequences for individuals and for society as a whole. On an individual level, people can either change their behaviour when a policy is implemented (e.g. fly less, recycle waste) or face the consequences of an environmental policy (e.g. face changes in the landscape or pay higher taxes). On a societal level, environmental policies, if effective, generally have positive consequences for society, for example because of reduced levels of harmful emissions and the protection of ecosystems and species. In some cases, negative collective consequences may occur as well, for example wind turbine parks may damage landscapes and wildlife protection ordinances may negatively affect economic welfare.

Many environmental policies have negative individual consequences (e.g. higher financial costs), but positive collective consequences (e.g. improved environmental quality). As such, the acceptability of many policy measures can be described as a **social dilemma** (see also Chapter 21), because individual and collective consequences are at odds.

29.3 THEORETICAL FRAMEWORK TO EXPLAIN THE ACCEPTABILITY OF POLICY MEASURES

Assuming that the acceptability of environmental policies reflects a social dilemma, a relevant theoretical framework explaining which factors determine acceptability is the **greed-efficiency-fairness (GEF) hypothesis** (Wilke 1991; see also Chapter 21), which states that in a social dilemma, people a priori want to maximize their own outcomes, but also want to preserve collective resources and distribute outcomes fairly. Thus, it can be argued that the acceptability of environmental policies is related to three main factors: (i) individual policy outcomes, (ii) collective policy outcomes, and (iii) the perceived fairness of the distribution of policy outcomes.

29.3.1 Individual Policy Outcomes

Policy measures may be perceived as unacceptable when people expect that they will have negative consequences for themselves (Jakobsson et al. 2000). In general, the acceptability of environmental policies decreases when people expect an infringement on their freedom or if the costs for not complying with these policies are too high. For example, the implementation of a fishing or agricultural quota is usually seen as a strong infringement on the freedom of fisherman or farmers, because they are restricted in the amount of products they can catch or grow. Those who do not comply with these quotas usually face severe consequences, such as high fines.

The extent to which policies infringe people's freedom, and thus affect their acceptability levels, depends on policy features. Policies can target **efficiency behaviour,** referring to the adoption of energy-efficient solutions such as electric cars or house insulation. This usually implies a single action or behavioural change on an infrequent basis. Policies can also target **curtailment behaviour,** which refers to changes in user behaviour that typically have to be made on a frequent basis, e.g. reducing shower times or thermostat settings. Policies targeting efficiency behaviour are generally more positively evaluated than those targeting curtailment behaviour (De Groot and Schuitema 2012). Even though efficiency behaviours typically require large investments, curtailment behaviours generally require more effort and reduce people's freedom to move. Consequently, policies that target efficiency behaviour are usually more acceptable than policies that target curtailment behaviour.

One strategy to enhance the acceptability of environmental policies is to compensate individuals for possible negative consequences of these measures, which can be realized by implementing a package of policy measures instead of single policies. To illustrate, individuals are more likely to find **push measures** (i.e. measures aimed at making environmentally unfriendly behaviour less attractive) acceptable when **pull measures** (i.e. measures aimed at making environmentally friendly behaviour more attractive) are implemented at the same time, because in that case desired changes are facilitated and made more attractive (Banister 2008; see Box 29.1). For example, higher taxes on flying may be more acceptable if high-speed railways are built at the same time.

29.3.2 Collective Policy Outcomes

The GEF hypothesis states that people do not always focus on their self-interests; they also want to use collective resources efficiently. This implies that environmental policies are more acceptable when people expect that collective problems will reduce after these policies are implemented (Gärling et al. 2008), that is,

BOX 29.1 PUSH VERSUS PULL MEASURES

Push measures are aimed at making environmentally unfriendly behaviour less attractive. Examples are taxes on fossil energy use or fuels and land reforms. In contrast, pull measures are aimed at making environmentally friendly behaviour more attractive, such as subsidizing solar panels, or improving the quality of public transport. In general, push measures are more effective in changing individual's behaviour. As a result, push measures are often perceived as less fair and acceptable than pull measures, because they are seen as an infringement on one's freedom (Eriksson et al. 2006). However, push measures are also more likely to have positive collective outcomes, as they are more likely to result in behavioural change. If push measures are indeed effective in reducing collective problems, acceptability judgements may become more positive as far as people believe that the problems will reduce and they understand and agree that it is important that they do so.

when the policies are believed to be effective. This is more likely to be achieved when policies have clear objectives (Schuitema et al. 2010b).

As another example, push measures are often more effective in changing behaviour than pull measures, and consequently they are often also believed to be more effective (see also Box 29.1). However, the acceptance levels of push measures depend on how many others find a policy acceptable: if a policy is considered to be acceptable by a majority (implying a strong **social norm,** see Chapter 18), this policy is seen as more acceptable than when the same policy is considered acceptable by a minority (implying a weak social norm) (De Groot and Schuitema 2012). This is probably because people feel more certain that others support a policy too, and as a result, the chance of positive outcomes for them increases.

Sometimes it is found that people perceive pull measures as more effective than push measures (e.g. Eriksson et al. 2008). However, these might be strategic perceptions, in that people might say that push measures are less effective than pull measures because they find push measures unacceptable and hope that pull measures will be implemented instead.

One reason why policy effectiveness is important for the acceptability of policies is that many people value the environment and consider the interests of the collective (see also Chapters 17 and 22). In addition, a reduction in collective problems may benefit individuals as well, depending on the extent to which they are affected by these collective problems. For example, reductions in car use may improve local air quality and thus reduce health problems, or may reduce travel times if congestion decreases.

The acceptability of environmental policies is generally higher when people are aware of and concerned about environmental problems (Eriksson et al. 2006). This is probably the case when problems are clearly visible.

Hence, environmental policies are likely to be more acceptable when they are implemented in areas that face serious (environmental) problems. Environmental concerns may also affect the perceived effectiveness of policies. For example, a study in Sweden showed that people with a high environmental concern believed more strongly that environmental policies would increase urban environmental quality than those with a low environmental concern (Loukopoulos et al. 2005).

Research suggests that the acceptability of policy measures increases when people actually experience the benefits of such policies after they are implemented. For example, experiencing the advantages of wind turbines increases acceptability levels, despite initial resistance against this policy (Wolsink 2007) and a study in Wales showed that carrier bag charges were more acceptable after they were implemented (Poortinga et al. 2013). This suggests that public support can increase after an environmental policy is implemented because of the experienced benefits. However, this implies that when policy outcomes are negative or less positive than expected, public support may not change over time, or even decrease after policies are implemented. This happened for example in Lyon, France, where a tax scheme had to be revised significantly after it had been implemented, due to public resistance (Raux and Souche 2004).

29.3.3   *Fair Distribution of Policy Outcomes*

The third assumption of the GEF hypothesis is that people have a desire to distribute outcomes fairly, referring to **distributive fairness** (Tyler 2000). But how should outcomes be distributed to make policies fair and thus acceptable? Fairness judgements are based on comparing policy outcomes with a reference point. Three types of comparisons can be made, based on different fairness principles and resulting in different policy outcomes: **intrapersonal**, **interpersonal**, and **intergenerational comparisons** (see Figure 29.1).

Intrapersonal comparison refers to a comparison of individual policy outcomes with an internal reference point or previous outcomes, independent of the outcomes of others. An example is comparing outcomes of a pricing policy with the absolute amount of money that one is willing to pay for certain goods, such as electricity. An increase in electricity taxes will be evaluated as unfair and unacceptable if the resulting electricity price is higher than this internal norm. A second reference point could be one's current situation. For example, you can consider policies that encourage the establishment of wind turbines unfair and unacceptable if you believe that wind turbines damage your view, and make you feel that you are worse off than before.

Interpersonal comparisons imply that people compare the outcomes of a policy for them personally with the outcomes of individuals or groups in the population. Firstly, one's own outcomes can be compared to that of others, that is, one may find a policy unfair if the outcomes of that policy affect oneself more strongly than others. To illustrate, a fisherman may consider a fishing quota on codfish as unfair and unacceptable, because that will affect his business negatively, but will not affect his colleague who fishes herring.

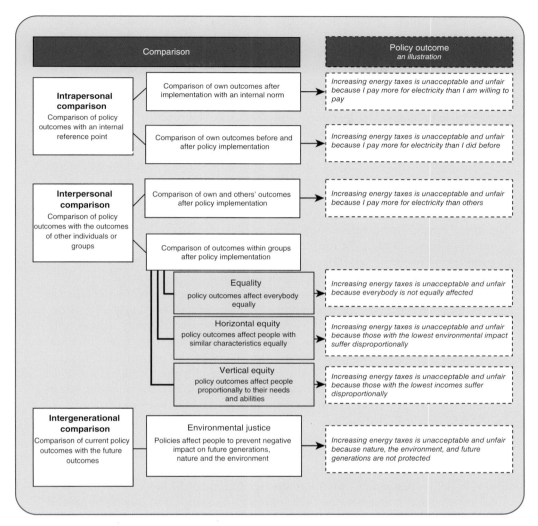

Figure 29.1 *Overview of comparisons used to evaluate policy outcomes.*
Source: Adapted from Schuitema et al. (2011).

Next, outcomes across groups can also be compared. In this respect, two relevant fairness principles are **equality** and **equity**. Equality implies that a policy affects all individuals to the same extent. To illustrate, a ban on light bulbs may be seen as fair and acceptable because it affects everybody equally. On the other hand, the placement of wind turbines may be perceived as unfair and unacceptable, because wind turbines affect those who live close-by more negatively than those living further away and thus do not affect everyone equally. Resistance to these facilities can occur if these facilities have negative consequences for local communities, for example as the result of noise or odour nuisances, health and safety risks, or losses in terms of the economic value of their property.

Equity implies that all people are *relatively* equally affected by policy outcomes. A distinction can be made between **horizontal** and **vertical equity**.

Horizontal equity implies that people with similar characteristics are equally affected by policy measures, such as one's impact on the environment. For example, a policy can be considered as unfair and unacceptable if those who have a small impact on the environment (e.g. use little energy, water, or space) are equally or more strongly affected by environmental policies than those who have a large environmental impact. Vertical equity implies that people are affected in proportion to their needs and abilities. For example, income-dependent car taxes may be evaluated as more fair and acceptable, because the relative changes in costs for low and high-income groups would be the same. In other words, policies may be seen as unfair and unacceptable if low-income groups are equally (or even more strongly) affected than high-income groups.

Finally, intergenerational comparisons imply that people compare current policy outcomes with outcomes for future generations and effects on nature and the environment (referring to a policy outcome that reflects **environmental justice**; Clayton 2000). An example of environmental justice is that wildlife protection laws may be seen as fair and acceptable if people believe they will protect nature, the environment, and future generations.

Few studies have examined how policy outcomes based on different fairness principles are related to the evaluation of fairness and acceptability of environmental policies. Clayton (2000) found that environmental justice was considered to be the most important principle in resolving two environmental conflicts, that is, a conflict concerning the ability of the government to place restrictions on the way private landowners may develop their land and a conflict about whether national parks should be made accessible to the public or left in their natural state. Also, environmental justice was the best predictor of fairness and acceptability judgements of various environmental pricing policies, next to other principles such as equity and equality (Schuitema et al. 2011). Environmental justice typically reflects a concern with collective considerations, but may also reflect self-interest to some extent, that is, individuals may also benefit when policy outcomes are distributed on the basis of environmental justice, for example because they appreciate better local air quality or natural water sources.

29.4   PROCEDURAL FAIRNESS AND ACCEPTABILITY OF ENVIRONMENTAL POLICIES

Fair procedures and decision-making processes lead to greater compliance with these decisions and increase trust in the decision-makers, which are important preconditions for environmental policies to be accepted. Procedural fairness refers to the perceived fairness of the procedures and decision-making processes used before and during the implementation of environmental policies, that is, the extent to which decision procedures meet basic societal values and norms of fairness (see also Chapters 17 and 18). This is related to trust, reflecting the expectation that another party can be depended on to fulfil its commitments. Public involvement is often seen as a key factor to increase perceptions of procedural fairness and trust in authorities, because it allows people to express their views. However, public involvement is only effective when people's views are considered seriously.

Another important determinant of procedural fairness and trust is consistency of decision-making procedures over time. It is important that procedures follow the same rules, that is, open and informative communication and authorities keeping to their commitments. Related to this, acceptability depends on the consistency between policy measures across policy sectors (Banister 2008). For example, a mixed message is given if prices for grey and green energy increase simultaneously, which may reduce acceptability for environmental policies in general.

29.5   HOW CAN PUBLIC SUPPORT INCREASE OVER TIME? AN ILLUSTRATION

After long debates, the Swedish government agreed on a seven-month congestion charge trial in Stockholm, starting in January 2006. Motorized vehicles were charged during office hours every time they passed a charging point. Some exceptions were made, such as for taxis, emergency vehicles, and low-emission vehicles. Also, public transport was expanded and more parking places were created near train stations.

Before the trial, acceptability of the congestion charge was low. People were sceptical about the positive effects of the congestion charge whereas they expected large cost increases (Schuitema et al. 2010a). Moreover, the trust in the government was low, mainly due to political issues. As a result strong negative reactions against the congestion charge from the public and the media were observed before the trial started (Isaksson and Richardson 2009).

After the trial, acceptability was much higher than beforehand, which was reflected in the results of a referendum held after the trial: 51.3% of the inhabitants of Stockholm city voted in favour of a permanent implementation of the congestions charge, whereas 45.5% voted against the scheme. As a result, since 2007 the congestion charge has been permanently in place.

Why did acceptability of the congestion trial increase? There are several possible explanations. Firstly, public transport was improved, which facilitated behavioural change and compensated car users somewhat for the negative consequences of the charge. Secondly, the congestion charge reduced congestion and pollution levels decreased, while accessibility increased. These positive effects were not merely reported by the government and the media, but the public also expressed the fact that they actually experienced these effects (Schuitema et al. 2010a). At the same time, the negative effects were not as big as they had expected. More specifically, after the charge was implemented, people believed that congestion, parking problems, and pollution had decreased more, while increases in travel costs turned out to be less high then expected beforehand. No significant differences were found in the extent to which people expected reductions in their own car use and crowdedness in public transport (see Figure 29.2). Thirdly, an important aim of the charge was to reduce pollution

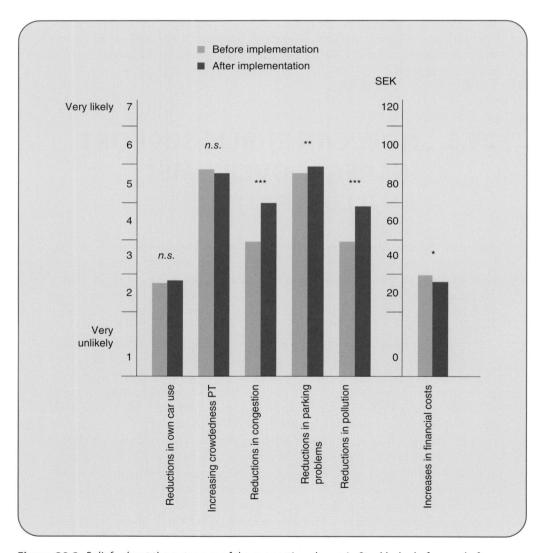

Figure 29.2 *Beliefs about the outcomes of the congestion charge in Stockholm before and after implementation.*
Source: Adapted from Schuitema et al. (2010a). SEK = Swedish Kronor (January 2006: 1 SEK ≈ 0,11 Euro); PT = Public Transport. ***$p < 0.001$; **$p < 0.01$; *$p < 0.05$; *n.s.* = not significant.

levels in Stockholm, which complies with the fairness principle of environmental justice. As discussed before, environmental justice plays an important role in judgements on fairness and acceptability of environmental policies. Finally, the trial period, which 'forced' people to experience the (positive) effects of the scheme, was followed by a referendum, which probably enhanced the feeling that fair procedures were followed (see Hensher and Li 2013). The congestion charge in Stockholm is not a unique case; very similar effects were found after the introduction of a congestion charge in Gothenburg (Nilsson et al. 2016).

29.6   SUMMARY

In this chapter we have given an overview of factors that influence the acceptability of environmental policies. We explained that the acceptability of policy measures can be seen as a social dilemma. We then proposed and discussed three key variables that predict the acceptability of environmental policies: (i) individual policy outcomes – acceptability decreases if people expect negative consequences for themselves after their implementation; (ii) collective policy outcomes – acceptability increases if people expect collective problems to be reduced after their implementation; and (iii) outcomes distribution – acceptability increases if outcomes are distributed fairly. We also explained how fair procedures and decision-making processes can enhance acceptability judgements. Finally, we described a real-life example to illustrate how acceptability of environmental policies can increase over time.

GLOSSARY

acceptability   Either a type of non-activist behaviour in the public sphere or an attitude towards a policy measure before a policy measure is implemented.

attitude   Evaluation of an entity with some degree of favour or disfavour.

curtailment behaviour   Changes in user behaviour, which typically implies behavioural changes on a frequent basis.

distributive fairness   An evaluation of the fairness of the distribution of outcomes.

efficiency behaviour   The adoption of energy-efficient solutions, which typically implies a single action.

environmental justice   Policies affect people in order to prevent a negative impact on future generations, nature, and the environment.

equality   Policies affect all people to the same extent.

equity   Policies affect people in proportion to individual characteristics, needs, or abilities.

greed-efficiency-fairness hypothesis   Hypothesis that states that in a social dilemma, people a priori want to maximize their own outcomes, but also want to preserve collective resources and distribute outcomes fairly.

horizontal equity   Policies affect people with similar characteristics equally.

intergenerational comparison   A comparison of current outcomes with outcomes for future generations and effects on nature and the environment.

interpersonal comparison   A comparison of outcomes with those of other individuals or groups, or among individuals and groups.

intrapersonal comparison   A comparison of outcomes with an internal reference point, independent of the outcomes of others.

procedural fairness   An evaluation of the fairness of procedures used in the decision-making process on environmental policies.

pull measures   Policy measures that aim to increase the attractiveness of environmentally friendly behaviour.

push measures   Policy measures that aim to reduce the attractiveness of environmentally unfriendly behaviour.

social dilemma   A conflict between individual and collective interests; a social dilemma has two basic characteristics: (i) each individual is better off when they act in their own interest and (ii) all individuals are better off when they cooperate.

social norm   What is commonly done or (dis)approved.

trust   The expectation that another party can be depended on to fulfil its commitments.

vertical equity   Policies affect people in proportion to their needs and abilities.

SUGGESTIONS FOR FURTHER READING

Gärling, T. and Steg, L. (2007). *Threats from Car Traffic to the Quality of Urban Life: Problems, Causes, and Solutions*. Amsterdam: Elsevier.

Schade, J. and Schlag, B. (2003). *Acceptability of Transport Pricing Strategies*. Oxford: Elsevier Science.

REVIEW QUESTIONS

1. Why is it important to study the acceptability of environmental policies?
2. How can acceptability of environmental policies be defined?
3. Which fairness principles can be distinguished? Which fairness principles are particularly important for the acceptability of environmental policies?
4. How can the acceptability of policy measures be increased?

30 Processes of Change

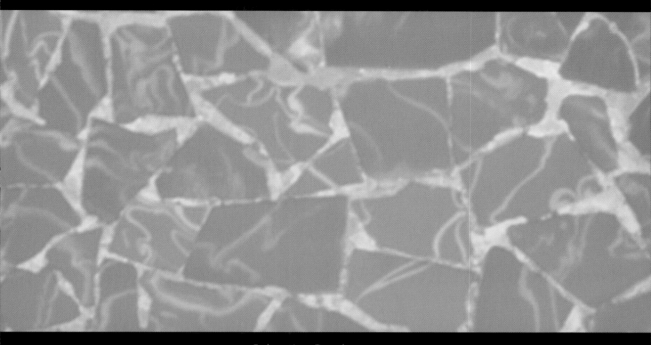

Sebastian Bamberg
FH Bielefeld University of Applied Science, Germany

Maxie Schulte
FH Bielefeld University of Applied Science, Germany

CHAPTER OUTLINE

30.1 INTRODUCTION

Environmental psychology looks back on a rich tradition of modelling environmental behaviours (see Part II of this book). However, comprehensive models that explicitly aim to explain the conditions or process of changing these behaviours are surprisingly scarce.

This chapter begins by presenting Lewin's (1952) theory of change, which was a pioneer work in the field. The next two sections introduce two additional perspectives on behavioural change: behavioural change as self-regulation, and behavioural change as transition through a sequence of qualitatively different change stages. These are followed by a section that translates the aforementioned ideas into the field of environmental behaviour by presenting the integrative stage model of self-regulated behavioural change. The last section demonstrates the implications of this framework for the design of systematic interventions.

30.2 LEWIN'S THEORY OF CHANGE

During World War II, Lewin (1948) explored ways to influence Americans to change their dietary habits (e.g. to eat internal organs or whole grain bread). He found that when group members were involved in and encouraged to discuss the issues themselves, and were able to make their own decisions as a group, they were far more likely to change their eating habits than when they just attended lectures providing corresponding information, recipes, and advice.

To explain his findings, Lewin (1952) developed the theory of change. Lewin assumed that behavioural change is made up of three steps, namely **unfreezing**, **moving,** and **refreezing** (see Figure 30.1). During the first step, unfreezing, situations indicating that important goals of a person or a group are not being met, create a motivation for change. As a consequence, present behavioural practices are rejected in favour of new ones that, however, need to be learned. Therefore, during the second step, moving, people need to develop and test new behavioural practices for reaching their goals. Interventions aimed at supporting behavioural change can be helpful during the moving stage. It is then that people are open to new sources of information, new concepts, or new ways of looking at old information. During the final step, refreezing, the person or group stabilizes this new behaviour. As will be shown, Lewin's ideas can still be discerned in newer theoretical approaches of behavioural change.

Environmental Psychology: An Introduction, Second Edition. Edited by Linda Steg and Judith I. M. de Groot.

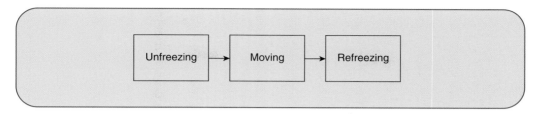

Figure 30.1 *Lewin's three-step change theory.*
Source: Adapted from Jackson (2005).

30.3 BEHAVIOURAL CHANGE: A SELF-REGULATION PROCESS STEERED BY FEEDBACK LOOPS

Self-regulation refers to the efforts made by humans to change their thoughts, feelings, desires, and actions in relation to a personally important goal (Carver and Scheier 1998). As in Lewin's theory of change, self-regulation research assumes that a person starts to think about change when there is information indicating that important personal goals are not being met. Based on the insight that goals are a central part of human personality, self-regulation is construed as a dynamic motivational system of setting goals, developing strategies to achieve these goals, appraising progress, and revising goals and strategies accordingly (Baumeister 2005; De Ridder and de Wit 2006).

30.3.1 Goals as Reference Values in a Feedback Loop

The central function of a goal is to provide a reference value for the **feedback loop** through which behaviour is regulated (Carver and Scheier 1998). The reference value (goal) contributes information on intentions and desires. This determines the target of the system. In addition, the feedback loop includes an input function, a comparator, and an output function (see Box 30.1).

30.3.2 Hierarchical Organization of Goals and Feedback Loops

A second idea central to the self-regulation model (Carver and Scheier 1998) is that goals differ in abstraction: a hierarchical organization of superordinate and subordinate feedback loops guides behavioural self-regulation. In this hierarchy, a higher-order feedback loop yields the reference value (goal) for the feedback loop just below it. Consequently, the goals specified as outputs become more concrete and restricted as one moves from higher to lower levels of the hierarchy.

The self-regulation model (Carver and Scheier 1998) proposes a three-level hierarchy of feedback loops (see Figure 30.2): The highest level (labelled **be-goal**

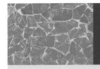

BOX 30.1   THE FEEDBACK LOOP

The thermostat is a commonly used example for a feedback loop. The system has an input function (sensor), constantly sampling current air temperature. This input information goes to the device that compares the sensed value to the thermostat's setting (reference value). As long as the two values are not discernably different, nothing else happens.

However, if the comparator detects that the current air temperature is lower than the thermostat setting, it sends a message that turns on the heater, which begins to dump heat into the room (output). If the thermostat finds there is no longer a difference between the room temperature and its setting, it requests the heater to stop.

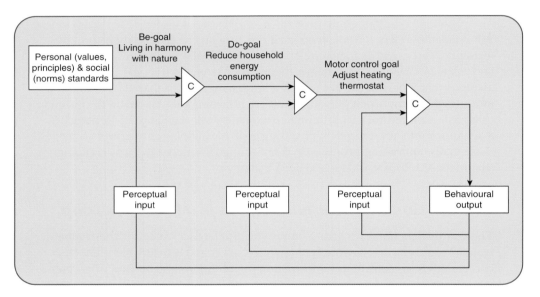

Figure 30.2 *Three-level hierarchy depicting the organization of goals and control processes.*
Source: Adapted from Carver and Scheier (1998).

level) reflects goals associated with a person's vision of an ideal self, ideal relationship, or ideal society. The reference values (goals) at this level are very abstract (e.g. living in harmony with nature). The output purpose on the be-goal level is to provide goals for the next level down, which is called the **do-goals** level. Do-goals (e.g. reducing household energy consumption) specify the course of action to reach the be-goals. A do-level goal specifies a general course of action but still contains decision points in which many details are left out. The goals established at the do-goal level supply the input for the lowest level, the **motor control goal level**. The task of the motor control level is to implement a do-goal by performing a sequence of specific actions (e.g. turning the heating down).

30.3.3 *The Importance of Self-Focus*

Although the main assumption is that be-goals function as the highest goals for human behaviour, everyday behaviour is not assumed to be directly regulated by these abstract goals (Carver and Scheier 1998). Most habitualized, everyday behaviour is regulated more effectively on the lower do-goal level. People need to be in a specific psychological state – **self-focus** – to be able to consciously compare their actual behaviour (and, hence, their actual self) with their be-goals (i.e. their ideal self). When people recognize a discrepancy between their current behaviour and their be-goals, they are motivated to alter their behaviour to conform more closely to these goals (e.g. Scheier et al. 1984).

30.4 BEHAVIOURAL CHANGE: IT TAKES TIME TO OVERCOME RESISTANCE TO CHANGE

By describing behavioural change as a transition through the sequence of the three stages of unfreezing, moving, and refreezing, the theory of change (Lewin 1952) stressed the temporal dimension of behavioural change and considered it a process rather than an event. The transtheoretical model (TTM; Prochaska and Velicer 1997) presents a more detailed version of behavioural change as a process. Like the theory of change, the TTM characterizes behavioural change as a transition through a sequence of qualitatively distinct stages in which people face specific hindrances. To overcome these sources of resistance, people need stage-specific skills and strategies. The TTM describes the following five **stages of change** (see Figure 30.3).

1. **Precontemplation** is the stage in which people are not intending to take action in the foreseeable future and avoid reading, talking, or thinking about their problem behaviours. This may be because they are not (fully) aware of the negative consequences of their behaviour, or they may have tried to change a number of times, without success, and have become demoralized as a consequence.

2. **Contemplation** is the stage in which people become aware that they might need to make a change. They recognize both the pros and cons of change. The concurrence of the costs and benefits of change may produce profound feelings of ambivalence, keeping people stuck at this stage for long periods of time.

3. **Preparation** is the stage in which people intend to take specific actions in the immediate future.

4. **Action** is the stage in which people actually change their behaviour. Since action can be observed from the outside, many theories have equated behavioural change with this stage.

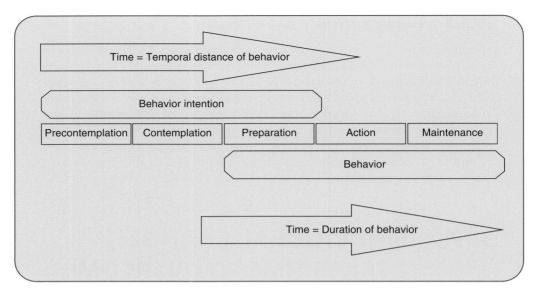

Figure 30.3 *The temporal dimension for the stages of change postulated by the transtheoretical model.*
Source: Velicer et al. (1998).

5. **Maintenance** is the stage in which people are working on preventing relapse. They do not make changes as frequently as people in the action stage do. People are less tempted to relapse, and they become increasingly confident that they can keep up their change of behaviour.

The TTM assumes that in most cases behavioural change is not a linear but a cyclical process. Barriers and resistances can keep people fixated at an early stage of change for a long period of time. Frequently, they relapse back to the beginning of the process.

30.5 THE STAGE MODEL OF SELF-REGULATED BEHAVIOURAL CHANGE

In the literature the TTM has been criticized as a descriptive model that does not provide a convincing theoretical rationale for the postulated five stages as well as the processes triggering stage transition (e.g. West 2005). The stage model of self-regulated behavioural change (SSBC) developed by Bamberg (2013a, b, see also Klöckner 2015) provides such a theoretical rationale. For this purpose, the SSBC combines assumptions from the model of action phases (Gollwitzer 1990) with popular behaviour models from social and

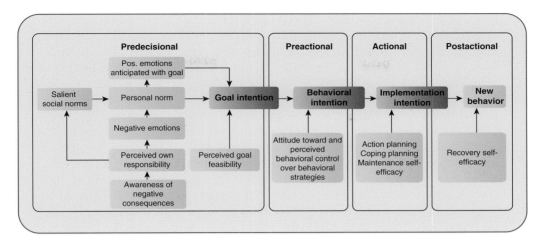

Figure 30.4 *A self-regulation model of voluntary behavioural change.*

environmental psychology, i.e. the theory of planned behaviour (Ajzen 1991) and the norm activation theory (Schwartz and Howard 1981) (see Chapter 22). The main assumption of the SSBC is that people can change even strongly habitualized behaviour (see Chapter 24), if they are motivated to do so. However, this process requires several steps that range from abstract motivation to concrete behavioural change. The SSBC describes this process as a series of four stages: (i) predecision stage, (ii) preaction stage, (iii) action stage, and (iv) postaction stage (see Figure 30.4).

A successful behavioural change follows these four stages but setbacks and repetitions may occur between stages. Each stage has its specific challenge, and transitioning from one stage to the next means to cross a threshold of setting a specific intention. In the predecision stage, the individual addresses the question of why behavioural change is necessary. Drawing upon the example of reducing car use voluntarily, the question in this stage is: 'Why is it important to reduce my car use?' Once the **goal intention** of reducing car use has been set, the individual proceeds to the preaction stage. This goal intention is a general intention to take action: 'In the next few weeks, I intend to reduce my car use'. This intention is fuelled by an activated personal norm to reduce car use. The personal norm is defined as a feeling of moral obligation to act. It is triggered by an awareness of negative consequences of one's behaviour, ascribing responsibility for these consequences, and the presence of salient social norms indicating that one is socially expected to reduce car use. Hence, the variables and mechanisms determining the goal intention are derived from the norm activation theory (Schwartz and Howard 1981). The SSBC predicts that a goal intention is generated when a sufficiently strong personal norm has been triggered. This personal norm is activated once a person becomes aware of the negative consequences of car use (e.g. for the environment, quality of urban life), accepts their personal responsibility for these consequences, and feels social pressure or support to reduce their car use.

During the preaction stage, the relevant question is: 'Which action should I take to reduce my car use?' Here, the person evaluates their attitude towards different alternatives such as walking, using public transportation, cycling, and how easy they perceive the implementation of these alternatives to be (perceived behavioural control (PBC)). Attitude and PBC are two constructs taken from the theory of planned behaviour (Ajzen 1991; see Chapter 22) and they pave the way for the next step: developing a **behavioural intention**. Here, the person picks a behaviour with the best attitude–difficulty balance for themself. This behavioural intention (e.g. 'In the next few weeks, I intend on using my bicycle instead of my car to commute to work') marks the transition from the preaction to the action stage. In the action stage, the implementation of the chosen behaviour needs to be planned. The obstacle to address is: 'How do I implement my intended changes?' The ability to make plans and remove barriers is the main driving force during this stage, and the transition to the last stage is marked by forming an **implementation intention**, e.g. 'Tomorrow morning at 7 a.m., I intend on taking bus number 5 to Victoria Road, the closest bus stop to my company's building'. In the final postaction stage, behavioural changes need to be stabilized, and relapses to old behavioural patterns have to be dealt with. The ability to recover from relapse is the main variable predicting whether a new behaviour can be stabilized and become a habit.

Altogether, the greatest strength of the SSBC lies in its detailed description of the tasks a person has to solve in the four stages as well as the specific cognitive mindset people adopt for solving them. The model assumes that the transition through the four stages is marked by three critical transition points, each reflecting the successful solution of stage-specific tasks: goal intention, behavioural intention, and implementation intention.

30.6 IMPLICATIONS FOR INTERVENTIONS

The ultimate goal of the SSBC is to provide a theoretical framework for the development of systematic interventions. One practical implication of considering behavioural change as a transition process is that instead of thinking of one single intervention for all, specific intervention packages can be matched to meet the needs and barriers of specific stages. For instance, interventions targeting people at earlier stages of change are more likely to be successful if they concentrate on providing information that can increase both problem awareness and perceived personal responsibility. Interventions designed to activate social and personal norms are likely to be important in this stage, as well. People who have set a goal intention need information concerning the availability and the pros and cons of different behavioural alternatives. People who already intended to switch to an alternative behaviour probably benefit most from interventions supporting the implementation and initiation of this intention,

Table 30.1 *Stage-tailored intervention strategies.*

Stage of change	Intervention strategies
Precontemplation	Intervention type I: Make social and personal norms salient (e.g. Goldstein and Cialdini 2007) Intervention type II: Enhance problem awareness and self-focus (e.g. Prochaska et al. 2002) Intervention type III: Enhance goal setting and goal commitment (e.g. McCalley and Midden 2002)
Contemplation	Intervention type IV: Provide information about the pros and cons of different behavioural alternatives and enhancing perceived behavioural control (e.g. Fishbein and Ajzen 2010)
Preparation/Action	Intervention type V: Support behavioural planning (e.g. Gollwitzer 1999)
Maintenance	Intervention type VI. Provide behavioural feedback (e.g. McCalley and Midden 2002) Intervention type VII: Prevent the temptation to relapse (e.g. Marlatt and Donovan 2005)
General strategies	Provide social support (e.g. Hogan et al. 2002) Change objective context conditions (see Chapter 21)

e.g. detailed behavioural planning. Table 30.1 proposes a way to combine the stage-specific change mechanisms postulated by the SSBC with different intervention types (see also Chapter 26).

30.7 EMPIRICAL VALIDATION OF THE SSBC

Measurement instruments of all SSBC's constructs have been developed and tested in different behavioural contexts (e.g. Bamberg 2013a, b; Klöckner 2014). Additionally, first correlational evidence for the SSBC's assumptions with regard to the relationships between the various constructs integrated in the model has been provided (Bamberg 2013a). Beyond that, the SSBC has been applied in a social marketing campaign with intervention modules based on the SSBC. This study showed that such specific interventions reduced motor car use significantly (Bamberg 2013b; see Box 30.2).

Also, Klöckner (2014) examined central SSBC premises by studying the decision-making process when purchasing e-cars. For this purpose, participants repeatedly completed measures of the SSBC over a period of 60 days. This design allowed for directly testing the chronological dynamics of behaviour change processes. The results supported the following SSBC assumptions: (i) In 85% of

BOX 30.2   EVALUATION OF AN SSBC-BASED SOCIAL MARKETING CAMPAIGN TO REDUCE CAR USE

To test the effectiveness of SSBC as guideline for intervention designs, Bamberg (2013b) developed and evaluated an SSBC-based social marketing campaign aiming at promoting car use reduction. Based on an initial diagnosis of their current stage membership, participants were assigned to the corresponding interventional module. The stage-specific intervention elements consisted of personal phone calls and information leaflets/ handouts/ literature, aiming at activating and changing the underlying social-cognitive constructs present during the formation of the three intention types. A randomized controlled trial was used for evaluating the campaign's efficacy. The results indicated that participants in the intervention group used public transport significantly more and used the car significantly less than the control group. Exhibiting a large effect size ($d = 0.56$), the car reduction impact of the SSBC-based intervention was about three times stronger than the effects found for traditional social marketing campaigns.

all transitions observed, participants moved a single stage forward or backward; (ii) Transitions from one stage to the next were preceded by changes in the respective intention. These intentions were meaningful predictors for subsequent behavioural change; (iii) Prior changes in the stage-specific social-cognitive constructs predicted changes of intentions.

Finally, there is evidence of how the SSBC can be used as a theoretical foundation for constructing a web-based behaviour change support system for environmentally friendly mobility behaviour (Bamberg et al. 2015a). Thus, the results of the presented studies lend strong support to the causal relationships postulated by the SSBC and show that the SSBC provides an effective framework for designing interventions for behavioural change.

30.8   SUMMARY

This chapter presented an overview of theoretical models that explicitly focus on the process of change. We argue that behaviour change theories focus on a self-regulating process including goal setting, developing strategies to achieve these goals, and feedback loops. Based on these assumptions the TTM was developed assuming that people need to pass through a sequence of qualitatively distinct stages to change their behaviour. Specifically designed to provide a theoretical rationale to explain the processes of change in relation to environmental behaviours, the SSBC was introduced. This model assumes that successful behaviour change follows four stages with stage-specific challenges and stage-specific social-cognitive constructs influencing behavioural change. Theories of change represent the foundation for the systematic design, implementation, and evaluation of interventions to underpin effective environmental policy planning and delivery. Stage theories replace 'one-fits-all' intervention approaches with intervention packages adapted to specific stages of behavioural change.

GLOSSARY

action   Fourth stage postulated by the TTM in which people successfully and consistently perform an intended behaviour.

be-goals   Goals associated with a person's vision of an ideal self, ideal relationship, or ideal society.

behavioural intention   A person's specific aim to engage in a particular action.

contemplation   Second stage postulated by the TTM in which people are starting to think seriously about changing their behaviour but have not yet acted upon the thought.

do-goals   Goals which specify the course of action that individuals want to take to reach their be-goals.

feedback loop   Central unit of Carver and Scheier's (1998) self-regulation model. A feedback loop consists of four elements: an input function, a reference value (goal), a comparator, and an output function.

goal intention   The will to achieve a goal without a concrete procedural plan of how to accomplish it.

implementation intention   Concrete procedural plan on how, when, and where to act to reach an intended goal.

maintenance   Fifth stage postulated by the TTM in which people perform the new behaviour for six months or more.

motor-control-goals   Sequence of specific actions individuals want to use to reach their 'do'-goals.

moving   Second stage of change postulated by Lewin in which people are open to new sources of information, new concepts, or new ways of looking at old information.

precontemplation   First stage postulated by the TTM in which people are not sufficiently aware of the negative implications of their actions, and are not thinking about behavioural change.

preparation   Third stage postulated by the TTM in which people are preparing themselves and their social world for a change in their behaviour.

refreezing   Third stage of change postulated by Lewin in which a person's new behaviour is stabilized at a new equilibrium.

self-focus   Psychological state in which people compare their actual self with their ideal self.

self-regulation   Efforts that are made to change thoughts, feelings, desires, and actions to meet a personally important goal.

stages of change   Assumption that behavioural change is best characterized as a transition through qualitatively different stages.

unfreezing   First stage of change postulated by Lewin in which present conceptions and practices are rejected in favour of new ones.

SUGGESTIONS FOR FURTHER READING

Darnton, A. (2008). *Reference Report: An Overview of Behavior Change Models and their Uses.* London: Centre for Sustainable Development, University of Westminster.

Gollwitzer, P.M. (1990). Action phases and mind-sets. In: *Handbook of Motivation and Cognition: Foundations of Social Behavior*, vol. 2 (ed. E.T. Higgins and R.M. Sorrentino), 53–92. New York, NY: Guilford.

Klöckner, C.A. (2015). *The Psychology of pro-Environmental Communication: Beyond Standard Information Strategies.* Basingstoke: Palgrave Macmillan.

Prochaska, J.O. and Velicer, W.F. (1997). The transtheoretical model of health behavior change. *American Journal of Health Promotion* 12: 38–48.

Weinstein, N.D., Rothman, A.J., and Sutton, S.R. (1998). Stages theories of health behavior. *Health Psychology* 17: 290–299.

REVIEW QUESTIONS

1. Describe the three stages of Lewin's theory of change.
2. What is the function of a goal within a feedback loop?
3. What is the distinction between the SSBC's predecision and action stage?
4. What kind of intervention could be used for promoting the transition from predecision to preaction stage?

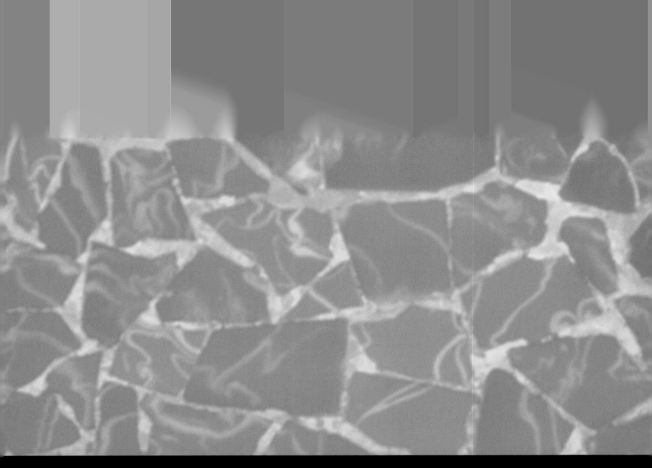

Wander Jager
University of Groningen, The Netherlands

Nick Gotts
Independent Researcher, UK

CHAPTER OUTLINE

31.1   INTRODUCTION

Human behaviour has a substantial impact on changes in environmental systems. Sometimes this influence is deliberate, as in the installation and management of irrigation systems. At other times it is accidental, as in the loss of topsoil and pollution of rivers due to agricultural practices. Such situations involve many people, who are likely to influence each other's behaviour in important ways.

Many drivers affect environmental behaviour, including social factors such as social learning and social norms (see also Chapter 18). To gain more insight into the complex interactions taking place within social environmental systems, scientists increasingly make use of computer simulation models. These models allow a better understanding of how individual environmental behaviour is affected by the behaviour of other people, and how the aggregate of individual behaviours affects the environment, which in turn influences the social system and individual behaviour. This chapter will elucidate the principles of **social complexity** that apply to social environmental systems, and describe a few agent-based simulations that have been developed in studying such systems. Following that, some guidelines for developing and using agent-based models are discussed.

31.2   AN INTRODUCTION TO SOCIAL COMPLEXITY

Social systems are often classified as **complex adaptive systems** in which individuals, groups, and populations can change their behaviour so as to enhance their quality of life. As a result, global phenomena (on a macro level) **emerge** from interactions between individuals (on a micro level). Additionally, such global phenomena may determine individual behavioural freedom, which is described as **downward causation**.

When humans interact with the environment, an additional layer of complexity is added. For example, intensified fishing to gain individual profit may affect the ecosystem by depleting fish stocks, which in turn affects the social system, such as less profit for fishermen. If all fish as they please, fish stocks may fall (a global phenomenon) as a combined result of individual behaviours, and as a consequence many fishermen may face bankruptcy and be forced to find other means of income.

Environmental Psychology: An Introduction, Second Edition. Edited by Linda Steg and Judith I. M. de Groot.
© 2019 John Wiley & Sons Ltd. Published 2019 by John Wiley & Sons Ltd.

Whereas societies most of the time display a relatively stable state, sometimes fast and unexpected changes occur, for example due to new technology or political changes. Social complexity theory shows how even small changes may give rise to cascades of effects, and as a result society may enter a turbulent, and thus less predictable state, bearing possible unforeseen and major implications (Jager and Edmonds 2015). For example, the Mayan culture is said to have collapsed due to exhaustion of agricultural potential and overhunting of large game (Emery 2007). Essential for social complexity is that humans formulate and employ ideas about how their social systems function, what their future is likely to be, and what it should be (Gotts 2007). While this opens up possibilities for managing social environmental systems (e.g. by legal enforcement), it also adds to the complexity of the system, as moral and political choices are involved, sometimes leading to conflicts between adherents of different perspectives. **Social simulation** provides a tool for studying the complexity of social environmental systems by systematically exploring how interactions between individuals, and between individuals and their environment, may result in aggregate outcomes that in turn affect individual behaviour.

31.3   SOCIAL SIMULATION AS A METHODOLOGY

The core element of the methodology of social simulation is the representation of individuals by interacting computer-coded **agents**. The use of agents makes it possible to conduct simulation experiments on problems that involve individual differences and complex interactions within large groups of people, such as possible consumer responses to increasing droughts.

You may be familiar with the concept of agents through videogames such as 'The Sims'. However, the behaviour of simulated people in popular videogames, although graphically very compelling, is typically not based on sound behavioural theory. Early social simulation models also used very simple models of human behaviour that were not soundly based (e.g. Schelling 1971). Later studies showed that the scientific relevance and practical applicability of simulation models benefited greatly from using behavioural theory and empirical data to program agents, as the outcomes of such models were more in line with what happens in the real world (e.g. Jager et al. 2000; Mosler and Martens 2008; Schwarz and Ernst 2009).

A key challenge in developing a simulation model for a specific domain is to select the most relevant theories on behaviour (see Chapter 22 for an overview). First, the model developer should identify which behaviours are of interest and then identify the key drivers and underlying behavioural processes for this behaviour (see Box 31.1 for an example). Next, the researcher has to find or develop a theoretical framework that applies to these drivers and processes. This theoretical framework is used to explicate the variables and concepts used

BOX 31.1   AN EXAMPLE OF A SIMPLE SIMULATION MODEL

Schelling (1971) developed a very simple yet illustrative social simulation model that demonstrates how spatial segregation may emerge if agents prefer to live next to similar others. The model consists of two types of agents (red and green) living in a space. The agents are happy if a critical number of direct neighbours (e.g. 50%) have the same colour. If agents become unhappy, they move to another place. The model demonstrated that even when this critical value is quite low (e.g. 30%), still a complete segregation will emerge, thus resulting in green and red neighbourhoods. To play with the model visit: http://luis.izqui.org/models/schelling; you can vary the number of agents and their critical values. More social simulation models can be found at: http://www.openabm.org.

in modelling the agents, resulting in a causal and computational model (see Schlüter et al. 2017). If necessary, the researcher may conduct a study to obtain data on the variables and concepts, thus constructing a population of simulated agents that represents variations in drivers and decision processes as identified in the population. As interactions between people are pivotal in many cases (e.g. in public opinion formation, in market dynamics, or in innovation diffusion processes), it is important to collect empirical data on how different people are connected and influence each other as well.

31.4   SOCIAL SIMULATION OF ENVIRONMENTAL BEHAVIOUR

In this section we discuss two studies that used behavioural theory for formalizing agents to study the complexities of human behaviour in interaction with the environment.

31.4.1   Using Theory in Simulation Models: Formalizing Processes of Attitude Change

Positive attitudes towards environmental protection can encourage pro-environmental behaviour (see Chapter 22). It is important to study how such positive attitudes develop, and whether they can be brought about by campaigning. A key theory that focuses on processes of attitude change is the **elaboration likelihood model** (ELM; Petty and Cacioppo 1986). The ELM distinguishes (i) a central route of persuasion, via which attitude change is the result of cognitive processing of the arguments provided, and (ii) a peripheral route of persuasion, via which attitude change is a result of simple cues – such as the number of arguments and attractiveness of the source – that require little cognitive processing.

The ELM has been used to develop a simulation model to study the effects of different environmental campaigns and to explore how these attitude changes influence social interactions in networks of people, resulting in additional word-of-mouth based attitude change (Mosler and Martens 2008). The study simulated a population of 10 000 interacting agents, and systematically varied population characteristics (e.g. involvement in environmental issues, which affects the likelihood of central versus peripheral processing of information) and type of campaign (e.g. arguments versus cues). In the simulation runs, campaigns were most effective in changing attitudes if strong arguments were provided to a population that was highly involved in environmental issues. Because the agents were motivated to process arguments, strong arguments resulted in the largest pro-environmental attitude shift, especially when agents had many social contacts who spread the arguments by word of mouth. However, for a population that was only weakly involved in environmental issues, the use of cues in the campaign resulted in the strongest attitude change. In general, this social simulation suggested that a campaign not only has direct effects, but also indirect effects as discussions between people carry on after the campaign stops, and cause additional changes in opinion. These findings demonstrate that agent-based simulations embodying well-established behavioural theory can help develop practical recommendations for socially complex systems – although empirical validation of such recommendations through longitudinal studies remains important.

31.4.2   *Using Theory and Data in Models: Diffusion of Environmental Innovations*

Considering droughts and decreasing water supplies in South Germany, the diffusion of three water-saving devices was studied: a shower-head, a toilet flush, and a rain harvesting system (Schwarz and Ernst 2009). The researchers simulated the purchase of these devices using a multitheoretical framework, including elements from innovation diffusion theory, lifestyle study (originating from sociology), the theory of planned behaviour (see Chapter 22) and social network theory. This framework was first tested on the empirical data on the spread of the aforementioned devices, which revealed that attitudes and perceived behavioural control had an important impact on the adoption of water-saving innovations, whereas communication in social networks was less important. Five innovation characteristics were particularly important (though the order of importance differed for the three innovations): environmental performance, ease of use, cost savings, compatibility with existing infrastructure, and investment costs.

Based on these outcomes, an agent-based simulation was developed where 11 915 agents were distributed over a grid of 2383 spatial cells representing

Southern Germany, including densely crowded cities and less-populated rural areas. Using the empirical data, each spatial cell was filled with a number of agents having certain lifestyles, connectivity and possibilities to install rain-harvesting systems. The decision-making of the agents was based on a multi-attribute subjective utility function, where attitude, social norms, and behavioural control were combined. Moreover, different lifestyles were conceptualized by attaching different values to these utilities. For example, postmaterialist agents were believed to consider more information in deciding to adopt than traditionalist, hedonist, and mainstream agents. Whereas information campaigns had a positive effect on the diffusion of all three innovations, subsidizing was only effective for the rain-harvesting system, mainly due to the relatively high costs associated with installing such a system.

This simulation model demonstrates which factors can influence water consumption in decades to come in a specific geographic region facing possible droughts. It exemplifies that agent-based modelling can be used to develop long-term scenarios that combine potential environmental developments (droughts), behavioural responses of a representative and spatial distributed population, and policy measures addressing different types of people. In particular, the model revealed the impacts of different policy strategies and provided insight on which lifestyle groups might be more influenced by these strategies.

31.5 INTEGRATING SOCIAL SIMULATION INTO ENVIRONMENTAL MODELLING

Social simulation models, as discussed in the Section 31.4, consider the environment as a passive entity that does not affect agents' behaviour. To capture human–environment dynamics, agent-based models can be integrated into models simulating environmental systems (Schlüter et al. 2017). Currently, rural land use is the most common application area, followed by water use. Below, we discuss three recent social environmental simulation models developed within these domains.

31.5.1 The Lakeland Study

The 'Lakeland study' aimed to investigate how choices between fishing and mining of agents having multiple needs (subsistence, leisure, identity, and freedom) affect the quality of a lake, and how, in turn, the quality of the lake affects the choices of the agents (Jager et al. 2000). The study made a distinction between outcome-maximizing (*Homo economicus*) agents versus more psychology-based (*Homo psychologicus*) agents. While *Homo economicus* agents selected the best goal satisfying behaviour out of all possible behaviours, *Homo psychologicus* agents could also base their decision on cognitively less-demanding strategies such as considering just the behaviour of friends, simply imitating friends, or behaving habitually. Agents could switch between these strategies depending on how satisfied they were and how uncertain they felt, for example due to deviating from the social norm.

The majority of *Homo economicus* agents immediately went mining when the mine was opened, causing a drop in fishing and increasing the market price for fish, and in response a majority went back to fishing. This resulted in an oscillating pattern between mining and fishing, finally resulting in an equilibrium state. In contrast, at first only a few dissatisfied *Homo psychologicus* agents switched to mining. Due to social influence, many more agents went mining than in the *Homo economicus* condition, causing a strong increase in pollution of the lake, which decreased the fish stock and drove the last fishermen to the mine as well. This was reflected in an **S-curve transition** from a fishing towards a mining society. By increasing the psychological realism of agents the effects were closer to what often happens in reality, but also more detrimental to the environment than if profit maximization assumptions were used. This illustrates the importance of using realistic behavioural assumptions in agent-based modelling.

31.5.2 *Companion Modelling: A Study of Rice Production and Labour Migrations in North-East Thailand*

Companion modelling involves developing an agent-based model in close collaboration with the group of people represented in the model itself (for a review, see Robinson et al. 2007). An example is a model of rice production and migration in search of work in north-east Thailand, developed in collaboration with farmers in this region (Naivinit et al. 2010).

The model has three parts: a hydro-climatic model, a model of rice crop growth, and a behavioural model of farming households. The hydro-climatic model is spatially explicit, and represents rainfall, and a series of storage tanks and rice paddies at different elevations, with water flowing from one paddy to the next. In the rice crop model, rice is divided into early-maturing and late-maturing types, which have different optimal moments for activities such as planting, transplanting, and harvesting. The lack of water at particular times (hydro-climatic model) can lead to partial or total loss of a particular type of crop. In the behavioural model the age of an individual influences their labour status (dependent, farmer, or migrant), while household income, gender, marital status, and migration experience influence the decision to migrate or not. The development of the behavioural model involved consulting husbands and wives from selected households. Their decisions on planting, rice transplantation, harvesting, and migrating were identified and validated through six successive cycles of refinement, involving role-playing games in which the participants took part, semistructured interviews, plenary discussion, and field surveys.

Nine different scenarios were explored using the final simulation model, varying in the availability of water and labour.

The results indicated that water availability is insufficient to explain labour migration patterns, because farmers had alternative ways to avoid complete crop failure, such as borrowing seedlings from their neighbours even when water was unavailable at crucial times. The participating farmers recognized the model as sufficiently accurate and complete, and presented it themselves to visiting students and academics. Participants felt they had gained new agro-ecological knowledge they could use directly. For example, farmers adopted a wider perspective on agricultural activities, and decided to diversify their pro-duction, adapting to changes in water supply. Hence the model contributed to understanding the social ecological dynamics in the system and revealed prom-ising strategies to cope with varying water supplies. Yet, the development of the model was time-consuming (three years) and costly, and has had only local effects so far.

31.5.3   *Integrating Multiple Models of a Socioenvironmental System: Water Use in the Danube Basin*

The model of water-saving device innovation discussed in Section 31.4.2 (Schwarz and Ernst 2009) is part of a larger model (GLOWA-Danube: Ernst et al. 2008) aimed at building a decision support system dealing with water use in the Upper Danube catchment in Germany. The core of this project is a simu-lation system, DANUBIA, which integrates 16 natural science and socioeco-nomic simulation models (Barthel et al. 2010), addressing rivers, groundwater, land-surface, atmosphere, and actors. Here, we discuss (i) the household model, which deals with the use of water of drinkable quality, and (ii) the water supply model, which links to the state of both the supply infrastructure and the water resources, to test whether and how consumer demand can be met within known or projected technical, economic, and ecological constraints. The household model was developed on the basis of empirical data on domestic water use of different lifestyle groups with different values and different water-use decision strategies. It appeared to be valid as the simulated water use closely matched records of actual annual household water use in subareas with different mixes of types of household. It was used to project possible household water use over the period 2000–2035, in a scenario assuming very dry conditions – one possible outcome of climate change – to test how water shortages might affect house-hold behaviour.

The water supply model included over 1700 water supply agents, drawing in total from over 8000 water sources. Both sources and supply agents were located in a simulated space representing the area. The model took account of seasonal variations in air temperature and expected changes in the population. Suppliers informed household actors about the quantity and quality of available water resources. Scenario analysis showed that water-saving innovations, such as water-saving shower heads and toilets are likely to diffuse, and thus allow appreciated habits to persist while decreasing the water demand per capita. The full model offers a tool to explore how variations in the environmental system (i.e. water supplies) affect social systems (i.e. water consumption of households), and what measures appear to be effective to manage water demand. Simulating such a social environmental system provides valuable insights in how to cope with an uncertain future.

31.6   KEY STEPS IN BUILDING AGENT-BASED MODELS

Agent-based simulations of human–environment systems are increasingly being used to explore environmental issues and as a test bed for policy-making (Jager and Ernst 2017). A key value of these agent-based models is their capacity to support decision-making in practical settings. The following steps are essential in developing and using simulation models.

31.6.1   Development of Models

Starting with a sound theoretical and empirical basis, relevant stakeholders or, if this is unrealistic due to time constraints, an advisory group, should be recruited both to obtain relevant information and to get them involved in the modelling process. Depending on the issue being modelled, the stakeholders may include representatives from the general population, managers from industry, policymakers, and environmental and behavioural experts. Once a model has been developed, stakeholders can be invited to evaluate the ease of use and relevance of successive versions. Also, the calibration of the model can start: empirical data on distributions of behaviours, opinions, abilities, and preferences of the relevant population can be incorporated into the population of agents. The model will indicate what data are required. At the end of this developmental process, ideally a theoretical sound and empirically validated simulation tool is available that is endorsed by the stakeholders involved.

31.6.2   Using Models

Once a first version of the model is completed, the modellers can conduct scenario analyses. Stakeholders can be interviewed to provide information on likely scenarios (e.g. drought) and on policies they want to test. For example, a certain tax regime may be coupled with economic developments to explore its effects under different economic conditions. Complex systems may confront stakeholders with unforeseen, and by nature unpredictable, outcomes which require adaptive responses. Therefore, it is essential to have an empirically valid model of the underlying processes, as this increases the trust of stakeholders in the model in case the results are counterintuitive to their initial expectations. A viable option is to conduct the simulation in a management-game setting, with stakeholders being invited to interact with the model to manage developments as they appear (Jager and Van der Vegt 2015). This allows stakeholders to experience the potential impacts of their policies, which would not be possible using informed participation processes. Moreover, this opens the possibility of exploring whether deliberate cascade effects can be stimulated in social systems, which requires the identification of tipping points, where once a critical number of people adopt new behaviour (e.g. non-smoking inside), new social norms may develop that create favourable conditions for additional policies (see Nyborg et al. 2016). This may stimulate discussions between stakeholders, and hence contribute to a more integrated vision of system management.

In general, developing theoretically sound simulation tools fed with adequate empirical data, which offer an accessible interface for stakeholders, will deepen understanding of human–environment interactions, and aid the development of integrated policies that are both effective and acceptable in managing their complexities.

31.7 SUMMARY

This chapter has provided an introduction to how simulation, in particular the simulation of human behaviour, can contribute to the understanding and management of complex human–environment interactions. The essence of agent-based modelling resides not in the development of predictive models, but rather of models that capture the complexity of these systems, offering a tool to stakeholders to explore possible management strategies. We first discussed the relevance of social influences in environmental systems. Next, we explained the principles of social complexity, elucidating how large-scale effects may emerge from local interactions and in turn constrain those interactions. We explained the methodology of social simulation, and provided examples of simulation models of environmental behaviour, and of how such simulation models can be integrated into environmental models. We concluded by discussing key steps in the development and use of simulation models.

GLOSSARY

agent A computer-coded model representing a single human or other decision-maker, equipped with rules prescribing how different factors and decision processes cause their behaviour. Linking agents in a network of interactions results in an agent-based model.

complex adaptive system   A system with components that respond to environmental changes to increase their well-being or survival.

downward causation   Effects of emergent large-scale phenomena on behaviour at the local level.

elaboration likelihood model   A theoretical model of persuasion distinguishing between processing arguments (central route of persuasion, likely when motivation and capabilities are high) and processing cues such as source attractiveness (peripheral route of persuasion, likely when motivation and capabilities are low).

emergence   The origination of a large-scale phenomenon due to local interactions.

S-curve transition   A change between two states of a system that begins slowly, accelerates, and then slows again as it nears completion, producing a stretched 'S' shape when graphed.

social complexity   The notion that social phenomena at a large scale may arise from interactions and individual choices at a local level, and in turn affect these local phenomena.

social simulation   A methodology to study interactions between groups of people by defining individuals as computer-programmed agents equipped with rules prescribing which factors and decision processes cause their behaviour, and letting these agents interact.

SUGGESTIONS FOR FURTHER READING

Jager, W. and Ernst, A. (2017). Social simulation in environmental psychology. Introduction of the special issue. *Journal of Environmental Psychology* 52: 114–118.

Waldrop, M.M. (1992). *Complexity: The Emerging Science at the Edge of Order and Chaos*. New York, NY: Simon and Schuster.

A library of social simulation models: http://www.openabm.org

The European Social Simulation Association (ESSA): www.essa.eu.org

REVIEW QUESTIONS

1. Social simulation may be used to reveal emergent phenomena in socio-environmental systems. Give three examples of emergent phenomena where the behaviour of populations affects the environment.

2. Explain how empirical data on human behaviour can be used in formalizing an agent-based model. Give an example of the type of data that can be used, and explain why it is critical to use such data.

3. Discuss how simulation models can support policy-making in social environmental systems.

4. How would you formalize the theory of planned behaviour for consumers considering investing in a private solar power system? (See e.g. Schlüter et al. 2017, for a supporting framework.)

32 Environmental Issues in Low- and Middle-Income Countries

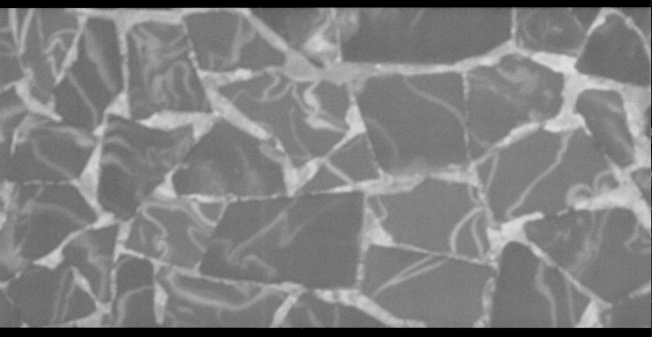

Nadja Contzen
University of Groningen, The Netherlands

Hans-Joachim Mosler
Swiss Federal Institute of Aquatic Science and Technology (EAWAG), Switzerland

Silvie Kraemer-Palacios
Swiss Federal Institute of Aquatic Science and Technology (EAWAG), Switzerland

CHAPTER OUTLINE

32.1 INTRODUCTION

Environmental issues in **low- and middle-income countries**[1] (LMICs) are manifold and often severe: natural disasters with devastating consequences occur frequently (CRED 2016); rapid economic growth has led to massive resource consumption and environmental degradation (UNFPA 2013); urban populations produce huge amounts of solid waste that pollute soil and water (Pakpour et al. 2014); industries and motorized transportation contribute to deathly air pollution (GBD 2015 Risk Factors Collaborators (GBD-RFC) 2016); and part of the population lives in degrading conditions in slums (UN-HABITAT 2014). Many of these problems are furthered by rapid population growth and urbanization (UNFPA 2013).

Especially in low-income countries, solutions to these environmental problems are often challenging, due to lack of technical know-how, finances, and administrative management. Environmental psychology may contribute to understanding and solving these problems, through better understanding of the effects of environmental conditions on well-being (e.g. Part I of the book), environmental awareness and behaviour (Part II), and behaviour change interventions (e.g. Part III).

Unfortunately, research on these topics is often limited to **high-income countries**. Yet, it is key also to apply the theories, concepts, intervention, and methods in LMICs to understand and solve environmental problems in these countries that are of global relevance, and to test the generalizability of findings and explore potential cultural differences. This chapter illustrates the application of environmental psychological research in LMICs. We discuss environmental risk perception and concern, residential environment and well-being, and behaviour (change).

32.2 ENVIRONMENTAL RISK PERCEPTION, ENVIRONMENTAL CONCERN, AND CLIMATE CHANGE PERCEPTION

32.2.1 *Environmental Risk Perception*

Environmental risks are among the 10 leading risk factors for premature death in LMICs but not in high-income countries (GBD-RFC 2016). Natural disasters

---

[1] This Chapter focuses on environmental issues in Asia and Africa. For research in Latin America, see Chapter 25.

Environmental Psychology: An Introduction, Second Edition. Edited by Linda Steg and Judith I. M. de Groot.

occur disproportionally in LMICs (CRED 2016). Low-income countries experience the severest consequences with unmatched rates of death and destroyed livelihoods per disaster. A better understanding of environmental risk perception in LMICs is essential because it affects risk preparedness and adaptation (Ainuddin et al. 2014). However, most studies on environmental risk perception target high-income countries (see Chapter 2).

In China, where air pollution is the fifth-leading health risk factor (GB-RFC 2016), students rated air pollution as the second likeliest environmental risk, after water pollution (Zhang et al. 2013). However, they ranked its severity only 14th, indicating underestimation. In the Yangtze River Delta the general population, but not students, rated floods and earthquakes as riskier than nuclear power (Ge et al. 2011). Possibly, their risk perception was affected by recurring floods in the region and a severe earthquake in China shortly before data collection. Research in Pakistan revealed that people were aware of the high seismic risk in the region but had rather fatalistic attitudes (Ainuddin et al. 2014). This may be due to low income, inhibiting people from engaging in preparedness measures, such as making buildings earthquake resistant (see Chapter 22, Section 22.3 Protection Motivation Theory).

32.2.2 Environmental Concern

Environmental concern can foster pro-environmental behaviour (see Chapter 17). The postmaterialism hypothesis suggests that environmental concern is low in LMICs (Pampel 2014): because people struggle with the most pressing material needs, they cannot afford to care about the environment. Interestingly, contradicting this hypothesis, environmental concern was high across all socioeconomic groups in LMICs (Pampel 2014). Possibly, populations in LMICs depend more strongly on the environment: their survival is directly affected by poor environmental conditions, which motivates environmental concern. Alternatively, environmental concern might be rooted in traditional cultures prevalent in many LMICs that perceive nature as sacred and thus worth protecting (Byers et al. 2001). A study in Nigeria, however, found that although environmental concern was high, traditional conservation principles had been abandoned to secure short-term survival (Chokor 2004).

32.2.3 Climate Change Perception

Whilst CO_2 emissions per capita are highest in high-income countries and have majorly increased in middle-income countries (PBL 2014), climate-related disasters primarily hit LMICs (CRED 2016). LMICs' climate change perception is thus essential for climate change adaptation as well as mitigation (see Chapter 3).

In a study in China, perceived climate change risk was high and predicted by **cultural worldviews** (Xue et al. 2014). High **egalitarianism** and low **fatalism** were associated with higher perceived risk. This in turn predicted support for climate change mitigation policy and mitigation behaviour. Neither **hierarchism** nor

individualism predicted risk perception, although the latter was associated with lower policy support.

In a climate-vulnerable Bangladeshi village, males, Hindus, and younger people were more concerned about climate change (Haq and Ahmed 2017). Many saw climate change as a wish of god. Others mentioned human activities, such as deforestation as well as sinful behaviour, as the cause. Similar notions of weather as a reward for good or punishment for bad behaviour have been found in other LMICs (World Bank 2015). These narratives, instead of being challenged, could serve as a foundation for presenting the scientific consensus of anthropogenic climate change to communities.

32.3 RESIDENTIAL ENVIRONMENT AND WELL-BEING

Continued rural–urban migration causes rapidly growing urban populations in LMICs (UNFPA 2013). The majority of the migrants end up in devastating conditions in urban slums. The remaining rural population often faces similar hardship. But residential environments also affect the well-being of wealthier city-dwellers.

32.3.1   Slums and Public Housing

One third of the LMICs' urban population lives in slums (UN-HABITAT 2014). In Africa, the number goes up to 60%. Slums are usually characterized by grave overcrowding, precarious housing and neighbourhood quality, insecure tenure, and a poor or non-existent safe water and sanitation infrastructure that causes pollution of water sources and soil by human faeces. These characteristics represent environmental stressors that may harm physical, and psychological well-being (see Chapters 4 and 12).

Environmental stressors were strongly associated with mental health in slums in Mumbai (Subbaraman et al. 2014) and Accra (Greif and Dodoo 2015). In Mumbai, nearly a quarter of the respondents were at high risk for a mental disorder (Subbaraman et al. 2014). Qualitative findings suggested that the slums' illegal status contributed most to psychological distress due to insecure tenure and complete lack of basic services. Interestingly, in Accra's slums, **social capital** benefited mental health among the poorest and least physically healthy dwellers but was an emotional burden for the others (Greif and Dodoo 2015).

Public housing programmes aim to increase slum dwellers' well-being through improved housing quality and secure tenure. Women in Ahmedabad who had moved from slums to public housing reported better physical and mental health than those remaining in slums (Vaid and Evans 2016). The differences in health were largely explained by observed housing quality.

The downsides of the relocation were decreased social ties, suggesting that these should actively be promoted in public housing programmes.

32.3.2   Communal Spaces

Research highlights the importance of communal spaces where social interaction takes place (see Chapter 12). Yet, good quality communal spaces are usually non-existent in slums and also not a given in wealthier urban neighbourhoods in LMICs. Higher quality and use of communal spaces increased place-based social relations and place attachment in urban China (Zhu and Fu 2016). These were in turn associated with higher neighbourhood participation (Zhu and Fu 2016) and well-being (Yip et al. 2013). Communal spaces are also relevant for recreational activities (see Chapter 6). The availability, aesthetic quality, and safety of communal spaces explained children's average time spent outdoors in Dhaka (Islam et al. 2016), and adults' sporting activities in Hangzhou (Su et al. 2014).

32.3.3   Rural Communities

Rural populations in LMICs often face a severe lack of basic services, including water and sanitation infrastructure, that hampers physical and psychological health. A study on sanitation-related psychosocial stress among women in Indian villages revealed that two-thirds of the respondents had no access to any sanitation facility but practised open defecation (Sahoo et al. 2015). During sanitation activities (e.g. defecation, urination, bathing, and menstrual management) women encountered three broad types of stressors: environmental (e.g. long distance to uncomfortable sites with walls to cross), social (e.g. insufficient privacy or social restriction of sites), and sexual stressors (e.g. being watched or sexually assaulted). While all stressors were experienced, social stressors were most prevalent.

32.4   BEHAVIOUR AND BEHAVIOUR CHANGE

Many environmental problems in LMICs could be reduced by changing people's behaviour through interventions. However, interventions are still uncommon in LMICs. Two types of behaviour seem particularly relevant to understand and promote: (i) behaviours that improve environmental quality, including resource conservation, sustainable transportation, and recycling, and (ii) behaviours that protect health from adverse environmental impacts, including safe water consumption and sanitation, and handwashing.

32.4.1   *Resource Conservation*

Many households in rural and slum areas in LMICs have no access to electricity or running water (e.g. Contzen 2015). For them, energy and water are scarce goods that are traditionally conserved. Overall, however, resource consumption has drastically increased in LMICs (UNFPA 2013). This threatens natural resources and supply reliability – water and power cuts are often a daily reality in LMICs, sometimes lasting for hours or even days. Experiencing supply breaks might make resource scarcity tangible and thus motivate conservation. Indeed, in a study in China that applied an extended theory of planned behaviour (TPB, see Chapter 22), past experience with power cuts was associated with increased electricity savings (Wang et al. 2011). Perceived economic benefits and subjective norm had additional positive effects, while discomfort caused by saving was associated with lower electricity savings.

In Iran, where water scarcity is high, the agricultural sector consumes 90% of the freshwater (Yazdanpanah et al. 2014), making farmers' water conservation (e.g. reuse of waste water) essential. A study that applied an extended TPB found that subjective norm and perceived risk of a water crisis explained farmers' conservation behaviour via intention (Yazdanpanah et al. 2014). Further, farmers who used their own water source or shared it with few people felt higher responsibility and stronger subjective norms and thus conserved more water.

32.4.2   *Sustainable Transportation*

Most cities in LMICs face serious traffic problems, including daylong traffic jams and high air pollution (Zailani et al. 2016). The main causes are unreliable public transportation and a strong growth in private motorized transportation. A study in Kuala Lumpur investigated use of the fairly good public transportation based on an extended TPB (Zailani et al. 2016). Attitude, perceived behavioural control, and past behaviour explained the intention to use public transportation.

A study in Bangalore city found that although most participants had cycled during childhood (96%), cycling had dropped drastically in adulthood (5.3%; Verma et al. 2016). Shifting to motorized transport was perceived as a natural process that increased comfort and status because it signalled prosperity. Interestingly, people who continued cycling found it equally unsafe as those who had stopped.

32.4.3   *Recycling*

Household waste production has drastically increased (Pakpour et al. 2014). The adverse environmental impacts are especially severe in LMICs: garbage collection occurs irregularly if at all, waste disposal facilities are insufficiently available, and waste is often dumped untreated in landfills. Recycling could help mitigate the waste problem and conserve natural resources. However, recycling is uncommon and often insufficiently organized by local authorities. All the more important is the role of households in recycling (see Figure 32.1).

Figure 32.1 *Riverbank next to the scenic 14 falls near Thika, Kenya. Source: Photo by Nadja Contzen.*

Several studies applied the TPB to explain household recycling behaviour in LMICs. In Turkey, housewives' recycling behaviour was explained by intention, perceived behavioural control (directly and through intention), and subjective norm through intention (Arı and Yılmaz 2016). In Iran, where an extended TPB was applied, attitude, subjective norm, perceived behavioural control, intention, moral obligation, self-identity, action planning, and recycling behaviour – all measured at baseline – predicted recycling behaviour one year later (Pakpour et al. 2014). A study in Santiago de Cuba applied an extended TPB to explain recycling, composting, and reuse (direct use of a material for a second purpose; Mosler et al. 2008). Attitudes and to a lesser extent perceived behavioural control explained all three behaviours. Interestingly, for recycling and composting the attitude component reflecting behaviour pleasantness was more relevant, whereas for reuse cost–benefit considerations were more relevant. Subjective norm was highly predictive for recycling (a rather public behaviour), moderately predictive for composting, and not predictive for reuse (a more private behaviour).

A study in Lahore highlights the critical contribution of scavengers to recycling and reuse in LMICs (Asim et al. 2012). Scavengers recover recyclable materials (such as metal, bottles, dry breads) directly from landfills and sell it to junkshops and recycling industries (via middlemen). Despite their vital environmental contribution, they are not recognized by the government: they suffer from regular harassments by officials and face high health and safety threats.

32.4.4   *Water, Sanitation, and Hygiene*

Unsafe water consumption, unsafe sanitation, and lack of handwashing are among the ten leading risk factors for premature death in low-income countries (GBD-RFC 2016). The common lack of access to safe water and sanitation infrastructure (see Section 32.3) contributes significantly to the elevated risk. Such water, sanitation and hygiene (WaSH) behaviours have been studied in LMICs applying the **RANAS approach** (Mosler 2012; see Box 32.1).

Safe water kiosks – small shops that sell treated water in slums and villages – are a low-cost option to compensate for the lack of a safe water infrastructure. A study in Kenya found that service satisfaction, perceived costs, social norms, self-efficacy beliefs, action control, and commitment explained consumption of kiosk water (Contzen 2015). In a cluster-randomized controlled trial in Bangladesh, reminders and implementation intentions were applied to promote the use of arsenic-safe wells (Inauen and Mosler 2014). The techniques were expected to increase commitment, descriptive norm, and recovery self-efficacy, in turn affecting behaviour. Switching to safe wells was indeed higher when these techniques were applied compared to health information alone. However, even without governmental provision of basic services, healthy behaviour options are often available (see Figure 32.2).

A method regularly applied in LMICs to stop open defecation is **community-led total sanitation (CLTS)**. A study in Mozambique revealed that participation

BOX 32.1   HANDWASHING PROMOTION IN ETHIOPIA

Contzen et al. (2015) tested two handwashing interventions in Ethiopian villages. These had been developed based on the RANAS approach (Mosler 2012), a multitheoretical framework to design WaSH interventions in LMICs. The approach's main idea is to tailor interventions to the targeted population through (i) identification of the psychological factors that predict the behaviour in the targeted population and (ii) selecting interventions expected to affect precisely these factors. The considered psychological factors are those specified in well-known theories (e.g. TPB; see Chapter 22).

In the Ethiopian villages, baseline results suggested (i) intervening on social norms,

impediments, such as having run out of water, and forgetting and (ii) to simplify the handwashing technique (Contzen et al. 2015). Two interventions were selected for this purpose: public commitment and promotion of handwashing-stations. All participants received a standard educational intervention. The effects of the two additional interventions were compared with the standard education intervention only. Pre-post data analysis revealed that the population-tailored interventions, and especially the handwashing-station promotion, performed better than the standard education intervention.

Figure 32.2 *Women and children fetching water at a borehole in Kancharo, Borana Zone, Ethiopia. Source: Photo by Nadja Contzen.*

in CLTS was associated with latrine ownership through social capital, perceived vulnerability for diarrhoea, perceived costs, social norms, and confidence in ability to rebuild a damaged latrine (Harter et al. 2017). Latrine ownership was strongly associated with using it, and thus with the stopping of open defecation.

In highly contaminated environments, as found in slums and rural areas in LMICs, hands are quickly (re)contaminated. Regular handwashing with soap is thus vital to reduce infectious diseases. A field experiment in Ethiopian villages revealed that public commitment and handwashing-station promotion increased handwashing more than a standard education intervention (see Box 32.1).

32.5   SUMMARY

Environmental problems in LMICs are difficult to manage with the limited resources these countries have. Environmental psychology can provide relevant theories, concepts, interventions, and methods with which these problems can be understood and tackled. Also, it is essential to apply these theories, concepts, interventions, and methods in LMICs to probe their generalizability and investigate potential cultural differences.

This chapter has discussed environmental psychological research in LMICs. The reviewed studies suggest that in LMICs: (i) **environmental risk perceptions** are not always accurate; (ii) levels of environmental and climate change concern are high; (iii) climate change concern predicts mitigating behaviour; (iv) residential environments and related stressors have a major impact on health and well-being; (v) (extended versions of) the TPB can explain various pro-environmental behaviours; (vi) psychological factors can explain and interventions can promote WaSH behaviours; and (vii) a common lack of private means and public infrastructure often limits people's capabilities to engage in adaptive, pro-environmental or health-promoting behaviours. These findings parallel results from high-income countries supporting the generalizability of (environmental) psychological theories, concepts, interventions, and methods to other economic, social, and cultural contexts. Yet, the evidence stems primarily from studies in certain LMICs (e.g. China) where research is expanding, and tests only certain theories (e.g. TPB). Future research should expand to additional, especially low-income, countries and apply other theories and concepts, such as the value-belief-norm theory (see Chapter 22).

GLOSSARY

community-led total sanitation   Approach to trigger community-led latrine construction to stop open defecation.

cultural worldviews   Individuals' views about how society should be structured; assumed to influence environmental risk perception.

egalitarianism   Worldview that all people are equal and deserve equal rights.

fatalism   Worldview that most events are predetermined and therefore inevitable.

hierarchism   Worldview that monolithic power structures should be in place.

high-income countries   Countries with highest levels of material well-being and a gross national income (GNI) per capita of $12 476 or more.

individualism   Worldview that autonomy and personal gain should be furthered.

low- and middle-income countries   Countries with low to medium levels of material well-being and GNI per capita of maximal $1025 (low-income countries) or $1026–$12 475 (middle-income countries).

RANAS approach   A multi-theoretical framework to design WaSH interventions in LMICs.

social capital   Networks, shared values, and understandings in society enabling people to trust each other, facilitating cooperation and reciprocal support.

SUGGESTIONS FOR FURTHER READING

Schmuck, P. and Schultz, W.P. (2002). *Psychology of Sustainable Development*. Norwell, MA: Kluwer Academic.

World Bank (2015). *World Development Report 2015: Mind, Society, and Behavior*. Washington, DC: World Bank.

REVIEW QUESTIONS

1. How can environmental psychology contribute to solving environmental problems in LMICs?
2. Why is environmental risk perception of high relevance in LMICs?
3. Are people in LMICs more or less environmentally concerned than people in high-income countries? Why?
4. How do the living environments in LMICs affect people's well-being?
5. What are the peculiarities of promoting (pro-environmental) behaviours in LMICs?

33 Conclusion: Summary, Trends, and Future Perspectives in Environmental Psychology

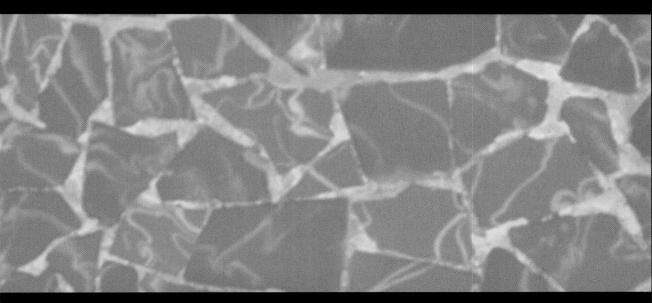

Agnes E. van den Berg
University of Groningen, The Netherlands

Linda Steg
University of Groningen, The Netherlands

CHAPTER OUTLINE

33.1 SUMMARY AND KEY FINDINGS

The environment in which we live influences people's lives in many ways, but reciprocally this environment is also a product of human activities. **Environmental psychology** studies this reciprocal relationship between humans and the environment. This book aims to provide an introduction into this rapidly evolving and dynamic field of research. This second edition has been substantially revised and updated to reflect the current state of the field. New chapters have been added that address important topics in the field, including climate change risks, place attachment, the importance of nature for children, emotions and pro-environmental behaviour, symbolic aspects of environmental behaviour, and the role of group processes in environmental issues, attitudes, and behaviours. The core part of this new edition of the book now comprises a total of 31 chapters, written by more than 60 leading authors in the field. The chapters have been organized into three parts. Part I includes 14 chapters discussing environmental influences on humans. Part II comprises 10 chapters focusing on factors that influence environmental behaviour. Part III includes seven chapters discussing ways to promote pro-environmental behaviour.

In this concluding chapter, we will first summarize the main findings of each part of the book. Next, we will discuss some general **trends** and developments, followed by a discussion of key challenges for future research in environmental psychology.

33.1.1 Part I: Environmental Influences on Human Behaviour and Well-Being

Part I starts with three chapters on negative influences of the environment on humans. Two of these chapters address classic themes in environmental psychology: environmental risk perception and environmental stress. These chapters emphasize the crucial role of people's perceptions in understanding negative impacts of the environment on human behaviour and well-being. The other chapter addresses climate change as a unique environmental problem. It gives an overview of the psychological processes that influence people's understanding of and concerns about climate change.

The next six chapters discuss the predominantly positive influences of the natural environment on humans. The extensive research activity in this domain

Environmental Psychology: An Introduction, Second Edition. Edited by Linda Steg
and Judith I. M. de Groot.
© 2019 John Wiley & Sons Ltd. Published 2019 by John Wiley & Sons Ltd.

is illustrative of the recent, more positive outlook of environmental psychology as a field that aims to create sustainable environments that support human well-being. A recurrent theme in these chapters is the important function of nature and urban green space as a source of health, well-being, and residential satisfaction. The newly added chapter on children and the natural environment (Chapter 10) builds the case for children as a special group of interest for whom access to nature may have life-long positive consequences. In Chapters 8 and 9, people's more ambivalent responses to wild nature and wild animals are acknowledged and discussed.

The next three chapters of Part I focus on impacts of urban environments on human behaviour and well-being. These chapters illustrate the continuing importance of the residential environment for quality of life. Indeed, as noted in Chapter 11 'even the most outdoors-oriented people spend most of their lives in one building or another'. Much of the more recent work in this domain has been aimed at translating insights from fundamental studies on the determinants of urban environmental quality into integrated practical models and approaches. For example, in Chapter 11, biophilic design and evidence-based design are discussed as two recent design approaches that aim to translate insights from environmental psychology into building designs that satisfy users' needs and improve their well-being. In Chapters 12 and 13, various multidimensional models for measuring and predicting residential satisfaction and quality of life are presented.

Chapter 14 discusses how people form emotional bonds to places, and presents different components and types of place attachments. Chapter 15 discusses the way insights on how environmental cues, such as the presence of others or signs of littering, can affect our environmental behaviour.

33.1.2   *Part II: Factors Influencing Environmental Behaviour*

Part II opens with a review of ways to measure environmental behaviour (Chapter 16). In this review, new approaches to measuring environmental behaviour are presented and the importance of complementing behavioural measures with measures of environmental impact are emphasized. Subsequent chapters highlight values (Chapter 17), social norms (Chapter 18), emotions (Chapter 19), and symbolic aspects (Chapter 20) as key factors influencing environmental behaviour. Some notable findings include the growing evidence for biospheric values as predictors of pro-environmental behaviour (Chapter 17), the empirical demonstration that disorder (e.g. graffiti, littering) can rapidly spread via the principle of cross-norm inhibition (Chapter 18), and the recognition of emotions and symbolic aspects as powerful determinants of environmental behaviour (Chapters 19 and 20). Chapter 21 reviews factors that promote cooperation in social dilemmas. Chapter 22 provides an integrative perspective by providing an overview of models that describe the combined influences of multiple determinants of environmental behaviour.

Chapter 23 discusses why environmental attitudes and behaviours do not solely depend on individual characteristics but are also affected by group memberships and group processes associated with group memberships. Next, Chapter 24 reflects on the habitual nature of many environmental behaviours, and presents different models and approaches to describe, explain, predict, and change habitual environmental behaviours. Finally, Chapter 25 discusses environmental psychology from a Latin American perspective. This chapter illustrates the growing interest in environmental psychology in Latin America, providing important insights into the applicability of relevant theories and methods in a different cultural context.

33.1.3 Part III: Encouraging Pro-Environmental Behaviour

The first three chapters of Part III discuss informational strategies (Chapter 26), rewards and penalties (Chapter 27), and persuasive technology (Chapter 28) as three strategies for behavioural change. Chapter 26 concludes that the provision of information alone, although still widely used, is not very effective in producing behaviour change. Several suggestions for improving the effectiveness of informational strategies, such as the provision of tailored information, are discussed. Policymakers often use environmental taxes and other monetary strategies to change people's behaviours. However, as shown in Chapter 27, there is a risk in providing monetary consequences for pro-environmental behaviours because these consequences may reduce people's moral motivation to act pro-environmentally. Chapter 27 provides guidelines for effectively announcing and delivering monetary interventions. Chapter 28 discusses persuasive technology as a relatively new approach that uses technology to give 'smart' feedback about environmental behaviour, or to provide immersive experiences that simulate the possible environmental consequences of behaviour.

Building on the insight that interventions can only be successful if they are accepted by the public, Chapter 29 discusses factors such as procedural and distributive fairness that influence the public acceptability of policy measures that aim to encourage pro-environmental behaviour. The last three chapters of Part III address relatively new and thus far less studied topics in environmental psychology. In Chapter 30, a stage model of behavioural change is presented that integrates different psychological theories on the processes underlying behavioural change. Chapter 31 discusses recent advances in agent-based modelling as a computer-based technique that can be used to simulate changes in complex social environmental systems. Finally, Chapter 32 gives an overview of the application of theories, concepts, and methods of environmental psychology in low- and middle-income countries. Many recent studies are discussed that show the relevance of environmental psychology to solving environmental problems in low- and middle-income countries. However, as yet environmental psychology is not tapped to its fullest potential in those parts of the world where it is probably most needed.

33.2 GENERAL TRENDS AND DEVELOPMENTS

In this section, we will discuss three general, overarching trends and developments as they emerge from this book.

33.2.1 Positive Interactions Between Humans and Environments

Traditionally, environmental psychology has focused primarily on studying the negative impacts of the environment on humans (e.g. detrimental effects of crowding or noise on health) and the negative impacts of humans on the environment (e.g. negative impacts of energy use on environmental quality). Applications of this research have been aimed mostly at the development of strategies to reduce these negative impacts. However, the growing concern for **sustainability**, as discussed in the introductory chapter of this book, has stimulated a trend towards studying positive transactions between humans and the environment, such as health-promoting effects of natural environments and positive contributions of pro-environmental behaviour to environmental quality and quality of life (Gifford 2007; Giuliani and Scopelliti 2009; Venhoeven et al. 2013). As part of this trend, interventions are increasingly aimed at supporting and encouraging pro-environmental behaviour, rather than merely on discouraging environmentally harmful behaviour.

In the five years since the publication of the first edition of the book, the positive outlook of environmental psychology has been further strengthened and extended. In Part I, much attention is paid to the positive effects of nature and natural environments as well as to positive contributions of well-designed, liveable urban environments to quality of life. In this domain, increasing attention is paid to the benefits of nature for children and to place attachment as an emotional bond to places that matter in people's lives. In Part II the focus is on understanding pro-environmental behaviour by identifying positive behavioural determinants of pro-environmental behaviour such as biospheric values, pro-environmental social norms, symbolic meaning, and anticipated positive affect. Indeed, the growing evidence that many people engage in pro-environmental behaviour because it makes them feel good, as discussed in Chapter 19, suggests that truly sustainable solutions that promote environmental quality without compromising human well-being can be achieved. Part III focuses on interventions, incentives, and techniques that support and encourage pro-environmental choices. Some notable examples are monetary incentives that support people's moral obligations to behave pro-environmentally and the use of interactive lighting feedback to make pro-environmental behaviour less demanding.

Although this book is mostly based on research in Western, industrialized countries, there are indications that the trend towards studying human–environment interactions also applies to other parts of the world. A review of studies in Latin American countries, as discussed in Chapter 25, reveals that the focus of environmental psychology research in this region has also shifted from an early focus on the negative influence of environmental conditions on well-being and behaviour, to a focus on the positive effects of environmental conditions and the gratifying impact of pro-environmental behaviour. Furthermore, a review of studies in low- and middle-income countries, as described in Chapter 32, illustrates how environmental psychology can contribute to solving the many environmental problems in less wealthy countries in the world.

33.2.2   Integrative Approaches

A second trend that is reflected in every part of this book is the development of integrative models and approaches. Whereas in the early years of environmental psychology the focus was often on studying relationships between single environmental conditions (e.g. crowding) and single outcome variables (e.g. physiological stress), contemporary research strives for integrative models and approaches that combine multiple influences and relationships among environmental and human conditions. This trend can be related to a growing interest in understanding and solving complex societal problems, which is increasingly replacing the traditional focus on individual problems (Bonnes and Bonaiuto 2002). In general, for research to be applicable to 'real-world problems', it is important to provide a comprehensive picture that integrates the manifold environmental, social, and psychological aspects of these problems.

The continuing trend towards integrative models and approaches is clearly illustrated in the chapters on urban environmental quality, place attachment, and quality of life in Part I of this book. In these chapters, multidimensional measures are presented that comprise comprehensive sets of positive and negative aspects of environmental quality and quality of life. The trend towards integrative approaches is also echoed in the fact that this book does not include any chapters on single (negative) aspects of environmental quality, such as noise or crowding, which used to figure prominently in previous introductions to environmental psychology (e.g. Bell et al. 2001; Gifford 2007). The new, integrative approach is also gaining ground in research on factors that determine environmental behaviour, as discussed in Part II of this book. In particular, Chapter 16 discusses multidimensional measures that integrate different environmental behaviours, while Chapter 22 discusses theories like goal framing theory that integrate different determinants of environmental behaviour. In Part III of the book, an integrated self-regulation model of behavioural change is presented that links different intervention types to different stage-specific change mechanisms (see Chapter 30).

33.2.3   From One Psychology to Multiple Psychologies

A third overarching trend is the development of multiple subfields or 'psychologies' within environmental psychology. This trend, which has also been described by Giuliani and Scopelliti (2009), can be considered as a **counter-trend** against the more unifying trends towards sustainability as a central guiding principle of the field and the development of integrative approaches. This counter-trend involves the development of more or less independent subfields with their own research topics and theoretical and empirical paradigms. Some established examples of psychologies as discussed in this book include the research on human–nature relationships, urban environmental quality, and pro-environmental behaviour. In addition, several emerging subfields, such as the study of climate change perceptions, place attachment, persuasive technologies, and agent-based modelling can be identified.

The development of new psychologies within environmental psychology has many positive consequences, such as a more in-depth analysis of the specific phenomenon of interest, the development and test of sound theories, a refinement of methods, and a stimulation of collaborations with other disciplines. For example, the recent emergence of the subfield of restorative environments research has yielded new insights and theories on the psychological mechanisms underlying recovery from stress and mental fatigue. It has led to the development of a new paradigm for studying and measuring restorative processes, and it has stimulated a collaboration with medical scientists to properly measure and diagnose stress. As another example, research on environmental behaviour has yielded important insights into how pro-environmental actions can be promoted via the strengthening of values and norms. It has led to the development of new methods for assessing environmental behaviour (i.e. the Campbell paradigm and measures of direct and indirect energy use of households), and it has stimulated collaboration with environmental scientists for assessing the environmental impacts of behaviour, thereby increasing the potential societal impact of this research. However, as noted by Giuliani and Scopelliti (2009), a drawback of the development of psychologies within environmental psychology is that it impedes the realization of a coherent and unifying theoretical framework as previously anticipated by pioneers of environmental psychology such as Craik (1973), Wapner (1995), and Proshansky (1987). Moreover, fragmentation of the field can lead to a decreased collaboration and weakening of the networks within environmental psychology. This latter issue may be partly countered by organizing more joint activities that facilitate collaboration and exchange, such as the publication of this book and the organization of international conferences and summer schools.

33.3 CHALLENGES FOR FUTURE RESEARCH

While the field of environmental psychology has continued to advance over the past years to the stage where it has become an active contributor to a more sustainable society, many challenges for future research still exist. In this last section of the book, we discuss three major challenges that apply to the field as a whole. These challenges address the need for further integration, further development of theories and models, and further engagement of environmental psychologists with environmental problems.

33.3.1 *Further Integration*

An important issue on the research agenda of environmental psychology is the need for further integration within and between the different subdomains that study environmental influences on behaviour (see Part I of this book) and human influences on the environment (see Part II and III of this book). In each of these domains, integrative models and solutions have focused either on combining multiple (positive and negative) environmental determinants of human behaviour or on combining multiple (positive and negative) individual determinants of environmental behaviour. However, little progress has been made towards integration within and between these domains.

Within the domains that study influences of the environment on humans, and influences of humans on the environment, further integration can be achieved by considering the combined influence of 'people and place components' at different scale levels (Stamps 1996; Steg et al. 2014a; Winkel et al. 2009). To this end, **multilevel models** have become widely available that enable the study of the effects of contextual and individual factors and their interaction on variables of interest. In recent years, such models have increasingly become a prominent analytical approach in studies on environmental influences on human behaviour, as described in Part I of this book. Multilevel modelling has also gained ground in research on pro-environmental behaviour. For example, a recent large-scale study in 30 countries used multilevel modelling to explain cross-national differences in environmental behaviour in terms of both national and individual variables (Pisano and Lubell 2017).

Between the domains of environmental influences on humans and human influences on the environment, the challenge for further integration lies in identifying and encouraging human–environment interactions that contribute to environmental quality as well as human well-being. In this book, this challenge is addressed by research showing that environmental policies may safeguard quality of life. Notably, research on emotions and environmental behaviour reveals that engaging in behaviour that benefits the environment can actually make people feel good, and research on persuasive technologies proposes solutions that alleviate the cognitive demand of monitoring environmental behaviour. A further example is research showing that energy-saving street lighting may not only benefit the environment, but also make people feel safe (Boomsma and Steg 2014a, b). Another example concerns the stimulation of contact with nature (especially in children) as a means to stimulate connectedness to nature, which in turn can foster pro-environmental behaviour (Kals et al. 1999; see also Chapter 14).

33.3.2   *Further Development of Theories and Methods*

Another major challenge for environmental psychology is to connect with theoretical and methodological developments within mainstream psychology. Three developments seem particularly promising with regard to human–environment transactions. First, a substantial body of research has accumulated that suggests much of human behaviour is driven by automatic, presumably largely unconscious, processes (Bargh and Ferguson 2000). This research has yielded important new models and theories about the implicit regulation of behaviour (Strack and Deutsch 2004), along with innovative methods for studying implicit processes (Gawronski and Payne 2010; Greenwald and Banaji 1995). These developments are beginning to find their way to environmental psychology (see Chapters 15, 18, 24, and 28). However the full potential of theories and methods for studying implicit processes has not yet been realized.

Second, there has been a shift from theories that emphasize 'cold' cognitive determinants of behaviour to theories that emphasize 'hot' emotional influences (Loewenstein 1996). The role of emotion in behaviour continues to be highly debated. Nevertheless, it is clear that a comprehensive account of human behaviour should address the fact that people's choices and decisions are often influenced by their passions and emotional impulses. The importance of emotions in understanding human behaviour is increasingly recognized in environmental psychology, as illustrated, for example, in Chapter 2 on risk perception, Chapter 8 on ambivalence towards landscapes, Chapter 9 on human dimensions of wildlife, and Chapter 19 on emotions and pro-environmental behaviour. However, the research on environmental behaviour in particular still remains dominated by rational-decision-making models (for a review, see Steg and Vlek 2009). A major task for research on environmental behaviour is to develop models that incorporate emotions without losing the rigour and structure that are the main strengths of existing models (see Loewenstein 1996).

Third, a biological revolution has taken place in many areas of psychology, with an increasing emphasis on the use of **neuroscience** methods to study brain processes that underlie people's thoughts and behaviour (Heatherton and Wheatly 2010). Among other things, this revolution has led to a widespread use of **neuroimaging** techniques for mapping which areas of the brain are activated when people engage in certain behaviours. Neuroimaging techniques can provide valuable insights into the location and functions of brain areas that are associated with human–environment transactions, such as the perception of natural or urban environments, the experience of guilt when engaging in environmentally harmful behaviour, or experience of positive emotions when acting pro-environmentally. However, so far these methods have scarcely been applied in environmental psychology.

33.3.3   *Further Engagement*

A final urgent challenge for environmental psychology is to move towards a greater engagement with the problems that are studied (Gifford 2007, 2008).

As demonstrated in this book, environmental psychology has increasingly embraced sustainability as a central focus of research, delivering many valuable insights and tools for promoting sustainability at local and global levels. However, environmental psychology is not yet a major player in sustainability science. To really make a difference in the struggle to save the planet from environmental and societal degradation, environmental psychologists need to become more engaged.

There are several lines of actions that environmental psychologists can take to strengthen their position in the sustainability debate. One is to improve and expand the academic infrastructure for education and research so that more and better research can be done. Since an academic infrastructure for environmental psychology is still lacking in many countries of the world, there is much to be gained from this endeavour. As illustrated in the chapters on environmental psychology in Latin America and low- and middle-income countries, attempts to establish or strengthen the academic infrastructure of environmental psychology are probably most effective in those countries and regions of the world where the consequences of environmental problems are most strongly felt and sustainable solutions are most needed.

Another line of action for environmental psychologists is to further increase the political relevance and applicability of their work. For example, by modelling the outcomes of different policy choices, environmental psychologists can directly inform policymakers on the effectiveness of environmental policies, thereby increasing the chances that the most effective and sustainable policies are implemented. Moreover, by examining factors influencing the acceptability of environmental policies, environmental psychologists can advise policymakers on how to increase the public support needed to successfully implement such policies. By publishing research outcomes in professional journals or magazines for a general audience, environmental psychologists can increase the chances that their findings are actually adopted and applied. Environmental psychologists may even enter the political arena themselves and become 'green lobbyists' (Gifford 2007, 2008). However, such a direct political engagement may be one step too far for many environmental psychologists who strive to maintain a more objective position.

Finally, we would like to draw attention to recent initiatives that aim to foster knowledge sharing between science, governments, industry, and civil society, such as the establishment of the international PERSON platform that brings together knowledge of different disciplines in social sciences and humanities on ways to encourage a sustainable energy transition (see person. eu). Such initiatives can play a crucial role in engaging groups of citizens, industry, and policymakers globally to explore effective and acceptable ways to reduce environmental problems. By taking a leading role in these initiatives, environmental psychologists can show their engagement and contribute to interdisciplinary and transgovernmental solutions that truly make a difference for present and future generations.

GLOSSARY

counter-trend   A trend that goes against the general direction in which a discipline or something else is moving.

environmental psychology   A subfield of psychology that studies the interplay between individuals and the built and natural environment.

multilevel models   Statistical models of parameters that vary at more than one level (e.g. individual and contextual factors). Also known as hierarchical linear models.

neuroimaging   The use of techniques such as functional magnetic resonance imaging (fMRI) or positron emission tomography (PET scans) to image or 'map' the structure and/or function of the brain.

neuroscience   The scientific study of the nervous system.

sustainability   Using, developing, and protecting resources at a rate and in a manner that enable people to meet their current needs and ensure that future generations can meet their own needs; achieving an optimal balance between environmental, social, and economic qualities.

trend   The general direction in which a discipline or something else tends to move.

SUGGESTIONS FOR FURTHER READING

Gifford, R. (2014). Environmental psychology matters. *Annual Review of Psychology*, 65, 541–579.

Giuliani, M. V., & Scopelliti, M. (2009). Empirical research in environmental psychology: past, present, and future. *Journal of Environmental Psychology*, 29(3), 375–386.

Steg, L., & Vlek, C. (2009). Encouraging pro-environmental behaviour: an integrative review and research agenda. *Journal of Environmental Psychology*, 29, 309–317.

REVIEW QUESTIONS

1. Describe three major trends in environmental psychology.
2. Describe three main challenges for environmental psychology.
3. Give an example of a case or problem in which the influences of individual and contextual factors on perceptions, evaluations, or behaviour are examined simultaneously.

Aarts, H. and Dijksterhuis, A. (2000). Habits as knowledge structures: automaticity in goal-directed behavior. *Journal of Personality and Social Psychology* 78 (1): 53–63.

Aarts, H., Verplanken, B., and van Knippenberg, A. (1997). Habit and information use in travel mode choices. *Acta Psychologica* 96: 1–14.

Abrahamse, W. and Steg, L. (2009). How do socio-demographic and psychological factors relate to households' direct and indirect energy use and savings? *Journal of Economic Psychology* 30: 711–720.

Abrahamse, W. and Steg, L. (2013). Social influence approaches to encourage resource conservation: a meta-analysis. *Global Environmental Change* 23 (6): 1773–1785.

Abrahamse, W., Steg, L., Vlek, C., and Rothengatter, T. (2005). A review of intervention studies aimed at household energy conservation. *Journal of Environmental Psychology* 25: 273–291.

Abrahamse, W., Steg, L., Vlek, C., and Rothengatter, J.A. (2007). The effect of tailored information, goal setting and feedback on household energy use, energy related behaviors and behavioral determinants. *Journal of Environmental Psychology* 27: 265–276.

Abrams, D., Wetherell, M., Cochrane, S. et al. (1990). Knowing what to think by knowing who you are: self-categorization and the nature of norm formation, conformity, and group polarization. *British Journal of Social Psychology* 29: 97–119.

Abu-Gazzeh, T.M. (1998). The use of the street as a playground in Abu Nuseir, Jordan. *Environment and Behavior* 30: 799–831.

Adeola, F.O. (1996). Environmental contamination, public hygiene, and human health concerns in the third world: the case of Nigerian environmentalism. *Environment and Behavior* 28: 614–646.

Adger, W.N., Barnett, J., Chapin, F.S. III, and Ellemer, H. (2011). This must be the place: underrepresentation of identity and meaning in climate change decision-making. *Global Environmental Politics* 11: 1–25.

Ahmadi, E. (2009). An evaluation of the influence of gasoline rationing plan on mobility pattern in Iran. In: *8th Biennial Conference on Environmental Psychology* (ed. H. Gutscher, H.-J. Mosler, B. Meyer, et al.), 127. Zurich: Institute of Psychology.

Aiello, A., Ardone, R., and Scopelliti, M. (2010). Neighbourhood planning improvement: physical attributes, cognitive and affective evaluation and activities in two neighbourhoods in Rome. *Evaluation and Program Planning* 33 (3): 264–275.

Ainuddin, S., Routray, J.K., and Ainuddin, S. (2014). People's risk perception in earthquake prone Quetta city of Baluchistan. *International Journal of Disaster Risk Reduction* 7: 165–175.

Environmental Psychology: An Introduction, Second Edition. Edited by Linda Steg and Judith I. M. de Groot.

Ajzen, I. (1985). From intentions to actions: a theory of planned behavior. In: *Action-Control: From Cognition to Behavior* (ed. J. Kuhl and J. Beckman), 11–39. Heidelberg, Germany: Springer.

Ajzen, I. (1991). The theory of planned behavior. *Organizational Behavior and Human Decision Processes* 50 (2): 179–211.

Allen, J. and Balfour, R. (2014). *Natural Solutions for Tackling Health Inequalities*. London: Institute of Health Equity. Retrieved from https://www.instituteofhealthequity.org/projects/natural-solutions-to-tackling-health-inequalities/natural-solutions-to-tackling-health-inequalities.pdf.

Almanza, E., Jerrett, M., Dunton, G. et al. (2012). A study of community design, greenness, and physical activity in children using satellite, GPS and accelerometer data. *Health & Place* 18 (1): 46–54.

Altherr, A.M., Mosler, H.-J., Tobias, R., and Butera, F. (2008). Attitudinal and relational factors predicting the use of solar water disinfection: a field study in Nicaragua. *Health Education & Behaviour* 35: 207–220.

Altman, I. (1975). *The Environment and Social Behavior: Privacy, Personal Space, Territory and Crowding*. Monterey, CA: Brooks/Cole.

Alvey, A.A. (2006). Promoting and preserving biodiversity in the urban forest. *Urban Forestry & Urban Greening* 5 (4): 195–201.

Amedeo, D.M. and Golledge, R.G. (2003). Environmental perception and behavioral geography. In: *Geography in America at the Dawn of the 21st Century* (ed. G.L. Gaile and C.J. Willmott), 133–148. Oxford, NY: Oxford University Press.

Anable, J. and Gatersleben, B. (2005). All work and no play? The positive utility of travel for work compared to leisure journeys. *Transportation Research Part A: Policy and Practice* 39: 163–181.

Andreoni, J. (1990). Impure altruism and donations to public goods: a theory of warm-glow giving. *The Economic Journal* 100 (401): 464–477.

Andrews, F.M. and Withey, S.B. (1976). *Social Indicators of Well-Being: America's Perception of Life Quality*. New York, NY: Plenum.

Annerstedt, M., Jönsson, P., Wallergård, M. et al. (2013). Inducing physiological stress recovery with sounds of nature in a virtual reality forest—results from a pilot study. *Physiology and Behavior* 118: 240–250.

Antrop, M. (1998). Landscape change: plan or chaos? *Landscape and Urban Planning* 41 (3–4): 155–161.

Antrop, M. (2004). Landscape change and the urbanization process in Europe. *Landscape and Urban Planning* 67 (1–4): 9–26.

Appleton, J. (1975). *The Experience of Landscape*. New York, NY: Wiley.

Appleyard, D. and Craik, K.H. (1974). The Berkeley environmental simulation project: its use in environmental impact assessment. In: *Environmental Impact Assessment: Guidelines and Commentary* (ed. T.G. Dickert and K.R. Downey), 121–125. Berkeley, CA: University of California Extension.

Arı, E. and Yılmaz, V. (2016). A proposed structural model for housewives' recycling behavior: a case study from Turkey. *Ecological Economics* 129: 132–142.

Armitage, R. (2007). Sustainability versus safety: confusion, conflict and contradiction in designing out crime. In: *Imagination for Crime Prevention: Essays in Honor of Ken Pease*, vol. 21 (ed. G. Farrell, K.J. Bowers, S.D. Johnson and M. Townsley), 81–110. Crime Prevention Studies. Monsey, NY: Criminal Justice Press and Willan Publishing.

Arroyo, E., Bonanni, L., and Selker, T. (2005). Waterbot: Exploring feedback and persuasive techniques at the sink. *Conference proceedings of CHI 2005* (pp. 631–639). Reading, USA: ACM Press.

Asch, S.E. (1951). Effects of group pressure upon the modification and distortion of judgment. In: *Groups, Leadership, and Men* (ed. H. Guetzkow), 177–190. Pittsburg, PA: Carnegie Press.

Asch, S.E. (1956). Studies of independence and conformity: a minority of one against a unanimous majority. *Psychological Monographs* 70 (9): 1–70.

Asensio, O.I. and Delmas, M.A. (2015). Nonprice incentives and energy conservation. *Proceedings of the National Academy of Sciences* 112 (6): E510–E515.

Asim, M., Batool, S.A., and Chaudhry, M.N. (2012). Scavengers and their role in the recycling of waste in Southwestern Lahore. *Resources, Conservation & Recycling* 58: 152–162.

Austin, J., Hatfield, D.B., Grindle, A.C., and Bailey, J.S. (1993). Increasing recycling in office environments: the effects of specific, informative cues. *Journal of Applied Behavior Analysis* 26: 247–253.

Babisch, W. and Kim, R. (2011). Conclusions. In: *Burden of Disease from Environmental Noise*. World Health Organization.

Bachmann, W. and Katzev, R. (1982). The effects of non-contingent free bus tickets and personal commitment on urban bus ridership. *Transportation Research* 16A: 103–108.

Bailey, E., Devine-Wright, P., and Batel, S. (2016). Investigating varieties of people-place relations across the life course: the relation between 'life-place trajectories' and responses to a power line proposal. *Journal of Environmental Psychology* 48: 200–211.

Baird, J.C., Cassidy, B., and Kurr, J. (1978). Room preference as a function of architectural features and user activities. *Journal of Applied Psychology* 63: 719–727.

Bamberg, S. (2003). Implementation intention versus monetary incentive comparing the effects of interventions to promote the purchase of organically produced food. *Journal of Economic Psychology* 23: 573–587.

Bamberg, S. (2006). Is a residential relocation a good opportunity to change people's travel behaviour? Results from a theory-driven intervention study. *Environment and Behavior* 38: 820–840.

Bamberg, S. (2013a). Changing environmentally harmful behaviors: a stage model of self-regulated behavioral change. *Journal of Environmental Psychology* 34: 151–159.

Bamberg, S. (2013b). Applying the stage model of self-regulated behavioral change in a car use reduction intervention. *Journal of Environmental Psychology* 33: 68–75.

Bamberg, S. and Schmidt, S. (2003). Incentives, morality or habit? Predicting students' car use for university routes with the models of Ajzen, Schwartz and Triandis. *Environment and Behavior* 35: 264–285.

Bamberg, S., Behrens, G., Papendick, M. et al. (2015a). Development of a theory-driven, web-based behavioral change support system for environmentally friendly mobility behaviour. In: *Social Marketing – Global Perspectives, Strategies and Effects on Consumer Behavior* (ed. W.D. Evans), 109–120. New York, NY: Nova Science Publishers.

Bamberg, S., Rees, J., and Seebauer, S. (2015b). Collective climate action: determinants of participation intention in community-based pro-environmental initiatives. *Journal of Environmental Psychology* 43: 155–165.

Bandura, A. (1977). *Social Learning Theory*. New York, NY: Prentice-Hall.

Banister, D. (2008). The sustainable mobility paradigm. *Transport Policy* 15: 73–80.

Barcena Ibarra, A. and Byanyima, W. (2016). Latin America is the world's most unequal region. Here's how to fix it. Accessed 20 Sept 2018: https://www.weforum.org/agenda/2016/01/inequality-is-getting-worse-in-latin-america-here-s-how-to-fix-it?utm_content=buffere0fff&utm_medium=social&utm_source=facebook.com&utm_campaign=buffer

Bargh, J.A. and Ferguson, M.J. (2000). Beyond Behaviorism: on the automaticity of higher mental processes. *Psychological Bulletin* 126: 925–945.

Bargh, J.A., Gollwitzer, P.M., Lee-Chai, A. et al. (2001). Automated will: nonconscious activation and pursuit of behavioral goals. *Journal of Personality and Social Psychology* 81: 1014–1027.

Barker, R. and Wright, H. (1955). *Midwest and Its Children: The Psychological Ecology of an American Town*. New York, NY: Harper and Row.

Baron, J. and Spranca, M. (1997). Protected values. *Organizational Behavior and Human Decision Processes* 70: 1–16.

Bartels, G. and Nelissen, W. (2001). *Marketing for Sustainability: Towards Transactional Policy-Making*. Amsterdam: IOS Press.

Barthel, R., Janisch, S., Nickel, D. et al. (2010). Using the multiactor approach in GLOWA-Danube to simulate decisions for the water supply sector under conditions of global climate change. *Water Resources Management* 24: 239–275.

Barton, J., Bragg, R., Wood, C., and Pretty, J. (2016). *Green Exercise: Linking Nature, Health and Well-Being*. London and New York: Routledge.

Batalha, L. and Reynolds, K.J. (2012). ASPIRing to mitigate climate change: superordinate identity in global climate negotiations. *Political Psychology* 33 (5): 743–760.

Baum, A. and Valins, S. (1977). *Architecture and Social Behavior: Psychological Studies of Social Density*. Hillsdale, NJ: Erlbaum.

Baumeister, R.F. (1982). A self-presentational view of social phenomena. *Psychological Bulletin* 91 (1): 3–26.

Baumeister, R.F. (1993). Understanding the inner nature of low self-esteem: uncertain, fragile, protective, and conflicted. In: *Self-esteem* (ed. R.F. Baumeister), 201–218. New York, NY: Plenum Press.

Baumeister, R.F. (2005). *The Cultural Animal: Human Nature, Meaning, and Social Life*. New York, NY: Oxford University Press.

Baumeister, R.F., Bratlavsky, E., Finkenauer, C., and Vohs, K.D. (2001). Bad is stronger than good. *Review of General Psychology* 5: 323–370.

Bechtel, R., Corral-Verdugo, V., and Pinheiro, J. (1999). Environmental beliefs system: U.S., Brazil and Mexico. *Journal of Cross Cultural Psychology* 30: 122–128.

Becker, L.J. (1978). Joint effect of feedback and goal setting on performance: a field study of residential energy conservation. *Journal of Applied Psychology* 63: 428–433.

Becker, F.D. and Poe, D.B. (1980). The effects of user-generated design modifications in a general hospital. *Journal of Nonverbal Behavior* 4: 195–218.

Belk, R. (1988). Possessions and the extended self. *The Journal of Consumer Research* 15 (2): 139–168.

Bell, S. (1999). *Landscape: Pattern, Perception and Process*. London: E & FN Spon.

Bell, P.A., Greene, T.C., Fisher, J.D., and Baum, A. (2001). *Environmental Psychology*, 5e. Fort Worth: Harcourt College Publishers.

Bem, D.J. (1972). Self-perception theory. In: *Advances in Experimental Social Psychology* (ed. L. Berkowitz), 1–62. New York, NY: Academic Press.

Benjamin, L. (2007). *A Brief History of Modern Psychology*. Malden, MA: Blackwell.

Berenguer, J. (2007). The effect of empathy in proenvironmental attitudes and behaviors. *Environment and Behavior* 39: 269–272.

Bethwaite, J. and Tompkinson, P. (1993). The ultimatum game - understanding the taste for fairness. *Economic Notes* 22: 37–48.

Beute, F. and de Kort, Y. (2014). Natural resistance: exposure to nature and self-regulation, mood, and physiology after ego-depletion. *Journal of Environmental Psychology* 40: 167–178.

Beveridge, C.E. (1977). Frederick Law Olmsted's theory of landscape design. *Nineteenth Century* 3: 38–43.

Biel, A. and Thøgersen, J. (2007). Activation of social norms in social dilemmas: a review of the evidence and reflections on the implications for environmental behaviour. *Journal of Environmental Psychology* 28: 93–112.

Biel, A., Dahlstrand, U., and Grankvist, G. (2005). Habitual and value-guided purchase behavior. *Ambio* 34 (4–5): 360–365.

Binder, C. and Mosler, H.-J. (2007). Waste-resource flows of short-lived goods in Santiago de Cuba. *Resources, Conservation and Recycling* 51: 265–283.

Bishop, I.D. and Rohrmann, B. (2003). Subjective responses to simulated and real environments: a comparison. *Landscape and Urban Planning* 65: 261–277.

Bishop, I.D., Ye, W.S., and Karadaglis, C. (2001). Experiential approaches to perception response in virtual worlds. *Landscape and Urban Planning* 54 (1–4): 117–125.

Bixler, R.D. and Floyd, M.F. (1997). Nature is scary, disgusting, and uncomfortable. *Environment and Behavior* 29 (4): 443–467.

Blaison, C. and Hess, U. (2016). Affective judgment in spatial context: how places derive affective meaning from the surroundings. *Journal of Environmental Psychology* 47: 53–65.

Bliuc, A.M., McGarty, C., Thomas, E.F. et al. (2015). Public division about climate change rooted in conflicting socio-political identities. *Nature Climate Change* 5 (3): 226–229.

Bockarjova, M. and Steg, L. (2014). Can protection motivation theory predict pro-environmental behavior? Explaining the adoption of electric vehicles in the Netherlands. *Global Environmental Change* 28: 276–288.

Bodner, R. and Prelec, D. (2003). Self-signaling and diagnostic utility in everyday decision making. In: *Collected Essays in Psychology and Economics* (ed. I. Brocas and J. Carillo), 105–126. Oxford: Oxford University Press.

Böhm, G. (2003). Emotional reactions to environmental risks: consequentialist versus ethical evaluation. *Journal of Environmental Psychology* 23: 199–212.

Böhm, G. and Pfister, H.-R. (2005). Consequences, morality, and time in environmental risk evaluation. *Journal of Risk Research* 8: 461–479.

Böhm, G. and Pfister, H.-R. (2015). The perceiver's social role and a risk's causal structure as determinants of environmental risk evaluation. *Journal of Risk Research* doi: 10.1080/13669877.2015.1118148.

Bolderdijk, J.W., Knockaert, J., Steg, E.M., and Verhoef, E.T. (2011). Effects of pay-as-you-drive vehicle insurance on young drivers' speed choice: results of a Dutch field experiment. *Accident Analysis and Prevention* 43: 1181–1186.

Bolderdijk, J.W., Gorsira, M., Keizer, K., and Steg, L. (2013a). Values determine the (in)effectiveness of informational interventions in promoting pro-environmental behavior. *PLoS One* 8 (12): e83911.

Bolderdijk, J.W. and Steg, L. (2015). Promoting sustainable consumption: the risks of using financial incentives. In: Handbook of research in sustainable consumption (ed. J. Thogersen and L. Reisch), 328–342. Cheltenham, UK: Edward Elgar.

Bolderdijk, J.W., Steg, L., Geller, E.S. et al. (2013b). Comparing the effectiveness of monetary versus moral motives in environmental campaigning. *Nature Climate Change* 3 (4): 413–416.

Bolderdijk, J.W., Steg, L., and Postmes, T. (2013c). Fostering support for work floor energy conservation policies: accounting for privacy concerns. *Journal of Organizational Behavior* 34: 195–210.

Bonaiuto, M. and Bonnes, M. (1996). Multiplace analysis of urban environment. A comparison between a large and a small Italian City. *Environment and Behavior* 28 (6): 699–747.

Bonaiuto, M. and Fornara, F. (2017). Residential satisfaction and perceived urban quality. In: *Reference Module in Neuroscience and Biobehavioral Psychology* (ed. J. Stein), 1–5. Oxford, UK: Elsevier.

Bonaiuto, M., Fornara, F., and Bonnes, M. (2003). Indexes of perceived residential environment quality and neighbourhood attachment in urban environments: a confirmation study on the city of Rome. *Landscape and Urban Planning* 65: 41–52.

Bonaiuto, M., Bonnes, M., and Continisio, M. (2004). Neighborhood evaluation within a multiplace perspective on urban activities. *Environment and Behavior* 36 (1): 41–69.

Bonaiuto, M., Fornara, F., Alves, S. et al. (2015). Urban environment and well-being: cross-cultural studies on perceived residential environment quality indicators (PREQIs). *Cognitive Processing* 16 (Suppl. 1): 165–169.

Bond, T.G. and Fox, C.M. (2001). *Applying the Rasch Model: Fundamental Measurement in the Human Sciences*. Mahwah, NJ: Erlbaum.

Bonnes, M. and Bonaiuto, M. (2002). Environmental psychology: from spatial physical environment to sustainable development. In: *Handbook of Environmental Psychology* (ed. R. Bechtel and A. Churchman), 28–54. New York, NY: Wiley.

Bonnes, M. and Carrus, G. (2017). Environmental psychology, overview. In: *Reference module in Neuroscience and Biobehavioral Psychology*. doi: 10.1016/B978-0-12-809324-5.05554-1.

Bonnes, M., Mannetti, I., Secchiaroli, G., and Tanucci, G. (1990). The city as a multi-place system. An analysis of people-urban environment transactions. *Journal of Environmental Psychology* 10 (1): 37–65.

Bonnes, M., Uzzell, D., Carrus, G., and Kelay, T. (2007). Inhabitants' and experts' assessments of environmental quality for urban sustainability. *Journal of Social Issues* 63: 59–78.

Bonnes, M., Passafaro, P., and Carrus, G. (2011). The ambivalence of attitudes toward urban green areas: between proenvironmental worldviews and daily residential experience. *Environment and Behavior* 43 (2): 207–232.

Boomsma, C. and Steg, L. (2014a). Feeling safe in the dark: examining the effect of entrapment, lighting levels, and gender on feelings of safety and lighting policy acceptability. *Environment and Behavior* 46 (2): 193–212.

Boomsma, C. and Steg, L. (2014b). The effect of information and values on acceptability of reduced street lighting. *Journal of Environmental Psychology* 39: 22–31.

Botzat, A., Fischer, L.K., and Kowarik, I. (2016). Unexploited opportunities in understanding liveable and biodiverse cities. A review on urban biodiversity perception and valuation. *Global Environmental Change* 39: 220–233.

Bourassa, S.C. (1991). *The Aesthetics of Landscape*. London: Belhaven Press.

Bowler, D., Buyung-Ali, L., Knight, T., and Pullin, A. (2010). A systematic review of evidence for the added benefits to health of exposure to natural environments. *BMC Public Health* 10 (1): 456.

Boyes, W.J. (1996). Understanding, fairness and reputation in the ultimatum game. *Economic Notes* 25: 21–32.

Boykoff, M. and Boykoff, J. (2004). Bias as balance: global warming and the U.S. prestige press. *Global Environmental Change* 14 (2): 125–136.

Bragg, R. and Atkins, G. (2016). *A Review of Nature-Based Interventions for Mental Health Care*. London: Natural England. Retrieved from http://publications.naturalengland.org.uk/publication/4513819616346112.

Bratt, C., Stern, P.C., Matthies, E., and Nenseth, V. (2015). Home, car use, and vacation. *Environment and Behavior* 47 (4): 436–473.

Brehm, J.W. (1966). *A Theory of Psychological Reactance*. New York, NY: Academic Press.

Brewer, M.B. and Kramer, M.R. (1986). Choice behavior in social dilemmas: effects of social identity, group size, and decision framing. *Journal of Personality and Social Psychology* 50: 543–549.

Brickman, P., Coates, D., and Janoff-Bulman, R. (1978). Lottery winners and accident victims: is happiness relative? *Journal of Personality and Social Psychology* 37: 917–927.

Bright, A.D., Manfredo, M.J., and Fulton, D.C. (2000). Segmenting the public: an application of value orientations to wildlife planning in Colorado. *Wildlife Society Bulletin* 28 (1): 218–226.

Broadbent, D.E. (1958). *Perception and Communication*. New York, NY: Academic Press.

Bronzaft, A.L. (1981). The effect of a noise abatement program on reading ability. *Journal of Environmental Psychology* 1: 215–222.

Brown, G. and Gifford, R. (2001). Architects predict lay evaluations of large contemporary buildings: whose conceptual properties? *Journal of Environmental Psychology* 21: 93–99.

Brown, B.B. and Perkins, D.D. (1992). Disruptions in place attachment. In: *Place Attachment* (ed. I. Altman and S. Low), 279–304. Boston, MA: Springer.

Brown, B. and Werner, C. (2012). Health physical activity and eating: environmental support for health. In: *Oxford Handbook of Environmental and Conservation Psychology* (ed. S. Clayton), 459–484. New York, NY: Oxford University Press.

Buchan, N.R., Croson, R.T.A., and Dawes, R.M. (1999). Who's with me? The role of group boundaries on trust and reciprocity: A cross-culture study. Paper presented at the EAESP meeting in Oxford.

Buhyoff, G.J., Hull, R.B., Lien, J.N., and Cordell, H.K. (1986). Prediction of scenic quality for southern pine stands. *Forest Science* 32 (3): 769–778.

Buijs, A.E. (2009). Lay people's images of nature: comprehensive frameworks of values, beliefs, and value orientations. *Society & Natural Resources: An International Journal* 22 (5): 417–432.

Buijs, A.E., Elands, B.H.M., and Langers, F. (2009). No wilderness for immigrants: cultural differences in images of nature and landscape preferences. *Landscape and Urban Planning* 91 (3): 113–123.

Burke, E. (1757). *A Philosophical Enquiry into the Origin of Our Ideas of the Sublime and Beautiful*. London: Dodsley.

Burke, P.J. (2006). Identity change. *Social Psychology Quarterly* 69 (1): 81–96.

Bustos, M., Flores, H.L.M., and Andrade, P.P. (2005). Residential water use: a model of personal variables. In: *Designing Social Innovation - Planning, Building, Evaluating* (ed. B. Martens and A. Keul), 147–154. Cambridge, MA: Hogrefe & Huber.

Byers, B.A., Cunliffe, R.N., and Hudak, A.T. (2001). Linking the conservation of culture and nature: a case study of sacred forests in Zimbabwe. *Human Ecology* 29 (2): 187–218.

Cackowski, J.M. and Nasar, J.L. (2003). The restorative effects of roadside vegetation: implications for automobile driver anger and frustration. *Environment and Behavior* 35 (6): 736–751.

Camacho-Cervantes, M., Schondube, J.E., Castillo, A., and MacGregor-Fors, I. (2014). How do people perceive urban trees? Assessing likes and dislikes in relation to the trees of a city. *Urban Ecosystems* 17 (3): 761–773.

Campbell, T.H. and Kay, A.C. (2014). Solution aversion: on the relation between ideology and motivated disbelief. *Journal of Personality and Social Psychology* 107 (5): 809–824.

Cannon, W.B. (1932). *The Wisdom of the Body*. New York, NY: Norton.

Canter, D. (ed.) (1970). *Architectural Psychology*. London: Royal Institute of British Architects.

Canter, D. (1985). Intention, meaning and structure: social action in its physical context. In: *Discovery Strategies in the Psychology of Action* (ed. G.P. Ginsburg, M. Brenner and M. von Cranach), 35–171. Orlando, FL: Academic Press.

Capaldi, C.A., Passmore, H.-A., Nisbet, E.K. et al. (2015). Flourishing in nature: a review of the benefits of connecting with nature and its application as a wellbeing intervention. *International Journal of Wellbeing* 5 (4): 1–16.

Capstick, S., Whitmarsh, L., Poortinga, W. et al. (2015). International trends in public perceptions of climate change over the past quarter century. *WIREs: Climate Change* 6 (1): 35–61.

Capstick, S.B., Pidgeon, N.F., Corner, A.J. et al. (2016). Public understanding in Great Britain of ocean acidification. *Nature Climate Change* 6 (8): 763–767.

Carlson, A. (2009). *Nature and Landscape: An Introduction to Environmental Aesthetics*. New York, NY: Columbia University Press.

Carrus, G., Passafaro, P., and Bonnes, M. (2008). Emotions, habits and rational choices in ecological behaviours: the case of recycling and use of public transportation. *Journal of Environmental Psychology* 28: 51–62.

Carrus, G., Lafortezza, R., Colangelo, G. et al. (2013). Relations between naturalness and perceived restorativeness of different urban green spaces. *Psyecology* 4 (3): 227–244.

Carrus, G., Scopelliti, M., Lafortezza, R. et al. (2015). Go greener, feel better? The positive effects of biodiversity on the well-being of individuals visiting urban and peri-urban green areas. *Landscape and Urban Planning* 134: 221–228.

Carvalho, M., George, R.V., and Anthony, K.H. (1997). Residential satisfaction in condominios exclusivos (gate-guarded neighbourhoods) in Brazil. *Environment and Behavior* 29: 734–768.

Carver, C.S. and Scheier, M.F. (1990). Origins and functions of positive and negative affect: a control-process view. *Psychological Review* 97: 19–35.

Carver, C.S. and Scheier, M.F. (1998). *On the Self-Regulation of Behavior*. New York, NY: Cambridge University Press.

Chaiken, S. and Trope, Y. (eds.) (1999). *Dual-Process Theories in Social Psychology*. New York, NY: Guilford Press.

Chao, Y. and Lam, S. (2011). Measuring responsible environmental behavior: self-reported and other-reported measures and their differences in testing a behavioral model. *Environment and Behavior* 43: 53–71.

Chapman, D. and Thomas, G. (1944). Lighting in dwellings. In: *The Lighting of Buildings*, Post war building studies No. 12. London: HMSO.

Chawla, L. (2015). Benefits of nature contact for children. *Journal of Planning Literature* 30 (4): 433–452.

Cheskey, E. (2001). How schoolyards influence behavior. In: *Greening School Grounds: Creating Habitats for Learning* (ed. T. Grant and G. Littlejohn). Toronto: New Society Publishers.

Chokor, B.A. (2004). Perception and response to the challenge of poverty and environmental resource degradation in rural Nigeria: case study from the Niger Delta. *Journal of Environmental Psychology* 24 (3): 305–318.

Christopher, A. and Schlenker, B. (2000). The impact of perceived material wealth and perceiver personality on first impressions. *Journal of Economic Psychology* 21: 1–19.

Chu, P.Y. and Chiu, P.F. (2003). Factors influencing household waste recycling behaviour: test of an integrated model. *Journal of Applied Social Psychology* 33: 604–626.

Cialdini, R.B. (2003). Crafting normative messages to protect the environment. *Current Directions in Psychological Science* 12: 105–109.

Cialdini, R.B. and Trost, M.R. (1998). Social influence: social norms, conformity, and compliance. In: *Handbook of Social Psychology*, 4e, vol. 2 (ed. D. Gilber, S. Fiske and G. Lindzey), 151–192. Boston: McGraw-Hill.

Cialdini, R.B., Reno, R.R., and Kallgren, C.A. (1990). A focus theory of normative conduct - recycling the concept of norms to reduce littering in public places. *Journal of Personality and Social Psychology* 58: 1015–1026.

Cialdini, R.B., Kallgren, C.A., and Reno, R.R. (1991). A focus theory of normative conduct: a theoretical refinement and reevaluation of the role of norms in human behavior. In: *Advances in Experimental Social Psychology*, vol. 24 (ed. M.P. Zanna), 201–234. San Diego, CA: Academic Press.

Cialdini, R.B., Demaine, L.J., Sagarin, B.J. et al. (2006). Managing social norms for persuasive impact. *Social Influence* 1 (1): 3–15.

Clayton, S. (2000). Models of justice in the environmental debate. *Journal of Social Issues* 56: 459–474.

Clayton, S., Manning, C.M., and Hodge, C. (2014). *Beyond Storms & Droughts: The Psychological Impacts of Climate Change*. Washington, DC: American Psychological Association and ecoAmerica.

Clayton, S., Devine-Wright, P., Stern, P. et al. (2015). Psychological research and global climate change. *Nature Climate Change* 5: 640–646.

Cleary, A., Fielding, K.S., Bell, S.L. et al. (2017). Exploring potential mechanisms involved in the relationship between eudaimonic wellbeing and nature connection. *Landscape and Urban Planning* 158: 119–128.

Cohen, S. (1978). Environmental load and the allocation of attention. In: *Advances in Environmental Psychology*, The Urban Environment, vol. 1 (ed. A. Baum, J.E. Singer and S. Valins), 1–29. Hillsdale, NJ: Erlbaum.

Cohen, S. (1980). Aftereffects of stress on human performance and social behavior: a review of research and theory. *Psychological Bulletin* 88 (1): 82–108.

Coley, R.L., Kuo, F.E., and Sullivan, W.C. (1997). Where does community grow? The social context created by nature in urban public housing. *Environment and Behavior* 29 (4): 468–494.

Coley, R.L., Leventhal, T., Lynch, A.D., and Kull, M. (2013). Relations between housing characteristics and the well-being of low-income children and adolescents. *Developmental Psychology* 49 (9): 1775.

Collado, S. and Staats, H. (2016). Contact with nature and children's restorative experiences: an eye to the future. *Frontiers in Psychology* 7: 1885.

Collado, S., Staats, H., Corraliza, J.A., and Hartig, T. (2017). Restorative environments and health. In: *Handbook of Environmental Psychology and Quality of Life Research* (ed. G. Fleury-Bahi, E. Pol and O. Navarro), 127–148. Cham: Springer International.

Colvin, R.M., Witt, G.B., and Lacey, J. (2015a). The social identity approach to understanding socio-political conflict in environmental and natural resources management. *Global Environmental Change* 34: 237–246.

Colvin, R.M., Witt, G.B., and Lacey, J. (2015b). Strange bedfellows or an aligning of values? Exploration of stakeholder values in an alliance of concerned citizens against coal seam gas mining. *Land Use Policy* 42: 392–399.

Cone, J.D. and Hayes, S.C. (1980). *Environmental Problems/Behavioral Solutions*. Monterey, CA: Brooks/Cole.

Contzen, N. (2015). *Factors explaining the use of safe water kiosks in Kenya*. Poster presented at the 2015 Water and Health Conference, Chapel Hill, USA.

Contzen, N., Meili, I.H., and Mosler, H.J. (2015). Changing handwashing behaviour in southern Ethiopia: a longitudinal study on infrastructural and commitment interventions. *Social Science & Medicine* 124: 103–114.

Cook, A.J., Kerr, G.N., and Moore, K. (2002). Attitudes and intentions towards purchasing GM food. *Journal of Economic Psychology* 23: 557–572.

Cornelissen, G., Pandelaere, M., Warlop, L., and Dewitte, S. (2008). Positive cueing: promoting sustainable consumer behavior by cueing common environmental behaviors as environmental. *International Journal of Research in Marketing* 25 (1): 46–55.

Cornelius, R.R. (1996). *The Science of Emotion: Research and Tradition in the Psychology of Emotion*. Upper Saddle River: Simon and Schuster.

Corner, A., Whitmarsh, L., and Xenias, D. (2012). Uncertainty, scepticism and attitudes towards climate change: biased assimilation and attitude polarisation. *Climatic Change* 114: 463–478.

Corraliza, J. and Berenguer, J. (2000). Environmental values, beliefs, and actions: a situational approach. *Environment and Behavior* 32: 832–848.

Corraliza, J., Collado, S., and Bethelmy, L. (2012). Nature as a moderator of stress in urban children. *Procedia-Social and Behavioral Sciences* 38: 253–263.

Corral-Verdugo, V. (1997). Environmental psychology in Latin America: efforts in critical situations. *Environment and Behavior* 29: 163–168.

Corral-Verdugo, V. (2002). A structural model of pro-environmental competency. *Environment and Behavior* 34: 531–549.

Corral-Verdugo, V. (2010). *Psicología de la sustentabilidad. [Psychology of Sustainability]*. Mexico City: Trillas.

Corral-Verdugo, V. and Pinheiro, J. (2009). Environmental psychology with a Latin American taste. *Journal of Environmental Psychology* 29: 366–374.

Corral-Verdugo, V., Bechtel, R.B., and Fraijo, S.B. (2002). Environmental beliefs and water conservation: an empirical study. *Journal of Environmental Psychology* 23: 247–257.

Corral-Verdugo, V. and Frías-Armenta, M. (2006). Personal normative beliefs, antisocial behaviour, and residential water conservation. *Environment and Behavior* 38: 406–421.

Corral-Verdugo, V., García, C., and Frías, M. (eds.) (2010). *Psychological Approaches to Sustainability*. New York, NY: Nova Science Publishers.

Costa-Font, J., Mossialos, E., and Rudisill, C. (2009). Optimism and the perceptions of new risks. *Journal of Risk Research* 12 (1): 27–41.

Council of Europe (2000). *Presentation of the European Landscape Convention*. Strasbourg: Council of Europe.

Covington, J. and Taylor, R.B. (1989). Gentrification and crime: robbery and larceny changes in appreciating Baltimore neighborhoods during the 1970s. *Urban Affairs Quarterly* 25: 142–172.

Craig, J.M., Logan, A.C., and Prescott, S.L. (2016). Natural environments, nature relatedness and the ecological theater: connecting satellites and sequencing to shinrin-yoku. *Journal of Physiological Anthropology* 35 (1): 1–10.

Craik, K.H. (1970). Environmental psychology. In: *New Directions in Psychology*, vol. 4 (ed. K.H. Craik, B. Kleinmuntz, R.L. Rosnow, et al.), 1–121. New York, NY: Holt, Rinehart, and Winston.

Craik, K.H. (1973). Environmental psychology. *Annual Review of Psychology* 24: 403–422.

Craik, K. and Feimer, N. (1987). Environmental assessment. In: *Handbook of Environmental Psychology*, vol. 2 (ed. D. Stokols and I. Altman), 891–918. New York, NY: Wiley.

Craik, K.H. and Mckechnie, G.H. (1974). *Perception on Environmental quality: Preferential judgments versus comparative appraisals*. Berkeley: CA, Institute of Personality Assessment and Research.

Craik, K.H. and Zube, F. (eds.) (1976). *Perceiving Environmental Quality: Research and Application*. New York, NY: Plenum Press.

CRED (2016). *Poverty & Death: Disaster Mortality 1996–2015*. Brussels, Belgium: CRED.

Cronon, W. (1996). The trouble with wilderness, or getting back to the wrong nature. *Environmental History* 1: 7–28.

Csikszentmihalyi, M. (1990). *Flow: the psychology of optimal experience*. New York: Harper Collins.

Daamen, D.D.L., Staats, H., Wilke, H.A.M., and Engelen, M. (2001). Improving environmental behavior in companies. The effectiveness of tailored versus non-tailored interventions. *Environment and Behavior* 33: 229–248.

Dake, K. (1991). Orienting dispositions in the perception of risk: an analysis of contemporary worldviews and cultural biases. *Journal of Cross-Cultural Psychology* 22: 61–82.

Damasio, A.R. (1999). *The Feeling of What Happens: Body and Emotion in the Making of Consciousness*. New York, NY: Harcourt Brace.

Daniel, T.C. (2001). Whither scenic beauty? Visual landscape quality assessment in the 21st century. *Landscape and Urban Planning* 54 (1–4): 267.

Daniel, T.C. and Boster, R.S. (1976). *Measuring Landscape Esthetics: The Scenic Beauty Estimation Method*. U.S. Department of Agriculture, Forest Service, Rocky Mountain Range and Experiment Station.

Daniel, T.C. and Meitner, M.M. (2001). Representational validity of landscape visualizations: the effects of graphical realism on perceived scenic beauty of forest vistas. *Journal of Environmental Psychology* 21 (1): 61–72.

Daniel, T.C. and Vining, J. (1983). Methodological issues in the assessment of landscape quality. In: *Behavior and the Natural Environment* (ed. I. Altman and J.F. Wohlwill), 39–84. New York, NY: Plenum Press.

Davidov, E. (2007). Explaining habits in a new context – the case of travel mode choice. *Rationality and Society* 19 (3): 315–334.

Davis, J. (2010). *Young Children and the Environment*. Melbourne: Cambridge University Press.

Dawes, R.M. (1980). Social Dilemmas. *Annual Review of Psychology* 32: 169–193.

Dawes, R.M., McTavish, J., and Shaklee, H. (1977). Behavior, communication, and assumptions about other people's behavior in commons dilemma situation. *Journal of Personality and Social Psychology* 35: 1–11.

De Campos, C.B. and Bonfim, Z.A.C. (2014). Psicologia ambiental: revisando, revisitando e ressignificando [Environmental psychology: reviewing, revisiting and resignifying]. *Psico* 45 (3): 290–291.

De Dominicis, S., Fornara, F., Cancellieri, U.G. et al. (2015). We are at risk, and so what? Place attachment, environmental risk perceptions and preventive coping behaviours. *Journal of Environmental Psychology* 43: 66–78.

De Groot, I. (1967). Trends in public attitudes toward air pollution. *Journal of the Air Pollution Control Association* 17: 679–681.

De Groot, M. (2010). *Humans and nature. Public visions on their interrelationship*. Dissertation. Nijmegen: Radboud University.

De Groot, M. and De Groot, W.T. (2009). 'Room for river' measures and public visions in the Netherlands: a survey on river perceptions among riverside residents. *Water Resources Research* 45 (7): W07403.

De Groot, J.I.M. and Schuitema, G. (2012). How to make the unpopular popular? Policy characteristics, social norms and the acceptability of environmental policies. *Environmental Science & Policy* 19–20: 100–107.

De Groot, J.I.M. and Steg, L. (2006). Impact of transport pricing on quality of life, acceptability, and intentions to reduce car use: an exploratory study in five European countries. *Journal of Transport Geography* 14: 463–470.

De Groot, J.I.M. and Steg, L. (2008). Value orientations to explain environmental attitudes and beliefs: how to measure egoistic, altruistic and biospheric value orientations. *Environment and Behavior* 40: 330–354.

De Groot, J.I.M. and Steg, L. (2009a). Mean or green? Values, morality and environmental significant behavior. *Conservation Letters* 2: 61–66.

De Groot, J.I.M. and Steg, L. (2009b). Morality and prosocial behavior: the role of awareness, responsibility, and norms in the norm activation model. *Journal of Social Psychology* 149 (4): 425–449.

De Groot, W.T. and Van den Born, R.J.G. (2003). Visions of nature and landscape type preferences: an exploration in the Netherlands. *Landscape and Urban Planning* 63 (3): 127–138.

De Groot, J.I.M., Steg, L., and Poortinga, W. (2013). Values, perceived risks and benefits, and acceptability of nuclear energy. *Risk Analysis* 33 (2): 307–317.

De Groot, J., Thøgersen, J., and Schubert, I. (2016). Morality and green consumer behaviour: a psychological perspective. In: *Ethics and Morality in Consumption* (ed. D. Shaw, M. Carrington and A. Chatzidakis), 57–74. London, UK: Routledge.

De Kort, Y.A.W., IJsselsteijn, W.A., Kooijman, J., and Schuurmans, Y. (2003). Virtual laboratories: comparability of real and virtual environments for environmental psychology. *Presence: Teleoperators and Virtual Environments* 12 (4): 360–373.

De Lucio, J.V., Mohamadian, M., Ruiz, J.P. et al. (1996). Visual landscape exploration as revealed by eye movement tracking. *Landscape and Urban Planning* 34 (2): 135–142.

De Ridder, D.T.D. and de Wit, J.B.F. (eds.) (2006). *Self-Regulation in Health Behavior*. London, UK: Wiley.

De Vries, S. (2010). Nearby nature and human health: looking at the mechanisms and their implications. In: *Open Space: People Space 2, Innovative Approaches to Researching Landscape and Health* (ed. C. Ward Thompson, P. Aspinall and S. Bell), 75–94. Abingdon: Routledge.

De Vries, S. (2016). Greener surroundings mean less ADHD. *Wageningen World* 1: 8.

De Vries, S. and Wilke, H. (1992). Constrained egoism and resource management under uncertainty. In: *Social Dilemmas: Theoretical Issues and Research Findings* (ed. W. Liebrand, D.M. Messick and H.A.M. Wilke), 81–99. Oxford: Pergamon.

De Vries, S., Verheij, R.A., Groenewegen, P.P., and Spreeuwenberg, P. (2003). Natural environments - healthy environments? An exploratory analysis of the relationship between greenspace and health. *Environment and Planning A* 35 (10): 1717–1731.

De Vries, S., Van Dillen, S.M., Groenewegen, P.P., and Spreeuwenberg, P. (2013). Streetscape greenery and health: stress, social cohesion and physical activity as mediators. *Social Science and Medicine* 94: 26–33.

De Vries, S., Verheij, R., and Smeets, H. (2015). *Groen en gebruik ADHD-medicatie door kinderen: de relatie tussen de hoeveelheid groen in de woonomgeving en de prevalentie van AD (H) D-medicatiegebruik bij 5-tot 12-jarigen*. Alterra Wageningen UR.

De Young, R. (1990–1991). Some psychological aspects of living lightly: desired lifestyle patterns and conservation behavior. *Journal of Environmental Systems* 20 (3): 215–227.

De Young, R. (2000). Expanding and evaluating motives for environmentally responsible behavior. *Journal of Social Issues* 56: 509–526.

Dempsey, F. (1914). Nela Park: a novelty in the architectural grouping of industrial buildings. *Architectural Record* 35: 469–504.

Deutsch, M. (1975). Equity, equality, and need: what determines which value will be used as the basis of distributive justice? *Journal of Social Issues* 31: 137–149.

Deutsch, M. (1985). *Distributive Justice: A Social Psychological Perspective*. New Haven: Yale University Press.

Deutsch, M. and Gerard, H.B. (1955). A study of normative and informational social influences upon individual judgment. *Journal of Abnormal & Social Psychology* 51: 629–636.

Devine-Wright, P. (2009). Rethinking NIMBYism: the role of place attachment and place identity in explaining place-protective action. *Journal of Community & Applied Social Psychology* 19 (6): 426–441.

Devine-Wright, P. (2013). Explaining 'NIMBY' objections to a power line: The role of personal, place attachment and project-related factors. *Environment and Behavior* 45 (6): 761–781.

Devlin, K. (1990). An examination of architectural interpretation: architects versus non architects. *Journal of Architectural and Plannifng Research* 7: 235–244.

Di Masso, A., Dixon, J., and Durrheim, K. (2014). Place attachment as discursive practice. In: *Place Attachment: Advances in Theory, Methods and Applications* (ed. L. Manzo and P. Devine-Wright), 75–86. London: Routledge.

Díaz, E.M., Tapia, K.M., Estrada, C., and Leiva-Bianchi, M. (2012). Red semántica de terremoto y maremoto en personas expuestas directa y vicariamente [Semantic network of earthquake and seaquake concepts among people exposed directly and vicariously]. *Psicologia em Estudo* 17 (4): 557–565.

Diaz-Serrano, L. and Stoyanova, A.P. (2010). Mobility and housing satisfaction: an empirical analysis for 12 EU countries. *Journal of Economic Geography* 10 (5): 661–683.

Diener, E. (2000). Subjective well-being: the science of happiness and a proposal for a national index. *American Psychologist* 55 (1): 34–43.

Diener, E.F. (2011). Evaluaciones del progreso, la política y las políticas. In: *Conferencia Latinoamericana para la Medición del Bienestar y la Promoción del Progreso de las Sociedades, Ciudad de México*, 11–13 Mayo 2011. México: Organización para la Cooperación y el Desarrollo Económicos.

Diener, E., Emmons, R.A., Larsen, R.J., and Griffin, S. (1985). The satisfaction with life scale. *Journal of Personality Assessment* 49: 71–75.

Diener, E., Lucas, R.E., Schimmack, U., and Helliwell, J.F. (2009a). *Well-Being for Public Policy*. Oxford: Oxford University Press.

Diener, E., Lucas, R.E., and Scollon, C.N. (2009b). Beyond the hedonic treadmill: revising the adaptation theory of well-being. *The Science of Well-Being: Social Indicators Research Series* 37: 103–118.

Dittmar, H. (1992) *The social psychology of material possessions: To have is to be*. Harvester Wheatsheaf, Hemel Hempstead, UK; St. Martin's Press, New York.

Dittmar, H. (2004). Are you what you have? *The Psychologist* 17 (4): 206–210.

Dittmar, H. and Pepper, L. (1994). To have is to be: materialism and person perception in working-class and middle-class British adolescents. *Journal of Economic Psychology* 15 (2): 233–251.

Dixon, J. and Durrheim, K. (2004). Dislocating identity: desegregation and the transformation of place. *Journal of Environmental Psychology* 24 (4): 455–473.

Dolnicar, S. and Grün, B. (2009). Environmentally friendly behaviour. Can heterogeneity be improved among individuals and contexts/ environments be harvested for improved sustainable management? *Environment and Behavior* 41: 693–702.

Doran, B.J. and Lees, B.G. (2005). Investigating the spatiotemporal links between disorder, crime, and fear of crime. *The Professional Geographer* 57 (1): 1–12.

Dougherty, E.M., Fulton, D.C., and Anderson, D.H. (2003). The influence of gender on the relationship between wildlife value orientations, beliefs, and the acceptability of lethal deer control in Cuyahoga Valley National Park. *Society & Natural Resources* 16 (7): 603–623.

Dowdell, K., Gray, T., and Malone, K. (2011). Nature and its influence on children's outdoor play. *Journal of Outdoor and Environmental Education* 15 (2): 24.

Druckman, A. and Jackson, T. (2009). The carbon footprint of UK households 1990–2004: a socio-economically disaggregated, quasi-multi-regional input-output model. *Ecological Economics* 68 (7): 2066–2207.

Duffy, M., Bailey, S., Beck, B., and Barker, D.G. (1986). Preferences in nursing home design: a comparison of residents, administrators, and designers. *Environment and Behavior* 18: 246–257.

Dunlap, R.E. and Jones, R.E. (2002). Environmental attitudes and values. In: *Encyclopedia of Psychological Assessment*, vol. 1 (ed. R. Fernandez-Ballesteros), 364–369. London: Sage.

Dunlap, R.E., Van Liere, K.D., Mertig, A.G., and Jones, R.E. (2000). Measuring endorsement of the new ecological paradigm: a revised NEP scale. *Journal of Social Issues* 56: 425–442.

Dunn, M.J. and Searle, R. (2010). Effect of manipulated prestige car ownership on both sex attractiveness ratings. *British Journal of Psychology* 101: 69–80.

Dupont, L., Antrop, M., and Van Eetvelde, V. (2013). Eye-tracking analysis in landscape perception research: influence of photograph properties and landscape characteristics. *Landscape Research* 39: 417–432.

Dyment, J.E. and Bell, A.C. (2008). 'Our garden is colour blind, inclusive and warm': reflections on green school grounds and social inclusion. *International Journal of Inclusive Education* 12 (2): 169–183.

Dzhambov, A.M., Dimitrova, D.D., and Dimitrakova, E.D. (2014). Association between residential greenness and birth weight: systematic review and meta-analysis. *Urban Forestry & Urban Greening* 13 (4): 621–629.

Eagly, A. and Chaiken, S. (1993). *The Psychology of Attitudes*. NY: Harcourt, Brace Jovanovich.

Economic Commission for Latin America and the Caribbean (2010). *Statistical Year Book for Latin America and the Caribbean 2010*. Santiago de Chile: United Nations.

Ekkekakis, P. (2012). Affect, mood, and emotion. In: *Measurement in Sport and Exercise Psychology* (ed. G. Tenenbaum, R.C. Eklund and A. Kamata), 321–332. Champaign, IL: Human Kinetics.

Emery, K.F. (2007). Assessing the impact of ancient Maya animal use. *Journal of Nature Conservation* 15 (3): 184–195.

Eriksson, L., Garvill, J., and Nordlund, A. (2006). Acceptability of travel demand management measures: the importance of problem awareness, personal norm, freedom, and fairness. *Journal of Environmental Psychology* 26: 15–26.

Eriksson, L., Garvill, J., and Nordlund, A. (2008). Acceptability of single and combined transport policy measures: the importance of environmental and policy specific beliefs. *Transportation Research Part A: Policy and Practice* 42: 1117–1128.

Erman, T. (1996). Women and the housing environment: the experiences of Turkish migrant women in squatter and apartment housing. *Environment and Behavior* 28: 764–798.

Ernst, A., Schulz, C., Schwarz, N., and Janisch, S. (2008). Modelling of water use decisions in a large, spatially explicit, coupled simulation system. In: *Social Simulation: Technologies, Advances and New Discoveries* (ed. B. Edmonds, K.G. Troitzsch and C. Hernández Iglesias), 138–149. New York, NY: Hershey.

Evans, G.W. (2001). Environmental stress and health. In: *Handbook of Health Psychology* (ed. A. Baum, T. Revenson and J.E. Singer), 365–385. Hillsdale, NJ: Erlbaum.

Evans, G.W. (2004). The environment of childhood poverty. *American Psychologist* 59: 77–92.

Evans, G.W. (2006). Child development and the physical environment. *Annual Review of Psychology* 57: 423–451.

Evans, G.W. and Cohen, S. (1987). Environmental stress. In: *Handbook of Environmental Psychology*, vol. 1 (ed. D. Stokols and I. Altman), 571–610. New York, NY: Wiley.

Evans, G.W. and Cohen, S. (2004). Environmental stress. In: *Encyclopedia of Applied Psychology* (ed. C. Spielberger), 815–824. Oxford: Elsevier.

Evans, G.W. and Hygge, S. (2007). Noise and performance in children and adults. In: *Noise and Its Effects* (ed. L. Luxon and D. Prasher), 549–566. London: Wiley.

Evans, G.W. and Marcynyszyn, L.A. (2004). Environmental justice, cumulative environmental risk, and health among low- and middle-income children in upstate New York. *American Journal of Public Health* 94: 1942–1944.

Evans, G.W. and Stecker, R. (2004). The motivational consequences of environmental stress. *Journal of Environmental Psychology* 24: 143–165.

Evans, G.W., Bullinger, M., and Hygge, S. (1998a). Chronic noise exposure and physiological response: a prospective, longitudinal study of children under environmental stress. *Psychological Science* 9: 75–77.

Evans, G.W., Lepore, S.J., Shejwal, B.R., and Palsane, M.N. (1998b). Chronic residential crowding and children's well-being: an ecological perspective. *Child Development* 69: 1514–1523.

Ewert, A. (1986). Fear and anxiety in environmental education programs. *Journal of Environmental Education* 18: 33–39.

Ewert, A. and Galloway, G. (2009). Socially desirable responding in an environmental context: development of a domain specific scale. *Environmental Education Research* 15 (1): 55–70.

Ewert, A., Place, G., and Sibthorp, J. (2005). Early-life outdoor experiences and an individual's environmental attitudes. *Leisure Sciences* 27 (3): 225–239.

Faber Taylor, A. and Kuo, F.E. (2006). Is contact with nature important for healthy child development: state of the evidence. In: *Children and their Environments: Learning, Using, and Designing Spaces* (ed. C. Spencer and M. Blades), 124–158. New York, NY: Cambridge University Press.

Faber Taylor, A., Kuo, F.E., and Sullivan, W.C. (2002). Views of nature and self-discipline: evidence from inner city children. *Journal of Environmental Psychology* 22 (1–2): 49–63.

Fairclough, G., Lambrick, G., and McNab, A. (eds.) (1999). *Yesterday's World, Tomorrows Landscape. The English Heritage Historic Landscape Project 1992–1994*. London: English Heritage.

Farías, M.T. and Pinheiro, J.Q. (2013). Vivendo a vizinhança: Interfaces pessoa-ambiente na produção de vizinhanças "vivas". *Psicologia em Estudo, Maringá* 18 (1): 27–36.

Farjon, H., De Blaeij, A., De Boer, T. et al. (2016). *Citizens' Images and Values of Nature in Europe: A Survey in nine EU Member States*. The Hague: PBL Netherlands Environmental Assessment.

Fawcett, W., Ellingham, I., and Platt, S. (2008). Reconciling the architectural preferences of architects and the public: the ordered preference model. *Environment and Behavior* 40: 599–618.

Fehr, E. and Schmidt, K.M. (1999). A theory of fairness, competition, and cooperation. *Quarterly Journal of Economics* 114: 817–851.

Felippe, M.L. and Kuhnen, A. (2012). O apego ao lugar no contexto dos estudos pessoa-ambiente: Práticas de pesquisa. *Estudos de Psicologia, Campinas* 29 (4): 609–617.

Ferguson, M.A., Branscombe, N.R., and Reynolds, K.J. (2011). The effect of intergroup comparison on willingness to perform sustainable behavior. *Journal of Environmental Psychology* 31 (4): 275–281.

Festinger, L. (1957). *A Theory of Cognitive Dissonance*. Stanford, CA: Stanford University Press.

Field, C.B., Barros, V.R., Mastrandrea, M.D., et al. (2014). Summary for policymakers. In Climate change 2014: impacts, adaptation, and vulnerability. Part A: global and sectoral aspects. Contribution of Working Group II to the Fifth Assessment Report of the Intergovernmental Panel on Climate Change (pp. 1–32). Cambridge University Press.

Fielding, K.S. and Hornsey, M.J. (2016). A social identity analysis of climate change and environmental attitudes and behaviors: insights and opportunities. *Frontiers in Psychology* 7: 121.

Fielding, K.S., Terry, D.J., Masser, B.M., and Hogg, M.A. (2008). Integrating social identity theory and the theory of planned behaviour to explain decisions to engage in sustainable agricultural practices. *British Journal of Social Psychology* 47 (1): 23–48.

Fields, J.M. (1993). Effect of personal and situational variables on noise annoyance in residential areas. *Journal of the Acoustical Society of America* 93 (5): 2753–2763.

Finucane, M.L., Alhakami, A., Slovic, P., and Johnson, S.M. (2000). The affect heuristic in judgements of risks and benefits. *Journal of Behavioural Decision Making* 13: 1–17.

Fischhoff, B., Slovic, P., Lichtenstein, S. et al. (1978). How safe is safe enough? A psychometric study of attitudes towards technological risks and benefits. *Policy Sciences* 8: 127–152.

Fishbein, M. and Ajzen, I. (2010). *Predicting and Changing Behavior: The Reasoned Action Approach*. New York, NY: Psychology Press (Taylor & Francis).

Fjørtoft, I. (2004). Landscape as playscape: the effects of natural environments on children's play and motor development. *Children, Youth and Environments* 14 (2): 21–44.

Fleming, I., Baum, A., and Weiss, L. (1987). Social density and perceived control as mediators of crowding stress in high-density residential neighborhoods. *Journal of Personality and Social Psychology* 52 (5): 899–906.

Fleury-Bahi, G., Pol, E., and Navarro, O. (2017). *Handbook of Environmental Psychology and Quality of Life Research*. Cham: Springer.

Flint, C.G., Kunze, I., Muhar, A. et al. (2013). Exploring empirical typologies of human–nature relationships and linkages to the ecosystem services concept. *Landscape and Urban Planning* 120: 208–217.

Floriani, V. and Kennedy, C. (2008). Promotion of physical activity in children. *Current Opinion in Pediatrics* 20 (1): 90–95.

Fogg, B.J. (2003). *Persuasive Technology: Using Computers to Change What we Think and Do*. San Francisco: Morgan Kaufman.

Fornara, F., Bonaiuto, M., and Bonnes, M. (2010). Cross-validation of abbreviated perceived residential environment quality (PREQ) and neighbourhood attachment (NA) indicators. *Environment & Behavior* 42 (2): 171–196.

Förster, J. and Liberman, N. (2007). Knowledge activation. In: *Social Psychology: Handbook of Basic Principles*, 2e (ed. A.W. Kruglanski and E. Tory Higgins). New York, NY: Guilford Press.

Fraj, E. and Martinez, E. (2007). Ecological consumer behaviour: an empirical analysis. *International Journal of Consumer Studies* 31 (1): 26–31.

Fransson, N. and Gärling, T. (1999). Environmental concern: conceptual definitions, measurement methods, and research findings. *Journal of Environmental Psychology* 19: 369–382.

Frantz, C.M. and Mayer, F.S. (2009). The emergency of climate change: why are we failing to take action? *Analyses of Social Issues and Public Policy* 9 (1): 205–222.

Frewald, D.B. (1990). Preferences for older buildings: a psychological approach to architectural design. *Dissertation Abstracts International* 51 (1-B): 414–415.

Frey, B.S. and Jegen, R. (2001). Motivation crowding theory. *Journal of Economic Surveys* 15: 589–611.

Fried, M. (1963). Grieving for a lost home. In: *The Urban Condition* (ed. L.J. Duhl), 151–171. New York, NY: Basic Books.

Friedrichsmeier, T., Matthies, E., and Klöckner, C.A. (2013). Explaining stability in travel mode choice: an empirical comparison of two concepts of habit. *Transportation Research Part F: Traffic Psychology and Behaviour* 16: 1–13.

Frijda, N.H. (2009). Mood. In: *The Oxford Companion to Emotion and the Affective Sciences* (ed. D. Sander and K.R. Scherer), 258–259. New York, NY: Oxford University Press.

Fujii, S. and Gärling, T. (2003). Development of script-based travel mode choice after forced change. *Transportation Research Part F: Traffic Psychology and Behaviour* 6 (2): 117–124.

Fujii, S. and Kitamura, R. (2003). What does a one-month free bus ticket do to habitual drivers? An experimental analysis of habit and attitude change. *Transportation* 30: 81–95.

Fujii, S., Gärling, T., and Kitamura, R. (2001). Changes in drivers' perceptions and use of public transport during freeway closure – effects of temporary structural change on cooperation in a real-life social dilemma. *Environment and Behavior* 33 (6): 796–808.

Fullilove, M.T. (2014). 'The frayed knot:' What happens to place attachments in the context of serial forced displacement? In: *Place Attachment: Advances in Theory, Methods and Applications* (ed. L.C. Manzo and P. Devine-Wright), 141–153. London: Routledge.

Fulton, D.C., Manfredo, M.J., and Lipscomb, J. (1996). Wildlife value orientations: a conceptual and measurement approach. *Human Dimensions of Wildlife* 1 (2): 24–47.

Fyhri, A., Hjorthol, R., Mackett, R.L. et al. (2011). Children's active travel and independent mobility in four countries: development, social contributing trends and measures. *Transport Policy* 18 (5): 703–710.

Gamborg, C. and Jensen, F.S. (2016). Wildlife value orientations: a quantitative study of the general public in Denmark. *Human Dimensions of Wildlife* 21 (1): 34–46.

Ganzel, B.L., Morris, P.A., and Wethington, E. (2010). Allostasis and the human brain: integrating models of stress from the social and life sciences. *Psychological Review* 117: 134–174.

Gardner, G.T. and Stern, P.C. (2002). *Environmental Problems and Human Behavior*. Boston: Allyn & Bacon.

Gärling, T. and Schuitema, G. (2007). Travel demand management targeting reduced private car use: effectiveness, public acceptability and political feasibility. *Journal of Social Issues* 63: 139–153.

Gärling, T., Jakobsson, C., Loukopoulos, P., and Fujii, S. (2008). Public acceptability of road pricing. In: *Pricing in Road Transport: A Multi-Disciplinary Perspective* (ed. E.T. Verhoef, M.C.J. Bliemer, L. Steg and B. Van Wee), 193–208. Cheltenham, UK and Northampton, MA, USA: Edward Elgar.

Gatersleben, B. (2000). *Sustainable Household Metabolism and Quality of Life: Examining the perceived social sustainability of environmentally sustainable household consumption patterns.* PhD Dissertation, University of Groningen, Groningen.

Gatersleben, B. (2007). Affective and symbolic aspects of car use: a review. In: *Threats to the Quality of Urban Life from Car Traffic: Problems, Causes, and Solutions* (ed. T. Gärling and L. Steg), 219–234. Amsterdam: Elsevier.

Gatersleben, B. (2010). The car as a material possession: exploring the link between materialism and car ownership and use. In: *Auto Motives: Understanding Car Use Behaviours* (ed. K. Lucas, E. Blumenberg and R. Weinberger), 137–150. Bradford: Emerald.

Gatersleben, B., Steg, L., and Vlek, C. (2002). Measurement and determinants of environmentally significant consumer behavior. *Environment and Behavior* 34: 335–365.

Gatersleben, B., Murtagh, N., and Abrahamse, W. (2012). Values, identity and pro-environmental behaviour. *Contemporary Social Science* 9 (4): 374–392.

Gattig, A. and Hendrickx, L. (2007). Judgmental discounting and environmental risk perception. *Journal of Social Issues* 63: 21–39.

Gawronski, B. and Payne, B.K. (2010). *Handbook of Implicit Social Cognition: Measurement, Theory, and Applications*. New York: Guilford Press.

GBD 2015 Risk Factors Collaborators (GBD-RFC) (2016). Global, regional, and national comparative risk assessment of 79 behavioural, environmental and occupational, and metabolic risks or clusters of risks in 188 countries, 1990–2013: a systematic analysis for the global burden of disease study 2013. *The Lancet* 380 (9859): 2224–2260.

Ge, Y., Xu, W., Gu, Z.H. et al. (2011). Risk perception and hazard mitigation in the Yangtze River Delta region, China. *Natural Hazards* 56 (3): 633–648.

Geiger, N. and Swim, J. K. (2018). Gendered impressions of issue publics as predictors of climate activism. Under review.

Geiger, N., Middlewood, B.L., and Swim, J.K. (2017). *Psychological, Social, and Cultural Barriers to Communicating about Climate Change*. Oxford Research Encyclopedia.

Geiger, N., Swim, J.K., Fraser, J., and Flinner, K. (2017). Catalyzing public engagement with climate change through informal science learning centers. *Science Communication* 39 (2): 221–249. doi: 10.1177/1075547017697980.

Geller, E.S. (2002). The challenge of increasing proenvironmental behavior. In: *Handbook of Environmental Psychology* (ed. R. Bechtel and A. Churchman), 541–553. New York, NY: Wiley.

Geller, E.S. (2016). Actively caring for mother earth. In: *Applied Psychology: Actively Caring for People* (ed. E.S. Geller), 594–623. New York, NY: Cambridge University Press.

Geller, E.S., Winett, R.A., and Everett, P.B. (1982). *Environmental Preservation: New Strategies for Behavior Change*. New York, NY: Pergamon Press.

Genereux, R.L., Ward, L.M., and Russell, J.A. (1983). The behavioral component of the meaning of places. *Journal of Environmental Psychology* 3: 43–55.

Ghassemi, R. and Becerik-Gerber, B. (2011). Transitioning to integrated project delivery: potential barriers and lessons learned. *Lean Construction Journal 2011* 32–52.

Gibson, J.J. (1979). *The Ecological Approach to Visual Perception*. Hughton Mifflin Company.

Gifford, R. (1980). Environmental dispositions and the evaluation of architectural interiors. *Journal of Research in Personality* 14: 386–399.

Gifford, R. (2007). *Environmental Psychology: Principles and Practice*, 4e. Colville WA: Optimal Books.

Gifford, R. (2008). Psychology's essential role in climate change. *Canadian Psychology* 49: 273–280.

Gifford, R. (2014). Environmental psychology matters. *Annual Review of Psychology* 65: 541–580.

Gifford, R. and Lacombe, C. (2006). Housing quality and children's socioemotional health. *Journal of Housing and the Built Environment* 21: 177–189.

Gifford, R. and Martin, M. (1991). A multiple sclerosis centre program and post-occupancy evaluation. In: *Design Innovation: The Challenge of Cultural Change* (ed. W.F.E. Preiser and J. Vischer). New York, NY: Van Nostrand Reinhold.

Gifford, R., Hine, D.W., Muller-Clemm, W. et al. (2000). Decoding modern architecture: understanding the aesthetic differences of architects and laypersons. *Environment and Behavior* 32: 163–187.

Gifford, R., Hine, D.W., Muller-Clemm, W., and Shaw, K.T. (2002). Why architects and laypersons judge buildings differently: cognitive and physical bases. *Journal of Architectural and Planning Research* 19: 131–147.

Gilavand, A. and Jamshidnezhad, A. (2016). The effect of noise in educational institutions on learning and academic achievement of elementary students in Ahvaz, South-West of Iran. *International Journal of Pediatrics* 4 (3): 1453–1463.

Gilbert, D.T. and Wilson, T.D. (2000). Miswanting. In: *Thinking and Feeling: The Role of Affect in Social Cognition* (ed. J. Forgas), 178–197. Cambridge: Cambridge University Press.

Gillis, A.R. (1997). High rise housing and psychological strain. *Journal of Health and Social Behavior* 18: 418–431.

Giuliani, M.V. (2003). Theory of attachment and place attachment. In: *Psychological Theories for Environmental Issues* (ed. M. Bonnes, T. Lee and M. Bonaiuto), 137–170. Aldershot: Ashgate.

Giuliani, M.V. (2004). Residential preferences and attachment across the lifespan. In: *Encyclopedia of Applied Psychology*, vol. 3 (ed. C. Spielberger), 259–266. San Diego: Elsevier/Academic Press.

Giuliani, M.V. and Scopelliti, M. (2009). Empirical research in environmental psychology: past, present, and future. *Journal of Environmental Psychology* 29 (3): 375–386.

Glass, D.C. and Singer, J.E. (1972). *Urban Stress: Experiments on Noise and Social Stressors.* New York, NY: Academic Press.

Gneezy, U. and Rustichini, A. (2000). A fine is a price. *Journal of Legal Studies* 29: 1–17.

Gobster, P.H. (1999). An ecological aesthetic for forest landscape management. *Landscape Journal* 18 (1): 54–64.

Göckeritz, S., Schultz, P.W., Rendón, T. et al. (2010). Descriptive normative beliefs and conservation behavior: the moderating role of personal involvement and injunctive normative beliefs. *European Journal of Social Psychology* 40: 514–523.

Goldenberg, J., Pyszczynski, T., Greenberg, J. et al. (2001). I am *not* an animal: mortality salience, disgust, and the denial of human creatureliness. *Journal of Experimental Psychology: General* 130: 427–435.

Goldstein, N.J. and Cialdini, R.B. (2007). Using social norms as a lever of social influence. In: *The Science of Social Influence* (ed. A.R. Pratkanis), 167–192. New York, NY: Psychology Press.

Goldstein, N.J., Cialdini, R.B., and Griskevicius, V. (2008). A room with a viewpoint: using social norms to motivate environmental conservation in hotels. *Journal of Consumer Research* 35: 472–482.

Gollwitzer, P.M. (1990). Action phases and mind-sets. In: *Handbook of Motivation and Cognition: Foundations of Social Behavior*, vol. 2 (ed. E.T. Higgins and R.M. Sorrentino), 53–92. New York, NY: Guilford.

Gollwitzer, P.M. (1999). Implementation intentions: strong effects of simple plans. *American Psychologist* 54: 493–503.

Golob, T.F., Recker, W.W., and Levine, D.W. (1990). Safety of freeway median high occupancy vehicle lanes: a comparison of aggregate and disaggregate analyses. *Accident Analysis & Prevention* 22: 19–34.

Gómez-Limón, J. and Lucío, J.V.d. (1999). Changes in use and landscape preferences on the agricultural-livestock landscapes of the central Iberian Peninsula (Madrid, Spain). *Landscape and Urban Planning* 44 (1): 165–175.

Gotts, N.M. (2007). Resilience, panarchy and world-systems analysis. *Ecology and Society* 12 (1): 24.

Graf, J., Meierhofer, R., Wegelin, M., and Mosler, H.-J. (2008). Water disinfection and hygiene behaviour in an urban slum in Kenya: impact on childhood diarrhoea and influence of beliefs. *International Journal of Environmental Health Research* 18 (5): 335–355.

Granada, H. (2002). *Psicología y ambiente: Introducción temática. [Psychology and Environment: A Thematic Introduction].* Barranquilla: Ediciones Uninorte.

Granada, H. and Molina Cortés, C. (2015). Conocimiento y valoración de la calidad ambiental de la Reserva Forestal Bosque de Yotogo: perspectiva psicoambiental. *Psicología desde El Caribe* 32 (3): 442–458.

Greenberg, J., Solomon, S., and Pyszczynski, T. (1997). Terror management theory of self-esteem and cultural worldviews: empirical assessments and conceptual refinements.

In: *Advances in Experimental Social Psychology*, vol. 29 (ed. M. Zanna), 61–139. London: Academic Press.

Greenwald, A.G. and Banaji, M.R. (1995). Implicit social cognition: attitudes, self-esteem, and stereotypes. *Psychological Review* 102: 4–27.

Gregory, R., Lichtenstein, S., and MacGregor, D. (1993). The role of past states in determining reference points for policy decisions. *Organizational Behavior and Human Decision Processes* 55: 195–206.

Greif, M.J. and Dodoo, F.N.A. (2015). How community physical, structural, and social stressors relate to mental health in the urban slums of Accra, Ghana. *Health & Place* 33: 57–66.

Griffiths, I.D. and Langdon, F.J. (1968). Subjective response to road traffic noise. *Journal of Sound and Vibration* 8: 16–32.

Griskevicius, V., Tybur, J., and Van den Bergh, B. (2010). Going green to be seen: status, reputation, and conspicuous conservation. *Journal of Personality and Social Psychology* 98: 392–404.

Groat, L. (1982). Meaning in post-modern architecture: an examination using the multiple sorting task. *Journal of Environmental Psychology* 2: 3–22.

Groat, L. and Canter, D. (1979). Does post-modernism communicate? *Progressive Architecture* 12: 84–87.

Guevara, J. and Mercado, S. (2002). *Temas selectos de Psicología Ambiental UNAM, GRECO*. México: Fundación Unilibre.

Gulwadi, G.B. (2006). Seeking restorative experiences: elementary school teacher's choices for places that enable coping with stress. *Environment and Behavior* 38 (4): 503–520.

Günther, H. and Neto, I. (2015). Comportamento no trânsito: Uma perspectiva da psicologia ambiental. In: *Pesquisas sobre comportamento no transito* (ed. H. Günther, F. de Cristo, I. Neto and Z. Oliveira Feitosa), 29–49. Laboratório de Psicologia Ambiental Universidade de Brasília, Casa do Psicologo.

Guski, R. (1999). Personal and social variables as co-determinants of noise annoyance. *Noise and Health* 1 (3): 45–56.

Hafer, C.L. and Olson, J.M. (2003). An analysis of empirical research on the scope of justice. *Personality and Social Psychology Review* 7: 311–323.

Hagerhall, C.M. (2001). Consensus in landscape preference judgments. *Journal of Environmental Psychology* 21: 83–92.

Hägerhäll, C.M., Laike, T., Kuller, M. et al. (2015). Human physiological benefits of viewing nature: EEG response to exact and statistical fractal patterns. *Nonlinear Dynamics, Psychology, and Life Sciences* 19 (1): 1–12.

Haider, M., Kerr, K., and Badami, M. (2013). Does commuting cause stress? The public health implications of traffic congestion. *The Public Health Implications of Traffic Congestion* (August 2, 2013).

Hale, L., Hill, T.D., and Burdette, A.M. (2010). Does sleep quality mediate the association between neighborhood disorder and self-rated physical health? *Preventive Medicine* 51 (3): 275–278.

Hale, L., Hill, T.D., Friedman, E. et al. (2013). Perceived neighborhood quality, sleep quality, and health status: evidence from the survey of the health of Wisconsin. *Social Science & Medicine* 79: 16–22.

Ham, J. and Midden, C. (2010). Ambient persuasive technology needs little cognitive effort: The differential effects of cognitive load on lighting feedback versus factual feedback. *Conference proceedings of Persuasive 2010* (pp. 132–142). Heidelberg: Springer.

Ham, J., Midden, C., and Beute, F. (2009). Can ambient persuasive technology persuade unconsciously? Using subliminal feedback to influence energy consumption ratings of household appliances. *Conference proceedings of Persuasive 2009, Claremont, USA* (pp. article no. 29). Heidelberg: Springer.

Ham, J., van Esch, M., Limpens, Y. et al. (2012). The automaticity of social behavior towards robots: the influence of cognitive load on interpersonal distance to approachable versus less approachable robots. In: *Proceedings of the Social Robotics* (ed. S.S. Ge et al.), 15–25. Berlin: Springer.

Hammen, C. (2005). Stress and depression. *Annual Review of Clinical Psychology* 1: 293–319.

Hanselmann, M. and Tanner, C. (2008). Taboos and conflicts in decision making: sacred values, decision difficulty and emotions. *Judgment and Decision Making* 3: 51–63.

Hanyu, K. (2000). Visual properties and affective appraisals in residential areas in daylight. *Journal of Environmental Psychology* 20 (3): 273–284.

Haq, S.M.A. and Ahmed, K.J. (2017). Does the perception of climate change vary with the socio-demographic dimensions? A study on vulnerable populations in Bangladesh. *Natural Hazards* 85 (3): 1759–1785.

Haramoto, E., Moyano-Díaz, E., Riffo, M., and Sepúlveda, O. (1994). *Evaluación del programa de viviendas progresivas en áreas rurales. [Evaluation of a Progressive Housing Program in Rural Areas]*. Santiago de Chile: Institute of Housing, Faculty of Architecture and Urbanism, University of Chile.

Hardin, G. (1968). The tragedy of the commons. *Science* 13: 1243–1248.

Hardisty, D.J., Johnson, E.J., and Weber, E.U. (2010). A dirty word or a dirty world? : Attribute framing, political affiliation, and query theory. *Psychological Science* 21: 86–92.

Harkins, S. and Szymanski, K. (1989). Social loafing and group evaluation. *Journal of Personality and Social Psychology* 56: 934–941.

Harland, P., Staats, H., and Wilke, H. (1999). Explaining proenvironmental behavior by personal norms and the theory of planned behavior. *Journal of Applied Social Psychology* 29: 2505–2528.

Hart, R. (1979). *Children's Experience of Place*. New York, NY: Irvington.

Harter, M., Mosch, S., and Mosler, H.-J. (2017). *How does community-led total sanitation affect latrine ownership? A quantitative case study from Mozambique*. Unpublished manuscript.

Hartig, T. (2007). Three steps to understanding restorative environments as health resources. In: *Open Space: People Space* (ed. C. Ward Thompson and P. Travlou), 163–179. London: Taylor & Francis.

Hartig, T., Korpela, K., Evans, G.W., and Gärling, T. (1996). *Validation of a Measure of Perceived Environmental Restorativeness* Göteborg Psychological Reports, vol. 26/7. Göteborg, Sweden: Göteborg University.

Hartig, T., Korpela, K., Evans, G.W., and Gärling, T. (1997). A measure of restorative quality in environments. *Scandinavian Housing and Planning Research* 14 (4): 175–194.

Hartig, T., Evans, G.W., Jamner, L.D. et al. (2003a). Tracking restoration in natural and urban field settings. *Journal of Environmental Psychology* 23 (2): 109–123.

Hartig, T., Johansson, G., and Kylin, C. (2003b). Residence in the social ecology of stress and restoration. *Journal of Social Issues* 59 (3): 611–636.

Hartig, T., Bringslimark, T., and Grindal Patil, C. (2008). Restorative environmental design: what, when, where, and for whom? In: *Biophilic Design* (ed. S.R. Kellert, J.H. Heerwagen and M.L. Mador), 131–151. Hoboken, NJ: Wiley.

Hartig, T., Mitchell, R., de Vries, S., and Frumkin, H. (2014). Nature and health. *Annual Review of Public Health* 35: 207–228.

Haslam, S.A., Eggins, R.A., and Reynolds, K.J. (2003). The ASPIRe model: actualizing social and personal identity resources to enhance organizational outcomes. *Journal of Occupational and Organizational Psychology* 76 (1): 83–113.

Hauer, E., Ahlin, F.J., and Bowser, J.S. (1982). Speed enforcement and speed choice. *Accident Analysis & Prevention* 14: 267–278.

Hay, C. and Forrest, W. (2008). Self-control theory and the concept of opportunity: the case for a more systematic union. *Criminology* 47: 1039–1072.

Heatherton, T.F. and Wheatley, T. (2010). Social neuroscience. In: *Advanced Social Psychology* (ed. R.F. Baumeister and E. Finkel), 575–612. New York: Oxford University Press.

Hellpach, W. (1911). *Geopsyche*. Leipzig: Engelmann.

Hennessy, D.A. (2008). The impact of commuter stress on workplace aggression. *Journal of Applied Social Psychology* 38 (9): 2315–2335.

Hensher, D.A. and Li, Z. (2013). Referendum voting in road pricing reform: a review of the evidence. *Transport Policy* 25: 186–197.

Hermann, N., Voß, C., and Menzel, S. (2013). Wildlife value orientations as predicting factors in support of reintroducing bison and of wolves migrating to Germany. *Journal for Nature Conservation* 21 (3): 125–132.

Hernandez, B., Hidalgo, M.C., Salazar-Laplace, M., and Hess, S. (2007). Place attachment and place identity in natives and non-natives. *Journal of Environmental Psychology* 27 (4): 310–319.

Herrmann, B., Thöni, B., and Gächter, S. (2008). Antisocial punishment across societies. *Science* 319: 1362–1367.

Herzog, H.A. and Burghardt, G.M. (1988). Attitudes towards animals: origins and diversity. *Anthrozoös* 1 (4): 214–222.

Herzog, T.R. and Stark, J.L. (2004). Typicality and preference for positively and negatively valued environmental settings. *Journal of Environmental Psychology* 24: 85–92.

Herzog, T.R., Maguire, C.P., and Nebel, M.B. (2003). Assessing the restorative components of environments. *Journal of Environmental Psychology* 23 (2): 159–170.

Herzog, T.R., Ouellette, P., Rolens, J.R., and Koenigs, A.M. (2010). Houses of worship as restorative environments. *Environment and Behavior* 42 (4): 395–419.

Hester, R. (2014). Do not detach! Instructions from and for community design. In: *Place Attachment: Advances in Theory, Methods and Applications* (ed. L. Manzo and P. Devine-Wright), 191–206. London: Routledge.

Heyman, J. and Ariely, D. (2004). Effort for payment. A tale of two markets. *Psychological Science* 15: 787–793.

Higgins, T. (1989). Self-discrepancy theory. What patterns of self beliefs cause people to suffer? *Advances in Experimental Social Psychology* 22: 93–136.

Hilbig, B.E., Zettler, I., Moshagen, M., and Heydasch, T. (2013). Tracing the path from personality – via cooperativeness – to conservation. *European Journal of Personality* 27: 319–327.

Hinkle, J..C. and Weisburd, D. (2008). The irony of broken windows policing: a micro-place study of the relationship between disorder, focused police crackdowns and fear of crime. *Journal of Criminal Justice* 36: 503–512.

Hipp, J.A., Gulwadi, G.B., Alves, S., and Sequeira, S. (2016). The relationship between perceived greenness and perceived restorativeness of university campuses and student-reported quality of life. *Environment and Behavior* 48 (10): 1292–1308.

Hiscock, R., Macintyr, S., Kearns, A., and Ellaway, A. (2003). Residents and residence. *Journal of Social Issues* 59: 527–546.

Hoffman, E. and Ortiz, F.A. (2009). Youthful peak experiences in cross-cultural perspective: implications for educators and counselors. In: *International Handbook of Education for Spirituality, Care and Wellbeing*, 469–489. Springer.

Hogan, B.E., Linden, W., and Najarian, B. (2002). Social support interventions: do they work? *Clinical Psychology Review* 22: 381–440.

Hogg, M.A. (2003). Social identity. In: *Handbook of Self and Identity* (ed. M.R. Leary and J.P. Tangney), 462–479. New York, NY: The Guilford Press.

Holland, R.W., Aarts, H., and Langendam, D. (2006). Breaking and creating habits on the working floor: a field-experiment on the power of implementation intentions. *Journal of Experimental Social Psychology* 42 (6): 776–783.

Homer, P.M. and Kahle, L.R. (1988). A structural equation test of the value-attitude-behaviour hierarchy. *Journal of Personality and Social Psychology* 54 (4): 638–646.

Horne, C. (2001). Sociological perspectives on the emergence of norms. In: *Social Norms* (ed. M. Hechter and K.-D. Opp), 3–34. New York, NY: Russell Sage.

Hornsey, M.J., Harris, E.A., Bain, P.G., and Fielding, K.S. (2016). Meta-analyses of the determinants and outcomes of belief in climate change. *Nature Climate Change* 6: 622–626.

Howe, P.D. and Leiserowitz, A. (2013). Who remembers a hot summer or a cold winter? The asymmetric effect of beliefs about global warming on perceptions of local climate conditions in the U.S. *Global Environmental Change* 23 (6): 1488–1500.

Huber, M., Knottnerus, J.A., Green, L. et al. (2011). How should we define health? *British Medical Journal* 343: d4163.

Hull, R.B. and Harvey, A. (1989). Explaining the emotion people experience in suburban parks. *Environment & Behavior* 21 (3): 323–345.

Hunka, A.D., De Groot, W.T., and Biela, A. (2009). Visions of nature in Eastern Europe: a Polish example. *Environmental Values* 18: 429–452.

Hygge, S., Evans, G.W., and Bullinger, M. (2002). A prospective study of some effects of aircraft noise on cognitive performance in school children. *Psychological Science* 13: 469–474.

IJsselsteijn, W.A. (2004). Presence in depth. Unpublished PhD dissertation, Eindhoven University of Technology, Department of Technology Management.

Imamoglu, C. (2000). Complexity, liking and familiarity: architecture and non-architecture Turkish students' assessments of traditional and modern house facades. *Journal of Environmental Psychology* 20: 5–16.

Inauen, J. and Mosler, H.J. (2014). Developing and testing theory-based and evidence-based interventions to promote switching to arsenic-safe wells in Bangladesh. *Journal of Health Psychology* 19 (12): 1483–1498.

Inglehart, R. (1997). *Modernization and Postmodernization*. Princeton, NJ: Princeton University Press.

IPCC (2013). Climate change 2013: The physical science basis. *Contribution of working group I to the fifth assessment report of the Intergovernmental Panel on Climate Change*. Cambridge: Cambridge University Press.

IPCC (2014). Climate Change 2014: Mitigation of climate change. *Contribution of working group III to fifth assessment report of the Intergovernmental Panel on Climate Change* (Edenhofer, O. et al. (Eds.)). Cambridge: Cambridge University Press.

Isaksson, K. and Richardson, T. (2009). Building legitimacy for risky policies: the cost of avoiding conflict in Stockholm. *Transportation Research Part A: Policy and Practice* 43: 251–257.

Islam, M.Z., Moore, R., and Cosco, N. (2016). Child-friendly, active, healthy neighborhoods: physical characteristics and children's time outdoors. *Environment & Behavior* 48 (5): 711–736.

Jackson, T. (2005). *Motivating Sustainable Consumption: A Review of Evidence on Consumer Behavior and Behavioral Change*. London: SDRN.

Jacobs, M.H. (2009). Why do we like or dislike animals? *Human Dimensions of Wildlife* 14 (1): 1–11.

Jacobs, M.H., Vaske, J.J., and Roemer, J.M. (2012). Toward a mental systems approach to human relationships with wildlife: the role of emotional dispositions. *Human Dimensions of Wildlife* 17 (1): 4–15.

Jacobs, M.H., Vaske, J.J., and Sijtsma, M.T. (2014). Predictive potential of wildlife value orientations for acceptability of management interventions. *Journal for Nature Conservation* 22 (4): 377–383.

Jager, W. and Edmonds, B. (2015). Policy making and modelling in a complex world. In: *Policy Practice and Digital Science: Integrating Complex Systems, Social Simulation and Public Administration in Policy Research* (ed. M. Janssen, M.A. Wimmer and A. Deljoo), 57–74. Cham: Springer.

Jager, W. and Ernst, A. (2017). Social simulation in environmental psychology. Introduction of the special issue. *Journal of Environmental Psychology* 52: 114–118.

Jager, W. and Van der Vegt, G. (2015). Management of complex systems: towards agent based gaming for policy. In: *Policy Practice and Digital Science: Integrating Complex Systems, Social Simulation and Public Administration in Policy Research* (ed. M. Janssen, M.A. Wimmer and A. Deljoo), 291–303. Cham: Springer.

Jager, W., Janssen, M.A., De Vries, H.J.M. et al. (2000). Behaviour in commons dilemmas: Homo economicus and Homo psychologicus in an ecological-economic model. *Ecological Economics* 35: 357–379.

Jakobsson, C., Fujii, S., and Gärling, T. (2000). Determinants of private car users' acceptance of road pricing. *Transport Policy* 7: 153–158.

Jakovcevic, A. and Steg, L. (2013). Sustainable transportation in Argentina: values, beliefs, norms and car use reduction. *Transportation Research Part F: Traffic Psychology and Behaviour* 20: 70–79.

Jakovcevic, A., Steg, L., Mazzeo, N. et al. (2014). Charges for plastic bags: motivational and behavioral effects. *Journal of Environmental Psychology* 40: 372–380.

James, W. (1890). *The Principles of Psychology*. New York, NY: Henry Holt and Company.

James, A.K., Hess, P., Perkins, M.E. et al. (2016). Prescribing outdoor play: outdoors Rx. *Clinical Pediatrics* 56 (6): 519–524.

Jans, L., Leach, C.W., Garcia, R., and Postmes, T. (2015). The development of group influence on in-group identification: a multi-level approach. *Group Processes and Intergroup Relations* 18 (2): 190–209.

Jansson, M., Fors, H., Lindgren, T., and Wiström, B. (2013). Perceived personal safety in relation to urban woodland vegetation – a review. *Urban Forestry & Urban Greening* 12 (2): 127–133.

Jenny, A., Hechavarria, F., and Mosler, H.-J. (2007). Psychological factors determining individual compliance with rules for common pool resource management: the case of a Cuban community sharing a solar energy system. *Human Ecology* 35 (2): 239–250.

Jensen, M. (1999). Passion and heart in transport – a sociological analysis on transport behaviour. *Transport Policy* 6: 19–33.

Joardar, S.D. (1989). Use and image of neighbourhood parks: a case of limited resources. *Environment and Behavior* 21: 734–762.

Johansson, M. and Karlsson, J. (2011). Subjective experience of fear and the cognitive interpretation of large carnivores. *Human Dimensions of Wildlife* 16 (1): 15–29.

Johansson, L.-O. and Svedsäter, H. (2009). Piece of cake? Allocating rewards to third parties when fairness is costly. *Organizational Behavior and Human Decision Processes* 109: 107–119.

Joireman, J.A., Lasane, T.P., Bennet, J. et al. (2001). Integrating social value orientation and the consideration of future consequences within the extended norm activation model of proenvironmental behaviour. *British Journal of Social Psychology* 40: 133–155.

Joireman, J.A., Van Lange, P.A.M., and Van Vugt, M. (2004). Who cares about the environmental impact of cars? Those with an eye toward the future. *Environment and Behavior* 36: 187–206.

Joireman, J., Truelove, H.B., and Duell, B. (2010). Effect of outdoor temperature, heat primes and anchoring on belief in global warming. *Journal of Environmental Psychology* 30: 358–367.

Jokela, M. (2015). Does neighbourhood deprivation cause poor health? Within-individual analysis of movers in a prospective cohort study. *Journal of Epidemiology and Community Health* 69: 899–904.

Jones-Rounds, M.L., Evans, G.W., and Braubach, M. (2014). The interactive effects of housing and neighbourhood quality on psychological well-being. *Journal of Epidemiology and Community Health* 68: 171–175.

Jongman, R.H.G. (2002). Homogenisation and fragmentation of the European landscape: ecological consequences. *Landscape and Urban Planning* 58: 211–221.

Jorgensen, B.S. and Stedman, R.C. (2006). A comparative analysis of predictors of sense of place dimensions: attachment to, dependence on, and identification with lakeshore properties. *Journal of Environmental Management* 79 (3): 316–327.

Jorgensen, A., Hitchmough, J., and Calvert, T. (2002). Woodland spaces and edges: their impact on perception of safety and preference. *Landscape and Urban Planning* 60 (3): 135–150.

Joye, Y. (2007). Architectural lessons from environmental psychology: the case of biophilic architecture. *Review of General Psychology* 11 (4): 305–328.

Joye, Y. and De Block, A. (2011). "Nature and I are two": a critical examination of the biophilia hypothesis. *Environmental Values* 20 (2): 189–215.

Joye, Y. and Van den Berg, A.E. (2011). Is love for green in our genes? A critical analysis of evolutionary assumptions in restorative environments research. *Urban Forestry & Urban Greening* 10: 261–268.

Joye, Y., Steg, L., Ünal, A.B., and Pals, R. (2016). When complex is easy on the mind: internal repetition of visual information in complex objects is a source of perceptual fluency. *Journal of Experimental Psychology: Human Perception and Performance* 42 (1): 103.

Joye, Y., Steg, L., Ünal, A.B., and Pals, R. (2016). When complex is easy on the mind: internal repetition of visual information in complex objects is a source of perceptual fluency. *Journal of Experimental Psychology: Human Perception and Performance* 42 (1): 103.

Joye, Y., Steg, L., Ünal, A.B., and Pals, R. (2016). When complex is easy on the mind: internal repetition of visual information in complex objects is a source of perceptual fluency. *Journal of Experimental Psychology: Human Perception and Performance* 42 (1): 103.

Kahan, D.M., Peters, E., Wittlin, M. et al. (2012). The polarizing impact of science literacy and numeracy on perceived climate change risks. *Nature Climate Change* 2: 732–735.

Kahn, I. Jr. and Kellert, P.H. (2002). *Children and Nature: Psychological, Sociocultural and Evolutionary Investigations*. Cambridge, MA: MIT press.

Kaiser, F.G. and Wilson, M. (2004). Goal-directed conservation behavior: the specific composition of a general performance. *Personality and Individual Differences* 36: 1531–1544.

Kaiser, F.G., Oerke, B., and Bogner, F.X. (2007). Behavior-based environmental attitude: development of an instrument for adolescents. *Journal of Environmental Psychology* 27: 242–251.

Kaiser, F.G., Byrka, K., and Hartig, T. (2010). Reviving Campbell's paradigm for attitude research. *Personality and Social Psychology Review* 14: 351–367.

Kallgren, C.A., Reno, R.R., and Cialdini, R.B. (2000). A focus theory of normative conduct: when norms do and do not affect behavior. *Personality and Social Psychology Bulletin* 26: 1002–1012.

Kals, E., Schumacher, D., and Montada, L. (1999). Emotional affinity toward nature as a motivational basis to protect nature. *Environment and Behavior* 31: 178–202.

Kamakura, W.A. and Mazzon, J.A. (1991). Value segmentation: a model for the measurement of values and value systems. *Journal of Consumer Research* 18: 208–218.

Kanagawa, M. and Nakata, T. (2007). Analysis of the energy access improvement and its socioeconomic impacts in rural areas of developing countries. *Ecological Economics* 62 (2): 319–329.

Kantola, S.J., Syme, G.J., and Campbell, N.A. (1984). Cognitive dissonance and energy conservation. *Journal of Applied Psychology* 69: 416–421.

Kaplan, S. (1995). The restorative benefits of nature: towards an integrative framework. *Journal of Environmental Psychology* 15: 169–182.

Kaplan, R. (2001). The nature of the view from home – psychological benefits. *Environment and Behavior* 33 (4): 507–542.

Kaplan, S. and Berman, M.G. (2010). Directed attention as a common resource for executive functioning and self-regulation. *Perspectives on Psychological Science* 5 (1): 43–57.

Kaplan, R. and Kaplan, S. (1989). *The Experience of Nature: A Psychological Perspective*. New York, NY: Cambridge University Press.

Kaplan, R. and Talbot, J.F. (1983). Psychological benefits of a wilderness experience. In: *Human Behavior and Environment: Advances in Theory and Research*, vol. 6 (ed. I. Altman and J.F. Wohlwill), 163–203. New York, NY: Plenum Press.

Kaplan, R., Kaplan, S., and Brown, T. (1989). Environmental preference: a comparison of four domains of predictors. *Environment and Behavior* 21: 509–530.

Kaplan, S., Bardwell, L.V., and Slakter, D.B. (1993). The museum as restorative environment. *Environment and Behavior* 725–742.

Karau, S. and Williams, K. (1993). Social loafing: a meta-analytic review and theoretical integration. *Journal of Personality and Social Psychology* 65: 681–706.

Karlin, B., Zinger, J.F., and Ford, R. (2015). The effects of feedback on energy conservation: a meta-analysis. *Psychological Bulletin* 141 (6): 1205.

Karmanov, D. and Hamel, R. (2008). Assessing the restorative potential of contemporary urban environment(s): beyond the nature versus urban dichotomy. *Landscape and Urban Planning* 86 (2): 115–125.

Kashima, Y., Paladino, A., and Margetts, E.A. (2014). Environmentalist identity and environmental striving. *Journal of Environmental Psychology* 38: 64–75.

Kay, A.C. and Ross, L. (2003). The perceptual push: the interplay of implicit cues and explicit situational construals on behavioral intentions in the prisoner's dilemma. *Journal of Experimental Social Psychology* 39: 634–643.

Kay, A.C., Wheeler, S.C., Bargh, J.A., and Ross, L. (2004). Material priming: the influence of mundane physical objects on situational construal and competitive behavioral choice. *Organizational Behavior and Human Decision Processes* 95: 83–96.

Kaźmierczak, A. (2013). The contribution of local parks to neighbourhood social ties. *Landscape and Urban Planning* 109 (1): 31–44.

Keizer, K., Lindenberg, S., and Steg, L. (2008). The spreading of disorder. *Science* 322: 1681–1685.

Keizer, K., Lindenberg, S., and Steg, L. (2011). The reversal effect of prohibition signs. *Group Processes and Intergroup Relations* 14 (5): 681–688.

Keizer, K., Lindenberg, S., and Steg, L. (2013). The importance of demonstratively restoring order. *PLoS One* 8 (6): 6–12.

Keller, C., Bostrom, A., Kuttschreuter, M. et al. (2012). Bringing appraisal theory to environmental risk perception: a review of conceptual approaches of the past 40 years and suggestions for future research. *Journal of Risk Research* 15: 237–256.

Kellert, S.R. (1976). Perceptions of animals in American society. *Transactions of the North American Wildlife and Natural Resources Conference* 41: 533–546.

Kellert, S.R. (1978). Attitudes and characteristics of hunters and anti-hunters. *Transactions of North American Wildlife and Natural Resources Conference* 43: 412–423.

Kellert, S.R. (1985). Public perceptions of predators, particularly the wolf and coyote. *Biological Conservation* 31: 167–189.

Kellert, S.R. (1996). *The Value of Life: Biological Diversity and Human Society*. Washington, DC: Island Press.

Kellert, S.R. and Berry, J.K. (1987). Attitudes, knowledge and behaviours towards wildlife as affected by gender. *Wildlife Society Bulletin* 15 (3): 363–371.

Kellert, S.R., Heerwagen, J., and Mador, M. (2011). *Biophilic Design: The Theory, Science and Practice of Bringing Buildings to Life*. Hoboken, New Jersey: Wiley.

Kelley, H.H. (1973). The processes of causal attribution. *American Psychologist* 28 (2): 107–128.

Kelz, C., Evans, G.W., and Röderer, K. (2015). The restorative effects of redesigning the schoolyard: a multi-methodological, quasi-experimental study in rural Austrian middle schools. *Environment and Behavior* 47: 119–139.

Kempton, W. (1991). Lay perspectives on global climate change. *Global Environmental Change* 1 (3): 183–208.

Kerr, N.L. (1983). Motivation losses in small groups: a social dilemma analysis. *Journal of Personality and Social Psychology* 45: 819–828.

Kerr, N.L. (1989). Illusion of efficiency: the effects of group size on perceived efficacy in social dilemmas. *Journal of Experimental Social Psychology* 25: 287–313.

Kerr, N.L. (1995). Norms in social dilemmas. In: *Social Dilemmas: Social Psychological Perspectives* (ed. D. Schroeder), 31–47. New York, NY: Pergamon Press.

Keulartz, J., Van der Windt, H., and Swart, J. (2004). Concepts of nature as communicative devices: the case of Dutch nature policy. *Environmental Values* 13: 81–99.

Kjellgren, A. and Buhrkall, H. (2010). A comparison of the restorative effect of a natural environment with that of a simulated natural environment. *Journal of Environmental Psychology* 30 (4): 464–472.

Klatte, M., Spilski, J., Mayerl, J. et al. (2016). Effects of aircraft noise on reading and quality of life in primary school children in Germany: results from the NORAH study. *Environment and Behavior* 49 (4): 390–424. doi: 10.1177/0013916516642580.

Klöckner, C.A. (2004). *How single events change travel mode choice – a life span perspective*. Paper presented at the 3rd ICTTP conference, Nottingham, UK.

Klöckner, C.A. (2014). The dynamics of purchasing an electric vehicle – a prospective longitudinal study of the decision-making process. *Transportation Research Part F: Traffic Psychology and Behaviour* 24: 103–116.

Klöckner, C.A. (2015). *The Psychology of Pro-Environmental Communication: Beyond Standard Information Strategies*. Basingstoke: Palgrave Macmillan.

Klöckner, C.A. and Matthies, E. (2004). How habits interfere with norm-directed behaviour: a normative decision making model for travel mode choice. *Journal of Environmental Psychology* 24 (3): 319–327.

Kluger, A.N. and DeNisi, A. (1996). The effects of feedback interventions on performance: a historical review, a meta-analysis, and a preliminary feedback intervention theory. *Psychological Bulletin* 119: 254–284.

Kollmuss, A. and Agyeman, J. (2002). Mind the gap: why do people act environmentally and what are the barriers to pro-environmental behavior? *Environmental Education Research* 8 (3): 239–260.

Koole, S.L. and Van den Berg, A.E. (2004). Paradise lost and reclaimed: an existential motives analysis of human-nature relations. In: *Handbook of Experimental Existential Psychology* (ed. J. Greenberg, S.L. Koole and T. Pyszczinsky), 86–103. New York, NY: Guildford.

Koole, S.L. and Van den Berg, A.E. (2005). Lost in the wilderness: terror management, action orientation, and nature evaluation. *Journal of Personality and Social Psychology* 88 (6): 1014–1028.

Kormos, C. and Gifford, R. (2014). The validity of self-report measures of proenvironmental behavior: a meta-analytic review. *Journal of Environmental Psychology* 40: 359–371.

Kozlowsky, M., Kluger, A., and Reich, M. (1995). *Commuting Stress*. New York, NY: Plenum.

Kraemer, S. and Mosler, H.-J. (2010). Persuasion factors influencing the decision to use a sustainable household water treatment technique. *International Journal of Environmental Health Research* 20 (1): 61–79.

Kraft, P., Rise, J., Sutton, S., and Røysamb, E. (2005). Perceived difficulty in the theory of planned behaviour: perceived behavioural control or affective attitude? *British Journal of Social Psychology* 44: 479–496.

Kreuter, M.W., Farrell, D., Olevitch, L., and Brennan, L. (1999). *Tailored Health Messages: Customizing Communication with Computer Technology*. Mahwah, NJ: Erlbaum.

Kruglanski, A.W. and Köpetz, C. (2009). What is so special (and non-special) about goals? A view from the cognitive perspective. In: *The Psychology of Goals* (ed. G.B. Moskowitz and H. Grant), 25–55. New York, NY: Guilford Press.

Kuo, M. (2015). How might contact with nature promote human health? Promising mechanisms and a possible central pathway. *Frontiers in Psychology* 6: 1093.

Kuo, F. and Faber Taylor, A. (2004). A potential natural treatment for attention-deficit/hyperactivity disorder: evidence from a national study. *American Journal of Public Health* 94: 1580–1586.

Kuo, F.E. and Sullivan, W.C. (2001). Aggression and violence in the inner city: effects of environment via mental fatigue. *Environment and Behavior* 33 (4): 543–571.

Kuropatwa, D. (2008). Natural fractal mosaic [Photograph], Retrieved June 9, 2011, from http://www.flickr.com/photos/dkuropatwa/2912488625. Made available under Creative Commons Licence.

Landeros-Mugica, K., Urbina-Soria, J., and Alcantara-Ayala, I. (2015). The good, the bad and the ugly: on the interactions among experience, exposure and commitment with reference to landslide risk perception in Mexico. *Natural Hazards* 80 (3): 1–23.

Lansing, J.S. and Kremer, J.N. (1994). Emergent properties of Balinese water temple networks: coadaptation on a rugged fitness landscape. In: *Artificial Life III* (ed. C.G. Langton), 201–223. Reading, MA: Addison-Wesley.

Larsen, L., Adams, J., Deal, B. et al. (1998). Plants in the workplace: the effects of plant density on productivity, attitudes, and perceptions. *Environment and Behavior* 30: 261–281.

Latané, B. and Darley, J.M. (1970). *The Unresponsive Bystander: Why Doesn't He Help?* New York, NY: Appleton-Century-Crofts.

Laumann, K., Gärling, T., and Stormark, K.M. (2001). Rating scale measures of restorative components of environments. *Journal of Environmental Psychology* 21 (1): 31–44.

Lazarus, R.S. (1966). *Psychological Stress and the Coping Process*. New York, NY: McGraw-Hill.

Lazarus, R.S. and Alfert, E. (1964). Short-circuiting of threat by experimentally altering cognitive appraisal. *Journal of Abnormal and Social Psychology* 69: 195–205.

Lazarus, R.S. and Cohen, J.B. (1977). Environmental stress. In: *Human Behavior and the Environment: Current Theory and Research* (ed. I. Altman and J.F. Wohlwill), 89–127. New York, NY: Plenum Press.

Lazarus, R.S. and Folkman, S. (1987). Transactional theory and research on emotions and coping. *European Journal of Personality* 1: 141–170.

Lazo, J.K., Kinnell, J.C., and Fisher, A. (2000). Expert and layperson perceptions of ecosystem risks. *Risk Analysis* 20: 179–193.

LeDoux, J. (1998). *The Emotional Brain: The Mysterious Underpinnings of Emotional Life*. New York, NY: Touchstone.

Lee, J.A. and Holden, S.J.S. (1999). Understanding the determinants of environmentally conscious behavior. *Psychology and Marketing* 16: 373–392.

Lee, T.H., Jan, F.H., and Yang, C.C. (2013). Conceptualizing and measuring environmentally responsible behaviours form the perspective of community-based tourism. *Tourism Management* 36: 454–468.

Lee, S.M., Conway, T.L., Frank, L.D. et al. (2016). The relation of perceived and objective environment attributes to neighborhood satisfaction. *Environment and Behavior*, published online January 18, 2016.

Leiserowitz, A., Thaker, J., Feinberg, G., and Cooper, D. (2013). Global warming's six Indias. Retrieved February, 2017: http://environment.yale.edu/climate-communication/article/Global-Warming-Six-Indias.

Lepore, S.J. and Evans, G.W. (1996). Coping with multiple stressors in the environment. In: *Handbook of Coping: Theory, Research, Applications* (ed. M. Zeidner and N.S. Endler), 350–377. Oxford: Wiley.

Lerner, J.S. and Keltner, D. (2001). Fear, anger, and risk. *Journal of Personality and Social Psychology* 81: 146–159.

Lerner, J.S. and Tiedens, L.Z. (2006). Portrait of the angry decision maker: how appraisal tendencies shape anger's influence on cognition. *Journal of Behavioral Decision Making* 19 (2): 115–137.

Levitt, L. and Leventhal, G. (1986). Litter reduction: how effective is the New York state bottle bill? *Environment and Behavior* 18: 467–479.

Lewandowsky, S., Gignac, G.E., and Vaughan, S. (2013). The pivotal role of perceived scientific consensus in acceptance of science. *Nature Climate Change* 3: 399–404.

Lewicka, M. (2011a). On the varieties of people's relationships with places: Hummon's typology revisited. *Environment and Behavior* 43 (5): 676–709.

Lewicka, M. (2011b). Place attachment: how far have we come in the last 40 years? *Journal of Environmental Psychology* 31 (2): 207–230.

Lewin, K. (1948). *Resolving Social Conflicts: Selected Papers on Group Dynamics*. New York, NY: Harper & Row.

Lewin, K. (1951). *Field theory in social science: selected theoretical papers* (ed. D. Cartwright). Oxford: Harpers.

Lewin, K. (1952). Group decision and social change. In: *Readings in Social Psychology* (ed. T.M. Newcomb and E.E. Hartley), 459–473. New York, NY: Holt.

Li, S. (2003). Recycling behaviour under China's social and economic transition: the case of metropolitan Wuhan. *Environment and Behavior* 35: 784–801.

Li, D. and Sullivan, W.C. (2016). Impact of views to school landscapes on recovery from stress and mental fatigue. *Landscape and Urban Planning* 148: 149–158.

Li, W., Moallem, I., Paller, K.A.P., and Gottfried, J.A. (2007). Subliminal smells can guide social preferences. *Psychological Science* 18: 1044–1049.

Li, Y., Johnson, E.J., and Zaval, L. (2011). Local warming daily temperature change influences belief in global warming. *Psychological Science* 22 (4): 454–459.

Liberman, V., Samuels, S.M., and Ross, L. (2004). The name of game: predictive power of reputations versus situational labels in determining prisoner's dilemma game moves. *Personality and Social Psychology Bulletin* 30: 1175–1185.

Lichtenstein, S., Slovic, P., Fischhoff, B. et al. (1978). Judged frequency of lethal events. *Journal of Experimental Psychology: Human Learning and Memory* 4: 551–578.

Liebrand, W.B.G. (1984). The effect of social motives, communication and group size on behaviour in an N-person multi-stage mixed-motive game. *European Journal of Social Psychology* 14: 239–264.

Lindenberg, S. (2008). Social rationality, semi-modularity and goal-framing: what is it all about? *Analyse & Kritik* 30: 669–687.

Lindenberg, S. and Steg, L. (2007). Normative, gain and hedonic goal frames guiding environmental behavior. *Journal of Social Issues* 65 (1): 117–137.

Lindenberg, S. and Steg, L. (2013). Goal-framing theory and norm-guided environmental behavior. In: *Encouraging Sustainable Behavior* (ed. H. van Trijp), 37–54. New York, NY: Psychology Press.

Lindvall, T. (1970). On sensory evaluation of odorous air pollutant intensities. *Nordisk. Hygienisk Tidskrift* (Suppl. 2): 1–181.

Locke, E.A. and Latham, G.P. (1990). *A Theory of Goal Setting and Task Performance*. Englewood Cliffs, NJ: Prentice Hall.

Loewenstein, G.F. (1996). Out of control: visceral influences on behavior. *Organizational Behavior and Human Decision Processes* 65: 272–292.

Loewenstein, G.F., Thompson, L., and Bazerman, M.H. (1989). Social utility and decision making in interpersonal contexts. *Journal of Personality and Social Psychology* 57: 426–441.

Lohr, V.I. and Pearson-Mims, C.H. (2005). Children's active and passive interactions with plants influence their attitudes and actions toward trees and gardening as adults. *HortTechnology* 15 (3): 472–476.

Lothian, A. (1999). Landscape and the philosophy of aesthetics: is landscape quality inherent in the landscape or in the eye of the beholder? *Landscape and Urban Planning* 44 (4): 177–199.

Loukopoulos, P., Jakobsson, C., Gärling, T. et al. (2005). Public attitudes towards policy measures for reducing private car use. *Environmental Science and Policy* 8: 57–66.

Louv, R. (2005). *Last Child in the Woods: Saving Our Children from Nature Deficit Disorder*. Chapel Hill: Algonquin Press.

Lu, S., Ham, J., and Midden, C. (2015). Persuasive technology based on bodily comfort experiences: The effect of color temperature of room lighting on user motivation to change room temperature. In: *Persuasive Technology. PERSUASIVE 2015*, Lecture Notes in Computer Science, vol. 9072 (ed. T. MacTavish and S. Basapur). Cham: Springer.

Lu, S., Ham, J., and Midden, C. (2016). The influence of color association strength and consistency on ease of processing of ambient lighting feedback. *Journal of Environmental Psychology* 47: 204–212.

Ludwig, J., Duncan, G.J., Gennetian, L.A. et al. (2012). Neighborhood effects on the long-term well-being of low-income adults. *Science* 337 (6101): 1505–1510.

Lynch, K. (1977). *Growing Up in Cities*. Cambridge, MA: MIT Press.

Maas, J., Verheij, R.A., Spreeuwenberg, P., and Groenewegen, P.P. (2008). Physical activity as a possible mechanism behind the relationship between green space and health: a multilevel analysis. *BMC Public Health* 8: 206.

Maas, J., Spreeuwenberg, P., Van Winsum-Westra, M. et al. (2009a). Is green space in the living environment associated with people's feelings of social safety? *Environment and Planning A* 41 (7): 1763–1777.

Maas, J., van Dillen, S.M.E., Verheij, R.A., and Groenewegen, P.P. (2009b). Social contact as a possible mechanism behind the relation between green space and health. *Health and Place* 15 (2): 586–595.

Maas, J., Verheij, R.A., de Vries, S. et al. (2009c). Morbidity is related to a green living environment. *Journal of Epidemiology and Community Health* 63 (12): 967–973.

Manetti, L., Pierro, A., and Livi, S. (2002). Explaining consumer conduct: from planned to self-expressive behavior. *Journal of Applied Social Psychology* 32 (7): 1431–1451.

Manetti, L., Pierro, A., and Livi, S. (2004). Recycling: planned and self-expressive behaviour. *Journal of Environmental Psychology* 24: 227–236.

Manfredo, M.J. (2008). *Who Cares About Wildlife? Social Science Concepts for Exploring Human-Wildlife Relationships and Conservation Issues*. New York, NY: Springer.

Manfredo, M.J., Teel, T.L., and Henry, K. (2009). Linking society and environment: a multi-level model of shifting wildlife value orientations in the Western United States. *Social Science Quarterly* 90 (2): 407–427.

Manfredo, M.J., Teel, T.L., and Dietsch, A.M. (2016). Implications of human value shift and persistence for biodiversity conservation. *Conservation Biology* 30 (2): 287–296.

Manzo, L.C. (2003). Beyond house and haven: toward a revisioning of place attachment. *Journal of Environmental Psychology* 23 (1): 47–61.

Manzo, L.C. (2014). Exploring the shadow side: place attachments in the context of stigma, displacement and social housing. In: *Place Attachment: Advances in Theory, Methods and Applications* (ed. L. Manzo and P. Devine-Wright), 178–190. London: Routledge.

Manzo, L. and Devine-Wright, P. (2013). *Place Attachment: Advances in Theory, Methods and Applications*. Oxford, UK: Routledge.

Marcus, C.C. (2006). *House as a Mirror of Self: Exploring the Deeper Meaning of Home*. Lake Worth, FL: Nicolas-Hays.

Maréchal, K. (2010). Not irrational but habitual: the importance of "behavioural lock-in" in energy consumption. *Ecological Economics* 69 (5): 1104–1114.

Markowitz, F.E., Bellair, P.E., and Liu, J. (2001). Extending social disorganization theory: Modeling the relationships between cohesion, disorder, and fear. *Criminology* 39: 293–319.

Marlatt, G.A. and Donovan, D.M. (2005). *Relapse Prevention: Maintenance Strategies in the Treatment of Addictive Behaviors*. New York, NY: Guilford Publications.

Marzluff, J.M. and Angell, T. (2005). *In the Company of Crows and Ravens*. New Haven, CT: Yale University Press.

Maslow, A.H. (1970). *Personality and Motivation*, vol. 1, 987. Harlow, England: Longman.

Masson, T. and Fritsche, I. (2014). Adherence to climate change-related ingroup norms: do dimensions of group identification matter? *European Journal of Social Psychology* 44 (5): 455–465.

Matthies, E., Kuhn, S., and Klöckner, C. (2002). Travel mode choice of women: the result of limitation, ecological norm, or weak habit? *Environment and Behavior* 34: 163–177.

Matthies, E., Klöckner, C.A., and Preißner, C.L. (2006). Applying a modified moral decision making model to change habitual car use: how can commitment be effective? *Applied Psychology: An International Review* 55: 91–106.

Mattos, T. and Pinheiro, J.Q. (2013). Vivendo a vizinhança: Interfaces pessoa-ambiente na produçao de vizinhanças 'vivas' [To dwell at a neigbourhood: The person-environment interfaces in the 'living' neighbourgood production]. *Psicologia em Estudo* 18 (1): 27–36.

Mayer, F.S. and Frantz, C.M. (2004). The connectedness to nature scale: a measure of individuals' feeling in community with nature. *Journal of Environmental Psychology* 24 (4): 503–515.

Mayer, F.S., Frantz, C.M., Bruehlman-Senecal, E., and Dolliver, K. (2009). Why is nature beneficial? *Environment and Behavior* 607–643.

Mayo, E. (1933). *The Human Problems of an Industrial Civilization*. New York, NY: Macmillan.

Mazur, A. (2006). Risk perception and news coverage across nations. *Risk Management* 8: 149–174.

McCalley, L.T. and Midden, C.J.H. (2002). Energy conservation through product-integrated feedback: the roles of goal-setting and social orientation. *Journal of Economic Psychology* 23: 589–603.

McDaniels, T., Axelrod, L.J., and Slovic, P. (1995). Characterizing perception of ecological risk. *Risk Analysis* 15: 575–609.

McDonald, R.I. (2016). Perceived temporal and geographic distance and public opinion about climate change. *Climate Science Oxford Research Encyclopedias*. Retrieved February, 2017 from http://climatescience.oxfordre.com/view/10.1093/acrefore/9780190228620.001.0001/acrefore-9780190228620-e-308

McDonald, S., Oates, C.J., Thyne, M. et al. (2015). Flying in the face of environmental concern: why green consumers continue to fly. *Journal of Marketing Management* 31: 1503–1528.

McEwen, B.S. (1998). Stress, adaptation, and disease: Allostasis and allostatic load. In: *Annals of the New York Academy of Sciences*, Neuroimmunomodulation: Molecular Aspects, Integrative Systems, and Clinical Advances, vol. 840 (ed. S.M. McCann, J.M. Lipton, E.M. Sternberg, et al.), 33–44. New York, NY: New York Academy of Sciences.

McEwen, B.S. (2002). *The End of Stress as we Know it*. Washington, DC: Joseph Henry Press.

McFarlane, B.L. (1994). Specialization and motivations of birdwatchers. *Wildlife Society Bulletin* 22: 361–370.

McGrath, J.J. (1970). *Social and Psychological Factors in Stress*. New York, NY: Holt.

McKenzie-Mohr, D. (2000). Fostering sustainable behavior through community-based social marketing. *American Psychologist* 55: 531–537.

Meijnders, A., Midden, C., and Wilke, H. (2001). Communications about environmental risks and risk reducing behaviour: the impact of fear on information processing. *Journal of Applied Social Psychology* 31: 754–777.

Meinig, D.W. (1979). The beholding eye: ten versions of the same scene. In: *The Interpretation of Ordinary Landscape: Geographical Essays* (ed. D.W. Meinig and J. Brinckerhoff Jackson), 33–48. New York, NY: Oxford University Press.

Mercado-Doménech, S., Ortega-Andeane, P., Luna-Lara, G., and Estrada-Rodríguez, C. (1994). *Factores psicológicos y ambientales de la habitabilidad de la vivienda. [Psychological and Environmental Factors of the Habitability of Housing]*. Mexico City: Faculty of Psychology, National University of Mexico.

Merziger, A. and Neumann, K. (2010). *Energy Neighbourhoods - Bet to win! The climate competition between municipalities and their citizens*. Summary Report for the Executive Agency for Competitiveness and Innovation (EACI), Berlin.

Messick, D.M. (1993). Equality as a decision heuristic. In: *Psychological Perspectives on Justice: Theory and Applications. Cambridge Series on Judgment and Decision Making* (ed. B.A. Mellers and J. Baron), 11–31. New York, NY, US: Cambridge University Press.

Messick, D.M. and Brewer, M.B. (1983). Solving social dilemmas: a review. In: *Review of Personality and Social Psychology*, vol. 4 (ed. L. Wheeler and P. Shaver), 11–44. Beverly Hills: Sage.

Messick, D.M. and McClelland, C.L. (1983). Social traps and temporal traps. *Personality and Social Psychology Bulletin* 9: 105–110.

Messick, D.M. and McClintock, C.G. (1968). Motivational basis of choice in experimental games. *Journal of Experimental Social Psychology* 4: 1–25.

Messick, D.M. and Schell, T. (1992). Evidence for an equality heuristic in social decision making. *Acta Psychologica* 80: 311–323.

Messick, D.M., Wilke, H., Brewer, M.B. et al. (1983). Individual adaptations and structural change as solutions to social dilemmas. *Journal of Personality and Social Psychology* 44: 292–309.

Metag, J., Füchslin, T., and Schäfer, M.S. (2015). Global warming's five Germanys: a typology of Germans' views on climate change and patterns of media use and information. *Public Understanding of Science* 23 (5): 1–18.

Midden, C. and Ham, J. (2009). Using negative and positive social feedback from a robotic agent to save energy. *Conference proceedings of Persuasive 2009, Claremont, USA* (pp. article no. 12). Heidelberg: Springer.

Midden, C., Kaiser, F., and Mccalley, L. (2007). Technology's four roles in understanding individuals' conservation of natural resources. *Journal of Social Issues* 63: 155–174.

Midden, C., Ham, J., Kleppe, M., et al. (2011). Persuasive power in groups: The influence of group feedback and individual comparison feedback on energy consumption behaviour. *Conference proceedings of Persuasive 2011*. Columbus, USA: OSU Press.

Midden, C.J.H., Ham, J., and Baten, J. (2015). Conforming to an artificial majority: Persuasive effects of a group of artificial agents. In: *Persuasive Technology* (ed. T. MacTavish and S. Basapur), 129–240. Heidelberg: Springer.

Milfont, R.L. and Duckitt, J. (2004). The structure of environmental attitudes: first- and second-order confirmatory factor analysis. *Journal of Environmental Psychology* 24: 289–303.

Milfont, T., Duckitt, J., and Cameron, L.D. (2006). A cross-cultural study of environmental motive concerns and their implications for pro-environmental behaviour. *Environment and Behavior* 38: 745–753.

Milgram, S. (1970). The experience of living in cities. *Science* 167 (3924): 1461–1468.

Milgram, S. (1974). *Obedience to Authority; an Experimental View*. New York, NY: Harper and Row.

Millennium Ecosystem Assessment (2005). *Ecosystems and Human Well-Being: Synthesis*. Washington, DC: Island Press.

Miller, G.E., Cohen, S., and Ritchey, A.K. (2002). Chronic psychological stress and regulation of pro-inflammatory cytokines: a glucocorticoid-resistance model. *Health Psychology* 21: 531–541.

Mitchell, R. and Popham, F. (2007). Greenspace, urbanity and health: relationships in England. *Journal of Epidemiology and Community Health* 61 (8): 681–683.

Mitchell, R. and Popham, F. (2008). Effect of exposure to natural environment on health inequalities: an observational population study. *Lancet* 372 (9650): 1655–1660.

Mo Jang, S. (2013). Framing responsibility in climate change discourse: ethnocentric attribution bias, perceived causes, and policy attitudes. *Journal of Environmental Psychology* 36: 27–36.

Mocelin Polli, G. and Vizeu Camargo, B. (2015). Representações Sociais do meio ambiente e da água. *Psicologia, Ciencia e Profissao* 35 (4): 1310–1326.

Mokhtarian, P.L. and Salomon, I. (2001). How derived is the demand for travel? Some conceptual and measurement considerations. *Transportation Research Part A: Policy and Practice* 35: 695–719.

Montero y López-Lena, M. (1997). Scientific productivity in environmental psychology in Mexico: a bibliometric analysis. *Environment and Behavior* 29: 169–197.

Moore, R.C. (1980). Collaborating with young people to assess their landscape values. *Ekistics* 47 (281): 128–135.

Moreno, R. and Urbina-Soria, J. (2008). *Impactos sociales del cambio climático en México. [Social Impacts of Climate Change In Mexico]*. Mexico City: National Institute of Ecology and the United Nations Program for Development.

Morrison, M., Duncan, R., Sherley, C., and Parton, K. (2013). A comparison between attitudes to climate change in Australia and the United States. *Australasian Journal of Environmental Management* 20 (2): 87–100.

Moscovici, S. (1985). Social influence and conformity. In: *Handbook of Social Psychology*, vol. 2 (ed. G. Lindzey and E. Aronson), 347–412. New York, NY: Random House.

Möser, G. and Bamberg, S. (2008). The effectiveness of soft transport policy measures: a critical assessment and meta-analysis of empirical evidence. *Journal of Environmental Psychology* 28: 10–26.

Moser, S. and Mosler, H.-J. (2008). Differences in influence patterns between groups predicting the adoption of a solar disinfection technology for drinking water in Bolivia. *Social Science & Medicine* 67: 497–504.

Mosler, H.-J. (2012). A systematic approach to behavior change interventions for the water and sanitation sector in developing countries: a conceptual model, a review, and a guideline. *International Journal of Environmental Health Research* 22 (5): 431–449.

Mosler, H.-J. and Martens, T. (2008). Designing environmental campaigns by using agent-based simulations: strategies for changing environmental attitudes. *Journal of Environmental Management* 88: 805–816.

Mosler, H.-J., Tamas, A., Tobias, R. et al. (2008). Deriving interventions on the basis of factors influencing behavioural intentions for waste recycling, composting, and reuse in Cuba. *Environment and Behavior* 40 (4): 522–544.

Moyano-Diaz, E. (2002). Theory of planned behavior and pedestrians' intentions to violate traffic regulations. *Transportation Research* 5: 169–175.

Moyano-Díaz, E., Juscksch Torquato, R., and Bianchi, A. (2014). Aportaciones a las ciencias de la salud: El comportamiento peatonal arriesgado de chilenos y brasileros. *Terapia Psicológica* 32 (3): 227–234.

Moyano-Díaz, E., Palomo-Vélez, G., and Moyano-Costa, P. (2015). Creencias ambientales e ideología en población chilena. *Universum* 30 (2): 219–236.

Mukherjee, B.N. (1993). Public response to air pollution in Calcutta proper. *Journal of Environmental Psychology* 13 (3): 207–230.

Mulder, L.B. (2008). The difference between punishments and rewards in fostering moral concerns in social decision making. *Journal of Experimental Social Psychology* 44: 1436–1443.

Münzel, T., Gori, T., Babisch, W., and Basner, M. (2014). Cardiovascular effects of environmental noise exposure. *European Heart Journal* 35 (13): 829–836.

Murtagh, N., Gatersleben, B., and Uzzell, D. (2012a). Multiple identities and travel mode choice for regular journeys. *Transportation Research, Part F – Traffic Psychology and Behaviour* 15 (5): 514–524.

Murtagh, N., Gatersleben, B., and Uzzell, D. (2012b). Self-identity threat and resistance to change: evidence from regular travel behaviour. *Journal of Environmental Psychology* 32 (4): 318–326.

Naciones Unidas, Comisión Económica para América Latina y el Caribe & Oxford Committee for Famine Relief (2016). *Tributación para un crecimiento inclusivo*. Santiago: Coediciones CEPAL.

Naivinit, W., Le Page, C., Trébuil, G., and Gajaseni, N. (2010). Participatory agent-based modeling and simulation of rice production and labor migrations in Northeast Thailand. *Environmental Modelling and Software* 25 (11): 1345–1358.

Nanistova, E. (1998). The dimensions of the attachment to birthplace and their verification after the 40 years following the forced relocation. *Sociológia* 30 (4): 377–394.

Nasar, J.L. (1981). Responses to different spatial configurations. *Human Factors* 23: 439–446.

Nasar, J.L. (1983). Adult viewers' preferences in residential scenes: a study of the relationship of environmental attributes to preference. *Environment and Behavior* 15: 589–614.

Nasar, J.L. (1989). Symbolic meanings of house styles. *Environment and Behavior* 21: 235–257.

Nasar, J.L. (1994). Urban design aesthetics: the evaluative qualities of building exteriors. *Environment and Behavior* 26: 277–401.

Nasar, J.L. and Fisher, B. (1993). 'Hot spots' of fear and crime: a multi-method investigation. *Journal of Environmental Psychology* 13 (3): 187–206.

Nasar, J.L. and Purcell, T. (1990). Beauty and the beast extended: knowledge structure and evaluations of houses by Australian architects and non-architects. In: *Culture, Space, History* (ed. H. Pamir, V. Imamoglu and N. Teymur), 107–110. Ankara, Turkey: Sevki Vanh Foundation for Architecture.

Nash, R. (1982). *Wilderness and the American Mind*, 3e. New Haven, CT: Yale University Press.

Nassauer, J.I. (1992). The appearance of ecological systems as a matter of policy. *Landscape Ecology* 6 (4): 239–250.

Nassauer, J.I. (1995). Messy ecosystems, orderly frames. *Landscape Journal* 14: 161–170.

Nassauer, J.I. (1997). Cultural sustainability: aligning aesthetics and ecology. In: *Placing Nature: Culture and Landscape Ecology* (ed. J.I. Nassauer), 67–83. Washington DC: Island Press.

Natural England (2009). *Childhood and Nature: A Survey on Changing Relationships with Nature across Generations*. Cambridgeshire: Natural England.

Nawab, B., Nyborg, I.L.P., Esser, K.B., and Jenssen, P.D. (2006). Cultural preferences in designing ecological sanitation systems in North West Frontier Province, Pakistan. *Journal of Environmental Psychology* 26 (3): 236–246.

Neal, D.T., Wood, W., and Quinn, J.M. (2006). Habits – a repeat performance. *Current Directions in Psychological Science* 15 (4): 198–202.

Newsome, D. and Rodger, K. (2013). Wildlife tourism. In: *The Routledge Handbook of Tourism and the Environment* (ed. A. Holden and D. Fennell), 345–358. New York, NY: Routledge.

Nielsen, A.B., Van den Bosch, M., Maruthaveeran, S., and Van den Bosch, C.K. (2014). Species richness in urban parks and its drivers: a review of empirical evidence. *Urban Ecosystems* 17 (1): 305–327.

Nigbur, D., Lyons, E., and Uzzell, D. (2010). Attitudes, norms, identity and environmental behaviour: using an expanded theory of planned behaviour to predict participation in a kerbside recycling programme. *British Journal of Social Psychology* 49 (2): 259–284.

Nilsson, M. and Küller, R. (2000). Travel behaviour and environmental concern. *Transportation Research Part D: Transport and Environment* 5: 211–234.

Nilsson, A., Schuitema, G., Jakobsson Bergstad, C. et al. (2016). The road to acceptance: attitude change before and after the implementation of a congestion tax. *Journal of Environmental Psychology* 46: 1–9.

Nisbet, E.K. and Zelenski, J.M. (2011). Underestimating nearby nature: affective forecasting errors obscure the happy path to sustainability. *Psychological Science* 22 (9): 1101–1110.

Nolan, J., Schultz, P.W., Cialdini, R.B. et al. (2008). Normative social influence is underdetected. *Personality and Social Psychology Bulletin* 34: 913–923.

Norberg-Schulz, C. (1980). *Genius Loci: Toward a Phenomenology of Architecture*. New York, NY: Rizzoli.

Nordh, H. and Hagerhall, C. (2009). *Identifying restorative elements in small urban parks using eye movement tracking*. Paper presented at the 2nd International conference on landscape and urban horticulture, Bologna, Italy.

Nordlund, A.M. and Garvill, J. (2002). Value structures behind pro-environmental behavior. *Environment and Behavior* 34: 740–756.

Nordlund, A.M. and Garvill, J. (2003). Effects of values, problem awareness, and personal norm on willingness to reduce personal car use. *Journal of Environmental Psychology* 23: 339–347.

Norgaard, K.M. (2011). *Living in Denial: Climate Change, Emotions, and Everyday Life*. Boston, MA: MIT Press.

Novaco, R., Kliewer, W., and Broquet, A. (1991). Home environmental consequences of commute travel impedence. *American Journal of Community Psychology* 19: 881–909.

Nyborg, K., Anderies, J.M., Dannenberg, A. et al. (2016). Social norms as solutions: policies may influence large-scale behavioral tipping. *Science* 354 (6308): 42–43.

Oakes, P.J., Haslam, S.A., and Turner, J.C. (1994). *Stereotyping and Social Reality*. Oxford, UK: Blackwell.

Obregón-Salido, F. and Corral-Verdugo, V. (1997). Systems of belief and environmental conservation behavior in a Mexican community. *Environment and Behavior* 29: 213–235.

Ode Sang, Å. and Tveit, M.S. (2013). Perceptions of stewardship in Norwegian agricultural landscapes. *Land Use Policy* 31: 557–564.

Ode Sang, Å., Hägerhäll, C., Miller, D., and Donaldson-Selby, G. (2014). The use of visualised landscapes in order to challenge and develop theory in landscape preference research. In: *Digital Landscape Architecture* (ed. W. Hayek, Fricker and Buhmann), 362–369. Zurich: Wichmann.

Ode Sang, A., Tveit, M.S., Pihel, J., and Hägerhäll, C.M. (2016). Identifying cues for monitoring stewardship in Swedish pasture landscapes. *Land Use Policy* 53: 20–26.

Ode, Å., Tveit, M., and Fry, G. (2008). Capturing landscape visual character using indicators: touching base with landscape aesthetic theory. *Landscape Research* 33 (1): 89–118.

Ode, Å., Fry, G., Tveit, M.S. et al. (2009). Indicators of perceived naturalness as drivers of landscape preference. *Journal of Environmental Management* 90 (1): 375–383.

Ode, Å., Tveit, M.S., and Fry, G. (2010). Advantages of using different data sources in assessment of landscape change and its effect on visual scale. *Ecological Indicators* 10 (1): 24–31.

Öhman, A. and Mineka, S. (2003). The malicious serpent: snakes as a prototypical stimulus for an evolved module of fear. *Current Directions in Psychological Science* 12: 5–9.

Ohta, H. (2001). A phenomenological approach to natural landscape cognition. *Journal of Environmental Psychology* 21 (4): 387–404.

Olekszechen, N., Battiston, M., and Kuhnen, A. (2016). Uso da bicicleta como meio de transporte nos estudos pessoa-ambiente. *Desenvolvimento.e Meio Ambiente* 36: 355–369.

Olivos, P. and Clayton, S. (2017). Self, nature and well-being: sense of connectedness and environmental identity for quality of life. In: *Handbook of Environmental Psychology and Quality of Life Research* (ed. G. Fleury-Bahi, E. Pol and O. Navarro), 107–126. Cham: Springer.

O'Neill, S. and Nicholson-Cole, S. (2009). 'Fear won't do it' promoting positive engagement with climate change through visual and iconic representations. *Science Communication* 30 (3): 355–379.

Onwezen, M.C., Antonides, G., and Bartels, J. (2013). The norm activation model: an exploration of the functions of anticipated pride and guilt in pro-environmental behaviour. *Journal of Economic Psychology* 39: 141–153.

Opotow, S. and Weiss, L. (2000). New ways of thinking about environmentalism: denial and the process of moral exclusion in environmental conflict. *Journal of Social Issues* 56 (3): 475–490.

Oreg, S. and Katz-Gerro, T. (2006). Behavior, and value-belief-norm theory. Predicting proenvironmental the theory of planned behavior cross-nationally: values. *Environment and Behavior* 38: 462–473.

Oregon Department of Environmental Quality (2004). *The Oregon Bottle Bill Fact Sheet*.

Oreskes, N. and Conway, E.M. (2010). *Merchants of Doubt: How a Handful of Scientists Obscured the Truth on Issues from Tobacco Smoke to Global Warming*. New York, NY: Bloomsbury Press.

Orians, G.H. (1980). Habitat selection: general theory and applications to human behavior. In: *The Evolution of Human Social Behavior* (ed. J.S. Lockard), 49–63. Amsterdam: Elsevier.

Orland, B., Budthimedhee, K., and Uusitalo, J. (2001). Considering virtual worlds as representations of landscape realities and as tools for landscape planning. *Landscape and Urban Planning* 54 (1–4): 139–148.

Ortega-Andeane, P. and Estrada-Rodríguez, C. (2010). Public health care center design and stress in female patients. *Australasian Medical Journal* 3: 598–603.

Ortega-Andeane, P., Mercado-Doménech, S., Reidl-Martínez, L., and Estrada-Rodríguez, C. (2005). *Estrés ambiental en instituciones de salud. [Environmental Stress in Health Institutions]*. Mexico City: UNAM.

Osbaldiston, R. and Schott, J.P. (2012). Environmental sustainability and behavioral science: meta-analysis of proenvironmental behavior experiments. *Environment and Behavior* 44 (2): 257–299.

Oskamp, S. (2000a). A sustainable future for humanity? How can psychology help? *American Psychologist* 55: 496–508.

Oskamp, S. (2000b). Psychology of promoting environmentalism: psychological contributions to achieving an ecologically sustainable future for humanity. *Journal of Social Issues* 56: 373–390.

Ostrom, E., Gardner, R., and Walker, J. (1994). *Rules, Games, and Common-Pool Resources*. Ann Arbor University of Michigan Press. ISBN: 13: 9780472065462.

Ouellette, J.A. and Wood, W. (1998). Habit and intention in everyday life: the multiple processes by which past behaviour predicts future behavior. *Psychological Bulletin* 124 (1): 54–74.

Özgüner, H. and Kendle, A.D. (2006). Public attitudes towards naturalistic versus designed landscapes in the city of Sheffield (UK). *Landscape and Urban Planning* 74 (2): 139–157.

Packer, J. (2008). Beyond learning: exploring visitors' perceptions of the value and benefits of museums experiences. *Curator* 51 (1): 33–54.

Page, R.A. (1977). Noise and helping behavior. *Environment and Behavior* 9 (1): 311–334.

Painter, J.E., Wansink, B., and Hieggelke, J. (2002). How visibility and convenience influence candy consumption. *Appetite* 38 (3): 237–238.

Pakpour, A.H., Zeidi, I.M., Emamjomeh, M.M. et al. (2014). Household waste behaviours among a community sample in Iran: an application of the theory of planned behaviour. *Waste Management* 34 (6): 980–986.

Palmer, J.F. and Hoffman, R.E. (2001). Rating reliability and representation validity in scenic landscape assessments. *Landscape and Urban Planning* 54 (1–4): 149–161.

Pals, R., Steg, L., Siero, F.W., and Van der Zee, K.I. (2009). Development of the PRCQ: a measure of perceived restorative characteristics of zoo attractions. *Journal of Environmental Psychology* 29 (4): 441–449.

Pampel, F.C. (2014). The varied influence of SES on environmental concern. *Social Science Quarterly* 95 (1): 57–75.

Pâquet, J. and Bélanger, L. (1997). Public acceptability thresholds of clearcutting to maintain visual quality of boreal balsam fir landscapes. *Forest Science* 43 (1): 46–55.

Páramo, P., Sandoval-Escobar, M., Jakovcevic, A. et al. (2015). Assessment of environmental quality, degree of optimism, and the assignment of responsibility regarding the state of the environment in Latin America. *Universitas Psychology* 14 (2): 605–613.

Park, S.H. (2006). *Randomized clinical trials evaluating therapeutic influences of ornamental indoor plants in hospital rooms on health outcomes of patients recovering from surgery.*

Unpublished Dissertation, Kansas State University, Manhattan, Kansas. Retrieved from http://krex.k-state.edu/dspace/bitstream/2097/227/1/Seong-HyunPark2006.pdf

Parsons, R. (1991). The potential influences of environmental perception on human health. *Journal of Environmental Psychology* 11: 1–23.

Pasquali, C.T., Hernández, M.H., and Muñoz, C.C. (1997). Study of environmental factors associated with primary health care. *Environment and Behavior* 2: 665–696.

Pato, C., Ros, M., and Tamayo, A. (2005). Creencias y comportamiento ecológico: Un estudio empírico con estudiantes brasileños. [Beliefs and ecological behavior: an empirical study with Brazilian students]. *Medio Ambiente y Comportamiento Humano* 6: 5–22.

Patterson, M.E. and Williams, D.R. (2005). Maintaining research traditions on place: diversity of thought and scientific progress. *Journal of Environmental Psychology* 25: 361–380.

PBL (2014). *Trends in Global CO$_2$ Emissions: 2014 Report*. The Hague, Netherlands: PBL Netherlands Environmental Assessment Agency.

Perlaviciute, G. (2009). *Residential well-being*. Unpublished Master thesis, Faculty of Social and Behavioral Sciences, University of Groningen, Groningen.

Peters, K., Elands, B., and Buijs, A. (2010). Social interactions in urban parks: stimulating social cohesion? *Urban Forestry & Urban Greening* 9 (2): 93–100.

Petty, R.E. and Cacioppo, J.T. (1986). The elaboration likelihood model of persuasion. In: *Advances in Experimental Social Psychology* (ed. L. Berkowitz), 123–205. New York, NY: Academic Press.

Petty, R. and Wegener, D. (1998). Attitude change: multiple roles for persuasion variables. In: *The Handbook of Social Psychology*, vol. 4 (ed. D. Gilbert, S. Fiske and G. Lindzey), 323–390. New York, NY: McGraw-Hill.

Pfister, H.-R. and Böhm, G. (2001). Decision making in the context of environmental risks. In: *Decision Making: Social and Creative Dimensions* (ed. C.M. Allwood and M. Selart), 89–111. Dordrecht: Kluwer Academic.

Pfister, H.-R. and Böhm, G. (2008). The multiplicity of emotions: a framework of emotional functions in decision making. *Judgment and Decision Making* 3: 5–17.

Pihel, J., Ode-Sang, Å., Hägerhäll, C., et al. (2014). Assessments and eye movements compared between photographs and visualizations of logged forest vistas. For what kind of assessments are visualisations a good representation of photographs? Peer reviewed proceedings Digital Landscape Architecture.

Pihel, J., Ode Sang, Å., Hagerhall, C., and Nyström, M. (2015). Expert and novice group differences in eye movements when assessing biodiversity of harvested forests. *Forest Policy and Economics* 56: 20–26.

Pinheiro, J.Q. (2003). Psicología Ambiental brasileira no início do século XXI. Sustentável? [Brazilian environmental psychology in the beginning of 21st century. Sustainable?]. In: *Construindo a psicología Brasileira: Desafios da ciencia e da práctica psicológica [Building Brazilian Psychology: Scientific Challenges and Psychological Practice]* (ed. O.H. Yamamoto and V.V. Gouveia), 279–313. São Paulo: Casa do Psicólogo.

Pisano, I. and Lubell, M. (2017). Environmental behavior in cross-national perspective: a multilevel analysis of 30 countries. *Environment and Behavior* 49 (1): 31–58.

Pol, E. (2006). Blueprints for a history of environmental psychology (I): from first birth to American transition. *Medio Ambiente y Comportamiento Humano* 7 (2): 95–113.

Pol, E. (2007). Blueprints for a history of environmental psychology (II): from architectural psychology to the challenge of sustainability. *Medio Ambiente y Comportamiento Humano* 8 (1/2): 1–28.

Pol, E., Guardia, J., Valera, S. et al. (2001). Cohesión e identificación en la construcción de la identidad social: La relación entre ciudad, identidad y sostenibilidad. [Cohesion and identification in the construction of social identity: relations between city, identity and sustainability]. *Revista Universidad de Guadalajara* 19: 40–48.

Poortinga, W., Steg, L., and Vlek, C. (2004). Values, environmental concern, and environmental behavior: a study into household energy use. *Environment and Behavior* 36: 70–93.

Poortinga, W., Whitmarsh, L., and Suffolk, C. (2013). The introduction of a single-use carrier bag charge in Wales: attitude change and behavioural spillover effects. *Journal of Environmental Psychology* 36: 240–247.

Poortinga, W., Calve, T., Jones, N. et al. (2016). Neighborhood quality and attachment: validation of the revised residential environment assessment tool. *Environment and Behavior*, published online March 2 2016 1–28.

Postmes, T., Haslam, S.A., and Swaab, R.I. (2005). Social influence in small groups: an interactive model of social identity formation. *European Review of Social Psychology* 16: 1–42.

Prochaska, J.O. and Velicer, W.F. (1997). The Transtheoretical model of health behavior change. *American Journal of Health Promotion* 12: 38–48.

Prochaska, J.O., Redding, C.A., and Evers, K.E. (2002). The Transtheoretical model and stages of change. In: *Health Behavior and Health Education: Theory, Research, and Practice* (ed. K. Glanz, C.E. Lewis and B.K. Rimer), 99–120. San Francisco: Jossey-Bass.

Proshansky, H.M. (1987). The field of environmental psychology: Securing its future. In: *Handbook of Environmental Psychology* (ed. D. Stokols and I. Altman), 1467–1488. New York: Wiley.

Proshansky, H.M., Ittelson, W.H., and Rivlin, L.G. (eds.) (1976). *Environmental Psychology: People and Their Physical Settings*, 2e. New York, NY: Holt, Rinehart & Winston.

Proshansky, H.M., Fabian, A.K., and Kaminoff, R. (1983). Place-identity: physical world socialization of the self. *Journal of Environmental Psychology* 3 (1): 57–83.

Purcell, A.T. (1986). Environmental perception and affect: a schema discrepancy model. *Environment and Behavior* 18: 3–10.

Rabinovich, A., Morton, T.A., Postmes, T., and Verplanken, B. (2012). Collective self and individual choice: the effects of intergroup comparative context on environmental values and behaviour. *British Journal of Social Psychology* 51 (4): 551–569.

Rapaport, A., Budescu, D.V., Suleiman, R., and Weg, E. (1992). Social dilemmas with uniformly distributed resources. In: *Social Dilemmas: Theoretical Issues and Research Findings* (ed. W. Liebrand, D.M. Messick and H. Wilke), 43–57. Oxford: Pergamon.

Raux, C. and Souche, S. (2004). The acceptability of urban road pricing: a theoretical analysis applied to the experience in Lyon. *Journal of Transport Economics and Policy* 38: 191–216.

Raymond, C.M., Brown, G., and Weber, D. (2010). The measurement of place attachment: person, community and environmental connections. *Journal of Environmental Psychology* 30: 422–434.

Reeves, B. and Nass, C. (1996). *The Media Equation: How People Treat Computers, Television, and New Media like Real People and Places*. New York, NY: Cambridge University Press.

Regoeczi, W.C. (2003). When context matters: a multilevel analysis of household and neighbourhood crowding on aggression and withdrawal. *Journal of Environmental Psychology* 23 (4): 457–470.

Regoeczi, W.C. (2008). Crowding in context: an examination of the differential responses of men and women to high-density living environments. *Journal of Health and Social Behavior* 49 (3): 254–268.

Reno, R., Cialdini, R., and Kallgren, C. (1993). The transsituational influence of social norms. *Journal of Personality and Social Psychology* 64: 104–112.

Reser, J.P., Bradley, G.L., and Ellul, M.C. (2014). Encountering climate change: "seeing" is more than "believing". *WIREs: Climate Change* 5 (4): 521–537.

Reyes, L. I. (2010). *Etnopsychometry development and validation of culturally relevant measures.* Presentation at the ICAP, July 10, 2010.

Rhodes, E., Axsen, J., and Jaccard, M. (2014). Does effective climate policy require well-informed citizen support? *Global Environmental Change* 29: 92–104.

Rishbeth, C. (2014). Articulating transnational attachments through on-site narratives. In: *Place Attachment: Advances in Theory, Methods and Applications* (ed. L. Manzo and P. Devine-Wright), 100–111. London: Routledge.

Riva, G., Vatalaro, F., Davide, F., and Alcañiz, M. (2004). *Ambient Intelligence: The Evolution of Technology, Communication and Cognition Towards the Future of Human-Computer Interaction.* Amsterdam: IOS Press.

Riva, M., Plusquellec, P., Juster, R.P. et al. (2014). Household crowding is associated with higher allostatic load among the Inuit. *Journal of Epidemiology and Community Health* 68 (4): 363–369.

Robinson, D.T., Brown, D.G., Parker, D.C. et al. (2007). Comparison of empirical methods for building agent-based models in land use science. *Journal of Land Use Science* 2 (1): 31–55.

Rogers, R.W. (1983). Cognitive and physiological processes in fear appeals and attitude change: a revised theory of protection motivation. In: *Social Psychophysiology: A Sourcebook* (ed. B.L. Cacioppo and R.E. Petty), 153–176. Guilford Press: London.

Roser-Renouf, C., Stenhouse, N., Rolfe-Redding, J. et al. (2015). Engaging diverse audiences with climate change: message strategies for global warming's six Americas. In: *Handbook of Environment and Communication* (ed. A. Hanson and R. Cox), 368–386. New York, NY: Routledge.

Roubroeks (2014). Smart humans, polite computer agents, and attentive objects: Processes underlying the automatic social behavior to non-human agents. Unpublished PhD thesis. Eindhoven University of Technology.

Roubroeks, M., Ham, J., and Midden, C. (2010). The dominant robot: Threatening robots cause psychological reactance, especially when they have incongruent goals. *Conference proceedings of Persuasive 2010* (pp. 174–184). Heidelberg: Springer.

Russell, J.A. and Feldman Barrett, L. (1999). Core affect, prototypical emotional episodes, and other things called emotion: dissecting the elephant. *Journal of Personality and Social Psychology* 76: 805–819.

Russell, J.A. and Pratt, G. (1980). A description of the affective quality attributed to environments. *Journal of Personality and Social Psychology* 38 (2): 311–322.

Rutkowski, G.K., Cruder, C.L., and Romer, D. (1983). Group cohesiveness, social norms, and bystander intervention. *Journal of Personality and Social Psychology* (3): 545–552.

Ryan, R.M., Weinstein, N., Bernstein, J. et al. (2010). Vitalizing effects of being outdoors and in nature. *Journal of Environmental Psychology* 30 (2): 159–168.

Sacchi, S., Riva, P., Brambilla, M., and Grasso, M. (2014). Moral reasoning and climate change mitigation: the deontological reaction toward the market-based approach. *Journal of Environmental Psychology* 38: 252–261.

Sachdeva, S. (2016). The influence of sacred beliefs in environmental risk perception and attitudes. *Environment and Behavior*, 1–18 doi: 10.1177/0013916516649413.

Sagerstrom, S.C. and Miller, G.E. (2004). Psychological stress and the human immune system: a meta-analytic study of 30 years of inquiry. *Psychological Bulletin* 130: 601–630.

Sahoo, K.C., Hulland, K.R., Caruso, B.A. et al. (2015). Sanitation-related psychosocial stress: a grounded theory study of women across the life-course in Odisha, India. *Social Science & Medicine* 139: 80–89.

Salingaros, N.A. (2004). *Anti-Architecture and Deconstruction*. Solingen, Germany: Umbau-Verlag.

Sally, D. (1995). Conversation and cooperation in social dilemmas. A meta-analysis of experiments from 1958 to 1992. *Rationality and Society* 7: 58–92.

Sánchez Miranda, M.P., De la Garza González, A., López Ramírez, E.O., and Morales Martínez, G.E. (2012). Escala de Preferencia Ambiental (EPA): Una propuesta para medir la relación entre individuos y su ambiente. *International Journal of Psychological Research* 5 (1): 66–76.

Sánchez, E., Wiesenfeld, E., and Cronick, K. (1987). Environmental psychology from a Latin American perspective. In: *Handbook of Environmental Psychology* (ed. D. Stokols and I. Altman), 1337–1357. New York, NY: Wiley.

Sang, N., Hägerhäll, C., and Ode, Å. (2015). The Euler character: a new type of visual landscape metric? *Environment and Planning B: Planning and Design* 42 (1): 110–132.

Saracci, R. (1997). The World Health Organisation needs to reconsider its definition of health. *British Medical Journal* 314 (7091): 1409–1410.

Scannell, L. and Gifford, R. (2010a). Defining place attachment: a tripartite organizing framework. *Journal of Environmental Psychology* 30: 1–10.

Scannell, L. and Gifford, R. (2010b). The relations between natural and civic place attachment and pro-environmental behavior. *Journal of Environmental Psychology* 30: 289–297.

Schaeffer, M., Street, S., Singer, J.E., and Baum, A. (1988). Effects of control on the stress reactions of commuters. *Journal of Applied Social Psychology* 18: 944–957.

Scheier, M.E. and Carver, C.S. (1985). Optimism, coping, and health: assessment and implications of generalized outcome expectancies. *Health Psychology* 4: 219–247.

Scheier, M.F., Fenigstein, A., and Buss, A.H. (1984). Self-awareness and physical aggression. *Journal of Experimental Social Psychology* 10: 264–273.

Schelling, T.C. (1971). Dynamic models of segregation. *Journal of Mathematical Sociology* 1: 143–186.

Scherbaum, C.A., Popovich, P.M., and Finlinson, S. (2008). Exploring individual-level factors related to employee energy-conservation behaviors at work. *Journal of Applied Social Psychology* 38 (3): 818–835.

Schlenker, B. and Leary, M. (1982). Social anxiety and self-presentation. A conceptualisation and model. *Psychological Bulletin* 92 (3): 641–669.

Schlüter, M., Baeza, A., Dressler, G. et al. (2017). A framework for mapping and comparing behavioural theories in models of social-ecological systems. *Ecological Economics* 131: 21–35.

Schuitema, G. and De Groot, J.I.M. (2015). Green consumerism: the influence of product attributes and values on purchasing intentions. *Journal of Consumer Behaviour* 14 (1): 57–69.

Schuitema, G., Steg, L., and Forward, S. (2010a). Explaining differences in acceptability before and acceptance after the implementation of a congestion charge in Stockholm. *Transportation Research Part A: Policy and Practice* 44: 99–109.

Schuitema, G., Steg, L., and Rothengatter, J.A. (2010b). The acceptability, personal outcome expectations and expected effects of transport pricing policies. *Journal of Environmental Psychology* 30: 587–593.

Schuitema, G., Steg, L., and Van Kruining, M. (2011). When are transport pricing policies fair and acceptable? *Social Justice Research* 24: 66–84.

Schultz, P.W. (1998). Changing behavior with normative feedback interventions: a field experiment on curbside recycling. *Basic and Applied Psychology* 21: 25–36.

Schultz, P.W. (2002). Knowledge, education, and household recycling: examining the knowledge-deficit model of behavior change. In: *New Tools for Environmental Protection* (ed. T. Dietz and P. Stern), 67–82. Washington DC: National Academy of Sciences.

Schultz, T. and Fielding, K. (2014). The common in-group identity model enhances communication about recycled water. *Journal of Environmental Psychology* 40: 296–305.

Schultz, P.W., Nolan, J.M., Cialdini, R.B. et al. (2007). The constructive, destructive, and reconstructive power of social norms. *Psychological Science* 18: 429–434.

Schultz, P.W., Shriver, C., Tabanico, J.J., and Khazian, A.M. (2004). Implicit connections with nature. *Journal of Environmental Psychology* 24 (1): 31–42.

Schultz, P.W., Khazian, A.M., and Zaleski, A.C. (2008). Using normative social influence to promote conservation among hotel guests. *Social Influence* 3: 4–23.

Schultz, P.W., Messina, A., Tronu, G. et al. (2016). Personalized normative feedback and the moderating role of personal norms: a field experiment to reduce residential water consumption. *Environment and Behavior* 48 (5): 686–710.

Schwartz, S.H. (1977). Normative influences on altruism. In: *Advances in Experimental Social Psychology*, vol. 10 (ed. L. Berkowitz), 222–280. New York, NY: Academic Press.

Schwartz, S.H. (1992). Universals in the content and structure of values: theoretical advances and empirical tests in 20 countries. In: *Advances in Experimental Social Psychology* (ed. M. Zanna), 1–65. Orlando: Academic Press.

Schwartz, S.H. (1994). Are there universal aspects in the structure and contents of human values? *Journal of Social Issues* 50: 19–45.

Schwartz, S.H. (2006). A theory of cultural value orientations: explication and applications. *Comparative Sociology* 5: 136–182.

Schwartz, S.H. and Howard, J.A. (1981). A normative decision-making model of altruism. In: *Altruism and Helping Behaviour: Social, Personality and Developmental Perspectives* (ed. J.P. Rushton), 189–211. Hillsdale NJ: Erlbaum.

Schwartz, D., Bruine de Bruin, W., Fischhoff, B., and Lave, L. (2015). Advertising energy saving programs: the potential environmental cost of emphasizing monetary savings. *Journal of Experimental Psychology: Applied* 21: 158–166.

Schwarz, N. (1999). Self-reports: how questions shape the answers. *American Psychologist* 54: 93–105.

Schwarz, N. and Ernst, A. (2009). Agent-based modeling of the diffusion of environmental innovations – an empirical approach. *Technological Forecasting and Social Change* 76: 497–511.

Schweiger Gallo, I. and Gollwitzer, P.M. (2007). Implementation intentions: a look back at fifteen years of progress. *Psicothema* 19: 37–42.

Seligman, M.E.P. (1971). Phobias and preparedness. *Behavioral Therapy* 2: 307–320.

Seligman, C. and Katz, A.N. (1996). The dynamics of value systems. In: *The Psychology of Values: The Ontario Symposium*, vol. 8 (ed. C. Seligman, J.M. Olson and M.P. Zanna), 53–75. Hillsdale, NJ: Erlbaum.

Selye, H. (1956). *The Stress of Life*. New York, NY: McGraw-Hill.

Sentse, M., Dijkstra, J.K., Lindenberg, S. et al. (2010). The delicate balance between parental protection, unsupervised wandering, and adolescents' autonomy and its relation with antisocial behavior. The TRAILS study. *International Journal of Behavioral Development* 34: 159–167.

Sevenant, M. and Antrop, M. (2010). The use of latent classes to identify individual differences in the importance of landscape dimensions for aesthetic preference. *Land Use Policy* 27 (3): 827–842.

Seyranian, V. (2014). Social identity framing communication strategies for mobilizing social change. *The Leadership Quarterly* 25: 468–486.

Shanahan, D.F., Bush, R., Gaston, K.J. et al. (2016). Health benefits from nature experiences depend on dose. *Scientific Reports* 6: 28551.

Shang, H. and Bishop, I. (2000). Visual thresholds for detection, recognition and visual impact in landscape settings. *Journal of Environmental Psychology* 20: 125–140.

Shenassa, E.D., Daskalakis, C., Liebhaber, A. et al. (2007). Dampness and mold in the home and depression: an examination of mold-related illnesses and perceived control of one's home as possible depression pathways. *American Journal of Public Health* 97: 1893–1899.

Sheppard, S. and Picard, P. (2006). Visual-quality impacts of forest pest activity at the landscape level: a synthesis of published knowledge and research needs. *Landscape and Urban Planning* 77 (4): 321–342.

Sherif, M. (1936). *The Psychology of Social Norms*. Oxford, England: Harper.

Sherif, M. (1965). *The Psychology of Social Norms*. New York, NY: Octagon Books, Inc.

Shiraishi, M., Washio, Y., Takayama, C., et al. (2009). Using individual, social and economic persuasion techniques to reduce CO2 emissions in a family setting. *Conference proceedings of Persuasive 2009, Claremont, USA* (article no. 13). Heidelberg: Springer.

Shultz, W. and Tabanico, J. (2007). Self, identity, and the natural environment: exploring implicit connections with nature. *Journal of Applied Social Psychology* 37 (6): 1219–1247.

Shwartz, A., Turbé, A., Simon, L., and Julliard, R. (2014). Enhancing urban biodiversity and its influence on city-dwellers: an experiment. *Biological Conservation* 171: 82–90.

Siddiqui, R.N. and Pandey, J. (2003). Coping with environmental stressors by urban slum dwellers. *Environment and Behavior* 35: 589–604.

Sidman, M. (1989). *Coercion and its Fallout*. Boston, MA: Authors Cooperative.

Simion, F., Regolin, L., and Bulf, H. (2008). A predisposition for biological motion in the newborn baby. *Proceedings of the National Academy of Sciences of the USA* 105 (2): 809–813.

Sirgy, M.J. (1982). Self-concept in consumer behavior: a critical review. *Journal of Consumer Research* 9: 287–300.

Sirgy, M.J. and Johar, J.S. (1999). Toward an integrated model of self-congruity and functional congruity. *European Advances in Consumer Research* 4: 252–256.

Skinner, B.F. (1974). *About Behaviorism*. New York, NY: Appleton-Century-Crofts.

Sklenicka, P. and Molnarova, K. (2010). Visual perception of habitats adopted for postmining landscape rehabilitation. *Environmental Management* 46 (3): 424–435.

Sloot, D., Jans, L., and Steg, L. (2017a). The potential of environmental community initiatives - a social psychological perspective. In: *Outlooks on Applying Environmental Psychology Research* (ed. A. Römpke, G. Reese, I. Fritsche, et al.), 27–34. Bonn: BfN-Skripten.

Sloot, D., Jans, L., and Steg, L.(2017b). Community Energy Initiatives as Facilitators of Sustainable Energy Intentions: The Role of Initiative Involvement on Household and Community Intentions. Manuscript in progress.

Slovic, P. (1987). Perception of risk. *Science* 236: 280–285.

Slovic, P. (1999). Trust, emotion, sex, politics, and science: surveying the risk-assessment battle field. *Risk Analysis* 19: 689–701.

Smith, N. and Leiserowitz, A.A. (2012). The rise of global warming skepticism: exploring affective image associations in the United States over time. *Risk Analysis* 32 (6): 1021–1032.

Smith, N. and Leiserowitz, A. (2014). The role of emotion in global warming policy support and opposition. *Risk Analysis* 34 (5): 937–948.

Smith, J. and Louis, W. (2008). Do as we say and as we do: the interplay of descriptive and injunctive group norms in the attitude-behaviour relationship. *British Journal of Social Psychology* 47: 647–666.

Smith, L.G.E. and Postmes, T. (2009). Intra-group interaction and the development of norms which promote inter-group hostility. *European Journal of Social Psychology* 39 (1): 130–144.

Smith, S.M., Haugtvedt, C.P., and Petty, R.E. (1994). Attitudes and recycling: does the measurement of affect enhance behavioral prediction? *Psychology and Marketing* 11: 359–374.

Smith, J.R., Louis, W.R., Terry, D.J. et al. (2012). Congruent or conflicted? The impact of injunctive and descriptive norms on environmental intentions. *Journal of Environmental Psychology* 32 (4): 353–361.

Solari, C.D. and Mare, R.D. (2012). Housing crowding effects on children's wellbeing. *Social Science Research* 41 (2): 464–476.

Sommer, R. (1983). *Social Design: Creating Buildings with People in Mind*. Englewood Cliffs, NJ: Prentice-Hall.

Sonderskov, K.M. and Dinesen, P.T. (2016). Trusting the state, trusting each other? The effect of institutional trust on social trust. *Political Behavior* 38: 179–202.

Song, H. and Schwarz, N. (2009). If it's difficult to pronounce, it must be risky. *Psychological Science* 20 (2): 135–138.

Sreetheran, M. and van den Bosch, C.C.K. (2014). A socio-ecological exploration of fear of crime in urban green spaces – a systematic review. *Urban Forestry & Urban Greening* 13 (1): 1–18.

Staats, H.J., Wit, A.P., and Midden, C.Y.H. (1996). Communicating the greenhouse effect to the public: evaluation of a mass media campaign from a social dilemma perspective. *Journal of Environmental Management* 45: 189–203.

Staats, H., Harland, P., and Wilke, H.A.M. (2004). Effecting durable change. A team approach to improve environmental behavior in the household. *Environment and Behavior* 36: 341–367.

Stamps, A.E. (1996). People and places: Variance components of environmental preferences. *Perceptual and Motor Skills* 82,: 323–334.

Stamps, A.E. and Nasar, J.L. (1997). Design review and public preferences: effects of geographical location, public consensus, sensation seeking, and architectural styles. *Journal of Environmental Psychology* 17: 11–32.

Staufenbiel, S.M., Penninx, B.W., Spijker, A.T. et al. (2013). Hair cortisol, stress exposure, and mental health in humans: a systematic review. *Psychoneuroendocrinology* 38 (8): 1220–1235.

Steele, F. (1981). *The Sense of Place*. Boston: CBI Publishing Company.

Steg, L. (2003). Can public transport compete with the private car? *IATSS Research* 27 (2): 27–35.

Steg, L. (2005). Car use: lust and must. Instrumental, symbolic and affective motives for car use. *Transportation Research Part A: Policy and Practice* 39: 147–162.

Steg, L. and De Groot, J.I.M. (2010). Explaining prosocial intentions: testing causal relationships in the norm activation model. *British Journal of Social Psychology* 49: 725–743.

Steg, L. and De Groot, J.I.M. (2012). Environmental values. In: *The Oxford Handbook of Environmental and Conservation Psychology* (ed. S. Clayton), 81–92. New York, NY: Oxford University Press.

Steg, L. and Gifford, R. (2005). Sustainable transportation and quality of life. *Journal of Transport Geography* 13: 59–69.

Steg, L., Dreijerink, L., and Abrahamse, W. (2005). Factors influencing the acceptability of energy policies: testing VBN theory. *Journal of Environmental Psychology* 25: 415–425.

Steg, L., De Groot, J., Forward, S. et al. (2007). Assessing life quality in transport planning and urban design. In: *Land use and transport: European research towards integrated policies* (ed. S. Marshall and D. Banister), 215–241. Amsterdam: Elsevier.

Steg, L., De Groot, J.I.M., Dreijerink, L. et al. (2011). General antecedents of environmental behavior: relationships between values, worldviews, environmental concern, and environmental behavior. *Society and Natural Resources* 24 (4): 349–367.

Steg, L., Bolderdijk, J.W., Keizer, K.E., and Perlaviciute, G. (2014a). An integrated framework for encouraging pro-environmental behaviour: the role of values, situational factors and goals. *Journal of Environmental Psychology* 38: 104–115.

Steg, L., Perlaviciute, G., Van der Werff, E., and Lurvink, J. (2014b). The significance of hedonic values for environmentally relevant attitudes, preferences, and actions. *Environment and Behavior* 46 (2): 163–192.

Steg, L., Lindenberg, S., and Keizer, K. (2016). Intrinsic motivation, norms and environmental behaviour: the dynamics of overarching goals. *International Review of Environmental and Resource Economics* 9 (1–2): 179–207.

Steg, L. and Vlek, C. (2009). Social science and environmental behaviour. In: *Principles of Environmental Sciences* (ed. J.J. Boersma and L. Reijnders), 97–142. New York, NY: Springer-Verlag.

Steg, L., Vlek, C., and Slotegraaf, G. (2001). Instrumental-reasoned and symbolic-affective motives for using a motor car. *Transportation Research Part F: Traffic Psychology and Behaviour* 4: 151–169.

Steptoe, A. and Kivimäki, M. (2013). Stress and cardiovascular disease: an update on current knowledge. *Annual Review of Public Health* 34: 337–354.

Stern, P.C. (2000). Toward a coherent theory of environmentally significant behavior. *Journal of Social Issues* 56 (3): 407–424.

Stern, P.C., Dietz, T., Abel, T. et al. (1999). A value-belief-norm theory of support for social movements: the case of environmentalism. *Human Ecology Review* 6: 81–97.

Stern, P.C., Dietz, T., and Guagnano, G.A. (1998). A brief inventory of values. *Educational and Psychological Measurement* 58: 984–1001.

Stern, P.C., Dietz, T., Kalof, L., and Guagnano, G.A. (1995). Values, beliefs, and proenvironmental action: attitude formation toward emergent attitude objects. *Journal of Applied Social Psychology* 25: 1611–1636.

Stern, P.C., Dietz, T., Ruttan, V.W. et al. (eds.) (1997). *Environmentally Significant Consumption*. Washington, DC: National Academy Press.

Stern, P.C. and Gardner, G.T. (1981). Psychological research and energy policy. *American Psychologist* 36: 329–342.

Stets, J.E. and Burke, P.J. (2000). Identity theory and social identity theory. *Social Psychology Quarterly* 63: 224–237.

Stokols, D. (1972). On the distinction between density and crowding. *Psychological Review* 79: 275–277.

Stokols, D. (ed.) (1977). *Perspectives on Environment and Behavior*. New York, NY: Plenum Press.

Stokols, D. (1978). Environmental psychology. *Annual Review of Psychology* 29: 253–295.

Strack, F. and Deutsch, R. (2004). Reflective and impulsive determinants of social behavior. *Personality and Social Psychology Review* 8: 220–247.

Stradling, S.G., Meadows, M.L., and Beatty, S. (1999). *Factors Affecting Car Use Choices*. Edinburgh: Transport Research Institute, Napier University.

Strife, S. and Downey, L. (2009). Childhood development and access to nature: a new direction for environmental inequality research. *Organization & Environment* 22 (1): 99–122.

Strumse, E. (1996). Demographic differences in the visual preferences for agrarian land-scapes in Western Norway. *Journal of Environmental Psychology* 16: 17–31.

Stryker, S. and Burke, P.J. (2000). The past, present, and future of an identity theory. *Social Psychology Quarterly* 63: 284–297.

Su, M., Tan, Y.Y., Liu, Q.M. et al. (2014). Association between perceived urban built environment attributes and leisure-time physical activity among adults in Hangzhou, China. *Preventive Medicine* 66: 60–64.

Subbaraman, R., Nolan, L., Shitole, T. et al. (2014). The psychological toll of slum living in Mumbai, India: a mixed methods study. *Social Science & Medicine* 119: 155–169.

Suls, J. and Wheeler, L. (2000). A selective history of classic and neo-social compar- ison theory. In: *Handbook of Social Comparison: Theory and Research* (ed. J. Suls and L. Wheeler). New York, NY: Kluwer Academic.

Suls, J. and Wheeler, L. (2007). Psychological magnetism: a brief history of assimilation and contrast in psychology. In: *Assimilation and Contrast in Social Psychology* (ed. D.A. Stapel and J. Suls), 9–44. New York, NY: Psychology Press.

Sussman, R. and Gifford, R. (2012). Please turn off the lights: the effectiveness of visual prompts. *Applied Ergonomics* 43 (3): 596–603.

Sussman, R. and Gifford, R. (2013). Be the change you want to see. Modeling food composting in public places. *Environment and Behavior* 45 (3): 323–343.

Swim, J.K. and Bloodhart, B. (2018). The Intergroup foundations of climate justice. *Group Processes & Intergroup Relations* 21 (3): 472–496. doi: 10.1177/1368430217745366.

Swim, J.K. and Geiger, N. (2017). From alarmed to dismissive: self-categorization into the six Americas audience segments. *Environmental Communication*.

Swim, J.K. and Geiger, N. (2018). The gendered nature of stereotypes about climate change opinion groups. *Group Processes & Intergroup Relations* 21 (3): 438–456. doi: 10.1177/1368430217747406.

Tajfel, H. and Turner, J. (1979). An integrative theory of intergroup conflict. In: *The Social Psychology of Intergroup Relations* (ed. W.G. Austin and S. Worchel), 33–47. Monterey, CA: Brooks/Cole.

Talbot, J. and Frost, J.L. (1989). Magical playscapes. *Childhood Education* 66 (1): 11–19.

Tamas, A., Tobias, R., and Mosler, H.-J. (2009). Promotion of solar water disinfection: comparing the effectiveness of different strategies in a longitudinal field study in Bolivia. *Health Communication* 24 (8): 711–722.

Tanner, T. (1980). Significant life experiences: a new research area in environmental education. *The Journal of Environmental Education* 11 (4): 20–24.

Tanner, C. and Medin, D.L. (2004). Protected values: no omission bias and no framing effects. *Psychonomic Bulletin & Review* 11: 185–191.

Tanner, C., Medin, D.L., and Iliev, R. (2008). Influence of deontological vs. consequentialist orientations on act choices and framing effects: when principles are more important than consequences. *European Journal of Social Psychology* 38: 757–769.

Tapper, K., Jiga-Boy, G.M., Haddock, G. et al. (2012). Motivating health behaviour change: provision of cognitive support for health values. *The Lancet* 380: S71.

Taufik, D., Bolderdijk, J.W., and Steg, L. (2015). Acting green elicits a literal 'warm-glow'. *Nature Climate Change* 5: 37–40.

Taufik, D., Bolderdijk, J.W., and Steg, L. (2016). Going green? The relative importance of feelings over calculation in driving environmental intent in the Netherlands and the United States. *Energy Research & Social Science* 2: 52–62.

Taylor, P.W. (1981). The ethics of respect for nature. *Environmental Ethics* 3: 197–218.

Taylor, R.P. and Spehar, B. (2016). Fractal fluency: an intimate relationship between the brain and processing of fractal stimuli. In: *The Fractal Geometry of the Brain* (ed. A. Di Ieva), 485–496. New York, NY: Springer.

Teasdale, B. and Silver, E. (2009). Neighborhoods and self-control: toward an expanded view of socialization. *Social Problems* 56: 205–222.

Teel, T.L. and Manfredo, M.J. (2010). Understanding the diversity of public interests in wildlife conservation. *Conservation Biology* 24 (1): 128–139.

Teel, T.L., Manfredo, M.J., Jensen, F.S. et al. (2010). Understanding the cognitive basis for human-wildlife relationships as a key to successful protected area management. *International Journal of Sociology* 40 (3): 104–123.

Tenbrunsel, A. and Messick, D. (1999). Sanctioning systems, decision frames, and cooperation. *Administrative Science Quarterly* 44: 684–707.

Tenngart Ivarsson, C. and Hagerhall, C.M. (2008). The perceived restorativeness of gardens: assessing the restorativeness of a mixed built and natural scene type. *Urban Forestry & Urban Greening* 7 (2): 107–118.

Tetlock, P.E., Kristel, O.V., Elson, S.B. et al. (2000). The psychology of the unthinkable: taboo trade-offs, forbidden base rates, and heretical counterfactuals. *Journal of Personality and Social Psychology* 78: 853–870.

Thøgersen, J. (2006). Norms for environmentally responsible behaviour: an extended taxonomy. *Journal of Environmental Psychology* 26: 247–336.

Thøgersen, J. and Møller, B. (2008). Breaking car use habits: the effectiveness of a free one-month travelcard. *Transportation* 35: 329–345.

Thøgersen, J. and Ölander, F. (2002). Human values and the emergence of a sustainable consumption pattern: a panel study. *Journal of Economic Psychology* 23: 605–630.

Thøgersen, J. and Ölander, F. (2006). To what degree are environmentally beneficial choices reflective of a general conservation stance? *Environment and Behavior* 38: 550–569.

Thøgersen, J., Zhou, Y., and Huang, G. (2016). How stable is the value basis for organic food consumption in China? *Journal of Cleaner Production* 134: 214–224.

Thomas, E.F., McGarty, C., and Mavor, K. (2016). Group interaction as the crucible of social identity formation: a glimpse at the foundations of social identities for collective action. *Group Processes & Intergroup Relations* 19 (2): 137–151.

Thomson, H., Thomas, S., Sellstrom, E., and Petticrew, M. (2013). Housing improvements for health and associated socio-economic outcomes. *Cochrane Database of Systematic Reviews* 2: CD008657.

Thwaites, K. and Simkins, I. (2007). *Experiential Landscape*. London: Routledge.

Tjoelker, K. (2011). *Residential quality of life in the neighbourhoods of Friesland*. Unpublished Master thesis, Faculty of Social and Behavioral Sciences, University of Groningen, Groningen.

Tobias, R. (2009). Changing behaviour by memory aids: a social psychological model of prospective memory and habit development tested with dynamic field data. *Psychological Review* 116: 408–438.

Tomei, G., Fioravanti, M., Cerratti, D. et al. (2010). Occupational exposure to noise and the cardiovascular system: a meta-analysis. *Science of the Total Environment* 408: 681–689.

Triandis, H.C. (1977). *Interpersonal Behavior*. Monterey, CA: Brooks/Cole.

Trope, Y. and Liberman, N. (2010). Construal-level theory of psychological distance. *Psychological Review* 117: 440–463.

Truelove, H.B., Carrico, A.R., Weber, E.U. et al. (2014). Positive and negative spillover of pro-environmental behavior: an integrative review and theoretical framework. *Global Environmental Change* 29: 127–138.

Tuan, Y. (1974). *Topophilia*. Englewood Cliffs: Prentice-Hall.

Turner, J.C. (1985). Social categorization and the selfconcept: a social cognitive theory of group behaviour. In: *Advances in Group Processes: Theory and Research*, vol. 2 (ed. E.J. Lawler), 77–122. Greenwich, CT: JAI Press.

Turner, J.C. (1991). *Social Influence*. Belmont, CA: Thomson Brooks/Cole.

Turner, J.C., Hogg, M.A., Oakes, P.J. et al. (1987). *Rediscovering the Social Group: A Self-Categorization Theory*. Oxford, UK: Basil Blackwell.

Tveit, M.S. (2009). Indicators of visual scale as predictors of landscape preference: a comparison between groups. *Journal of Environmental Management* 90 (9): 2882–2888.

Tveit, M., Ode, Å., and Fry, G. (2006). Key concepts in a framework for analysing visual landscape character. *Landscape Research* 31 (3): 229–256.

Tversky, A. and Kahneman, D. (1974). Judgment under uncertainty: heuristics and biases. *Science* 185: 1124–1131.

Tversky, A. and Kahneman, D. (1981). The framing of decisions and the psychology of choice. *Science* 211: 453–458.

Twigger-Ross, C. and Uzzell, D. (1996). Place and identity processes. *Journal of Environmental Psychology* 16: 205–220.

Tyler, T.R. (2000). Social justice: outcome and procedure. *International Journal of Psychology* 35: 117–125.

Tyler, T. and Dawes, R.M. (1993). Fairness in groups: comparing the self-interest and social identity perspectives. In: *Psychological Perspectives on Justice: Theory and Applications* (ed. J. Baron), 87–108. New York, NY: Cambridge University Press.

Tyler, T.R. and Degoey, P. (1995). Collective restraint in social dilemmas. Procedural justice and social identification effects on support for authorities. *Journal of Personality and Social Psychology* 69: 482–497.

Ulrich, R.S. (1983). Aesthetic and affective response to natural environment. In: *Human Behavior and Environment: Advances in Theory and Research*, vol. 6 (ed. I. Altman and J.F. Wohlwill), 85–125. New York, NY: Plenum Press.

Ulrich, R.S. (1984). View through a window may influence recovery from surgery. *Science* 224 (4647): 420–421.

Ulrich, R.S. (1986). Human responses to vegetation and landscapes. *Landscape and Urban Planning* 13: 29–44.

Ulrich, R.S. (1993a). Aesthetic and affective responses to natural environment. In: *Human Behavior and the Environment*, vol. 6 (ed. I. Altman and J.F. Wohlwill), 85–125. New York, NY: Plenum.

Ulrich, R.S. (1993b). Biophilia, biophobia and natural landscapes. In: *The Biophilia Hypothesis* (ed. S.R. Kellert and E.O. Wilson), 73–137. Washington, DC: Island Press.

Ulrich, R.S. (1999). Effects of gardens on health outcomes: theory and research. In: *Healing Gardens: Therapeutic Benefits and Design Recommendations* (ed. C. Cooper-Marcus and M. Barnes), 27–86. New York, NY: Wiley.

Ulrich, R., Quan, X., Zimring, C. et al. (2004). *The Role of the Physical Environment in the Hospital of the 21st Century*. Martinez, CA: The Center for Health Design.

Ulrich, R.S., Simons, R.F., Losito, B.D. et al. (1991). Stress recovery during exposure to natural and urban environments. *Journal of Environmental Psychology* 11 (3): 201–230.

Ulrich, R.S., Zimring, C., Zhu, X. et al. (2008). A review of the research literature on evidence-based healthcare design. *Health Environments Research and Design Journal* 1 (13): 61–125.

UNFPA (2013). *Population Dynamics in the Post-2015 Development Agenda*. New York, NY: UNFPA, UNDESA, UN-HABITAT, IOM.

Unger, E., Diez-Roux, A.V., Lloyd-Jones, D.M. et al. (2014). Association of neighborhood characteristics with cardiovascular health in the multi-ethnic study of atherosclerosis. *Circulation: Cardiovascular Quality and Outcomes* 7 (4): 524–531.

UN-HABITAT. (2014). *October 6 World Habitat Day background paper*. Nairobi, Kenya.

United Nations Human Settlement Program (2001). *Urban environment—waste, thematic report of the general assembly*. Special session for an overall review & appraisal of the implementation of the Habitat Agenda, New York, 6–8 June, 2001. Retrieved from http://www.un.org/ga/Istanbul+5/70.pdf

Unsworth, K.L. and Fielding, K.S. (2014). It's political: how the salience of one's political identity changes climate change beliefs and policy support. *Global Environmental Change* 27: 131–137.

Urbina-Soria, J. and Flores-Cano, O. (2010). Movilidad en la zona metropolitana de la ciudad de México: Preferencias y opiniones de los usuarios. [Mobility in the Metropolitan Area of Mexico City: Users' Preferences and Opinions]

Urbina-Soria, J. and Martínez, J. (eds.) (2006). *Más allá del cambio climático: Las dimensiones psicosociales del cambio ambiental global*. Mexico: Secretaría de Medio Ambiente-Instituto Nacional de Ecología, Universidad Nacional Autónoma de Mëxico-Facultad de Psicología.

Urbina-Soria, J. and Ortega-Andeane, P. (1991). El estudio de las interacciones ambiente-comportamiento en México: Evolución y perspectiva [The study of environmental behaviour interactions in Mexico: evolution and perspective]. In: *La investigación del comportamiento en México [Behaviour Research in Mexico]* (ed. V. Colotla Espinoza), 371–378. Mexico City: National University of Mexico.

Urbina-Soria, J., Flores-Cano, O., and Andrade, R.J. (2010). Percepción de riesgos por el consumo y disposición de pilas primarias y secundarias en México. [Perception of risks by the consumption and disposition of primary and secondary batteries in Mexico]. In: *La psicología social en México*, vol. XIII (ed. S. Rivera, R. Diaz-Loving, I. Reyes, et al.), 1295–1301. [Social psychology in Mexico]. Mexico City: AMEPSO.

Vaid, U. and Evans, G.W. (2016). Housing quality and health: an evaluation of slum rehabilitation in India. *Environment and Behavior*. Advance online publication.

Valadez, R.A. and Landa, D.P. (2007). Health, environment and development: brief reflections. *Romanian Journal of Applied Psychology* 1: 69–76.

Van de Kragt, A., Orbell, J., and Dawes, R.M. (1983). The minimal contributing set as a solution to public goods problems. *American Political Science Review* 77: 112–122.

Van den Berg, A.E. (2012). *Buiten is gezond. Onderzoeksrapport publieksenquête De Friesland Zorgverzekeraar. [The healthy outdoors. Report of public survey by De Friesland health insurance company]*. Retrieved from http://www.agnesvandenberg.nl/Buiten_is_gezond.pdf.

Van den Berg, A.E., Hartig, T., and Staats, H. (2007a). Preference for nature in urbanized societies: stress, restoration, and the pursuit of sustainability. *Journal of Social Issues* 63 (1): 79–96.

Van den Berg, A.E., Joye, Y., and Koole, S.L. (2016a). Why viewing nature is more fascinating and restorative than viewing buildings: a closer look at perceived complexity. *Urban Forestry & Urban Greening* 20: 397–401.

Van den Berg, A.E., Koenis, R., and Van den Berg, M.M.H.E. (2007b). *Spelen in het groen: Effecten van een bezoek aan een natuurspeeltuin op het speelgedrag, de lichamelijke activiteit, de concentratie en de stemming van kinderen [Playing in Nature: Effects of a Visit to a Natural Playground on Children's Play Behaviour, Physical Activity, Concentration and Mood]*. Rapport 1600. Wageningen: Alterra.

Van den Berg, A.E. and Koole, S.L. (2006). New wilderness in the Netherlands: an investigation of visual preferences for nature development landscapes. *Landscape and Urban Planning* 78 (4): 362–372.

Van den Berg, A.E. and Ter Heijne, M. (2005). Fear versus fascination: an exploration of emotional responses to natural threats. *Journal of Environmental Psychology* 25 (3): 261–272.

Van den Berg, A. and Van den Berg, C. (2011). A comparison of children with ADHD in a natural and built setting. *Child: Care, Health and Development* 37 (3): 430–439.

Van den Berg, A.E., Vlek, C.A.J., and Coeterier, J.F. (1998). Group differences in the aesthetic evaluation of nature development plans: a multilevel approach. *Journal of Environmental Psychology* 18 (2): 141–157.

Van den Berg, A.E., Van Winsum-Westra, M., De Vries, S., and Van Dillen, S.M.E. (2010). Allotment gardening and health: a comparative survey among allotment gardeners and their neighbors without an allotment. *Environmental Health* 9: 74–86.

Van den Berg, M., Wendel-Vos, W., Van Poppel, M. et al. (2015). Health benefits of green spaces in the living environment: a systematic review of epidemiological studies. *Urban Forestry & Urban Greening* 14 (4): 806–816.

Van den Berg, A.E., Wesselius, J.E., Maas, J., and Tanja-Dijkstra, K. (2016b). Green walls for a restorative classroom environment: a controlled evaluation study. *Environment and Behavior* 49 (7): doi: 10.1177/0013916516667976.

Van den Bergh, B., Dewitte, S., and Warlop, L. (2008). Bikinis instigate generalized impatience in intertemporal choice. *Journal of Consumer Research* 35: 85–97.

Van den Born, R.J.G. (2008). Rethinking nature: public visions in the Netherlands. *Environmental Values* 17: 83–109.

Van der Linden, S.L., Leiserowitz, A.A., Feinberg, G.D., and Maibach, E.W. (2015). The scientific consensus on climate change as a gateway belief: experimental evidence. *PLoS One* 10 (2): e0118489.

Van der Werff, E., Steg, L., and Keizer, K. (2013a). It is a moral issue: the relationship between environmental self-identity, obligation-based intrinsic motivation and pro-environmental behaviour. *Global Environmental Change* 23 (5): 1258–1265.

Van der Werff, E., Steg, L., and Keizer, K. (2013b). The value of environmental self-identity: the relationship between biospheric values, environmental self-identity and environmental preferences, intentions and behaviour. *Journal of Environmental Psychology* 34: 55–63.

Van der Werff, E., Steg, L., and Keizer, K. (2014a). I am what I am, by looking past the present the influence of biospheric values and past behavior on environmental self-identity. *Environment and Behavior* 46 (5): 626–657.

Van der Werff, E., Steg, L., and Keizer, K. (2014b). Follow the signal: when past pro-environmental actions signal who you are. *Journal of Environmental Psychology* 40: 273–282.

Van Dillen, S.M.E., De Vries, S., Groenewegen, P.P., and Spreeuwenberg, P. (2011). Streetscape greenery and health: stress, social cohesion and physical activity as mediators. *Social Science and Medicine* 94: 26–33.

Van Doorn, J. and Verhoef, P.C. (2015). Drivers of and barriers to organic purchase behavior. *Journal of Retailing* 91 (3): 436–450.

Van Houwelingen, J.H. and Van Raaij, F.W. (1989). The effect of goal-setting and daily electronic feedback on in-home energy use. *Journal of Consumer Research* 16: 98–105.

Van Kempen, E. and Babisch, W. (2012). The quantitative relationship between road traffic noise and hypertension: a meta-analysis. *Journal of Hypertension* 30 (6): 1075–1086.

Van Kempen, E., Van Kamp, I., Fischer, P. et al. (2006). Noise exposure and children's blood pressure and heart rate: the RANCH project. *Occupational and Environmental Medicine* 63 (9): 632–639.

Van Kempen, E., Van Kamp, I., Lebret, E. et al. (2010). Neurobehavioral effects of transportation noise in primary schoolchildren: a cross-sectional study. *Environmental Health* 9 (25): 2–13.

Van Lange, P.A.M., Liebrand, W.B.G., Messick, D.M., and Wilke, H.A.M. (1992). Social dilemmas: the state of art; introduction and literature review. In: *Social Dilemmas: Theoretical Issues and Research Findings* (ed. W.B.G. Liebrand, D.M. Messick and H.A.M. Wilke), 3–28. Oxford: Pergamon.

Van Vliet, W. (1987). Housing in the third world. *Environment and Behavior* 19: 267–285.

Van Vugt, M. (2001). Community identification moderating the impact of financial incentives in a natural social dilemma: water conservation. *Personality and Social Psychology Bulletin* 27 (11): 1440–1449.

Van Vugt, M., John, P., Dowding, K., and Van Dijk, E. (2003). The exit of residential mobility or the voice of political action? Strategies for problem solving in residential communities. *Journal of Applied Social Psychology* 33 (2): 321–338.

Vaske, J.J., Jacobs, M.H., and Sijtsma, M.T.J. (2011). Wildlife value orientations and demographics in the Netherlands. *European Journal of Wildlife Research* 57 (6): 1179–1187.

Veitch, J., Salmon, J., and Ball, K. (2010). Individual, social and physical environmental correlates of children's active free-play: a cross-sectional study. *International Journal of Behavioral Nutrition and Physical Activity* 7 (1): 11.

Velarde, M.D., Fry, G., and Tveit, M. (2007). Health effects of viewing landscapes: landscape types in environmental psychology. *Urban Forestry & Urban Greening* 6 (4): 199–212.

Velicer, W.F., Prochaska, J.O., Fava, J.L. et al. (1998). Smoking cessation and stress management: applications of the Transtheoretical model of behavior change. *Homeostasis* 38: 216–233.

Venhoeven, L. (2016). *A look on the bright side of an environmentally-friendly life. Whether and why acting environmentally-friendly can contribute to well-being.* PhD thesis, University of Groningen, Faculty of Behavioural and Social Sciences.

Venhoeven, L.A., Bolderdijk, J.W., and Steg, L. (2013). Explaining the paradox: how pro-environmental behaviour can both thwart and foster well-being. *Sustainability* 5: 1372–1386.

Venhoeven, L.A., Bolderdijk, J.W., and Steg, L. (2016). Why acting environmentally friendly feels good: exploring the role of self-image. *Frontiers in Psychology* 7: 1846.

Verbeek, P. and Slob, A. (2006). Analyzing the relations between technologies and user behaviour: toward a conceptual framework. In: *User Behaviour and Technology Development* (ed. P. Verbeek and A. Slob), 385–399. Dordrecht: Springer.

Verberne, M.F., Ham, J., and Midden, J.H. (2015). Trusting a virtual driver that looks, acts, and thinks like you. *Human Factors* 57 (5): 895–909.

Verboom, J. and De Vries, S. (2006). *Topervaringen van kinderen met de natuur [Impressive Childhood Nature Experiences].* Wageningen: Alterra.

Verderber, S. and Moore, G.T. (1977). Building imagery: a comparative study of environmental cognition. *Man-Environment Systems* 7: 332–341.

Verma, M., Rahul, T.M., Reddy, P.V., and Verma, A. (2016). The factors influencing bicycling in the Bangalore city. *Transportation Research Part A: Policy and Practice* 89: 29–40.

Verplanken, B. (2006). Beyond frequency: habit as mental construct. *British Journal of Social Psychology* 45: 639–656.

Verplanken, B. and Aarts, H. (1999). Habit, attitude, and planned behaviour: is habit an empty construct or an interesting case of automaticity? *European Review of Social Psychology* 10: 101–134.

Verplanken, B., Aarts, H., van Knippenberg, A., and van Knippenberg, C. (1994). Attitude versus general habit: antecedents of travel mode choice. *Journal of Applied Social Psychology* 24 (4): 285–300.

Verplanken, B., Aarts, H., and van Knippenberg, A. (1997). Habit, information acquisition, and the process of making travel mode choices. *European Journal of Social Psychology* 27: 539–560.

Verplanken, B., Aarts, H., van Knippenberg, A., and Moonen, A. (1998). Habit versus planned behaviour: a field experiment. *British Journal of Social Psychology* 37 (1): 111–128.

Verplanken, B. and Holland, R.W. (2002). Motivated decision making: effects of activation and self-centrality of values on choices and behaviour. *Journal of Personality and Social Psychology* 82: 434–447.

Verplanken, B. and Orbell, S. (2006). Reflections on past behaviour: a self-report index of habit strength. *Journal of Applied Social Psychology* 33: 1313–1330.

Verplanken, B. and Roy, D. (2016). Empowering interventions to promote sustainable lifestyles: testing the habit discontinuity hypothesis in a field experiment. *Journal of Environmental Psychology* 45: 127–134.

Verplanken, B. and Wood, W. (2006). Interventions to break and create consumer habits. *American Marketing Association* 25 (1): 90–103.

Vikan, A., Camino, C., Biaggio, A., and Nordvik, H. (2007). Endorsement of the new ecological paradigm: a comparison of two Brazilian samples and one Norwegian sample. *Environment and Behavior* 39: 217–228.

Vlek, C. (2000). Essential psychology for environmental policy making. *International Journal of Psychology* 35: 153–167.

Vohs, K.D. (2015). Money priming can change people's thoughts, feelings, motivations, and behaviors: an update on 10 years of experiments. *Journal of Experimental Psychology: General* 144 (4): 86–93.

Volpp, K.G., John, L.K., Troxel, A.B. et al. (2008). Financial incentive-based approaches for weight loss: a randomized trial. *JAMA: The Journal of The American Medical Association* 300: 2631–2637.

Vos, P.E., Maiheu, B., Vankerkom, J., and Janssen, S. (2013). Improving local air quality in cities: to tree or not to tree? *Environmental Pollution* 183: 113–122.

Vossen, S., Ham, J., and Midden, C. (2010). What makes social feedback from a robot work? Disentangling the effect of speech, physical appearance and evaluation. *Conference proceedings of Persuasive 2010* (pp. 52–57). Heidelberg: Springer.

Walbe-Ornstein, S. (1997). Post-occupancy evaluation performed in elementary and high schools of Greater São Paulo, Brazil: the occupants and the quality of the school environment. *Environment and Behavior* 2: 236–263.

Walker, I., Thomas, G.O., and Verplanken, B. (2015). Old habits die hard: travel habit formation and decay during an office relocation. *Environment and Behavior* 47 (10): 1089–1106.

Walzer, M. (1983). *Spheres of Justice: A Defence of Pluralism and Equality*. New York, NY: Basic Books.

Wang, Z., Zhang, B., Yin, J., and Zhang, Y. (2011). Determinants and policy implications for household electricity-saving behaviour: evidence from Beijing, China. *Energy Policy* 39 (6): 3550–3557.

Wang, Y., Chau, C.K., Ng, W.Y., and Leung, T.M. (2016). A review on the effects of physical built environment attributes on enhancing walking and cycling activity levels within residential neighborhoods. *Cities* 50: 1–15.

Wapner, S. (1995). Toward integration: environmental psychology in relation to other subfields of psychology. *Environment and Behavior* 27: 9–32.

Ward, L.M. (1977). Multidimensional scaling of the molar physical environment. *Multivariate Behavioral Research* 12: 23–42.

Watson, D., Clark, L.A., and Tellegen, A. (1988). Development and validation of brief measures of positive and negative affect: the PANAS scales. *Journal of Personality and Social Psychology* 54: 1063–1070.

Weigel, R. and Weigel, J. (1978). Environmental concern. The development of a measure. *Environment and Behavior* 10: 3–14.

Weiner, B. (1995). *Judgments of Responsibility: A Foundation for a Theory of Social Conduct*. New York, NY: The Guilford Press.

Weinstein, N.D. (1980). Unrealistic optimism about future life events. *Journal of Personality and Social Psychology* 39: 806–820.

Weinstein, N.D., Rothman, A.J., and Sutton, S.R. (1998). Stages theories of health behavior. *Health Psychology* 17: 290–299.

Weinstein, N.D., Sandman, P.M., and Roberts, N.E. (1990). Determinants of self-protective behavior: home radon testing. *Journal of Applied Social Psychology* 20: 783–801.

Weisenfeld, E. (1994). *Contribuciones iberoamericanas a la psicología ambiental. [Latin American Contributions to Environmental Psychology]*. Caracas: Central University of Venezuela.

Weisenfeld, E. (1997). Construction of the meaning of a barrio house: the case of a Caracas barrio. *Environment and Behavior* 29: 34–63.

Wells, N.M. (2000). At home with nature: effects of 'greenness' on children's cognitive functioning. *Environment and Behavior* 32 (6): 775–795.

Wells, N.M. and Evans, G.W. (2003). Nearby nature: a buffer of life stress among rural children. *Environment and Behavior* 35 (3): 311–330.

Wells, N.M. and Lekies, K.S. (2006). Nature and the life course: pathways from childhood nature experiences to adult environmentalism. *Children Youth and Environments* 16 (1): 1–24.

Welsh, B.C. and Farrington, D.P. (2007). Improved street lighting and crime prevention. Report for The Swedish National Council for Crime Prevention. Stockholm Swedish Council for Crime Prevention, Information and Publications

West, R. (2005). Time for a change: putting the transtheoretical (stages of change) model to rest. *Addiction* 100: 1036–1039.

Wheeler, G., Thumlert, C., Glaser, L. et al. (2007). *Environmental Education Report: Empirical Evidence, Exemplary Models, and Recommendations on the Impact of Environmental Education on K-12 Students*. Olympia, WA: Office of Superintendent of Public Instruction.

White, K.M., Smith, J.R., Terry, D.J. et al. (2009). Social influence in the theory of planned behaviour: the role of descriptive, injunctive, and ingroup norms. *British Journal of Social Psychology* 48 (1): 135–158.

Whitfield, S.C., Rosa, E.A., Dan, A., and Dietz, T. (2009). The future of nuclear power: value orientations and risk perception. *Risk Analysis* 29: 425–437.

Whitmarsh, L. (2011). Scepticism and uncertainty about climate change: dimensions, determinants and change over time. *Global Environmental Change* 21: 690–700.

Whitmarsh, L. and O'Neill, S. (2010). Green identity, green living? The role of pro-environmental self-identity in determining consistency across diverse pro-environmental behaviours. *Journal of Environmental Psychology* 30: 305–314.

Whittaker, D., Vaske, J.J., and Manfredo, M.J. (2006). Specificity and the cognitive hierarchy: value orientations and the acceptability of urban wildlife management actions. *Society & Natural Resources* 19 (6): 515–530.

Wilke, H.A.M. (1991). Greed, efficiency and fairness in resource management situations. In: *European Review of Social Psychology*, vol. 2 (ed. W. Stroebe and M. Hewstone), 165–187. New York, NY: Wiley.

Williams, D.R. and Vaske, J.J. (2003). The measurement of place attachment: validity and generalizability of a psychometric approach. *Forest Science* 49 (6): 830–840.

Willig, C. (2001). *Introducing Qualitative Research in Psychology: Adventures in Theory and Method*. Buckingham: Open University Press.

Wilson, E.O. (1984). *Biophilia*. Cambridge, MA: Harvard University Press.

Wilson, M.A. (1996). The socialization of architectural preference. *Journal of Environmental Psychology* 16: 33–44.

Wilson, R. (2012). *Nature and Young Children: Encouraging Creative Play and Learning in Natural Environments*. New York, NY: Routledge.

Wilson, T.D., Wheatley, T., Meyers, J.M. et al. (2000). Focalism: a source of durability bias in affective forecasting. *Journal of Personality and Social Psychology* 78: 821–836.

Winkel, G., Saegert, S., and Evans, G.W. (2009). An ecological perspective on theory, methods, and analysis in environmental psychology: advances and challenges. *Journal of Environmental Psychology* 29 (3): 318–328.

Wit, A. and Wilke, H. (1998). Public good provision under environmental and social uncertainty. *European Journal of Social Psychology* 28: 249–256.

Wohlwill, J.F. (1970). The emerging discipline of environmental psychology. *American Psychologist* 25: 303–312.

Wolch, J., Jerrett, M., Reynolds, K. et al. (2011). Childhood obesity and proximity to urban parks and recreational resources: a longitudinal cohort study. *Health & Place* 17 (1): 207–214.

Wolcott, H.F. (2001). *Writing up Qualitative Research*. Thousand Oaks, CA: Sage.

Wolsink, M. (2007). Wind power implementation: the nature of public attitudes: equity and fairness instead of 'backyard motives'. *Renewable and Sustainable Energy Reviews* 11: 1188–1207.

Wood, W., Quinn, J.M., and Kashy, D.A. (2002). Habits in everyday life: thought, emotion, and action. *Journal of Personality and Social Psychology* 83 (6): 1281–1297.

Wood, W., Tam, L., and Guerrero Witt, M. (2005). Changing circumstances, disrupting habits. *Journal of Personality and Social Psychology* 88: 918–933.

Wooller, J.-J., Barton, J., Gladwell, V.F., and Micklewright, D. (2016). Occlusion of sight, sound and smell during green exercise influences mood, perceived exertion and heart rate. *International Journal of Environmental Health Research* 26 (3): 267–280.

World Bank (2015). *World Development Report 2015: Mind, Society, and Behavior*. Washington, DC: World Bank.

World Commission on Environment and Development (1987). *Our Common Future*. Oxford: Oxford University Press.

Wu, C.D., McNeely, E., Cedeño-Laurent, J.G. et al. (2014). Linking student performance in Massachusetts elementary schools with the "greenness" of school surroundings using remote sensing. *PLoS One* 9 (10): e108548.

Xue, W., Hine, D.W., Loi, N.M. et al. (2014). Cultural worldviews and environmental risk perceptions: a meta-analysis. *Journal of Environmental Psychology* 40: 249–258.

Yazdanpanah, M., Hayati, D., Hochrainer-Stigler, S., and Zamani, G.H. (2014). Understanding farmers' intention and behavior regarding water conservation in the Middle-East and North Africa: a case study in Iran. *Journal of Environmental Management* 135: 63–72.

Yerkes, R.M. and Dodson, J.D. (1908). The relation of strength of stimulus to rapidity of habit-formation. *Journal of Comparative Neurology and Psychology* 18: 459–482.

Yip, N.M., Leung, T.T.F., and Huang, R. (2013). Impact of community on personal well-being in urban China. *Journal of Social Service Research* 39 (5): 675–689.

Yu, K. (1995). Cultural variations in landscape preference: comparisons among Chinese subgroups and Western design experts. *Landscape and Urban Planning* 32 (2): 107–126.

Zaalberg, R. and Midden, C. (2010). Human responses to climate change: flooding experiences in the Netherlands. In: *The Social and Behavioural Aspects of Climate Change: Linking Vulnerability, Adaption and Mitigation* (ed. P. Martens and C.T. Chang), 157–176. Sheffield, UK: Greenleaf Publishing.

Zacharias, J. (2002, 2002). Choosing sustainability: the persistence of non-motorized transport in Chinese cities. In: *Culture, Environmental Action and Sustainability* (ed. R. Garcia Mira, J.M. Sabucedo Cameselle and J.R. Martinez), 219–229. Göttingen: Hogrefe.

Zailani, S., Iranmanesh, M., Masron, T.A., and Chan, T.H. (2016). Is the intention to use public transport for different travel purposes determined by different factors? *Transportation Research Part D: Transport and Environment* 49: 18–24.

Zainal Abidin, Z.A. and Jacobs, M.H. (2016). The applicability of wildlife value orientations scales to a muslim student sample in Malaysia. *Human Dimensions of Wildlife* 21 (6): 555–566.

Zajonc, R.B. (1980). Feeling and thinking: preferences need no inferences. *American Psychologist* 35 (2): 151–175.

Zanoli, R. and Naspetti, S. (2002). Consumer motivations in the purchase of organic food: a means-end approach. *British Food Journal* 104 (8): 643–653.

Zeisel, J. (1975). *Sociology and Architectural Design*. New York, NY: Russell Sage Foundation.

Zelenski, J.M. and Nisbet, E.K. (2014). Happiness and feeling connected: the distinct role of nature relatedness. *Environment and Behavior* 46 (1): 3–23.

Zhang, H. and Lin, S.-H. (2011). Affective appraisal of residents and visual elements in the neighborhood: a case study in an established suburban community. *Landscape and Urban Planning* 101 (1): 11–21.

Zhang, L., He, G.Z., Mol, A.P., and Lu, Y.L. (2013). Public perceptions of environmental risk in China. *Journal of Risk Research* 16 (2): 195–209.

Zhang, Y., van Dijk, T., Tang, J., and Berg, A.E. (2015). Green space attachment and health: a comparative study in two urban neighborhoods. *International Journal of Environmental Research and Public Health* 12 (11): 14342–14363.

Zhu, Y. and Fu, Q. (2016). Deciphering the civic virtue of communal space: neighborhood attachment, social capital, and neighborhood participation in urban China. *Environment & Behavior* 49 (2): 16–191.

Zimmer, M., Cabral, J.C.R., Borges, C.F. et al. (2013). Alterações psicológicas decorrentes da permanência na Antártica: Revisão sistemática. *Estudos de Psicologia Campinas* 30 (3): 415–423.

Zimring, C. and Bosch, S. (2008). Building the evidence base for evidence-based design: Editors' introduction. *Environment and Behavior* 40: 147–150.

Zube, E.H., Brush, R.O., and Fabos, J.G. (eds.) (1975). *Landscape Assessment: Values, Perceptions and Resources*. Stroudsburg, PA: Dowden, Hutchinson & Ross.

Zupancic, T., Westmacott, C., and Bulthuis, M. (2015). *The Impact of Green Space on Heat and Air Pollution in Urban Communities: A Meta-Narrative Systematic Review*. Vancouver, BC: David Suzuki Foundation.

Zweers, W. (2000). *Participating with Nature, Outline for an Ecologization of Our Worldview*. Utrecht: International Books.

Environmental Psychology: An Introduction, Second Edition. Edited by Linda Steg
and Judith I. M. de Groot.
© 2019 John Wiley & Sons Ltd. Published 2019 by John Wiley & Sons Ltd.